A Genealogist's Guide to

DISCOVERING YOUR African-American ANCESTORS

How to find and record your unique heritage

Franklin Carter Smith

Emily Anne Croom

BETTERWAY BOOKS
CINCINNATI, OHIO

www.familytreemagazine.com

About the Authors

FRANKLIN CARTER SMITH was born and raised in Claiborne County, Mississippi. He holds a B.A. from Alcorn State University, an M.P.A. from Drake University, and a Doctor of Jurisprudence from the University of Houston Law Center. He is a licensed attorney and currently is employed as a librarian with the Houston Public Library. He resides in Houston, Texas.

EMILY ANNE CROOM is a native Houstonian who taught public school history and worked in church music before concentrating full-time on genealogy—researching, writing, speaking, and teaching. She writes articles for several periodicals, and her other Betterway books are *Unpuzzling Your Past, The Unpuzzling Your Past Workbook, The Genealogist's Companion & Sourcebook*, and *The Sleuth Book for Genealogists*. She holds a B.A. in history from Texas Tech University and a B.A. in music and an M.A. in history from the University of Houston. She lives in Bellaire, Texas.

A Genealogist's Guide to Discovering Your African-American Ancestors. © 2003 by Franklin Carter Smith and Emily Anne Croom. Manufactured in the United States of America. All rights reserved. No part of this book may be reproduced in any form or by any electronic or mechanical means including information storage and retrieval systems without permission in writing from the publisher, except by a reviewer, who may quote brief passages in a review. Published by Betterway Books, an imprint of F&W Publications, Inc., 4700 East Galbraith Road, Cincinnati, Ohio 45236. (800) 289-0963. First edition.

Other fine Betterway books are available from your local bookstore or on our Web site at www.familytreemagazine.com. To subscribe to Family Tree Magazine Update, a free e-mail newsletter with helpful tips and resources for genealogists, go to http://newsletters.fwpublications.com.

07 06 05 04 03   5 4 3 2 1

Library of Congress Cataloging-in-Publication Data

Smith, Franklin Carter
    A genealogist's guide to discovering your African-American ancestors: how to find and record your unique heritage / Franklin Carter Smith and Emily Anne Croom.
        p.   cm.
    Includes bibliographical references (p.) and index.
    ISBN 1-55870-605-4 (pbk.: alk. paper)
    1. African Americans—Genealogy—Handbooks, manuals, etc. I. Croom, Emily Anne. II. Title.
E185.96.S6514   2003
929'.1'08996073—dc21
                                                              2002152014
                                                              CIP

Editor: Sharon DeBartolo Carmack, CG
Production editor: Brad Crawford
Production coordinator: Michelle Ruberg
Interior designer: Sandy Conopeotis Kent
Cover designer: Wendy Dunning
Icon designer: Cindy Beckmeyer

Table of Contents

Foreword

Since my earliest years, I have held a deep and abiding interest in the history of my ancestors. I was always fascinated by the stories my mother and her sisters told of their parents and their ancestors. Unfortunately, all my grandparents died before I was four. The absence of a grandparent generation left a void in my personal history. By learning more about my ancestral history, I hoped I would fill in the missing pieces of my personal puzzle.

I wasn't very far along in my search before I realized that some of the names mentioned over the years had been born during slavery. Yet, this fact never seemed to come up in conversations about these people. When I questioned my mother about this, I was told the "old folk" never spoke of slavery, and her generation knew better than to ask. The stories of my ancestors' lives during slavery died with them. Reliving the shame and humiliation they had experienced was something they were unwilling to consider.

My generation no longer shares their shame. I am unabashedly proud of their strength and perseverance. They endured and overcame trials and tribulations we can only imagine. For this reason, I feel it is my duty and obligation to document as best I can their life stories. Thus began a journey that has now become my personal quest.

When I started, only a few books on the market discussed the resources an African American would need to uncover the family's history. However, none of those books proposed a search strategy that would guide researchers through the maze of dead ends and other pitfalls they would encounter, especially when researching the pre–Civil War era. Without a search strategy, many researchers, either intimidated or overwhelmed by the vastness of such a project, end their search with 1870.

This book will show readers how to research their African-American ancestors into the pre–Civil War era. More than an exhaustive list of resources, this book guides the researcher, whether novice or experienced, through the genealogical quagmire. It will introduce the researcher to a step-by-step approach that should help eliminate much aimless wandering. Case studies and examples show the type of information found in these resources and how to apply the search strategies suggested. In addition to using the search strategy presented in this book, if you are thorough in your search, diligent in your approach, and allow imagination and instinct to be your guide, you can create, if not a portrait, at least a snapshot of your ancestors' lives.

My gratitude and thanks to my mother, Sylvia (Boines) Smith from whom I learned the importance of family. Thanks to Emily Anne Croom, without whose encouragement, direction, and cooperation this book would not have become reality. To Jacqueline Smith, the sister I never had, thanks for believing I could. My sincere appreciation to Audrey Ellison for reading the manuscript and Douglas Carter for allowing me a peek into his family.

Franklin Carter Smith

It has been a great pleasure to work again with Franklin Smith, whose good nature and talents for genealogy are remarkable. My appreciation extends also to loyal readers and students for all I learn from them and for reading and using my books. For this book, special thanks to Jane S. Blanks and Lugenia Parham-Evans of Houston for sharing some of their family documents and to Yvonne Corey of Brooklyn, New York, for sharing her family and cooperating in the research on them. Thank you to the volunteer librarians at the Bering (Houston) Family History Center, especially Tom Lyon, Pat Fite, and Shirley Chapman (thank you, too, Shirley, for reading the manuscript); to John Butler of the National Archives staff; to Chad, John, and Terry at the Nebraska State Historical Society; to the staff at Clayton Library, Center for Genealogical Research, Houston; and to Gay E. Carter, reference librarian, University of Houston-Clear Lake. Thanks to Lorie Szarek of Clearfield Company for permission to use material from the Charleston, South Carolina, city directories, and to the Nebraska State Historical Society for permission to print the photograph of the Jerry Shores family. And to my husband, Robert T. Shelby, my deep appreciation for his manuscript critique, research assistance, patience, and moral support.

Emily Anne Croom

ONE

In the Beginning

African-American genealogy is not only possible, but many are involved successfully in the search every day. You, too, can start uncovering your family's story. This book is designed to guide you, step by step, along the way.

Sooner or later, most people become curious about their heritage and their ancestors. Who were the people who came before you? How did their lives pave the way for you? Were you named for one or more of them?

People become involved in learning about their family's past for many reasons but usually because of an experience or a person who sparked their curiosity. Even those who had no interest in history as a school subject become enthusiastic genealogists when they begin learning about their own families. What created your interest?

No two family histories are exactly alike, yet enough similarities exist that we can generalize about how to get started and how to proceed. The first four chapters of this book are basic to the pursuit of family history. Even those with some research experience can often profit from a review of the basics. Thus, these four chapters focus on the process of working back in time from the present to 1870. They will encourage you to gather information within the family, in census records, and in numerous other public records that are available to researchers. These chapters will tell you what kind of information you might find and how to use it to plan the next step.

In African-American history and genealogy, the years 1865 to 1870 are pivotal. The end of the Civil War and the emancipation of thousands of slaves occurred in 1865. The 1870 federal census was the first nationwide census after the war and the first to name the recently freed slaves. For black genealogists, the censuses are interesting and important tools for determining the makeup of ancestral families in the late nineteenth century. Chapter two will focus on these records. Chapters three and four cover other kinds of post-1865 records of genealogical value. You need to learn all you can about your ancestral families in the twentieth and late nineteenth centuries before you start working in pre-1865 records.

Chapters five through nine discuss the information, process, and records you need in order to continue your genealogical search prior to 1865. The final three chapters are in-depth case studies that illustrate successful use of the methods and sources discussed in the previous chapters.

BASIC PRINCIPLES OF GENEALOGY

Genealogy is the study of lineages—parent-child relationships in each generation. Besides collecting information needed to link children and their parents, genealogists also collect family history—the personal and cultural details that add perspective, interest, and a sense of reality to lists of names and dates. The process of genealogy—gathering the information that links one generation to the previous one—is research, which takes place within the family and in libraries and other facilities.

Before you begin gathering information, consider some of the principles that successful genealogists follow.

Technique

1. Begin with yourself, and work backward to parents, grandparents, etc., one generation at a time, without skipping a generation.
2. Gather information on specific ancestors at specific times and places—for example, George and Betty Sims in Newland, Kentucky, in the 1920s and 1930s. Gather ancestral names and vital statistics (birth, marriage, and death dates and places), as well as names, dates, places, and relationships of siblings (brothers and sisters), cousins, and parents in each generation. Remember, several people may have had the same name; you need to know you are collecting information on the right ancestors in the right places at the right times. Learning about the extended family helps you do this. (Case studies throughout this book will illustrate this process.)
3. Organize the material you gather so that everything you learn about one person or one couple stays together in a three-ring binder or file folder. Organize your binders or filing system in such a way that you can find quickly any piece of information you have collected. There is no right or wrong way to organize, but it is better not to use spiral notebooks and the backs of envelopes. For consistency, it is usually best to use paper that is 8½ inches by 11 inches.
4. Be cautious in accepting what you read or hear, and be ready to double-check the information. Be serious about accuracy so you know you are claiming the correct ancestors.
5. Seek out sources closest in time to each ancestor's life. (See the other chapters of this book.)
6. Improve your chances of success by (a) being thorough—using many different source materials—and (b) focusing on one ancestor or one family at a time so that you can concentrate on details.

TWO BASIC CHARTS

Keeping your information organized is important so you can see what you have found and determine what you need to find next. Two charts that genealogists

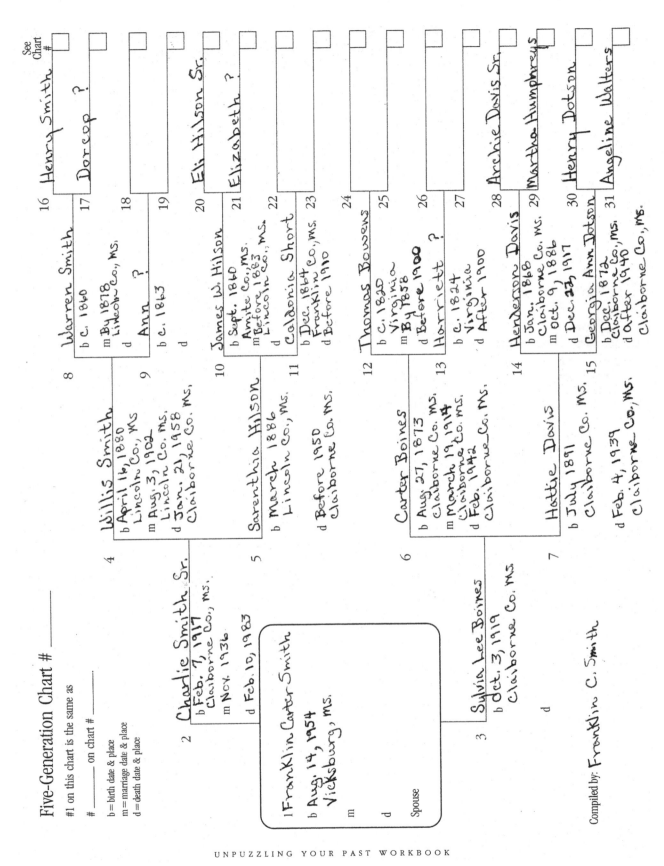

Five-Generation Chart # _____

#1 on this chart is the same as
_____ on chart # _____

b = birth date & place
m = marriage date & place
d = death date & place

1 Franklin Carter Smith
b Aug. 14, 1954
Vicksburg, MS.

m

d

Spouse

2 Charlie Smith, Sr.
b Feb. 7, 1917
Claiborne Co., MS.
m Nov. 1936
d Feb. 10, 1983

3 Sylvia Lee Boines
b Oct. 3, 1919
Claiborne Co. MS

d

4 Willis Smith
b April 16, 1880
Lincoln Co., MS
m Aug. 3, 1902
Lincoln Co., MS.
d Jan. 21, 1958
Claiborne Co. MS.

5 Sarenthia Hilson
b March 1886
Lincoln Co., MS.

d Before 1950
Claiborne Co. MS.

6 Carter Boines
b Aug. 27, 1873
Claiborne Co. MS.
m March 19, 1914
Claiborne Co. MS.
d Feb. 1942
Claiborne Co., MS.

7 Hattie Davis
b July 1891
Claiborne Co. MS.

d Feb. 4, 1939
Claiborne Co., MS.

8 Warren Smith
b c. 1860
m By 1878
Lincoln Co., MS.
d

9 Ann ?
b c. 1863
d

10 James W. Hilson
b Sept. 1860
Amite Co., MS.
m Before 1883
Lincoln Co., MS.
d

11 Caledonia Short
b Dec. 1864
Franklin Co., MS.
d Before 1910

12 Thomas Bowens
b c. 1820
Virginia
m By 1858
d Before 1900

13 Harriett ?
b c. 1824
Virginia
d After 1900

14 Henderson Davis
b Jan. 1868
Claiborne Co., MS.
m Oct. 9, 1886
d Dec. 22, 1917
Claiborne Co. MS

15 Georgia Ann Dotson
b Dec. 1872
Claiborne Co., MS.
d After 1940
Claiborne Co., MS.

16 Henry Smith

17 Dorcas ?

18

19

20 Eli Hilson Sr.

21 Elizabeth ?

22

23

24

25

26

27

28 Archie Davis Sr.

29 Martha Humphreys

30 Henry Dotson

31 Angeline Walters

See Chart #

Compiled by: Franklin C. Smith

Figure 1-1 Example of a pedigree chart.

use to summarize this information are the pedigree (or five-generation) chart and the family group sheet. See page 221, Appendix E, for a blank copy of each form.

The *pedigree or five-generation chart* is like a road map of you and your ancestors and shows each person's name and vital statistics. An example is shown in Figure 1-1 on page 3. Record information about yourself in box number one. On the rest of the chart, males are the even numbers; females are the odd numbers. Your father's information goes in area number two, and your mother's information goes in the number three space. Your father's father would be number four; your father's mother, number five; your mother's father, number six; and your mother's mother, number seven. Your eight great-grandparents' names will go in spaces eight through fifteen. As you identify your great-great-grandparents, their names will go in the last column on the chart. You can create additional charts as needed.

The *family group sheet* summarizes basic information on one nuclear family—parents and their children. Creating these charts for every family you study helps you sort out all the relatives and keep track of who fits where.

The version shown in Figures 1-2A and 1-2B on pages 5 and 6 also provides space for you to list the sources where you found each piece of information. The process is called documentation and is important for several reasons:

- It reminds you and shows anyone who sees your chart where you found the details you have recorded.
- It aids you or someone else in finding the same information again if the need arises.
- When used properly, it demonstrates that you have used appropriate sources in an attempt to be accurate.
- It adds credibility and quality to your efforts.

You will learn more about research, source materials, and documentation throughout this book.

TIPS FOR SUCCESS

1. In family and public records, expect names to be spelled in different ways. Regardless of whether family members were literate, clerks wrote the names in public records the way they heard them, thought they heard them, or saw them in other records. For example, Betty Roth could be Betsy Ross in one record and Elizabeth Rose in another. (*Betty* and *Betsy* are common nicknames for Elizabeth.) Priscilla Gregory could be recorded as Cela Grigrey.

2. As you research, take careful notes. It is helpful to date your notes and tell where you are using the source—library, courthouse, cemetery, National Archives branch, Aunt Mary Gregg's house, etc. On the pages of notes, identify

- the family to which the notes pertain
- the title or name of the source you are using
- a microfilm roll number if you are using microfilm
- the page numbers in the source where you find information

3. To document your research, it is helpful to write down the source information before you begin taking notes. On your notes, form is not critical; just

\di'fin\ *vb*

Definitions

Your father's side of the family is your *paternal* ancestors. Your mother's side is your *maternal* ancestors. *Paternal* comes from the Latin *pater*, "father." *Maternal* comes from the Latin *mater*, "mother." *Vital statistics* are the dates and places of a person's birth, marriage, and death.

Tip

See Also

See pages 106–107, for more information on names and nicknames.

Family Group Sheet of the ___Burton Clark___ Family

working copy

	Source #			Source #
Burton Clark Full name of husband	1,2,3 4,6	Birth date 1830-1842 Birth place N.C. Death date before 1915 Death place probably Pitt Co. NC Burial place		2,3 2,3,6 1
His father				
His mother with maiden name				
Anica/Anniky Daniels Full maiden name of wife	4,6	Birth date no later than 1839 based on ages of children Birth place Pitt Co. NC Death date before 1870 Death place probably Pitt Co. NC Burial place		2,4 6 2
Her father				
Her mother with maiden name				

Other Spouses Burton m 2ⁿᵈ Jane [Collins?] by 1870. Jane b 1835-1846 and d before 1912. May have had dau Judy

Source #s 1,2,3

Marriage date, place, etc.

by about 1853 based on ages of children

Source #s 2,4

Children of this marriage Birth order based on 1870 census	Birth date & place	Death date, place, & burial place	Marriage date, place & spouse
1. Susan Clark had son John T. Slade, dau Lizzie Slade Source #s 2,4,5	1854-1857 NC 2,4,5		m1-Isaac Slade, 24 Feb 1875, Pactolus, Pitt Co NC m 2-Lewis Allen, 3 Jan 1884, Greenville, Pitt Co NC 4
2. Sarah Clark Source #s 2	c 1859 NC 2		
3. J. Burton Clark Jr. had dau Hellen Source #s 2,3,4,8	1858-1861 NC 2,3,4	after 1900	Mary Clark, 13 Jan 1881 Pactolus, Pitt Co NC 4,8
4. David Clark (Rev.) had dau Bettie Source #s 2,4,6,9,10	1853-1863 Beaufort Co NC 2,6,9,10	18 Mar 1926 Swift Creek, Pitt Co NC. Bur. Johnson Mill Run Cem. 6	Laura Cannon, 27 Dec 1900, Deep Creek, Pitt Co NC 4,6,9,10
5. Ollie Clark Source #s 2,3,7,8	1862-1865 Pitt Co NC 2,3,7,8	5 Oct 1929 Pactolus, Pitt Co bur. Clark Graveyard 7	single 7,8
6. Olivia Clark child of which wife? Source #s 2	c 1867 NC 2		

Figure 1-2A Example of a family group sheet.

Source #   Sources (Documentation)

1	Marriage license #1787 of William Collins (age 40), son of <u>Bert & Jane Clark</u> (both deceased) to marry Louna (Leona) Croom, dated 20 Jan 1915, Craven Co., NC, FHL microfilm 0288286; marriage license #1113 of William Collins (39), son of <u>John and Jane Collins</u> (both deceased) to marry Hattie White, dated 15 Dec 1912, Craven Co., NC, FHL microfilm 0288285.
2	U.S. Census of 1870, roll 1155, Pitt Co., NC, Pactolus township, p. 182, <u>family</u> 158, Bert Clark (28 *sic*), Jane (24 *sic*), Susan (13), Sarah (11), Bert (9), Dave (7), Ollie (5), Olivia (3).
3	U.S. Census of 1880, roll 978, Pitt Co., NC, Pactolus twp, e.d. 129, sheet 55, <u>family</u> 508, Burton Clark (50), wife Jane (45), dau Ollie (15), dau Judy (9); sheet 54, family 502, Burton Clark (22).
4	Marriage record of <u>Burton Clark Jr.</u> (21), son of Burton and Anniky Clark, to marry Mary Clark (23), wedding 13 Jan 1881, Pactolus, Pitt Co., NC; marriage record of <u>Dave Clark</u>, son of Boston (*sic*) and Anica Clark, to marry Louisa (*sic*) Cannon, wedding 27 Dec 1900, Deep Creek, Pitt Co., NC; marriage record of <u>Susan Clark</u> (20), dau of Burton and Anniky Clark, to marry Isaac Slade (31), wedding 27 Feb 1875, Pactolus, Pitt Co., NC; marriage record of <u>Susan Slade</u> (26), dau of Burton Slade (*sic*), to marry Lewis Allen, wedding 3 Jan 1884, Greenville, Pitt Co., NC—all in Colored Marriages 1851–1924, FHL microfilm 0333704.
5	U.S. Census of 1880, Population Schedule, roll 978, Pitt Co., NC, e.d. 129, sheet 52, family 477, Isaac Slade, wife <u>Susan</u> (26), son John T. (3), dau Lizzie (4/12); Mortality Schedule, Roll 4, Pitt Co., NC, entry for Isaac Slade, deceased, NC Dept. of Archives and History, microfilm.
6	Death certificate of <u>David Clark</u>, Vol. 13:679, Pitt Co., NC, Death Register, Office of Register of Deeds–Vital Statistics, photocopy. Parents' names, birthplaces; wife's name; his age, death, burial, informant-Laura Clark of Grifton.
7	Death certificate of <u>Ollie Clark</u>, Vol. 16:639, Pitt Co., NC, ibid. No birth or parent info; death info, single, informant-Mary Clark of Washington.
8	U.S. Census of 1900, roll 1212, Pitt Co., NC, Pactolus twp, e.d. 95, sheet 3, family 43, <u>J.B. Clark</u> (b Apr 1859), married 19 years, wife Mary (b Apr 1860), only child Hellen (b July 1884), sister <u>Olia Clark</u> (b Dec 1862, single). Not found yet in 1910, 1920.
9	U.S. Census of 1910, Soundex, T1271, roll 30, C462, showing <u>Dave Clark</u> (57), wife Laura (47), dau Bettie (6), Pitt Co., NC. Finding info apparently contains error; couldn't find on census itself. Family not yet found in 1900.
10	U.S. Census of 1920, roll 1315, Pitt Co., NC, Swift Creek twp, e.d. 57, sheet 13A, family 249, <u>David Clark</u> (66), wife Laura (57), dau Bella/Bettie (16).

Figure 1-2B Reverse side of family group sheet, showing documentation.

write down the information. On your family group sheets or finished family histories, consistent form is more important and gives your work credibility and validity. The process involves writing down pertinent information about your source in order to create footnotes. It is easier to collect this information at the time you use the source instead of years later when you may have forgotten where you found the details.

Style manuals, such as *The Chicago Manual of Style* and the *MLA Handbook for Writers of Research Papers*, give additional help in citing published books and articles, electronic works, Internet sites, and various government documents. Croom's *Sleuth Book for Genealogists* also contains a detailed guide to documentation.

In documenting many genealogical materials, there is no hard-and-fast standard form to follow. Thus, you have a choice. The key is to write down enough information about the source that you or anyone else could find the same material again. The following are three examples:

Citing Sources

- Tombstone for Cora Greenapple, Pearly Gate Cemetery, Newtown, New County, California, copied by the compiler [that's you—you can list your name], 4 July 2001. [This citation identifies the source of information and where and when you saw it.]
- Birth certificate for Marietta Greenapple, no. 35, dated 23 May 1912, Old County, Texas, County Clerk's Office, Courthouse, Oldtown. [This citation identifies the document and where you found it.]
- Obituary of Gouldsberry Greenapple, *Newberry (Florida) Star*, 14 April 1928, clipping in possession of Barbery Thorne, Newberry, Florida, photocopied by compiler 5 May 2001. [This citation identifies the source of information and where and when you found it.]

The case studies and illustrations in this book are fully documented and cited; the endnotes appear at the end of the book, beginning on page 227. **As you read, please refer to the endnotes as they will enhance your understanding of the examples and the sources.** The endnotes are included for three reasons:

Important

1. to let you know that the examples and case studies are about real people, from actual research
2. to give you examples of how you might cite many kinds of documents in your own research, including published works, microfilm sources, letters and interviews, and original documents
3. to help you learn of sources you might want to try, especially if any of the people in the examples are your ancestors

CREATING A KNOWLEDGE BASE

Before researching in public records, gather information from the knowledge and records within the family. The names, dates, places, relationships, and other details you gather serve as a base on which to build.

Personal Knowledge

Begin by creating several family group sheets. First, from personal knowledge, start a group sheet for yourself with your parents and siblings. On family group sheets, list children in birth order if possible, and use full names if you know them. If you have children, start a group sheet showing you as the parent and listing your children.

Next, begin a group sheet for each of your parents in their childhood families with their parents; then, your grandparents with their siblings and parents. Again, use your personal knowledge, but realize you may need to make corrections and additions. If necessary, indicate the number of children in the family even if you cannot name them.

On separate paper or with an audio or a video recorder, interview yourself. Write or record your memories of your parents, grandparents, and other relatives. Include specific events such as holiday celebrations, personality traits, time spent with the ancestors you knew, and early memories of your children.

Consult Relatives and Family Artifacts

To add to the group sheet knowledge base, consult your siblings, cousins, parents, and other relatives. Check names, dates, places, and relationships with them. If they supply new information from memory, list your source as "Personal knowledge of [the person who told you]" or "Interview with [name] on [date]."

Hidden Treasures

Whenever possible, **try to locate records in the family to confirm or furnish details.** These records can include family Bibles, birth and death certificates, marriage certificates, family reunion or funeral programs, newspaper obituaries, labeled photographs, letters, scrapbooks, Social Security cards, driver's licenses, legal documents, military documents, and other items passed down from previous generations. From these records, you may learn full names, relationships, birth or death dates and places, marriage dates and places, burial sites, parents' names and birthplaces, where someone lived or worked at a certain time, or where relatives went to school. Any of this information—even details apart from vital statistics—can be helpful to later research.

Interview Letters

Sometimes you can get helpful information by writing letters to relatives. Leave space for them to answer and enclose a self-addressed, stamped envelope for the return to you. Keep this kind of letter relatively short and specific. E-mail is another helpful interview tool for short messages and questions.

You may also have success sending a family group sheet that you have started. Ask the correspondent to add to or correct what you have started.

"Mama always said . . . "

Idea Generator

Parents and grandparents, brothers and sisters, aunts and uncles, cousins and others will be an important part of your information gathering, both at the beginning and as you proceed with your research. Gather whatever you can—little details, nicknames, memories of a visit, next-door neighbors' names, where someone worked—because you never know which tidbit will prove helpful in furthering your search.

Sometimes, the relatives you consult will remember things differently. In addition, as you research, you may find some facts that disagree with what relatives have told you. At family gatherings, some will remain adamant that "Mama always told me this," and, therefore, they really do not want to hear anything different. They may even announce that you are wrong. If you have your facts documented from legitimate sources and have organized or presented your material in an understandable way, most of the relatives will appreciate your efforts and may even be amazed at all you have learned.

Have you ever played the "rumor" game in which you whisper something to the person nearest you? That person whispers it to the next person, and it spreads around the circle one person at a time. When the last person gets the message, he or she announces it to the group, and everyone laughs because the message is always different from what you originally said. Try something like "Uncle Harvey ate his hat while standing on the kitchen table" and see how it sounds at the end of the circle.

Family history is much like this. Ask your siblings about events in your childhood, and some of you will remember the same event differently. Ask your parents and their siblings about people or events in their childhoods. Some will remember little; some will remember differently; and some will argue about who is right. This can happen to family memories over the years.

Genealogists must be aware of "creative remembering" and the "Mama always told me" syndrome. Often, Mama was correct, and others report her statements accurately. At other times, either Mama was slightly off target or those reporting what she said did not remember her exact words. Therefore, gather whatever you can from family members, but expect some discrepancies or inaccuracies. Part of your role as a genealogist is to try to determine what information is accurate.

CONSULT THE ELDERS

Identify as many older living family members as possible. These can include parents, aunts and uncles, grandparents and their siblings, cousins, surviving spouses of deceased relatives, and even long-time family friends and neighbors. Seek out the "griot"—the person who is most knowledgeable about each family's history.

As soon as possible, contact these people via mail, e-mail, telephone, or personal visit. Each one can furnish information, if you ask the right questions. As you learn more, you may need to talk with an interviewee several times.

Interviews on tape can help preserve several aspects of family history. Remember that an audiotape is a memory of the person's voice as well as a source of information. Thus, audiotapes you make could help family members of the future feel a special kind of connection with ancestors they never met. In addition, speech patterns and voice inflections often carry over from one generation to the next in the same area. Thus, hearing your grandmother speak may tell you something of how your great-grandmother or other ancestors spoke.

General Interview Techniques

1. If potential interviewees do not know you, introduce yourself and explain your reason for the contact—to ask for information about family history. Ask for a convenient time to call or visit.

2. If they know you, briefly explain your interest in family history and ask for a time when they could share with you some of their memories of family history.

3. Prepare specific questions in advance and tailor them to fit each person's place in the family of your interest. Someone in your mother's family, for exam-

Oral History

ple, may or may not know details about people on your father's side of the family. Also, most people know more about relatives they knew personally than relatives who lived elsewhere or who died before the interviewee was born.

4. If you contact the interviewee by mail, try one of these ideas. (a) Number your questions so your correspondent can respond easily, and keep a copy of the questions you send. (b) Type your questions and leave room for answers; ask your correspondent to answer on the page and return it to you.

5. Ask for names, vital statistics, and relationships, but ask also about family stories, oral tradition, and how the ancestors lived their daily lives. Figure 1-3, on page 11, is part of an interview dealing with daily life and social history.

6. Ask about specific events and people the interviewees knew well. Word your questions to trigger memories, and try to get explanations in addition to yes and no answers. If you ask "Do you remember anything about Grandpa Brown?" you may get "No" for an answer. On the other hand, you could begin with "Mama always said Grandpa Brown had four sisters. What were their names? Who was Cassie?"

7. Try to find out about your ancestors as people—their character, their personality traits, and stories that illustrate these traits. Figure 1-4, on page 12, is part of such an interview.

8. If your interviewee has family artifacts, especially family Bibles or photographs, use these as triggers to conversation. Who were these people? How were they related to you (the interviewee)? What can you tell me about them? What was the occasion in the photograph?

9. Realize that failing memory may result in inaccurate information or mixed-up identities. However, record what you are told and later double-check what you can.

10. During an interview, record the conversation and/or take thorough notes. Label the tape or notes with your name, the interviewee's name, and the date and location of the visit. This information is your documentation of the information and the event: "Interview with Aunt Susan Wilson, 9 October 2000, at her home in Pleasant Valley, Arkansas, by Jane Clark, on audiotape."

11. Transcribe your notes soon after the interview while the conversation and details of family stories are fresh on your mind.

What If Some Relatives Won't Share?

Although most relatives will gladly share information and memories with those interested in family history, some relatives are reluctant to tell what they know. Genealogists cannot force people to talk, but knowing why some people decline may help you work out a strategy to help them overcome their unwillingness. Their hesitation may fall into one of several categories.

1. Some people may have had an unhappy or abusive childhood or marriage and prefer not to talk about it. One man did not want to remember anything prior to his marriage, and his family never knew the real reason. However, not long before he died, his son asked him for his parents' and siblings' names. These were the only clues the family had when they started working on family history. Research later suggested some reasons why the elder man may not have wanted to remember his early years.

For More Info

See Croom's comprehensive guide for beginning genealogists, *Unpuzzling Your Past*, 4th edition, chapters five through eight, for many examples of interview questions.

PORTION OF AN INTERVIEW WITH MRS. SYLVIA (BOINES) SMITH, BY FRANKLIN SMITH AT WILLOWS, MISSISSIPPI, 24 NOVEMBER 2001

What age were you when you started school?
I was about seven or eight years old [1926 or 1927].

How far from home was the school you attended?
Three or four miles or more.

How did you get to school?
I walked with my sisters. We left about 7:00 A.M. and got there about 8:00 A.M. We left school about 2:30 P.M. and got home about 4:00.

What month did you start school each year?
We started school after we had gathered all the crops in the fall.

What month was school out?
In March or April so we could start clearing the fields for planting.

Did you attend school on a regular basis during the school year?
I attended pretty regularly after we had finished gathering the crops. In the evening after school, we would finish gathering the crops.

When did you study and do homework?
In the evening when we came home from the fields. It would be night when we got home. We studied by kerosene lamp or light from the fireplace.

What subjects did you like most in school?
I liked spelling and arithmetic the best, and I was pretty good in English.

Were you issued books to study?
I did get some books, but I never had all the books I needed. I would copy my lessons from classmates' books at school or borrow classmates' books. My parents had to buy our books.

How many students were at the school?
At least fifteen and probably more. It was the only school for miles.

What did you eat for lunch?
Sometimes we brought our lunch and sometimes people from the neighborhood made soup and brought it to the school.

What kind of food did you take to school?
We made sandwiches from biscuits and jelly and homemade sausage. We didn't have light bread back then. We carried our lunches in a jelly bucket.

What did you have for breakfast?
Grits that were home-ground, biscuits and syrup or corn cakes and syrup and eggs and home-cured pork.

Figure 1-3 Interview about daily life.

This category could also include those who grew up in a variety of family homes or children's homes, foster homes, or other institutions and perhaps feel embarrassment, shame, or guilt. Genealogists probably cannot anticipate or lessen the emotions these relatives may feel but may encourage them to talk about other aspects of family history.

2. Relatives may not understand what genealogists want to know and why they want to know it. One aunt was, at first, rather talkative and then began hedging on answering questions. Not understanding her sudden change of atti-

---

PORTION OF AN INTERVIEW BY MAIL, WITH YVONNE COREY OF BROOKLYN, NEW YORK, BY EMILY CROOM, JANUARY 2002, ABOUT YVONNE'S GRANDFATHER, WILLIAM COLLINS

How old was your mother when her father died? Did she remember him?
My mother was 2 years old when he died. My mother always honored the father she never knew and kept his memory alive because her mother always spoke of him in a good way.

What do you know about William Collins's physical appearance?
My mother always told me that he was an exslave and looked like a red man with curly hair. That's what her mother told her when she was growing up. Some say Bill Collins was a Native American.

What kind of father was he?
My mother said her mother always told her William Collins was very good to his family. He took very good care of them the best he could at the time that he was with them. He was a farmer all of his life, and he worked very hard to take care of his family.

What do you know about him as a person?
His memory has lasted so long because he was different for that time. He was a very independent man under the worst circumstances during the 1800s [and early 1900s]. My mother said her mother said that both black and white feared him, if you crossed him. At that time, no black man would dare to bring attention to himself or his family in a bad way. What made William Collins stand apart from this was, when he was freed, I think, he thought he should act free. He was always moving from farm to farm. My mother said her mother told her, if the white man made him mad, he would move that night and would be waiting the next day when the white man would come to the house to make him move his family off of his farm. William Collins would say you're too damn late, I moved last night. That is one of the things he inspired me about: he was not afraid to stand up for what he thought was right.

Do you know how your grandparents got together, since William Collins was so much older than your grandmother?
I don't know how he met my grandmother. She always said she left home at twelve years old because her step-mother treated her so badly. She must have told him this as a child. William Collins must have felt sorry for her. I think they lived together for a while until she was at a marriage age. This is why there is such puzzlement about the age difference. William Collins knew he would not see his children grow up. When he was dying, so the story goes, he told my grandmother not to separate his children, and don't let anyone mistreat them. My grandmother married again, to a man who was crabby by nature, but she never let him mistreat her children. I think she always loved her first husband, William Collins.

Figure 1-4 Interview about an ancestor as a person.

tude, her nephew addressed the issue directly, saying that he sensed a reluctance on her part and wondered whether he had said anything to cause this change in their communication. She then explained an episode in her past that she had not wanted him to discover. He had to help her understand that this kind of episode was not what he, as the genealogist, was trying to uncover. In effect, she had completely misunderstood his quest as the family historian.

Individuals in this situation, or their relatives, may have had gambling, drinking, drug, mental, legal, or criminal problems. Some may have had an extramarital affair they later regretted; others may have divorced at a time and place where that action was considered unacceptable. They may wish to keep closed these or other personal chapters in their lives and may think the genealogist is asking too many probing questions. **Genealogists need to make clear that they are looking for information on their ancestors and interesting family stories and memories.** Some of these episodes may surface in the process, but genealogists are not seeking to open old wounds.

Reminder

3. Other relatives may possess family papers but "refuse to share" with the genealogist. One young woman made this complaint about her older brother, who lived out of town and had all their parents' papers. When she approached the subject directly, she learned that the brother had no idea what was in the boxes, was very busy, and felt it was too time-consuming and expensive to take boxes of papers to a photocopier and send her all the copies. However, he was glad for her to come for a visit, go through the papers, and make copies of whatever she wanted. Sometimes relatives even give key documents to the genealogist. Of course, if family history enthusiasts do not know what is in the papers, they cannot know what copies to request. And sometimes, in their eagerness, they may ask too much or want answers too fast.

4. Family members may want to hide secrets that the family has had for generations. These "skeletons in the closet" may include many of the situations already mentioned but happened so long ago that the relatives involved are no longer living. Most families have included individuals who broke the law, had bad habits, made poor choices, or had unfortunate things happen to them. Genealogists can accept such events as facts in the family history and decide how much to include in a compilation of the family's past.

One researcher learned why her grandmother had refused to talk: A great-grandparent had been a stagecoach robber on the western frontier. The researcher became very interested in studying that family and discovered that the robber's sister had been a published playwright. While not condoning what the robber did, the genealogist wanted to know all, and it certainly enlivened the family history.

If You Are an Elder in the Family

If you are among the elders in your family, you have irreplaceable memories of previous generations whom younger generations never knew. It is up to you to preserve the names and personal details. Write down or tape record your experiences with and memories of your parents, aunts and uncles, and grandparents. Preserve the stories; tell about the tough times and the good times. Even if you think no one in the family cares to know these things, someone someday will be thrilled at your efforts.

FAMILY GATHERINGS, REUNIONS, AND FUNERALS

Genealogists have an opportunity to learn new information whenever relatives gather—on holidays and at family reunions, birthday parties, weddings, graduations, anniversaries, and funerals. On these occasions, you may well have within arm's reach people you see regularly, some you seldom see, and some whom you are meeting for the first time. If you prepare in advance, you may be able to pick up valuable information while you are there.

Tip

Whether formally or informally, with or without charts in hand, at these events you often can

1. learn the names of and information about spouses and children of relatives
2. compare information and check details with other family members
3. hear stories about the honorees, the deceased, or ancestors
4. see family photographs on display
5. get programs or bulletins that contain genealogical information
6. exchange addresses and phone numbers with others who are interested in family history or those you would like to contact again later
7. hear family history from the elders
8. meet and talk with relatives who knew ancestors you never knew

Family reunions often draw together the larger extended family. Because these events are usually planned months in advance, you may have a greater opportunity because you can

- alert relatives to bring information you need
- ask relatives to bring photographs you would like to see
- arrange to interview key people
- prepare questions to ask and charts for people to fill out
- put together family history exhibits or programs to share what you and others have learned

For example, if someone is there from the same county as several of your ancestors, spend some time together and find out about the cemeteries where family members are buried, the churches they attended, the communities where they lived, and whether other descendants still live in the area. Perhaps arrange with this person to gather certain information for you or put you in contact with someone in the ancestral church or community.

Reminder

Although funerals are usually marked with sadness, they are also times to share memories and keep in touch. Grandmother's cousin, whom no one has seen in years, may show up for Grandmother's funeral and give you the opportunity to get information on your shared ancestors or identify a mystery person in an old family photograph.

On any of these occasions, you may learn valuable information—a "new" former residence of your grandparent in which to research or the location of important church records. The scientist Louis Pasteur is credited with the statement, "Chance favors only the prepared mind." This is certainly true in genealogy. If you have studied your genealogy material before attending the function, are familiar with what facts you have and what you lack, and are alert as you visit with relatives and friends at these gatherings, you may pick up some little tidbit that will become the key to discovering another generation of ancestors. As you gain experience, you will improve your ability to recognize these gems when they are tossed your way.

TWO

Census Records

See Also

See page 115 for information on slave census schedules; see pages 91–92, 120, and 129 for information on the free censuses of 1860 and earlier years.

After collecting whatever you can within the family, you are ready to begin looking at public records. Then, as you research in public records, you will continue to consult family members and family papers as needed. The goal of this research is to use what you learn from the family to

1. double-check what the family has told you
2. learn more about your ancestors
3. work back into the nineteenth century to 1870

Census records are among the most interesting and useful of the public resources and are often a good place to begin genealogical research. Because the first part of this book concentrates on research between the present and 1870, the censuses of that period and census research techniques are the focus of this chapter.

ABOUT CENSUS RECORDS

Since 1790, the United States government and many state governments have conducted censuses to count the population. Federal censuses enumerate the population every ten years in order to apportion representation in the House of Representatives in Congress. Federal and state censuses also collect demographic information for many purposes, such as public health statistics, but not for taxation as some people think. After seventy-two years, federal censuses become public records, available to researchers. For example, the 1930 census was opened in 2002.

The demographic questions on censuses from 1870 forward provide details about ancestors and their family members, including age, sex, race, birthplace, occupation, and, after 1880, each person's relationship to the head of the household. Even an ancestor's name on the list tells you the person was alive and in that place at that time—an important fact in your research. Appendix B, on

Figure 2-1 U.S. Census of 1870, roll 726, Claiborne County, Mississippi, Rocky Springs District, Port Gibson post office, handwritten p. 44.

page 208, summarizes basic census information from 1790 to 1930.

Figure 2-1, above, illustrates part of a page from the 1870 census of Claiborne County, Mississippi. Although the page reports a variety of birthplaces, most of these residents were born in Mississippi. **Notice in the birthplace column that the "Miss" abbreviation of Mississippi was written using the old-style double s, which can appear to be an *fs* or a *p.*** The state name at the top left-hand corner of the page illustrates both the old-style double s and the newer style that we use today. Line ten shows an infant age six months old (6/12), born in December 1869. Although most of these families were black, several individuals were mulatto, and one family was white (with the wife erroneously listed as black).

Unfortunately, most of the 1890 census burned early in the twentieth century. Fragments do exist, especially for Perry County, Alabama; the District of Columbia; Washington County, Georgia; and McDonough County, Illinois. Several other resources help fill the gap from some of the missing 1890 census schedules:

- 1885 censuses for Colorado, Dakota Territory, Florida, Nebraska, and New Mexico Territory (see chapter four)
- 1890 special census of Union (Civil War) veterans and widows—remaining fragments (see chapter three)
- 1890 territorial census for Oklahoma
- city directories for urban ancestors (see chapter four)
- state censuses in a number of states

Census Day

Although you cannot know for sure whether your ancestral families followed this rule, you need to be aware of it as you evaluate census records. Since 1790, Congress has designated one day in each census year as the official census day:

1790–1820	First Monday in August
1830–1900	June 1
1910	April 15
1920	January 1
1930, 1940	April 1

The information reported to the census takers was to be correct as of that day. Census takers were to explain the rule and request information accordingly:

- Each household or institution was to report all people living there on that day whether or not they were related.
- Babies born after census day but before the census taker's visit were not to be enumerated since they were not part of the household on census day.
- Household members who died after census day and before the census taker's visit were to be included in the enumeration because they were alive on census day.
- Ages reported in the census were supposed to be the age of each person on census day.

Mortality and Agriculture Schedules

Between 1850 and 1880, federal census takers collected information for several supplemental census schedules: mortality, agriculture, industry/manufacturing, and social statistics. The mortality schedules are the most genealogical because they report many of the deaths that occurred during the year prior to the census—for example, 1 June 1869 to 1 June 1870. Not all families reported deaths to the census taker, but many did. The information varied slightly from year to year but usually included the name, age, race, and gender of the deceased, the month and cause of death, and the length of illness if the person

Important

died of disease. **The lists included both the slave and free population. Some state censuses also included mortality schedules.**

For the agriculture schedules, census takers interviewed farmers to describe and place a value on their land, crops, livestock, and produce. For ancestors who owned, rented, or sharecropped land, these reports give interesting details about the family's life and farm. These schedules also help identify landowners, renters, and sharecropping farmers who lived near each other. Comparing such a list with the names of slaveholders in the slave schedules sometimes helps narrow the search for slave families. (See chapters six and seven.)

If the occupation given for your ancestors in the 1870 census was "farm laborer" or "works on farm" rather than "farmer," it is unlikely they will appear in the agriculture schedule. They probably worked on a farm for wages. If you find in the schedule your ancestors' neighbors who reported paying wages for the previous year, your ancestor may have worked for one of those neighbors.

In the 1870 census of Lincoln County, Mississippi, were these black inhabitants:[1]

1. John W. Smith, head of family 341, occupation given as "works on farm"
2. James R. Smith, head of family 342, occupation reported as "farm laborer" (brother of Henry, below)
3. Henry Smith, head of family 343, occupation given as "farm laborer"

None of these Smiths was listed in the Lincoln County agriculture schedule that year. However, a white neighbor, A.B. Lofton, head of family 344 and a farmer, and several other neighbors answered the agricultural questions.[2] Only two of those neighbors reported paying wages for the previous year. A.B. Lofton reported paying five hundred dollars in wages, and his son, Perry Lofton, reported paying $134 in wages. Because of their close proximity to the Smiths in the census, and thus probably in the neighborhood, chances are good that the Smiths may have worked for one or both Lofton families. Although research indicates that A.B. Lofton was not the likely slaveholder of these Smith families, a connection may exist between Lofton and the former slaveholder. It is doubtful that Lofton would have hired someone with whom he was not familiar.

Microfilm Source

The existing supplemental schedules are available on microfilm in research libraries, in state archives, and from rental libraries such as the Family History Library and Heritage Quest. A number of mortality schedules have been published for specific counties or states. However, researchers can check many ancestral counties fairly quickly because the microfilm is arranged by state and county. Except for the mortality schedules of very populous cities or counties, each county's report uses only a few pages.

The 1870 Census

The 1870 census is a pivotal record for African-American researchers. Why? This was the first census to name the population who had been slaves before the Civil War, which ended in 1865. Also, many Southerners, both black and white, moved after the Civil War, but large numbers remained in their pre-war locations until after 1870. Thus, finding your ancestral families in 1870 is often the gateway into pre–Civil War genealogy. (See chapter seven for more about the 1870 census.)

Working back one census at a time helps you gather valuable information on your family before you reach the 1870 census. The information you gather will help you identify the correct ancestral families in 1870 and begin your research in other records:

- You will learn which ancestors probably were children in 1870 and perhaps the names of one or both of their parents.
- You may obtain clues to the ancestral heads of household in 1870 and relatives who may have been living with them.
- You may learn of other related families who were living in the 1870 ancestral neighborhood.
- You may identify white families by the same surname as your family in censuses of 1870 and after; these could be important in your search.
- You may notice certain white families consistently enumerated near your family in censuses of 1870 and after; these could be important in your search.

Research Tip

WHERE TO FIND CENSUS RECORDS

Federal censuses are readily available to anyone with access to a microfilm reader because all the records are on microfilm. Many public and academic libraries have census microfilm for their county, state, or region. Some have complete national sets of census and Soundex microfilm through 1920. These include Clayton Library, part of Houston Public Library; Allen County Public Library, Fort Wayne, Indiana; Mid-Continent Public Library, Independence, Missouri; and Sutro Library, part of the California State Library, in San Francisco (except for the 1890 fragments). Check in your local area to learn which records are available near you.

In addition, the National Archives in Washington, DC, and its branches throughout the country have complete sets, as does the Family History Library in Salt Lake City. The Family History Library is an institution of the Church of Jesus Christ of Latter-day Saints and allows members and non-members to rent film through its Family History Centers throughout the world.

Rental of census microfilm is also possible through Heritage Quest in North Salt Lake [(800) 760-2455], <www.heritagequest.com>, and the National Archives Census Microfilm Rental Program, a private company in Annapolis Junction, Maryland [(301) 604-3699], <www.archives.gov/publications/microfilm_catalogs/how_to_rent_microfilm.html>.

Federal census records are also available as digitized images on CD-ROM from Heritage Quest, and, at this writing, digitized records of quite a few censuses are available by subscription at Ancestry.com. Scattered digitized and abstracted records are also online on various county pages on USGenWeb <www.usgenweb.org>. Many census schedules have been abstracted and published.

State and territorial censuses exist for many states, as do census substitutes created from tax and other lists. In addition to the Family History Library and

Microfilm Source

Sources

To find a Family History Center near you, look in your local telephone directory under the church's name and visit the Web site at www.familysearch .org. For more on the Family History Library, consult the Warrens' *Your Guide to the Family History Library.*

Heritage Quest catalogs, three books can help you identify censuses for your state(s) of interest.

- Croom, Emily Anne. *The Genealogist's Companion & Sourcebook*. Cincinnati: Betterway Books, 1994 or latest edition. Chapter two, on federal census records and finding aids, and chapter three, on state censuses.
- Lainhart, Ann S. *State Census Records*. Baltimore: Genealogical Publishing Co., 1992.
- Thorndale, William, and William Dollarhide. *Map Guide to the U.S. Federal Censuses, 1790–1920*. Baltimore: Genealogical Publishing Co., paperback, 1993.

When you find published abstracts of census records, remember that you need to look for the microfilm of the original record. Abstracts of records are often well done, but they are subject to human error in copying and publishing and are not as complete as the original records.

USING CENSUS RECORDS

Reminder

By interviewing family members and gathering information from family papers, you can create a list of family members who were alive in 1930 or 1920 to help you research the 1930 or 1920 census. **Genealogists work with known information to learn new information.** Thus, you need to begin by reading the most recent census available for the ancestors you are researching and work backward in time, as illustrated in the case study later in this chapter.

Another example of working from the known to the unknown occurs in the 1890–1930 censuses, which asked the population about property ownership. If an ancestor's census entry indicates he or she owned the family home or farm, you would want to use this information to try to learn, usually in county or federal land records, when the purchase took place, what the price was, and any other information given in the land record. Land records usually include the location of the land. This information may lead you to identify the church the family attended or a cemetery where family members are buried. (See chapters three and four for more on land records.)

Warning

The instructions to census takers varied from census to census. One of the columns that changed over the years was the designation for race or color, along with the census bureau's definition of each choice. **Researchers could interpret ancestral enumerations inaccurately if they are not aware of the changing choices and definitions.**[3]

- In 1870 and 1880, Chinese and Indian were added to White, Black, and Mulatto in the "color" column. *Mulatto* included "all persons having any perceptible trace of African blood." We cannot know whether the census taker asked the family or guessed, based on someone's appearance.
- For 1890, census takers were asked to write "white, black, mulatto, quadroon, octoroon, Chinese, Japanese, or Indian, according to the color or race of the person enumerated." *Black* was to mean anyone at least three-fourths Negro; *mulatto* was to describe persons who were three-eighths to five-eighths black; *quadroon* applied to persons one-fourth black; and *octoroon* referred to those with one-eighth or any trace of Negro ancestry.

- In 1900, the only printed choices were White, Black, Chinese, Japanese, or Indian.
- For 1910 and 1920, the choices were White, Black, Mulatto, Chinese, Japanese, Indian, and Other. *Mulatto* was to apply to persons "having some proportion or perceptible trace of negro blood."
- In 1930, Mexican was added to the choices. *Mulatto* was withdrawn; persons of mixed white and black parentage were to be reported as Negro. Those of mixed Indian and Negro blood were to be reported as Negro, unless the Indian blood was predominant and the person was considered an Indian in the community. By the same token, those of mixed white and Indian blood were to be reported as Indian, unless the person was accepted as white in the community.
- By 1940, the main choices were White, Negro, Indian, Chinese, Japanese, Filipino, Hindu, and Korean; the enumerator was to write in any other "race."

Tips For Success

As you research in census records, keep in mind these tips for success:

1. Read all available federal and state censuses for each ancestor.

2. Copy or photocopy every person and detail in the family's entry. Include people of different surnames; often they were relatives.

3. Use the Latin word *sic* (meaning "thus") in your notes to indicate obvious errors or surprises. This notation means that you copied what was given even though you question its accuracy. Such errors may occur in ages, names, birthplaces, and even the recording of males as females and vice versa.

4. Read several pages on either side of your family's entry to look for known relatives or other households by the same surname. Families of the same surname may or may not be related.

5. Be aware that ages of infants and, sometimes, young children were expressed in months as a fraction—5/12 for five months or 2 1/12 for two years and one month. You may see a newborn's age reported several ways—21/30 for twenty-one days old or 0/12 for less than one month old. Examples are shown in Figure 2-3, on page 25, and Figure 6-3, on page 117.

6. Expect ages and name spellings to vary. In five censuses, one individual could be listed as ages five, twelve, twenty-three, thirty-seven, and forty-eight years. Why? Many families did not keep written records of birthdays. (See also item nine on page 22, the case study on pages 82–84, and chapters three and six.)

7. In your notes, indicate any "negative evidence"—some detail that is missing or left blank, such as someone's birthplace or occupation. Doing this the first time you read the census keeps you from having to repeat your effort later when you realize that the information is not in your notes.

8. Write in your notes or on your photocopy enough information to create a footnote to document the family's entry on your family group sheet. There are many correct ways to create such a footnote; this is one example:

U.S. Census of 1880, roll 1256, New County, Texas, Newburg post office, e.d. 54, sheet 14, family 45, household of George Greenberry.

- census year
- roll number of the microfilm, or CD-ROM title, publisher, and number
- county and state
- town or post office name, ward number, or other finding information, if given
- enumeration district (e.d.) for censuses of 1880 and after
- page or sheet number (If two numbers are given, note which is a stamped number and which is handwritten.)
- family number
- name of the head of household or line number of the individual
- for online digital images, the full Web address of the image you use and the date you accessed it

9. Remember, we do not know (a) who furnished the family's information, (b) to what extent the informant knew the correct information or did not want to tell the truth, (c) whether the informant spoke in a way that was difficult for the census taker to understand, or (d) what the census taker thought he heard. Sometimes we find a census entry of an ancestral family that appears to be a different family because of discrepancies in the recorded information. Figure 2-2, on page 23, illustrates such a situation. Although the father's name was the only constant in the two entries, family sources and marriage records help determine that both entries were for the same family, and the names in the 1910 entry were correct.

INDEXES AND SOUNDEX

For many of the censuses between 1870 and 1930, indexes are available—on CD-ROM, in books and journals, on microfilm, and on the Internet. In 2001, Heritage Quest in North Salt Lake, Utah, released a CD-ROM, *African-Americans in the 1870 U.S. Federal Census*, as part of its Generations Archives' World Immigration Series (#ACD-0101). This index covers heads of household and persons living in a household of a different surname; it does not include all individuals.

CD Source

Also in 2001, **the Church of Jesus Christ of Latter-day Saints in Salt Lake City issued a set of fifty-five compact discs, called** *1880 United States Census and National Index,* **that is available in many libraries.** The database is searchable using many pieces of information, including name, age, race, and birthplace. These CD-ROM publications save researchers valuable time by (1) speeding up the process of locating ancestors on the census microfilm and (2) identifying households that had no children age ten and under and therefore were not included in the Soundex. (See the discussion of Soundex on page 24.)

What if you do not find your ancestral head of household listed in a statewide index?

- The family name may be spelled differently in the census; try variant spellings and similar names. (See also chapter six.)
- The head of household may be indexed under initials, nickname, or middle name. Anthony Davis could be enumerated and indexed as A. Davis, Tony Davis, or even J.A. Davis if, for example, his name was James Anthony Davis and you were not aware that he went by his middle name. The other

---

1900 AND 1910 CENSUS ENTRIES FOR THE RICHARD A. CROOM FAMILY

1900 entry*
Richard Croom, age 33, born June 1866
wife Lilla [*sic*], age 25, born September 1874

son Lee Andrew, age 4, born December 1895
son Allen, age 2, born January 1898
son Richard L., age 5/12, born March 1900

1910 entry**
Richard A. Croom, age 42, his 2nd marriage
wife Rosa P., age 31, her first marriage, this couple
   married for 5 years; mother of 3 children, all 3 living
dau Leona, age 13
dau Anna, age 11
son Lafayett [*sic*], age 9
son Marcillis, age 3
dau Flecta, age 2
dau Sue May, age 10/12

*U.S. Census of 1900, roll 1190, Craven County, North Carolina, township 3, e.d. 45, sheet 8, family 152, household of Richard Croom, all family members listed as black.

**U.S. Census of 1910, roll 1104, Craven County, North Carolina, Ft. Barnwell precinct, e.d. 17, sheet 10A, family 184, household of Richard A. Croom, all family members listed as mulatto.

What evidence indicates that the two census entries are for the same family?

1. The marriage of Richard Croom to Lila Hargett, 2 December 1894, is shown in the Craven County, North Carolina, Marriage Records, vol. 6 (1879–1898):65, FHL microfilm 0288298. This is consistent with the 1900 census entry.

2. The 1910 census reports that Rosa P. Croom, married five years to Richard by 1910, was the mother of three children and all three were living at the time of the 1910 census. The census record clearly shows the three younger children and the six-year gap between the birth of Lila's third child and Rosa's first. This information suggests that Lila died between 1900 and 1905 and that Richard married Rosa about 1905. Number 6 below supports this suggestion of Lila's death.

3. The knowledge and memories of three family members strenghten the evidence that Lee Andrew and Allen in the 1900 census were in fact the daughters Leona and Anna of the 1910 census and suggest that their brother Lafayette was probably named Richard Lafayette. First, in a telephone interview by Emily Croom, 19 September 2001, Ida Brown of Craven County, North Carolina, a step-daughter of Richard Croom, without prompting, named Richard's three wives—Lila Hargett, Rosa Barshield, and Catherine Chapman. The first two are consistent with the census entries and 1894 marriage license. County marriage records confirmed the third wife, Ida's mother.

4. In a telephone interview by Emily Croom, 6 April 2001, Lillie Dawson of Ft. Barnwell, North Carolina, daughter of Richard Croom's daughter Anna, named Richard's second and third wives (Rosa and Catherine), her mother's brother Lafayette, sister Leona, and half-brothers Marcill and Odell (not yet identified in other records). Her memory was consistent with the 1910 census entry.

5. In a letter to Emily Croom, 16 April 2001, Yvonne Corey of Brooklyn, New York, acknowledged that the 1910 family is the correct family, as she knew her grandmother Leona's sisters Anna and Flecta and one brother.

6. Richard's daughter Leona Croom married William Collins, according to the three family members and county marriage records—Craven County, North Carolina, Marriage Licenses, 1915–1919, license #1787, dated 20 January 1915, FHL microfilm 0288286. The license shows Louna [Leona] Croom as the daughter of Richard and Lila Croom; at the time of this marriage, Leona's father was still living and her mother was deceased. This marriage record helps identify the "son Lee Andrew" of the 1900 census as the daughter Leona of the 1910 census and the 1915 marriage record.

7. No contradictory evidence has been found to suggest that the two census entries were different families.

Figure 2-2 Evaluating discrepancies in census entries.

members of the household will help you know whether you have found the right person.

- The indexer may have misread the name.
- The family may have been living elsewhere; try a different state.
- The ancestor or family may have been living with a head of household other than the one you expect and thus was not indexed under the name you expect; you can read page by page in the county where you believe they were living.
- The indexer may have missed the family, so read the county page by page.
- The census taker may have missed the family in the census taking process, or parts of the schedule are missing.
- The family may have changed its surname.

Soundex

A special index called Soundex is available for certain census records between 1880 and 1930.

1. The 1880 Soundex is available for all states but only for households with children age ten and under.
2. The 1900 and 1920 Soundex is available for all states.
3. The 1910 Soundex is available for twenty-one states: Alabama, Arkansas, California, Florida, Georgia, Illinois, Kansas, Kentucky, Louisiana, Michigan, Mississippi, Missouri, North Carolina, Ohio, Oklahoma, Pennsylvania, South Carolina, Tennessee, Texas, Virginia, and West Virginia. (Some of these states have typewritten Miracode cards instead of handwritten Soundex cards. Instead of sheet and line numbers, Miracode cards give you the family number as a finding aid. Both use the coding system explained below.)
4. The 1930 Soundex is available for ten Southern states—Alabama, Arkansas, Florida, Georgia, Louisiana, Mississippi, North Carolina, South Carolina, Tennessee, Virginia—and parts of Kentucky (Bell, Floyd, Harlan, Kenton, Muhlenberg, Perry, and Pike counties) and West Virginia (Fayette, Harrison, Kanawha, Logan, McDowell, Mercer, and Raleigh counties).

Tip

Photocopy this section, and keep it with your research materials for reference.

The Soundex gives you the finding information you need to look for your ancestral families on the census microfilm—county, enumeration district number, sheet number, and beginning line number. Using this index is a necessary step in researching federal census records.

Soundex is an index based on the sounds in the surname. To use the Soundex, you must first create a code using the process on pages 25–26. Then, you find that code on the Soundex microfilm. This film shows cards, each containing a partial abstract of a household's census entry. (Because it is a partial abstract, it does not take the place of reading the census record itself.) The cards give you the advantage of surveying entire families rather than reading for only the name of the head of household as you would in most indexes. Households of all ethnic groups are mixed together on the Soundex, but the head of household is identified by race on the Soundex card.

Figure 2-3, on page 25, shows Soundex cards from the 1880 census, which

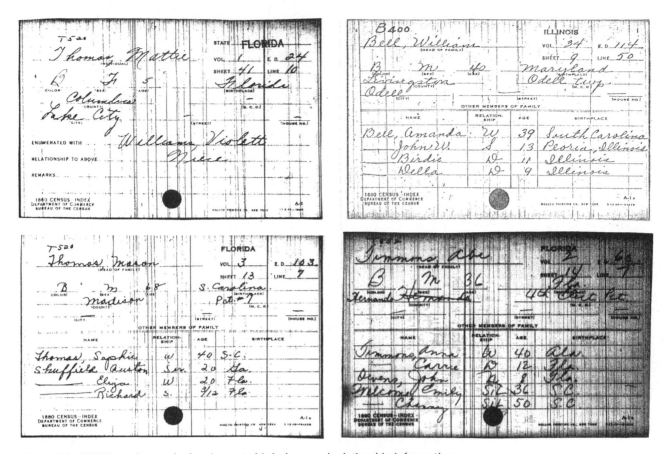

Figure 2-3 1880 Soundex cards showing age, birthplace, and relationship information.

are similar to the cards for later censuses. The family card for the Abe Timmons family illustrates a household with a nuclear family and three relatives of other surnames—a nephew and two sisters-in-law. The individual card for Mattie Thomas helps locate an individual living in a household of a different surname— a child living with her aunt, Violett Williams. The card for the William Bell family of Illinois shows one person for whom the census taker reported not only the state where the child was born but the city as well. The Mason Thomas household includes two families; notice that the infant was three months old, with the age indicated as 3/12.

Once the household Soundex abstracts were made, they were sorted by state and placed in a loose alphabetical order, according to the code. Several different names may have the same code because they contain similar sounds. In this way, the names Gill, Gilly, Galey, and Gale have the same code and are grouped together on the film. They are sorted alphabetically by the first name of the head of household. Names enumerated in the census only by initials appear first on the Soundex microfilm: A.B. Gill before Albert Gale and Andrew Gilly.

The Soundex Code

Here's how to create the code for your ancestors so that you can look for them in the Soundex and then in the census:

1. Write down the surname you are researching, and set aside the initial letter to begin the code, as in *A* for Armstead.
2. With the remaining letters, cross out all vowels and the letters *w*, *h*, and *y*.
3. With the remaining consonants, create the rest of the code—three (and only three) numbers from this chart. The code for the name Armstead uses only the *r*, *m*, and *s* and ignores the *t* and *d*.

Code numbers	Consonants
1	b, p, f, v
2	c, s, k, g, j, q, x, z
3	d, t
4	l
5	m, n
6	r

4. Put the code numbers with the initial letter to form the Soundex code. For Armstead, you would use "A-*r*-*m*-*s*" and get the code A652.
5. If you run out of consonants before you get a three-digit code, add zeros. Examples:
Kelsey (K *l* *s* + 0)—K420
Kelly (K *l* + 00)—K400
Key—K000
6. Double letters and consecutive letters with the same code count only once. Examples:
Hall, Hill, Hull (Double letters *ll* = 4)—H400
Lloyd (Double letters *Ll* begin the code and *d* = 3)—L300
Scardon (Consecutive letters *Sc* form the beginning of the code; the *r*, *d*, and *n* get the code numbers 6, 3, and 5)—S635
Griggs (The three consecutive letters *ggs* are coded once; *G* + *r* + *ggs*)—G620
7. Expect ancestral names to be spelled in various ways in records: Blount or Blunt, Armistead or Armstead. These variations do not change the Soundex code, but some do. One example is Garner (G656) and Gardner (G635).

For More Info

For more on using census records, see these books listed in the bibliography: Croom's *Genealogist's Companion & Sourcebook*; Croom's *Unpuzzling Your Past*, 4th edition; and Hinckley's *Your Guide to the Federal Census*.

Some Web sites, such as <www.archives.gov/research_room/genealogy/census/soundex.htm>, will figure the Soundex code for you. If you use such aids, be sure to get the codes for variant spellings of each surname. Also, review the codes supplied to you to check your understanding of the coding system.

When you find your family on the Soundex microfilm, copy or photocopy the entry, especially the finding information mentioned on page 24. Then find the roll of census microfilm for the state and county where the family lived; several counties may be on one roll of film. When you find the beginning of the county's pages, scroll to the enumeration district you need and then to the sheet number and line number where your family's enumeration begins. If the family is the last one on the page, check the next page in case their entry extends to it.

A CASE STUDY
The Search for Ancestors of Elizabeth "Lizzie" (Blount) Armstead

The remainder of this chapter is a case study that illustrates the value of census records in working back to 1870. The known ancestor was Lizzie Armstead, and her descendants wanted to learn more about her history. As it turned out, census records provided a great deal of information and showed the family's migration through three states and one grandfather's birth in another. Records in these states may provide further information on the family.

Case Study

In the case study, you will see what various census records reported about Lizzie and her family and how each piece of new information guided the search for more. Ages, birthplaces, and similarities in names became clues for the next step. Another important factor in this search was studying the cluster of Lizzie's relatives, not just focusing on Lizzie.

Although Lizzie's descendants had only sketchy information about her at the beginning, each tidbit became an important clue in the search. It is helpful to write out what is "known" as you start looking for the "unknown," as shown below.

Family members provided the following information about the target ancestor:

1. Lizzie was born in Lee County, Arkansas, a daughter of Fay and Mary Blount.
2. She married John Armstead in Lee County, Arkansas, and had two known children: a son Edgar and a daughter Jessie.
3. A sister, Captolia Blount, married Monroe Dukes.
4. Lizzie may have had another sister, Dee Anna Blount.
5. Lizzie's birth and death dates were unknown to the informant.
6. Lizzie's daughter Jessie was born in Arkansas before 1920.

Twentieth-Century Censuses

Since Lizzie's daughter Jessie was born before 1920, the 1920 census was a logical choice for starting the search. The 1920 Arkansas Soundex and census reported the following household:[4]

Notes

In the census records abstracted in this case study, members of the household had the same surname as the head of household unless otherwise noted.

1. John Armstead, age 45, born in Mississippi, as were his parents
2. Lizzie, wife, age 31, born in Arkansas, with parents reportedly born in Tennessee
3. Edgar, son, age 11, born in Arkansas, as were the other children
4. Jessie, daughter, age 9
5. John, daughter [sic], age 8
6. Berniece, daughter, age 6
7. Freddie, daughter, age 5
8. Charlotte Tottivor [sic], mother of the head of household, age 65, born in Mississippi, as were her parents

The age of the oldest child, Edgar (eleven years), suggested that John and Lizzie probably married before 1910 and therefore would be enumerated together in the 1910 census. Indeed, the Arkansas Soundex and Lee County census showed their household:[5]

1. John Armstead, age 34, born in Mississippi, as were his parents (consistent with 1920 census)
2. [wife], no first name recorded, age 24, born in Arkansas, father born in Alabama, mother born in Tennessee (mother's birthplace consistent with 1920 census)
3. Edcar [*sic*], son, age 2, born in Arkansas (consistent with 1920 census)
4. Scharllott [*sic*] Tolivor, mother of head of household, age 54, born in Mississippi, parents reportedly born in Alabama (different from 1920 census)

Age information in the two censuses allowed calculation of Lizzie's birth year between about 1886 and 1889—1910 minus 24 and 1920 minus 31. Thus, Lizzie would have been between eleven and fourteen years old in the 1900 census and probably a child in her parents' household.

The 1900 Arkansas Soundex revealed no candidate for Lizzie's father under the name Fay Blount, as the family remembered it. However, the Soundex showed the following Lee County household:[6]

1. Mary Blount, widow, age 37, born in Alabama, as were her parents
2. Dee Anna, daughter, age 18, born in Arkansas, as were the other children, with parents reportedly born in Alabama
3. Lizzie, daughter, age 13, reportedly born in 1887 (The 1900 census reported a month and year of birth for each individual.)
4. Captolia, daughter, age 10
5. James Blount, brother-in-law, age 29 (in conflict with the reported birth year of 1879, which suggested an age of 20 or 21 in 1900), born in Alabama, as were his parents

Because the eighteen-year-old Dee Anna, the oldest child at home, was born in Arkansas, Mary Blount and her deceased husband were likely in Arkansas by 1882, and he died probably after ten-year-old Captolia was born—about 1890 or during that decade. No other families in Mary's neighborhood showed obvious connections to her and her family. However, listed next to Mary in the census was forty-six-year-old Elias Weems, reportedly born in Alabama, as were his parents and Mary and James Blount. This birthplace similarity of the neighbors may have been mere coincidence, but it was worth noting.

The 1880 Census Presents A Challenge

Mary Blount's age of thirty-seven years in 1900, with a reported birth date of 1862, suggested that the earliest she and her husband, Fay Blount, would have appeared as a family would have been the 1880 census. However, the Soundex did not show them enumerated as a household. If daughter Dee Anna Blount, born about 1882, was indeed the first child born to the couple, they would not appear in the 1880 Soundex because the household contained no child age ten or under. In addition, it was possible that Mary and Fay Blount married after 1880.

In fact, the Blount entries in the 1880 Arkansas Soundex did not show Fay Blount or anyone of his approximate age and birthplace. Was Fay a nickname?

Was he not in Arkansas? A search for Mary's family in 1880 was not possible since her maiden name was not known at this time in the search.

What were the research options at this point?

- Search for a marriage record to try to determine when and where they married and learn Mary's maiden name.
- Read page by page the Lee County 1880 census, looking for one or both of the couple.
- Try a "cluster" approach.

Although any of these options would have been a legitimate choice, the decision was to search first for Mary Blount after 1900. Because she was not listed in either the 1910 or 1920 Soundex, the search turned next to Mary's cluster of relatives.

"Cluster genealogy" is the idea that ancestors lived among relatives, neighbors, and friends and that studying these people often helps you learn more about the ancestors. Besides, neighbors sometimes were also relatives.

The Cluster

One other known family member who might provide additional insight into the family was Lizzie's sister, and Mary and Fay Blount's daughter, Cappie (Captolia), who was known to have married Monroe Dukes. The 1920 Arkansas Soundex and census revealed this Dukes family in Lee County:[7]

1. R.M. Dukes, age 35, born in Mississippi, as were his parents
2. Capie, wife, age 28, born in Arkansas, as was her father, with Tennessee given as her mother's birthplace
3. Aliv [*sic*] V., daughter, age 9
4. Columbus, son, age 7
5. Pearline, daughter, age 5
6. Hattie, daughter, age 2 9/12 (two years, nine months)
7. Betty Russeau, aunt of the head of household, age 43

No other households in the immediate neighborhood showed apparent connections to this family. However, the search moved backward to 1910 and found this couple listed in Lee County:[8]

1. Monrow [*sic*] Dukes, age 25, married but with no children
2. Castora [*sic*], wife, age 20, born in Arkansas, with both parents born in Alabama (not Arkansas and Tennessee as reported in 1920)

The 1900 and 1910 censuses asked how many children a woman had borne and how many were still living; reported relationships were supposed to be the relationship to the head of household.

Enumerated next to this Dukes household in 1910 was this family:

1. Fred Williams, age 60
2. Mary, wife, age 46, married eight years (since about 1902), born in Alabama as were her parents, mother of six children, of whom three were living in 1910
3. Tishue, age 8, reported as daughter (a question needing further research)
4. Gussie, age 7, reported as daughter (a question needing further research)
5. Peter Turner, stepson to head of household, age 21
6. Sarah Murf, aunt to head of household, age 75
7. Elias Weems, father-in-law of head of household (thus Mary's father), age 88, born in Alabama

Was it possible that Mary Williams was the former Mary Blount? A number of facts pointed to this conclusion:

- At age forty-seven in 1910, Mary Williams would have been approximately the same age as thirty-six-year-old Mary Blount in 1900.
- Both Marys were born in Alabama, as were their parents.
- Mary Blount's remarriage after 1900 would explain why she was not found in the 1910 or 1920 census under the Blount name. (It was later confirmed in Lee County marriage records that Mary Blount married Fred Williams on 2 February 1902.[9])
- It was likely more than coincidence that in 1900 forty-six-year-old Elias Weems, possibly her brother, lived next to Mary Blount and that in 1910 Mary Williams's eighty-eight-year-old father of the same name was in her home.

Reminder

Discovering Mary Blount's maiden name was a significant find; identifying her father was a greater find. These breakthroughs do not immediately tell much about the Blount line—the original goal of discovering Lizzie (Blount) Armstead's heritage. However, **the mother's line is half the ancestors, and researchers must go where the information leads them.** The discovery of the Weems surname and specifically the eighty-eight-year-old Elias Weems allowed an expansion and extension of the search. (Because no relationship has been established between the two Weems men, they will be designated *senior* and *junior* due to their age differences.)

The elder Elias Weems had appeared in the 1910 Arkansas census. Could he be found there in previous censuses? No. Neither Elias Sr. nor Elias Jr. appeared in Arkansas censuses prior to 1900, the year when Elias Jr. was living next to Mary Blount.

Because both Eliases, Mary Blount Williams, James Blount, and supposedly Fay Blount (from his children's census reports of their father's birthplace) were born in Alabama, that state was the next target of census research. However, these families were not enumerated there prior to 1900.

The Cluster Expands

At this point in the search, a review of Elias Jr.'s family in the 1900 census indicated that his wife and child were born in Tennessee. Thus, the search expanded to a third state, Tennessee. Elias Weems Jr. was listed in the 1880 Tennessee Soundex in Haywood County; Elias Weems Sr. was not.

When Elias Jr.'s household was located in the census, Elias Sr. was found two houses away with the following family members, all reportedly born in Alabama.[10] They were not included in the Soundex because no child in the home was age ten or younger.

1. Elias Weems, age 56
2. Easter, daughter, age 21
3. Mary, daughter, age 18
4. Lizzie, daughter, age 16
5. Columbia, daughter, age 12

Something unexpected turned up in the Weems neighborhood. Several pages from Elias Sr.'s entry was the family of Sam Blount:[11]

1. Sam Blount, age 60, born in North Carolina, as were his parents
2. Agnes, wife, age 40, born in Georgia
3. Fayette, son, age 18, born in Alabama
4. Adline, daughter, age 16, born in Alabama
5. Phillis, daughter, age 14, born in Alabama
6. Frank, son age 13, born in Alabama
7. Jim, son, age 10, born in Tennessee
8. Rachel, daughter, age 8, born in Tennessee
9. Roxanna, daughter, age 7, born in Tennessee
10. Sam, son, age 5, born in Tennessee
11. Alex, son, age 3, born in Tennessee
12. Mary Perry, stepdaughter, age 13, born in Alabama

In this household was eighteen-year-old Fayette Blount, born in Alabama. Was Fayette the same as Fay Blount who married Mary Weems? Several factors seemed to support the possibility:

- Fayette, like Fay, was born in Alabama, as had been reported in 1900 as the birthplace of Mary's children's father.
- Fay's brother James Blount was listed in Mary's household in 1900, with a reported age of twenty-nine, and a ten-year-old Jim Blount was in Sam Blount's household in 1880. The two censuses indicated that James and Jim were about the same age (born about 1869–1870).

However, Jim's birthplace was given as Tennessee, not Alabama as reported for James in 1900. In addition, the 1900 census gave Alabama as the birthplace of James's parents, not North Carolina as reported for Sam Blount in 1880. Nevertheless, Haywood County, Tennessee, marriage records later confirmed that Fayette Blount married Mary Weems on 12 March 1881.[12]

In 1880, Sam's wife, Agnes Blount, was forty years old and reported as Georgia-born. She was too young to be Fayette's mother. The presence of a stepdaughter, Mary Perry, suggested that Agnes was Sam's second wife. Indeed, a marriage record for Samuel Blunt [sic] and Agnis [sic] Perry was later found in the Haywood County, Tennessee, records.[13] Based on the age of thirteen-year-old Frank, the last Blount child born in Alabama, Sam moved from Alabama after 1867 and by 1870, the approximate birth year of Jim, the first child reported with a Tennessee birthplace.

The Sam Blount family could not be found in the 1870 census for Tennessee. However, the Elias Weems Sr. family was enumerated in Haywood County with the following members:[14]

1. Elias Weems, age 51, born in Alabama
2. Elizabeth, age 44, born in Tennessee
3. Perry, age 20, born in Alabama
4. Harriett, age 16, born in Alabama
5. Elias Jr., age 18, born in Alabama
6. Ester, age 12, born in Alabama

Idea Generator

Birthplaces reported in these censuses for individuals and for their parents help you create a timeline to estimate where they were at a given time. In this case study, this information was essential.

7. Mary, age 9, born in Alabama
8. Elizabeth, age 5, born in Alabama
9. Claud, age 2, born in Tennessee
10. John White, age 21, born in Alabama
11. Malinda White, age 22, born in Alabama

Reminder

Because **relationships were not stated in the 1870 census**, it was not clear whether Elizabeth was Elias Sr.'s wife, nor could it be determined whether she was the mother of all the children. She was no longer in the household by 1880. In 1910, Elias Sr. (reported as eighty-eight years old in Mary Williams's household) was listed as a widower.

According to the ages and birthplaces of the children, Elias Weems Sr. left Alabama between 1865 and 1867. Although born in Alabama, Mary grew up in Tennessee. This fact could explain why Lizzie's census records consistently, but mistakenly, reported her mother of Tennessee birth.

The Search for Sam Blount

The Sam Blount household was not enumerated in Tennessee in 1870, but evidence suggested that the family may have been in Alabama. The ages and birthplaces of the children in the 1880 household had suggested that the family left Alabama between 1867 and 1870. In 1870, a family headed by S. Blount indeed was living in Cherokee County, Alabama.[15] Although the Emaline Blount in the 1870 census was not listed with the 1880 household and the ages and birthplaces of Sam Blount of 1880 and S. Blount of 1870 were different, the members of the two households were nearly identical. The 1870 census enumerated the following:

1. S. Blount, age 55, born in Georgia
2. Emaline, age 22, born in Georgia, occupation given as keeping house
3. Cynthia, age 17, born in Alabama
4. Zilpha [*sic*], age 16, born in Alabama
5. Lucinda, age 12, born in Alabama
6. Lafayette, age 10, born in Alabama, likely the Fay of the initial search
7. Adaline, age 9, born in Alabama
8. Phillis, age 7, born in Alabama
9. Frank, age 5, born in Alabama (reported as age 13 in 1880)
10. Jane, age 7 or 2 (difficult to read), born in Alabama
11. James, age 1, born in Alabama, the same birthplace as reported in Mary Blount's 1900 household
12. Jim [*sic*], age 6, born in Alabama (Both James and Jim were listed and in this order. Jim may have been the son of Emaline, who could easily have been Sam Blount's daughter rather than his wife.)

Warning

Without relationships stated, researchers can suggest but not assume how household members may have been related.

Apparently, Sam Blount moved his family to Tennessee in or shortly after 1870. Nevertheless, the Blount line had now been traced through three states—Arkansas, Tennessee, and Alabama—to the county in Alabama where Fay Blount may have been born. Although many gaps need filling and many resources need to be studied, the foundation is laid. The identification of the new

Blount and Weems ancestors and their whereabouts in 1870 may provide clues that could lead to information on their lives before the Civil War.

One clue for the Blount family is a possible connection to a white neighbor, T.R. Lowe, listed next to them in 1870. Circumstantial evidence in the census suggests a possible connection and thus warrants further investigation:

- Nearness of residence of the two families in 1870 could suggest pre–Civil War association in the same location.
- Listed in the T.R. Lowe household in 1870 was a thirty-five-year-old black male named E. Blount, a laborer, born in Georgia, a likely relative of Sam Blount.
- The ages and birthplaces of the children in both households suggest that both families may have arrived in Alabama from Georgia about the same time.

This evidence, though circumstantial, is the type from which a search strategy is formulated for the pre–Civil War years, as discussed in chapters six through nine of this book.

The search for the Blount ancestors illustrates (1) the importance of clues from the family as a background for census research and (2) the use of census records to augment and confirm family knowledge and build the framework for future research. Other sources—birth and death certificates and marriage records, among others—often verify or clarify the census information and provide additional facts. As you research, you will realize that census records provide much of the information you need in order to study the other records. In addition, for African Americans, few other records are as comprehensive and as readily available as the censuses.

THREE

Federal Sources

For More Info

For more information on records in these jurisdictions, see Croom's *Unpuzzling Your Past*, 4th edition, chapters 10-13, and Croom's *Genealogist's Companion & Sourcebook*.

Internet Source

For more information on Social Security and its history, visit the Web site at <www.ssa.gov/history/reports/briefhistory.html>.

Post–Civil War public resources abound in federal, state, local, and county jurisdictions. Each record group provides personal information about thousands of individuals—perhaps your ancestors. You will not find all your ancestors mentioned in all these records, but any of the records could have good genealogical information. Because it is beyond the scope of this book to discuss all conceivable records of use to genealogists, this chapter and the next will consider the most commonly useful public records. This chapter focuses on federal sources.

Besides census records, five types of federal records are particularly useful for African-American research after 1865:

- Social Security records
- Military records
- Archives of the Bureau of Refugees, Freedmen, and Abandoned Lands, commonly called the Freedmen's Bureau
- Archives of the Freedman's Savings and Trust Company
- Federal land files

SOCIAL SECURITY RECORDS

The Social Security Administration began issuing Social Security numbers and cards in November 1936, but not all occupations were eligible for coverage in the early years, and not all eligible persons applied for cards. At first, the "old age pension" part of Social Security covered mostly industrial workers who were employed on or after 1 January 1937. Over the years, the rules and procedures changed so that more individuals were eligible and paid into the system for assistance if they became disabled or when they retired.

Two kinds of records are sometimes available because of an ancestor's participation in the Social Security system. One database is the Social Security Death Index (SSDI), accessible online without cost at Ancestry.com and FamilySearch

.org, and on CD-ROM at many libraries. This index reports post-1936 deaths of millions of individuals with Social Security numbers, along with each person's birth year, death date and place, and the state where the person applied for a Social Security card. This index provides many researchers with information on ancestors and their siblings. If you do not find ancestors listed, remember that (1) not all deaths were reported and (2) not all ancestors who died after 1936 participated in Social Security.

The second record is the Social Security application (SS-5). If you find an ancestor mentioned in the death index or if you have the Social Security number of a deceased relative from a death certificate or family papers, you may want to get a copy of the person's original application. Figure 3-1, below, illustrates the genealogical value of the SS-5, showing the individual's name, birth date and place, parents' names with mother's maiden name, signature, and employment information at the time of the application. This information can help confirm family memory or provide new data.

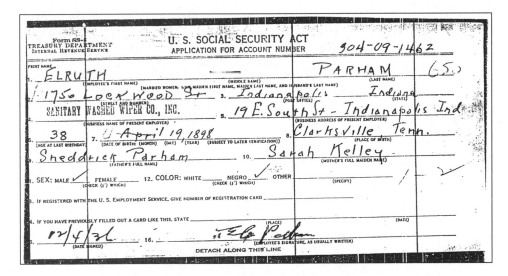

Figure 3-1 Social Security application (SS-5) for Elruth Parham, SS no. 304-09-1462, 4 December 1936, microprint copy from Freedom of Information Office, Social Security Administration, Baltimore, Maryland.

If the ancestor was listed on the Social Security Death Index on the Ancestry .com Web site, the site can generate a letter for you to send to the Social Security office in Baltimore, along with a twenty-seven-dollar search fee, in order to get a copy of the ancestor's application. If the ancestor was not listed on this index, you can send a copy of the death certificate (showing the Social Security number), a letter of request for a copy of the application, and your search fee to the Social Security Administration, Freedom of Information Act (or FOIA) Workgroup, 300 North Greene Street, P.O. Box 33022, Baltimore, Maryland 21290.

MILITARY RECORDS

African Americans in the United States have participated in military service since the colonial period. Records pertaining to colonial militia service are usually housed in state archives, and many have been abstracted and published. Thousands of federal military records exist at the National Archives in Washington, DC, for soldiers and sailors who served in military and naval forces since the American Revolution. However, the great majority of African Americans in military and naval forces served after 1861, the beginning of the Civil War.

Many kinds of records pertain to military units and their members, including muster rolls and other rosters, pay rolls, enlistment papers, official correspondence, files of court-martial cases, prisoner and casualty lists, burial records, "returns" and ship logs dealing with where units were and what they were doing, reports of engagements, and records of soldiers' homes for the aged or disabled. Some of these records mention individual servicemen and are beneficial for studying in depth an individual's service and life, along with his unit. Many of these records have been microfilmed. Other files, such as draft records and descriptive rolls of draftees, are not yet available on microfilm.

For more comprehensive information on military records and their availability, consult such books as these:

> *Black Studies: A Select Catalog of National Archives Microfilm Publications.* Washington, D.C.: National Archives Trust Fund Board, 1996.
>
> *Military Service Records: A Select Catalog of National Archives Microfilm Publications.* Washington, D.C.: National Archives Trust Fund Board, 1985. Consult the National Archives Web site, <www.archives.gov/public ations/microfilm_catalogs.html>, under "Subject Catalogs" for the online version of the *Black Studies* and *Military Service Records* catalogs. To learn of new microfilm publications, consult <www.archives.gov/research _room/genealogy/> under "Now Featuring—New Microfilm Publications."
>
> Morebeck, Nancy Justus. *Locating Union & Confederate Records: A Guide to the Most Commonly Used Civil War Records of the National Archives and Family History Library.* North Salt Lake, Utah: Heritage Quest, 2001.
>
> Neagles, James C. *U.S. Military Records: A Guide to Federal & State Sources.*

Identifying an Ancestor With Military Service

Sources

Some of these finding aids can help you determine whether an ancestor served:

- Family photographs, papers, tradition.
- The 1910 census, column 30, asked whether a man was a Civil War veteran; not all families answered the question.
- The 1930 census, columns 30 and 31, asked about military/naval service and in which war.
- The National Park Service Web site: <www.itd.nps.gov/cwss>.
- *Index to Compiled Service Records of Volunteer Union Soldiers Who Served With United States Colored Troops*, National Archives microfilm series M589.
- *General Index to Pension Files, 1861–1934*, National Archives microfilm series T288.
- Special 1890 census of Union veterans and widows.
- Numerous published indexes to and abstracts of service records and pension applications from different wars; these are found in many libraries.
- Hewett, Janet B., ed. *The Roster of Union Soldiers.* 33 vols. Wilmington, N.C.: Broadfoot Publishing Company, 1998. Created from military service records.

Compiled Service Records

The first records of individual service personnel that genealogists need to obtain are compiled military service records and/or pension records on file at the National Archives. To request a copy of service records before World War I, request form NATF 86 from the National Archives, 700 Pennsylvania Avenue NW, Washington, DC 20408, or 8601 Adelphi Road, College Park, Maryland 20740-6001. You can also send an e-mail request for forms to inquire@nara .gov; specify the form you need and your mailing address. To request a copy of a pension file, get form NATF 85. It is advisable to request copies of both records. For both order forms, you need to supply the serviceman's name, state from which he served, branch of service, unit if known, and birth and death dates and places if known. The forms contain instructions and information on cost.

Compiled military service records may include such details as the individual's rank and unit, enlistment and discharge dates, birthplace, wounds, hospitalization, and capture and release. These records were created from muster rolls, hospital records, regimental returns, and other documents prepared by military units. Check the microfilm *Index to Compiled Service Records of Volunteer Union Soldiers Who Served with United States Colored Troops*, National Archives publication M589. This alphabetical card index of African-American Civil War volunteers does not include those who served in state units. The microfilm is available at the National Archives and its branches, some research libraries, and the Heritage Quest rental program.

If you find evidence that an ancestor served, request a copy of the service record from the National Archives. At this writing, most Union Army military service records have not yet been microfilmed, although the process has begun. One National Archives project filmed in 2001 is over one hundred rolls of *Compiled Service Records of Volunteer Union Soldiers Who Served with the 8th–13th Infantry Regiments, United States Colored Troops* (M1821). In addition, a number of records—returns, descriptive books, muster rolls and the like—for one state unit are available on microfilm: *Records of the Fifty-Fourth Massachusetts Infantry Regiment (Colored), 1863–1865* (M1659).

An interesting article based on these compiled service records is "Preserving the Legacy of the United States Colored Troops," by Ms. Budge Weidman. Not only does the article include a brief history of the U.S.C.T., but it also shares some of the treasures the records contain. At this writing, **the article and others on African-American records appear on the National Archives Web site at <www.archi ves.gov/publications/prologue/summer_1997_table_of_contents.html>**. If you cannot access this URL, you can e-mail the National Archives at inquire@nara.gov to request a copy.

Pension Records

Of the two kinds of records, the pension files usually are more helpful for genealogists because they may contain information about the veteran's life and family. At least two National Archives microfilm indexes may be helpful in determining whether a serviceman, his widow, his minor children, or his aged parents applied for a pension:

Internet Source

You can request these forms online at www.archiv es.gov/global_pages/ inquire_form.html.

Internet Source

- *General Index to Pension Files, 1861–1934* (T288). This alphabetical publication generally pertains to service between 1861 and 1916, including post–Civil War service. The microfilm is available at major research libraries, the National Archives and its branches, the Heritage Quest rental program, and the Family History Library and through its Family History Centers.
- *Veterans Administration Pension Payment Cards, 1907–1933* (M850). This huge series of microfilm covers pensioners on the rolls during the given dates excluding World War I pensioners. The rolls are alphabetical by the surname of the pensioner. The microfilm is available at the National Archives and the Family History Library and through its Family History Centers. Check with individual National Archives branches and other libraries for their holdings.

To determine which roll of microfilm you need to use, see the alphabetical lists in the National Archives *Military Service Records* and *Black Studies* catalogs. These catalogs are online at <www.archives.gov/publications/microfilm_catalogs.html> under "Subject Catalogs."

Because Confederate pensions were programs only of the former Confederate and border states, the records are kept at the state archives, not the National Archives. However, rarely were blacks in Confederate service. Information on these pensions is available at <www.archives.gov/research_room/genealogy/military/confederate_pension_records.html>.

Pension Applications

Pensions for military and naval service began after the Revolutionary War and were at first limited to needy or disabled servicemen and widows or minor children whose husbands or fathers were killed in the war or served for a specified number of years. The promise of pensions or the granting of bounty land encouraged some men to volunteer for service. When the veteran applied for bounty land (for service between 1775 and 1855) or for a pension, he supplied information on his service; his birth date, birthplace, and residence; and information about his economic or health condition. A widow applying for a pension based on her husband's service had to verify their marriage, his service and death, and her age and residence. This evidence was sometimes in the form of documents, such as a family Bible record or marriage certificate, and sometimes in the form of affidavits from people who had known her and her husband for many years. Thus, the pension files may contain genealogical treasures.

Figure 3-2, on page 39, is an affidavit in support of a widow's application for a pension based on her husband's military service. Note the valuable information that it provides, even on people not related to the serviceman:

- The husband, Robert Short, had died before 26 August 1898, the date of the affidavit.
- Robert had been raised on the Heskah [Hezekiah] Short plantation, and the widow, Silvia Short, was using the former master's surname at the time of the affidavit.
- Hezekiah Short, age 78, of Jefferson County, Mississippi, said he bought

Sources

For records relating to service in World War I or II, write to the National Personnel Records Center, Military Personnel Records, 9700 Page Avenue, St. Louis, Missouri 63132-5100. See also <www.archives.gov/research_room/genealogy/research_topics/military.html> for information.

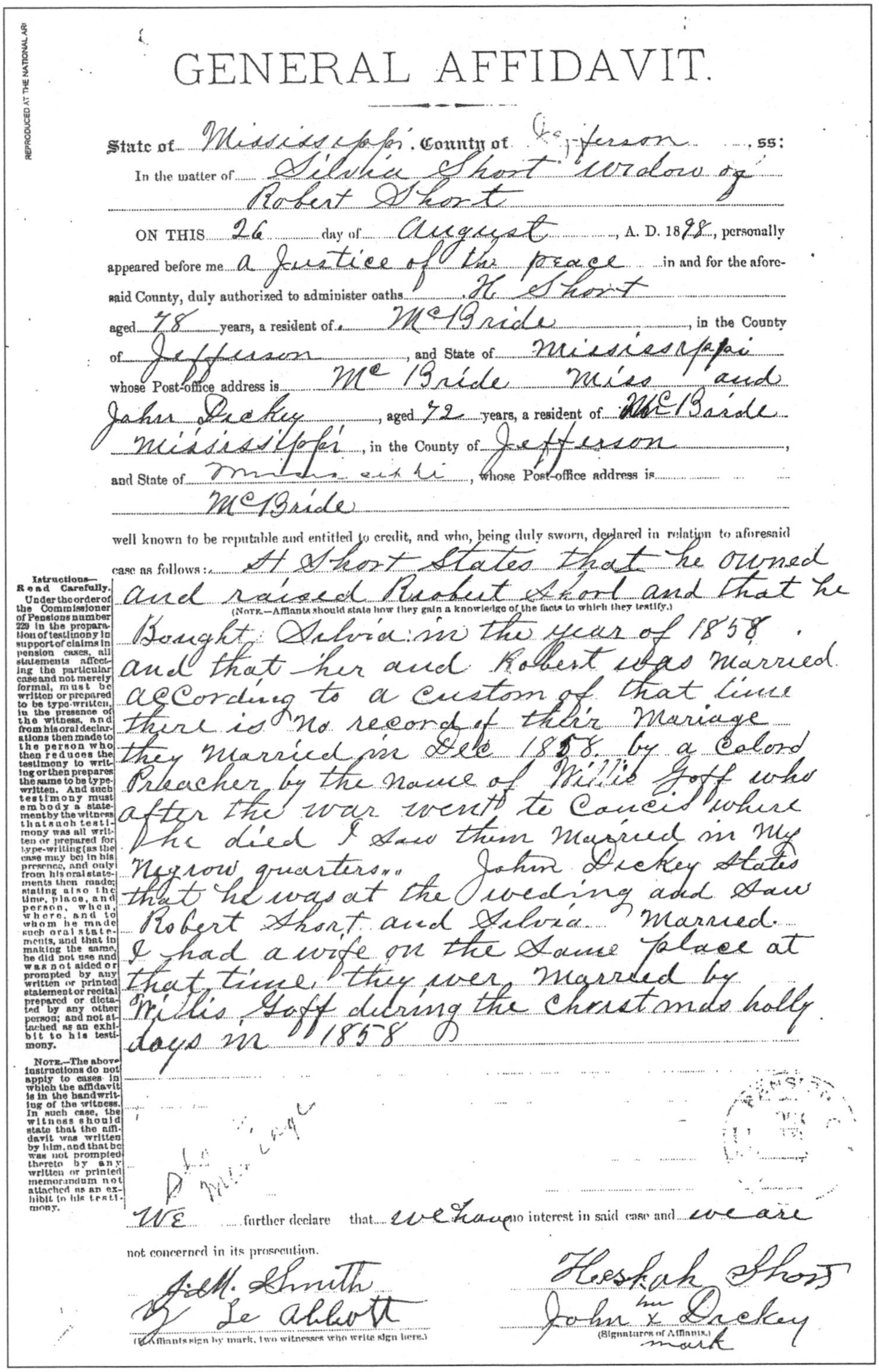

GENERAL AFFIDAVIT.

State of Mississippi County of Jefferson ss:

In the matter of Silvia Short widow of Robert Short

ON THIS 26 day of August, A. D. 1898, personally appeared before me a Justice of the peace in and for the aforesaid County, duly authorized to administer oaths H Short aged 78 years, a resident of McBride, in the County of Jefferson, and State of Mississippi whose Post-office address is Mc Bride Miss and John Dickey, aged 72 years, a resident of McBride Mississippi, in the County of Jefferson, and State of Mississippi, whose Post-office address is McBride

well known to be reputable and entitled to credit, and who, being duly sworn, declared in relation to aforesaid case as follows: H Short States that he owned and raised Robert Short and that he Bought Silvia in the year of 1858. and that her and Robert was married according to a custom of that time there is No record of their Mariage they Married in Dec 1858 by a Colord Preacher by the name of Willis Goff who after the war went to Cancis where he died I saw them Married in My Negrow quarters." John Dickey States that he was at the weding and saw Robert Short and Silvia Married. I had a wife on the Same place at that time, they wer Married by Willis Goff during the Christmas holly days in 1858

(NOTE.—Affiants should state how they gain a knowledge of the facts to which they testify.)

Instructions—Read Carefully. Under the order of the Commissioner of Pensions number 229 in the preparation of testimony in support of claims in pension cases, all statements affecting the particular case and not merely formal, must be written or prepared to be type-written, in the presence of the witness, and from his oral declarations then made to the person who then reduces the testimony to writing or then prepares the same to be typewritten. And such testimony must embody a statement by the witness that such testimony was all written or prepared for type-writing (as the case may be) in his presence, and only from his oral statements then made; stating also the time, place, and person, when, where, and to whom he made such oral statements, and that in making the same, he did not use and was not aided or prompted by any written or printed statement or recital prepared or dictated by any other person; and not attached as an exhibit to his testimony.

NOTE.—The above instructions do not apply to cases in which the affidavit is in the handwriting of the witness. In such case, the witness should state that the affidavit was written by him, and that he was not prompted thereto by any written or printed memorandum not attached as an exhibit to his testimony.

WE further declare that we have no interest in said case and we are not concerned in its prosecution.

J. M. Smith — Heskah Short

Le Abbott — John his x mark Dickey

(If Affiants sign by mark, two witnesses who write sign here.) (Signatures of Affiants.)

Figure 3-2 Pension application of Silvia Short, widow's file 662510, 18 September 1897, Civil War pension application files, Records of the Veterans Administration, Record Group 15, National Archives.

Silvia in 1858; in December 1858, Robert and Silvia married on his plantation.

- Willis Goff, the preacher who married the couple, lived and died in Cancis (Kansas) after the war.
- John Dickey, age 72, of Jefferson County said his wife lived on the Short plantation in 1858 and he was present at Robert and Silvia's wedding.

The Case of Joseph Paxton

Figure 3-3, on page 41, is the pension application of veteran Joseph Paxton, with answers to many of the questions genealogists ask regarding birth, marriages, military service, and children. This application also supplies the name of the plantation where the applicant was born and, thus, the name of his slaveholder.

Technique

It is also an example of the need to corroborate what you find in one record with other records. Because Paxton had been a slave before the Civil War, he probably did not know his own age with certainty and probably had no written records of family events. On the 1915 application, he reported his birth year as 1832 and his first marriage in 1850. The chart below evaluates Paxton's age as reported in his four census records and the pension application[1].

Since Paxton's 1900 census entry gave his birth month as August, we will use that month for purposes of illustration. Perhaps he did know that he was born in the summer. For example, census day was June 1 in 1870. Considering the previous August (1869) as Paxton's birth month, when he became thirty-six, subtract 36 from 1869 and estimate a birth year of 1833.

Estimating Joseph Paxton's Age from Census and Pension Records	
1 June 1870 census—age 36.	1869 − 36 = 1833 estimated birth year, age 17 at marriage
1 June 1880 census—age 40.	1879 − 40 = 1839 estimated birth year, age 11 at marriage
1 June 1900 census—age 68.	1899 − 68 = 1831 estimated birth year, age 19 at marriage
15 April 1910 census—age 75.	1909 − 75 = 1834 estimated birth year, age 16 at marriage
12 April 1915 application—	1832 stated birth year, age 18 at marriage

Custom and logic suggest that, if the 1850 marriage date is approximately correct, the most likely birth years would be 1831 or 1832, although 1833 and 1834 would be possible.

Many people in the past could not read and write, although some learned as adults to sign their names. Official documents such as marriage licenses and pension applications called for signatures. People who could not write their names made their mark, often an X or an initial, and the clerk filled in the name. Census records of 1850 and after identify each person's ability to read and write. All of Joseph Paxton's census entries indicate that he had not acquired either skill. His pension application seems to confirm the census reports since it appears to be written in the same handwriting throughout—that of a clerk.

Paxton's pension application also listed his children, their birth order, and birth dates. **Remember, this document was prepared in 1915, many years after the children were born.** Paxton probably did not remember the exact birth dates of all his children but was trying to be cooperative in getting something on paper so that his application could be processed. As shown in Figure 3-4, on page 42, the discrepancies in the pension paper and the 1870 and 1880 censuses are typical examples of what you may find as you research. However, the more you gather, the better you can evaluate what you find to try to discover the actual facts.

Reminder

None of Paxton's children were living with him in 1900 or 1910, nor did these censuses indicate that he had any children by his second wife. Some of the fourteen children shown in Figure 3-4, on page 42, may have died young

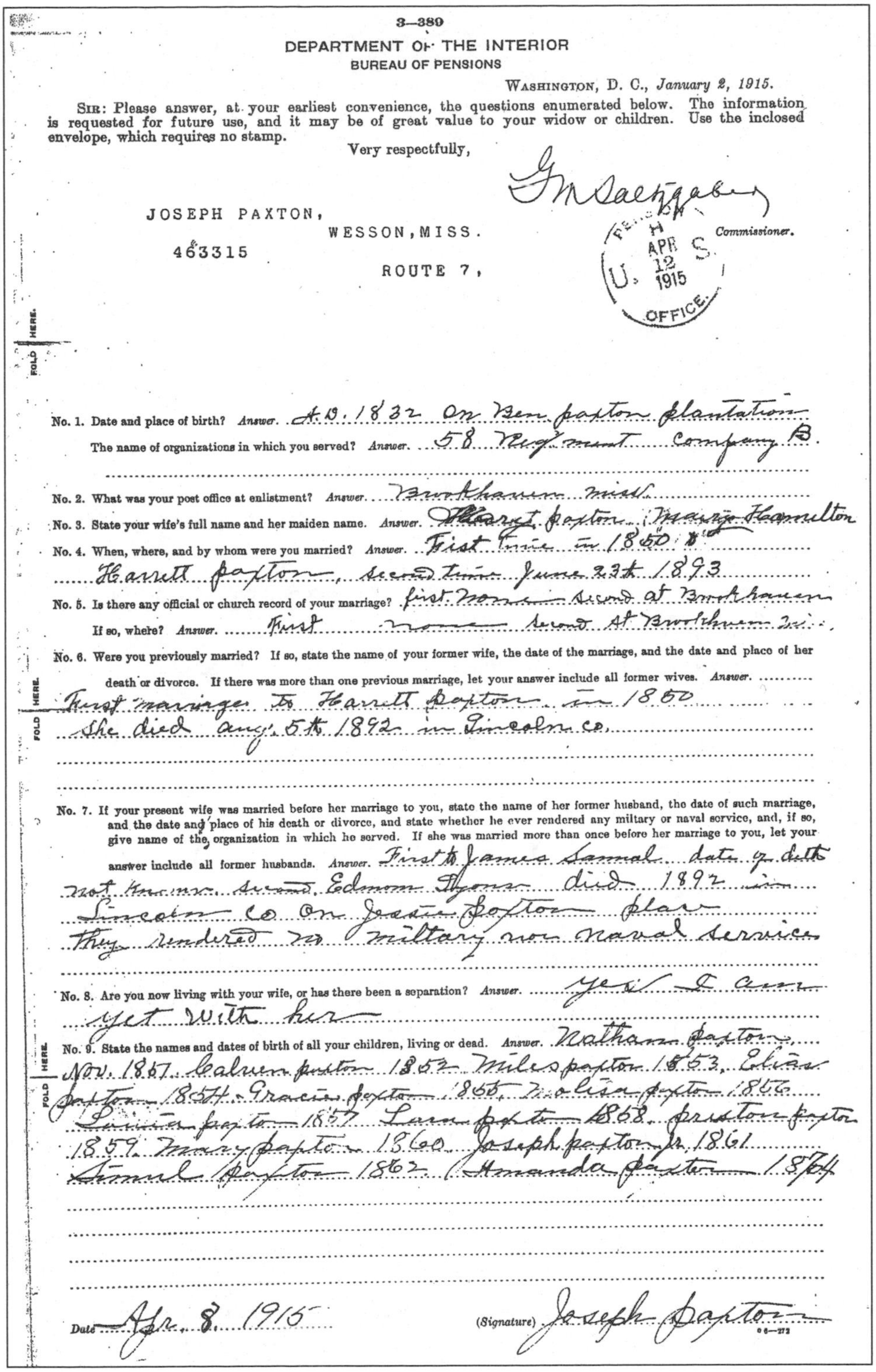

3–380

DEPARTMENT OF THE INTERIOR

BUREAU OF PENSIONS

WASHINGTON, D. C., *January 2, 1915.*

SIR: Please answer, at your earliest convenience, the questions enumerated below. The information is requested for future use, and it may be of great value to your widow or children. Use the inclosed envelope, which requires no stamp.

Very respectfully,

G M Saltzgaber

Commissioner.

JOSEPH PAXTON,
WESSON, MISS.
463315
ROUTE 7,

PENSION OFFICE APR 12 1915 U. S.

No. 1. Date and place of birth? *Answer.* A.D. 1832 On Ben paxton plantation

The name of organizations in which you served? *Answer.* 58 Regiment Company B.

No. 2. What was your post office at enlistment? *Answer.* Brookhaven miss.

No. 3. State your wife's full name and her maiden name. *Answer.* Harriet paxton Mary Hamilton

No. 4. When, where, and by whom were you married? *Answer.* First time in 1860 Harrett paxton, second time June 23th 1893

No. 5. Is there any official or church record of your marriage? first none second at Brookhaven

If so, where? *Answer.* First none second At Brookhaven ...

No. 6. Were you previously married? If so, state the name of your former wife, the date of the marriage, and the date and place of her death or divorce. If there was more than one previous marriage, let your answer include all former wives. *Answer.* First marriage to Harrett paxton in 1860 She died aug. 5th 1892 in Lincoln co.

No. 7. If your present wife was married before her marriage to you, state the name of her former husband, the date of such marriage, and the date and place of his death or divorce, and state whether he ever rendered any miltary or naval service, and, if so, give name of the organization in which he served. If she was married more than once before her marriage to you, let your answer include all former husbands. *Answer.* First to James Samal date of deth not known second Edmon Lyons died 1892 in Lincoln co On Jessie paxton place they rendered no miltary nor naval service

No. 8. Are you now living with your wife, or has there been a separation? *Answer.* yes I am yet With her

No. 9. State the names and dates of birth of all your children, living or dead. *Answer.* Nathan paxton, Nov. 1851 Calvin paxton 1852 Miles paxton 1853, Elias paxton 1854 Gracie paxton 1855 Malisa paxton 1856 Lucinda paxton 1857 Lara paxton 1858 preston paxton 1859 Mary paxton 1860 Joseph paxton Jr. 1861 Samuel paxton 1862 Amanda paxton 1864

Date Apr. 8. 1915 (*Signature*) Joseph paxton

Figure 3-3 Pension application of Joseph Paxton (private, Co. B, 58th Infantry Regiment, U.S. Colored Troops), file 463315, 8 April 1915, Civil War pension application files, Records of the Veterans Administration, Record Group 15, National Archives.

or moved to other locations. Research into vital records and other sources will no doubt shed more light on this family. The records abstracted here indicate that the first four children probably were the eldest four, even if the order is not firmly determined. From these sources, the youngest five appear to be in the correct order. The middle five are the ones whose birth order will require the most study.

COMBINING RECORDS TO STUDY AGES AND BIRTH ORDER OF JOSEPH PAXTON'S CHILDREN

Name, birth on pension application		Name, age in 1870 census		Name, age in 1880 census	
Nathan	b Nov, 1851	Nathan, 17,	b c 1852–1853	possibly found,	b c 1850
Calven	b 1852	Calvin, 10,	b c 1860	—	
Miles	b 1853	Miles, 11,	b c 1859	—	
Elias	b 1854	?Liza, 9, female,	b c 1861*	—	
Gracie	b 1855	Gracy, 3,	b c 1867	Gracy, 10,	b c 1870
Molisa	b 1856	Lizzie, 6,	b c 1874	Melissa, 15,	b c 1865
Louisa	b 1857	Luisa, 7,	b c 1863	Louisa, 20,	b c 1860
Lara	b 1858	—		Clara, 11/12,	b c 1879++
Preston	b 1859	P., male, 4,	b c 1866	—	
Mary	b 1860	Mary, 8/12,	b Oct 1869+	Mary, 8,	b c Oct 1871
Joseph Jr.	b 1861	—		Joseph, 6,	b c 1874
Simul	b 1862	—		Simeon, 5,	b c 1875
Amanda	b 1864/1874	—		Amanda, 3,	b c 1877
daughter, not on pension list		—		Willie, 2,	b c 1878

Note: Census records normally list members of the nuclear family in descending age order. The children are listed here in the order used in the pension application for ease of comparison.

*Sometimes, males are recorded as females and vice versa. Perhaps these were two different children, although Lias can be a nickname for Elias. This dilemma requires study in additional records.

+Obviously, since Mary was an eight-month-old infant in 1870, she would not have been eight years old in 1880, but that's what the family reported.

++Clara was reported as eleven months old in June 1880; at that time she was reported as currently ill from teething.

Figure 3-4

Notes

In estimating birth years from ages reported in census records, genealogists often use *c* or *ca*, from the Latin *circa*, "about." *Born* is abbreviated *b*. Thus *b c 1860*, as used in Figure 3-4, means "born about 1860."

1890 Special Census of Union Veterans and Widows

Most of the 1890 population schedules were destroyed by fire. Fortunately, more of the special veterans census survives. These schedules exist for the District of Columbia and the states in alphabetical order from Louisiana through Wyoming. It is estimated that about half the Kentucky schedules still exist but only fragments are available for the states from California to Kentucky. Many research libraries have the microfilm of this census. The forms asked for the name of the veteran, his rank and unit, the dates of his service, his residence in 1890, and information on wounds or disabilities. Widows of servicemen reported their names and their husbands' names, units, and service information.

Numerous veterans lived in New Orleans after the Civil War and thus reported their service in the 1890 veterans census. Since not all reported their units in the same way, the researcher needs to check what the census gives against the compiled service records index. For example, Joseph Harris and William James had served for three years and two months as privates in Company K of the 81st Colored Infantry—or eighty-first infantry regiment of U.S. Colored Troops (U.S.C.T.).[2] Octave Lavaux may have checked his discharge papers, as his entry showed his three-year service as a private in Company E of the 96th [Infantry], U.S.C.T.[3] Others said they had served with the Colored Heavy Artillery, the Colored Infantry, and the U.S. Colored Volunteers, but the regiment numbers and descriptions match the U.S.C.T.

Sometimes, veterans and widows reported aliases in this census. One example was George Thomas, alias George Washington, who had served as a private in Company F of the 58th Colored Infantry from August 1863 to September 1865. At his home in Caseyville District, Lincoln County, Mississippi, he told the census taker that he suffered from rheumatism because of exposure during his service.[4] He was indeed in the service during the arctic weather that rushed south from the Ohio Valley at New Year's 1864 and below normal temperatures of the following winter.[5] His researcher would want to study the whereabouts of his unit during these outbreaks and learn about the hardships of the soldiers at such times. His researcher would also need to keep in mind both of the names he reported, as he could be listed under either in records.

World War I Draft Registrations

Some twenty-four million World War I draft registration cards are available, by state, on microfilm through the Family History Library and at other research libraries. Copies of originals can be ordered from the National Archives branch at East Point, Georgia, for a ten-dollar fee. You must supply the registrant's name, residence in 1917, and birth date, if known or estimated. (See page 219 for the address.) Some cards are abstracted online at Ancestry.com.

The cards resulted from the Selective Service Act of 1917 and the implementing regulations. On 5 June 1917, 5 June 1918, and 24 August 1918, men between twenty-one and thirty years of age in the United States were supposed to register, unless they were already serving in the armed services. By the last registration day, 12 September 1918, men born between 13 September 1872 and 12 September 1900 were to register if they had not already done so.

Information on the cards varies, depending on the registration date, but generally included name, address, birth date, race, occupation, and employer. Some of the cards requested information on citizenship, birthplace, and name of the nearest relative. Men were asked to sign their card, but the information was written by a registrar. For various reasons, some men did not report their age, address, or other details accurately.

Figure 3-5, on page 44, is the registration card of Calvin Finch of Wilmington, California. He had not been required to register until the last registration day, 12 September 1918, because he was older than thirty. Since he was single in 1918 when he registered, he reported as his nearest relative his mother, Lu Finch, of Jefferson, Alabama. Such a record helps the genealogist work back to his place of origin. In fact, the 1880 census of Jefferson, Marengo County, Alabama, shows Louisa Finch, age thirty-eight, with her seven children, including Calvin, age five.[6]

Military Discharge Records

During the twentieth century, counties copied or collected military discharge papers from veterans and their families. Most of these were from World War I and World War II, but occasionally other records appear in the files. The papers are usually bound together in volumes in the office of the county clerk, the county recorder, the clerk of the superior court, the clerk of the circuit court, the recorder of deeds, or other office. Each state organizes its courthouses ac-

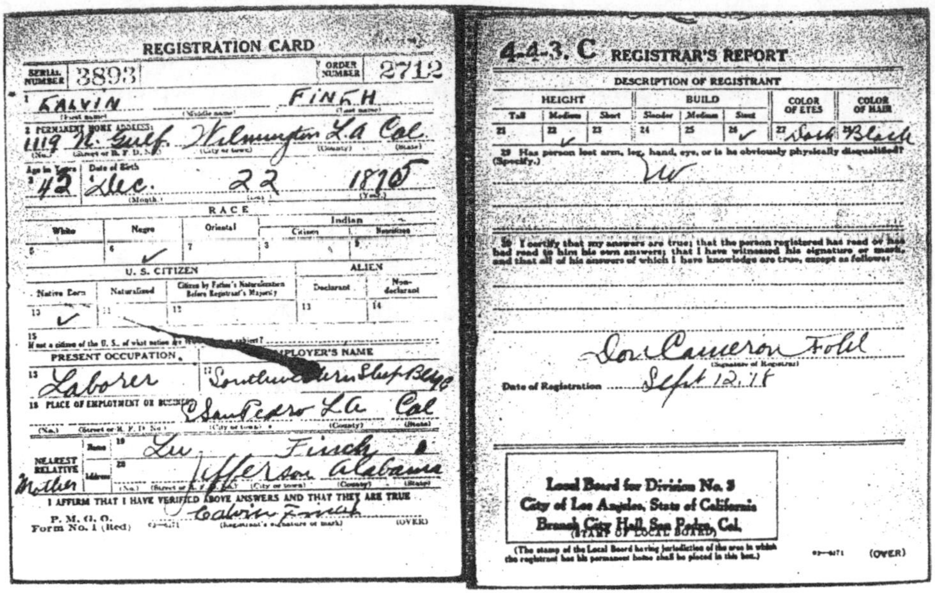

REGISTRATION CARD

SERIAL NUMBER 3893 ORDER NUMBER 2712

1 Calvin Finch
(First name) (Middle name) (Last name)

2 PERMANENT HOME ADDRESS: 1119 N. Gulf Wilmington L.A. Cal.
(No.) (Street or R. F. D. No.) (City or town) (County) (State)

3 Age in Years 42 4 Date of Birth Dec. 22 1875
(Month) (Day) (Year)

RACE

White	Negro	Oriental	Indian: Citizen	Indian: Noncitizen
5	6 ✓	7	8	9

U. S. CITIZEN: Native Born	U. S. CITIZEN: Naturalized	U. S. CITIZEN: Citizen by Father's Naturalization Before Registrant's Majority	ALIEN: Declarant	ALIEN: Non-declarant
10 ✓	11	12	13	14

15 If not a citizen of the U. S., of what nation are you a citizen or subject?

PRESENT OCCUPATION: 16 Laborer
EMPLOYER'S NAME: 17 Southwestern Shipbuilding [illegible]

18 PLACE OF EMPLOYMENT OR BUSINESS: San Pedro L.A. Cal
(No.) (Street or R. F. D. No.) (City or town) (County) (State)

NEAREST RELATIVE (Mother): 19 Name Lu Finch
20 Address Jefferson Alabama
(No.) (Street or R. F. D. No.) (City or town) (County) (State)

I AFFIRM THAT I HAVE VERIFIED ABOVE ANSWERS AND THAT THEY ARE TRUE

Calvin Finch
(Registrant's signature or mark)

P. M. G. O. Form No. 1 (Red) (OVER)

4-4-3. C REGISTRAR'S REPORT

DESCRIPTION OF REGISTRANT

HEIGHT: Tall	HEIGHT: Medium	HEIGHT: Short	BUILD: Slender	BUILD: Medium	BUILD: Stout	COLOR OF EYES	COLOR OF HAIR
21	22 ✓	23	24	25	26 ✓	27 Dark	28 Black

29 Has person lost arm, leg, hand, eye, or is he obviously physically disqualified? (Specify.) No

30 I certify that my answers are true; that the person registered has read or has had read to him his own answers; that I have witnessed his signature or mark, and that all of his answers of which I have knowledge are true, except as follows:

Don Cameron Ford
(Signature of Registrar)

Date of Registration Sept 12, 18

Local Board for Division No. 3
City of Los Angeles, State of California
Branch City Hall, San Pedro, Cal.
(STAMP OF LOCAL BOARD)

(The stamp of the Local Board having jurisdiction of the area in which the registrant has his permanent home shall be placed in this box.)

(OVER)

Figure 3-5 World War I draft registration of Calvin Finch, serial no. 3893, Los Angeles County, California, draft registrations, National Archives microfilm M1509, roll 30, Family History Library microfilm 1530800.

cording to state law, and the names of these clerks' offices vary from state to state.

A number of the volumes have been microfilmed and are available at the state archives or the Family History Library. Figure 3-6, on page 45, is a clerk's copy of the World War I honorable discharge of Private Phillip Vaughn of Cane Valley, Kentucky.

Other Military Records

Other records related to military service are available on microfilm. See the online or printed catalogs for more information.

M1872—*List of Mothers and Widows of American World War I Soldiers, Sailors, and Marines Entitled to Make a Pilgrimage to the War Cemeteries of Europe, 1930.*

M929—*Documents Relating to the Military and Naval Service of Blacks Awarded the Congressional Medal of Honor from the Civil War to the Spanish-American War.*

M1002—*Selected Documents Relating to Blacks Nominated for Appointment to the U.S. Military Academy During the 19th Century, 1870–1887.*

Parts of M665, M744, M617—Returns from the black units (including the Buffalo Soldiers) of Regular Army Infantry and Cavalry and military posts in the West after the Civil War.

If your research identifies free male ancestors of the early nineteenth century or eighteenth century, you would want to investigate the possibility that one or more served in the military in a colonial militia, Regular Army or Navy, or as a volunteer in the Revolutionary War, War of 1812, Indian Wars, or other engagements. The *Military Service Records* and *Black Studies* microfilm catalogs of the National Archives detail the microfilm collections relating to federal

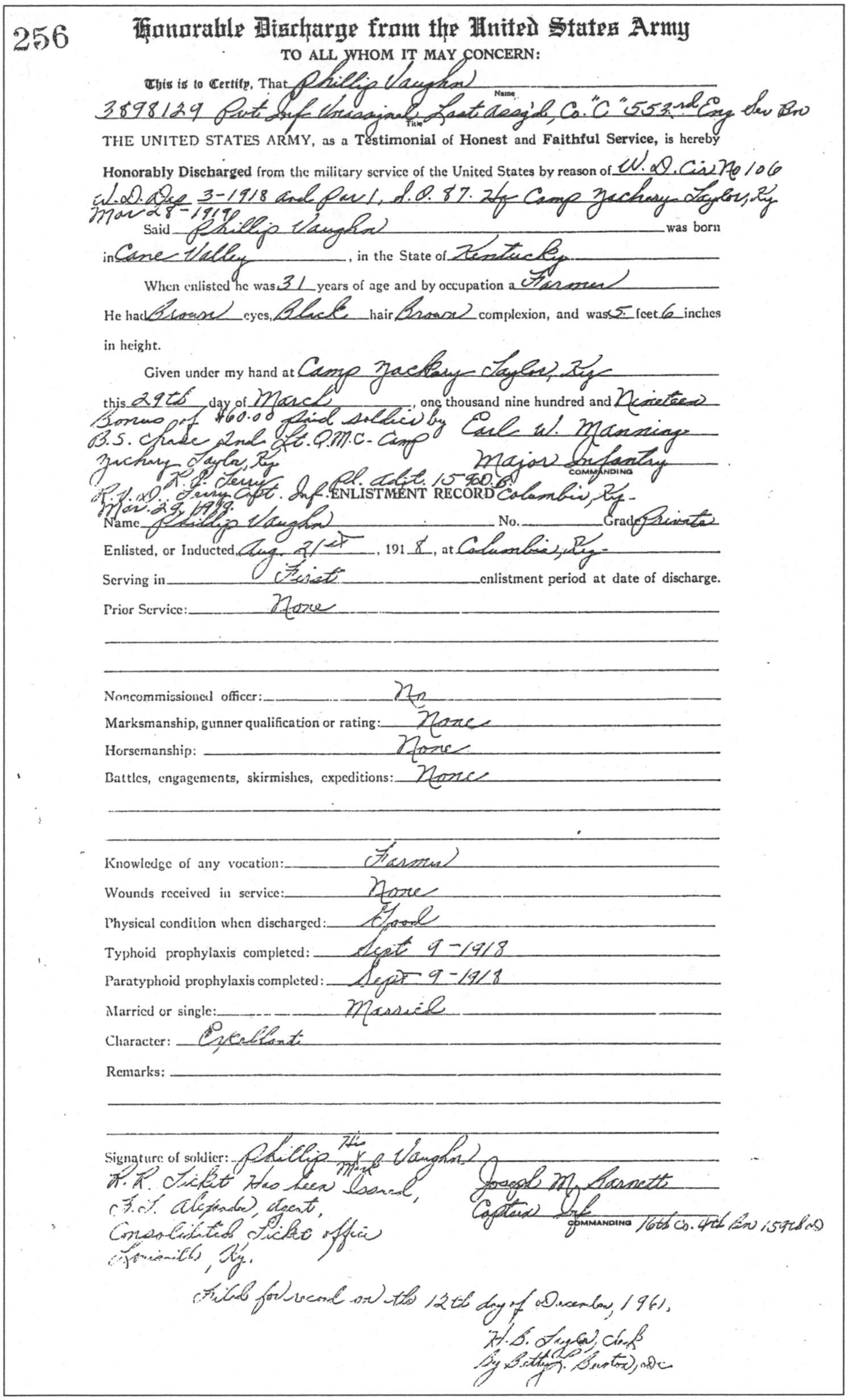

256

Honorable Discharge from the United States Army

TO ALL WHOM IT MAY CONCERN:

This is to Certify, That Phillip Vaughn
Name

3898129 Pvt. Inf. Unassigned, Last ass'd, Co. "C" 553rd Eng. Ser. Bn
Title

THE UNITED STATES ARMY, as a Testimonial of Honest and Faithful Service, is hereby **Honorably Discharged** from the military service of the United States by reason of W. D. Cir. No 106 W. D. Dec 3-1918 and Par 1, S. O. 87. Hq Camp Zachary Taylor, Ky Mar 28-1919

Said Phillip Vaughn was born in Cane Valley, in the State of Kentucky

When enlisted he was 31 years of age and by occupation a Farmer

He had Brown eyes, Black hair Brown complexion, and was 5 feet 6 inches in height.

Given under my hand at Camp Zachary Taylor, Ky this 29th day of March, one thousand nine hundred and Nineteen

Bonus of $60.00 paid soldier by B. S. Chase 2nd Lt. Q.M.C. Camp Zachary Taylor, Ky

Earl W. Manning
Major Infantry
COMMANDING

R. S. Terry
R. V. D. Terry Capt. Inf. Pl. Adjt. 1590 D.B. Columbia, Ky. Mar. 29, 1919

ENLISTMENT RECORD

Name Phillip Vaughn No. Grade Private

Enlisted, or Inducted Aug. 21st, 1918, at Columbia, Ky.

Serving in First enlistment period at date of discharge.

Prior Service: None

Noncommissioned officer: No

Marksmanship, gunner qualification or rating: None

Horsemanship: None

Battles, engagements, skirmishes, expeditions: None

Knowledge of any vocation: Farmer

Wounds received in service: None

Physical condition when discharged: Good

Typhoid prophylaxis completed: Sept 9-1918

Paratyphoid prophylaxis completed: Sept 9-1918

Married or single: Married

Character: Excellent

Remarks:

Signature of soldier: Phillip his X mark Vaughn

R. R. Ticket Has been Issued, F. S. Alexander, Agent, Consolidated Ticket office Louisville, Ky.

Joseph M. Garnett
Captain Inf.
COMMANDING 16th Co. 4th Bn 159th D.B.

Filed for record on the 12th day of December, 1961.
H. B. Taylor, Clerk
By Bethy L. Burton, DC

Figure 3-6 World War I military discharge of Phillip Vaughn (private, 3898129, Co. C, 553rd Eng. Ser. Battalion), Soldiers Discharge Book 1:256, County Clerk's Office, Courthouse, Adair County, Columbia, Kentucky.

government records. Published indexes, published histories, and records in state archives deal with colonial service.

Another helpful resource is Frederick H. Dyer's *Compendium of the War of the Rebellion* (reprint of 1908 original; Dayton, Ohio: Broadfoot/Morningside Press, 1994). Because this work gives capsuled histories of Union regiments, it could help you learn

- when or whether an ancestral unit changed names or commands, especially if records give different designations, for example, on the 1890 special census and the pension application
- what the abbreviations of a unit name mean
- which of two similarly named units the ancestor might have belonged to, based on which unit was organized nearest the ancestor's home
- which of several servicemen by the ancestor's name might be your ancestor, based on which unit was organized nearest the ancestor's home

BUREAU OF REFUGEES, FREEDMEN, AND ABANDONED LANDS

The Civil War left behind a vacuum, especially in the war-torn parts of the South. Freedom had finally come, but with considerable chaos and confusion and little help or guidance. Families uprooted by the war wanted to go home, find a new home, or rejoin relatives wherever they could find them. Some freedmen headed to the north and west, not really knowing where they were going or how they would survive on the way. Many freedmen stayed where they had been for years but still faced hunger and deprivation. Even many white families were hard-pressed to feed and clothe their families. Aid societies and religious organizations tried to help the needy, but the task was overwhelming. Early in 1865, Congress created the Bureau of Refugees, Freedmen, and Abandoned Lands within the War Department to try to address the needs of the thousands who were suffering.

For seven years, this "Freedmen's Bureau" worked to help former slaves and indigent whites, especially in the areas of daily necessities, education, health care, the transition to freedom, race relations, and work. Field offices existed in the former Confederate states—Alabama, Arkansas (which had jurisdiction also over Missouri and Kansas), Florida, Georgia, Louisiana, Mississippi, North and South Carolina, Tennessee, Texas, and Virginia—as well as Kentucky, the District of Columbia, and Maryland, with the last two also serving Delaware and West Virginia.

After the bureau was abolished, the records were collected and eventually were sent to the National Archives. For research purposes, the bureau's records can be divided into two groups: those filed with or created by the headquarters in Washington and those kept by the district offices and local field offices. Headquarters records have been microfilmed, and descriptions of these records are found in the National Archives Preliminary Inventory No. 174, *Preliminary Inventory of the Records of the Bureau of Refugees, Freedmen, and Abandoned Lands, Washington Headquarters*. Headquarters records have been microfilmed for Alabama, Arkansas, the District of Columbia, Georgia, Louisiana,

Mississippi, North and South Carolina, Tennessee, Texas, and Virginia. Researchers can find this microfilm at many research libraries, including some National Archives branches, and can rent it from Heritage Quest in North Salt Lake, Utah, or the Family History Library. Unfilmed files are available for searching at the National Archives in Washington, DC.

The vast majority of the field office records have not been microfilmed. Descriptions of field office records are in a three-part unpublished inventory, compiled by Elaine C. Everly and Willna Pacheli, entitled *Preliminary Inventory of the Records of the Field Offices of the Bureau of Refugees, Freedmen, and Abandoned Lands, Record Group 105* (NM-95).

Warning

- Part one includes descriptions for records of field offices in Alabama, Arkansas, the District of Columbia, Florida, Georgia, Kentucky, and Louisiana.
- Part two contains descriptions of records of field offices in Maryland and Delaware, Mississippi, Missouri, North Carolina, and South Carolina.
- Part three gives descriptions of records of field offices in Tennessee, Texas, and Virginia and records of the field offices of the Adjutant General's Office.

In 2000, President Clinton signed into law The Freedmen's Bureau Preservation Act (H.R. 5157), authorizing the preservation, indexing, and microfilming of all the remaining Freedmen's Bureau records. Until the preservation project is completed, the only way to access these genealogically rich documents is to visit the National Archives. Before visiting, request a copy of the pages of NM-95 that cover your ancestral state.

See Also

See Appendix D for information on the National Archives and its branches. If you know which files are relevant to your search before arriving, you can use your available time for research.

For the most part, the records of the bureau's superintendents of education in these states contain correspondence, some lists of teachers, statistical reports, and expense reports. These records are not particularly helpful to most genealogists, but many are available on microfilm.

Many of the surviving bureau records are correspondence about administrative business between the officials of the bureau, lists of staff members in the field offices, and reports on conditions in the black community. Some researchers find family members mentioned since many individuals sent letters asking bureau agents to help them locate missing relatives.

More family information appears in the records of the bureau's interaction with local residents, especially marriage records, labor contracts, records of relief, and transportation requests. These records differ from district to district and state to state, and not all are available for all the southern states. Nevertheless, you may benefit from reading these categories of microfilmed records when they exist for your ancestral state.

Microfilm Source

Marriage Records

Although marriage records and mentions of marriages may be tucked into letters in the commissioners' various files, the bureau records for Mississippi contain an impressive number of freedmen's marriage records. The grooms in these records reported residence in many places, including Chicago and Kentucky, and many were servicemen who often gave their units as their residence. For the most part, the brides were from the area around Vicksburg, on both sides of the Mississippi River. An interesting feature of these records is the question asked of both bride and groom about any previous partner.

One rather typical entry was the 5 June 1864 marriage of Robert Benson, mulatto, age forty-four, of Company C, 50th U.S.C.I. (Colored Infantry), and Louisa Massey, a quadroon, age twenty-seven, of Madison Parish, Louisiana.[7] Robert's parents were mulatto; Louisa's father was white and her mother mulatto. Robert had lived for twenty-six years with another woman, now deceased, with whom he had had two children. Louisa, a widow, had lived one year with her previous partner and had one child by him. This is an amazing amount of information in one record.

Labor Contracts and Indentures

For about half the former Confederate states, the bureau records include letters of apprenticeship, labor contracts, or other items dealing with work. The indentures of apprenticeship may state a parent's name, former slaveholder's name, approximate age of the child or teenage apprentice, and the conditions and term of service.

One indenture of apprenticeship is the contract, dated 14 September 1865, between James Sinclair, agent of the Bureau and "therefore legal Guardian of colored Orphans," and Archibald McMillan of Robeson County, North Carolina. Sinclair was binding to McMillan an orphan girl named Jane, age fifteen and former slave of Mrs. Effie McNeill. Jane was to live in McMillan's household as apprentice and servant until she became twenty-one; she was to serve faithfully and obediently "his lawful commands." In return, McMillan agreed to teach Jane to read and write, to furnish her sufficient diet, washing, lodging, apparel, and other necessities in sickness and in health.[8]

In this case, as in perhaps a number of other apprenticeships, the girl Jane has not yet been identified in the 1870 census in a McMillan household in Robeson County. Other county or census records may or may not suggest what happened to her or to the agreement.

Relief Records

Poverty permeated every corner of the South after the war. Many blacks and some whites were utterly destitute and bewildered. A considerable number of freedmen could have remained with the household of their former slaveholder and worked out some form of employment but chose to start afresh, out on their own. This move left many of them homeless and unemployed. Few of the former slaveholders and potential employers had cash with which to pay employees anyway; and many whites, former slaveholders or not, were bankrupt. Thus, other forms of compensation had to be worked out over time.

As the region struggled to come to grips with the many changes it faced, the Freedmen's Bureau provided some relief to the destitute in the form of seed, clothing, medicine, and food rations. The aid varied somewhat from place to place and according to the need. Many of those receiving food were elderly, ill, feeble, disabled, or orphaned; others were simply families with great needs. Likewise, the reports vary in the amount of detail they provide researchers

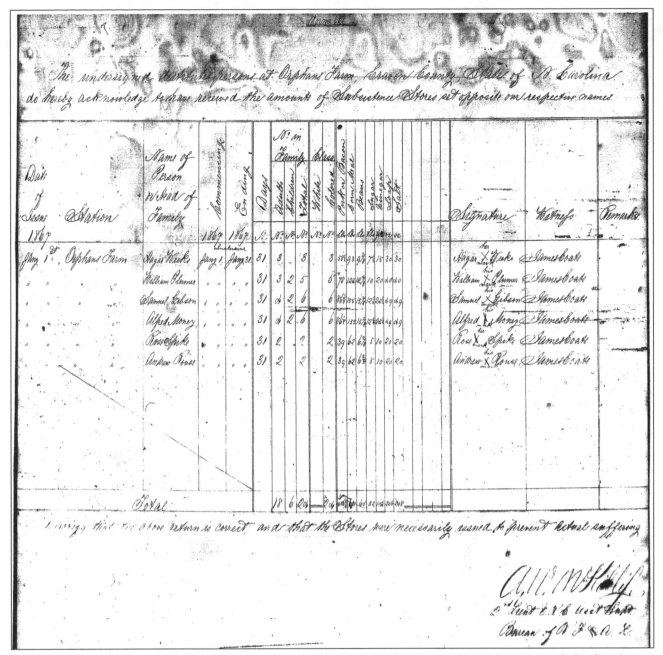

Figure 3-7 Superintendent's return of rations issued for January 1867 at Orphans Farm, Craven County, North Carolina, in *Receipts for Rations Issued, December 1866–July 1867, Records of the Assistant Commissioner for the State of North Carolina, Bureau of Refugees, Freedmen, and Abandoned Lands, 1865–1870,* National Archives microfilm M843, roll 35.

today, but they are microfilmed for most of the states in the region.

Figure 3-7, above, is a superintendent's report of rations issued to six families who were living at the Orphans Farm in Craven County, North Carolina. The six heads of families made their marks acknowledging receipt of rations for thirty-one days in January 1867. Although some whites received the same rations in that district of the state, this page shows only black families. The larger families received more food, apparently according to a set formula. The two-adult families received the following—all typical staple foods and supplies in the South at the time:

A gill is four fluid ounces of liquid, or one-half cup; thus the ration was five cups.

- 39 pounds of pork or bacon
- 62 pounds of corn meal
- 6 ⅞ pounds of beans
- 5 pounds of sugar
- 10 gills of vinegar
- 20 ounces of soap
- 20 ounces of salt

Transportation Requests

For several states, the microfilmed bureau files include records relating to transportation. These reports include specific requests for people in need of transportation and registers of those issued orders for government-supplied transportation. A few people approved for transportation were soldiers' wives and widows, teachers, military personnel, and bureau officials. The great majority were destitute freedmen; some were white refugees wanting to return home.

The South Carolina registers listed the names of those requesting transportation, the date, their occupation or status (in most cases, "destitute freedmen"), and their destination. Unfortunately, wives and children were not named, and not all the freedmen used a surname. Thus, the lists are of marginal genealogical value, unless the given name was somewhat unusual or a surname was used.

Figure 3-8, on page 51, shows freedmen and their families requesting transportation from Charleston to other South Carolina towns as well as Savannah and Augusta, Georgia. A considerable number in the same register asked to go to Richmond, Virginia, and eastern North Carolina.

Some registers and documents in the transportation files explained the reasons for the travel requests. Many people were trying to rejoin family members. As shown in Figure 3-8, Joe Middleton requested transportation to Savannah, Georgia, "to go after family." Figure 3-9, on page 52, shows a request of 15 August 1866, from the acting assistant commissioner in Columbia's bureau headquarters to the assistant adjutant general, possibly in the same city:

> Colonel, I have the honor to request transportation from this City [Columbia] to Richmond, Va, for Freedboy Samuel Smith. This boy has been transported thus far from Agusta [*sic*] Ga he desires to be sent to his parents. This will relieve the government from his support.

Most of the requests added the argument that helping people get to family who could support them would relieve the government of the expense of their care. The Bureau never had all the funds it could have used in its humanitarian efforts.

FREEDMAN'S SAVINGS AND TRUST COMPANY

Congress chartered the Freedman's Savings and Trust Company in March 1865 as a bank for freed slaves and their descendants. For nine years, the institution operated branches in thirty-three cities. Unfortunately, the bank failed in 1874, and many depositors lost the small sums they had saved.

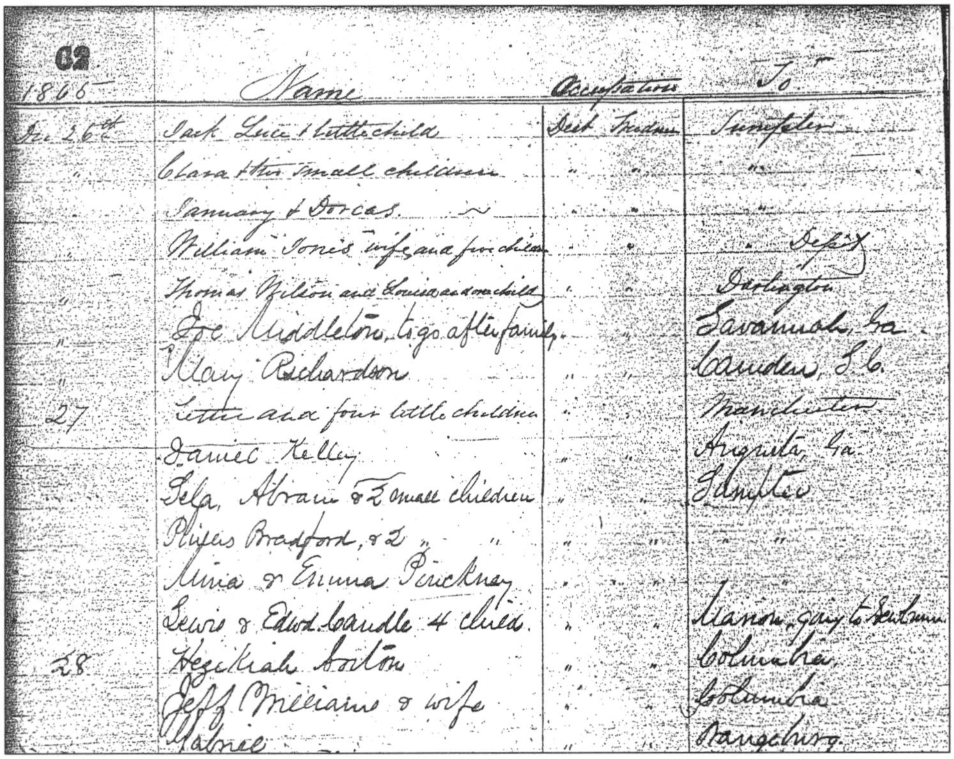

[Handwritten ledger page image — facsimile of the transportation request list]

Figure 3-8 List of requests for transportation, 26 and 27 December 1865, p. 62, in target 2, list of requests for transportation, 1 October 1865 to 31 December 1866, in Records Relating to Transportation, *Records of the Assistant Commissioner for the State of South Carolina, Bureau of Refugees, Freedmen, and Abandoned Lands, 1865–1870*, National Archives microfilm M869, roll 44.

The branches were in the cities and towns with considerable African-American populations. If your ancestors lived in rural areas, especially more than a few miles from the city, it is unlikely that they had accounts. However, you lose nothing by looking at the records. You may even find an ancestor's sibling or parent who had moved to the city. The microfilm is in many libraries.

Indexes to Deposit Ledgers

Basically, two kinds of records from the bank interest genealogists: the indexes to deposit ledgers and the registers of signatures of depositors. The undated indexes to deposit ledgers contain a number of clues for researchers:

- names of account holders who made deposits
- occasionally, the identities of their spouses
- evidence of these people being in a given place between 1865 and 1874
- personal identifiers, such as *Jr.* or *Sr.* with a name, an occupation, designation of *widow*, or an alias, which for a woman sometimes indicated her maiden name
- names of churches and organizations with accounts, which give clues for further research as well as indications of social, religious, educational, labor, and humanitarian activities in the town.

The deposit ledgers no longer exist, but the indexes survive for twenty-six identified branch offices:

- Alabama: Huntsville
- Arkansas: Little Rock
- District of Columbia: Washington

CD Source

Abstracts of Freedman's Bank depositor records are available on CD-ROM from the Family History Library and at many libraries; if you find a family member on the CD-ROM, check the information in the original on microfilm.

Figure 3-9 Letter to Lt. Col. H.W. Smith, Assistant Adjutant General, 15 August 1866, in target 5, transportation requests received, 20 April to 21 December 1866, in Records Relating to Transportation, *Records of the Assistant Commissioner for the State of South Carolina, Bureau of Refugees, Freedmen, and Abandoned Lands, 1865–1870,* National Archives microfilm M869, roll 44.

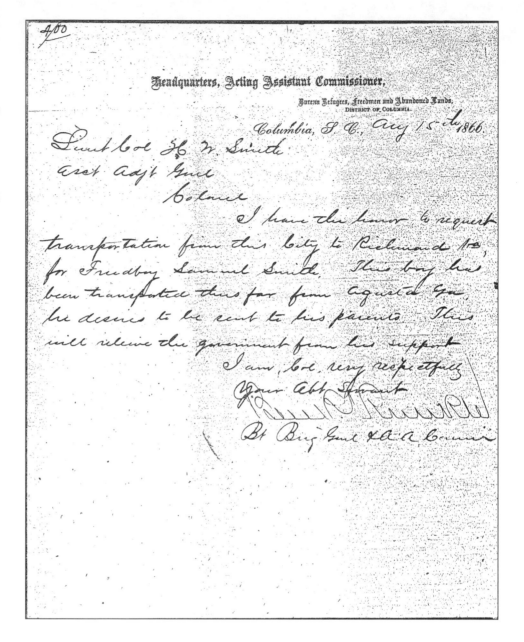

Notes

A few indexes exist from unidentified branches.

- Florida: Jacksonville, Tallahassee
- Georgia: Augusta, Savannah
- Kentucky: Lexington, Louisville
- Louisiana: New Orleans, Shreveport
- Maryland: Baltimore
- Mississippi: Natchez, Vicksburg
- Missouri: St. Louis
- New York: New York City
- North Carolina: New Bern, Raleigh, Wilmington
- Pennsylvania: Philadelphia
- South Carolina: Beaufort, Charleston
- Tennessee: Memphis, Nashville
- Virginia: Norfolk, Richmond

Registers of Signatures of Depositors

The more genealogically valuable of the bank records are the registers of signatures, which contain individual and family information. They often include age and birth information, occupation, parents' and siblings' names, spouse's and children's names, including relatives who were deceased. Some provide the former slaveholder's name; some indicate that the depositor was living several states away from his or her birthplace. A number of applications indicate the use of three or four surnames within the immediate family—good clues for investigation. All give useful family history information that suggests possibilities for further research.

The following are some of the genealogical gems in these records:

- Mrs. Ellen Baptiste Lubin of New Orleans said she was free before the war.[9]
- Ancel Bunton of New Orleans was born in Sumner County, Tennessee, the slave of Sumpter Turner and the son of William and Annie Bunton.[10]
- In New York City, Violet Ann Shields reported that her husband, George, was a seaman. She did not sign her application because she "has to have her spectacles to write," and apparently did not have them with her, or perhaps did not want to admit she could not write.[11]
- Atlanta depositor Robert Hammonds said his wife was Ann, but his son, Scott, in Mississippi was the child of Martha Jones; his father, Sy, had emigrated to Liberia thirty years before, about 1840.[12]
- William Guilford, a resident of Thomaston in Upson County, Georgia, had an account in the Atlanta branch (about sixty miles from his residence), was a harness maker, and was serving in the Georgia legislature at age twenty-six.[13]
- Peter Williams of Atlanta, son of William Fletcher and Millie Pugerson, worked as a drayman but was also a university student.[14]

Notes

A drayman drove a freight wagon.

Figure 3-10, on page 54, shows the 1870 depositor record of Elbot Greene of Atlanta. Notice he had lived in five different Georgia counties and mentioned four family surnames, all different from the slaveholder's name. Curiously, he bore the surname Greene, was born in Greene County around Greensboro, and his father was Jimmy Greenwood. The 1870 census listed him as Elbert Green in Atlanta's fourth ward.[15]

These registers are available for the same cities as the indexes to deposit ledgers, with the following differences:

- Registers are also available for Mobile, Alabama; Atlanta, Georgia; Columbus, Mississippi; Lynchburg, Virginia.
- No register is available for Jacksonville, Florida.

FEDERAL LAND RECORDS

Land is surveyed when it changes hands so that the title to the land is precise and all parties know the boundaries. In the United States, most of the states fall into two broad categories according to the way their land is surveyed and described—state land states and federal land, or public land, states.

Figure 3-10 Depositor record of Elbot Greene, #258, in register of Atlanta, Georgia, 15 January 1870–2 July 1874, *Registers of Signatures of Depositions in Branches of the Freedman's Savings and Trust Company, 1865–1874*, National Archives microfilm M816, roll 6.

No. 258 Record for Elbot Greene.

Date of Application, March 17, 1870.

Where born, was in Greensboro Ga at his first recollection

Where brought up, In Putnam + Houston + Bibb Co with Col. Holt

Residence, Near Georgia R.R. Shop. Mr Shears lot.

Age, 50 about he thinks.

Complexion, Black

Occupation, Works on Car Trucks

Works for State Rail Road.

Wife, Clemantine.

Children, Billy Cummings + John + Charley + Mary all in Augusta in Atlanta. Hannah and some others (dead) Sally + Harriet are living but where he does not know

Father, Jimmy Greenwood died in Putnam Co about 27 years ago.

Mother, Betty Cooper died at Putnam Co. before father

Brothers, Jim + Rupert the last in Leagrange..

Sisters, Lukey + Rose + Harriet. he knows nothing of them or their whereabouts.

Signature, Elbot his X Greene
mark

Notes

Metes and bounds: system of land survey and description using natural landmarks (trees, creeks), artificial landmarks (rock pile, stake in the prairie), and adjoining property lines, along with measurements (rods, poles, yards) and compass directions (as in "north ten degrees west").

State Land States

The twenty state land states are those whose land never belonged to the federal government. They include (1) the thirteen original states, (2) the five states that came out of them—Maine and Vermont in New England, Kentucky, Tennessee, and West Virginia, and (3) Texas and Hawaii, both of which entered the United States after being independent republics. These states generally use a metes and bounds system to describe land location and boundaries: "north along the creek bank to a pin oak sapling," "west thirty degrees south to a rock pile," and "along William Caldwell's line to the beginning." In addition, some areas in these states are surveyed on a grid system similar to the public land states.

Because land in these states did not belong to the federal government originally, land transactions are county or town records, not federal records. (See
chapter four.)

Public Land States

The other thirty states are public land states. The federal government acquired
and controlled these lands before organizing them as territories and later accepting them as states. Most of the land in these states was surveyed according
to a "rectangular survey system" into grids, like a checkerboard. The larger
squares—townships—are fairly standard in size: thirty-six square miles, or six
miles on each side.

Townships are described in the records and located on maps with a township
and range number: Township 8 North, Range 3 East, or T8N R3E. The numbers
are counted from two main surveying lines called a base line and meridian.
(You can study the land records without knowing the location of these two
lines.) Most counties have several townships and ranges within their boundaries. For the counties you research, get maps that show these designations and
you can easily determine where a given piece of land is located.

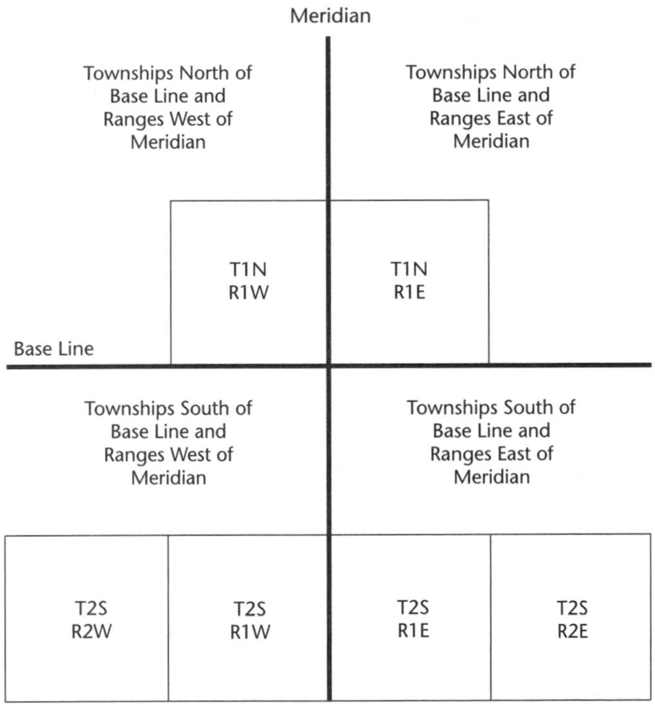

Meridian

Townships North of
Base Line and
Ranges West of
Meridian

Townships North of
Base Line and
Ranges East of
Meridian

T1N
R1W

T1N
R1E

Base Line

Townships South of
Base Line and
Ranges West of
Meridian

Townships South of
Base Line and
Ranges East of
Meridian

T2S
R2W

T2S
R1W

T2S
R1E

T2S
R2E

Townships are normally divided into thirty-six sections, each one square mile
or about 640 acres. On page 56 is a typical township divided into its thirty-six
sections. Notice the pattern by which the sections are numbered. As Figure 7-
1, on page 127, illustrates, sections can be sold whole or can be divided into
smaller tracts. A tract of land described as the "NE1/4 of S1 T2S R2E" is the
northeast quarter of Section 1 in Township 2 South, Range 2 East. As a quarter
section, the tract contains about 160 acres. The western half of a section would
be labeled W2 or W1/2. The northwest quarter of the northwest quarter of

section 5 would be labeled NW1/4 (or NW4) NW1/4 S5. Some townships may not have all thirty-six sections because of the terrain or a natural feature such as a swamp or lake that eliminates one or more sections.

6	5	4	3	2	1
7	8	9	10	11	12
18	17	16	15	14	13
19	20	21	22	23	24
30	29	28	27	26	25
31	32	33	34	35	36

When plotting and studying land ownership, as in Figure 7-1, note that someone living, for example, in section 1 of a township can be near neighbors to someone in a different section, township, or range. This diagram illustrates such a corner section and the neighboring land.

S35 T3N R2W	S36 T3N R2W	S31 T3N R1W
S2 T2N R2W	S1 T2N R2W	S6 T2N R1W
S11 T2N R2W	S12 T2N R2W	S7 T2N R1W

Federal Land Records

When land became United States property, it was considered public land or public domain. The government opened land offices to take charge of surveying and distributing the land. A person who acquired a piece of this federal land was a *patentee*, one who received a land patent. Congress passed several laws regulating the sale of land. Thus, some patentees did not have to pay more than a small filing fee if they met other requirements.

When all requirements were met, the patentee received a final certificate or a patent certificate indicating title to that land. The land office staff sent copies of the paperwork to Washington, DC, and these eventually went to the National Archives. Thus, if you discover an ancestor with a federal land patent, you can purchase a copy of his or her land entry file from the National Archives. Request the proper form by mail or via e-mail to inquire@nara.gov or use the online request at <www.archives.gov/global_pages/inquire_form.html>. On the form, you must provide the person's name, the legal description of the land, the land office if you can determine it, and the document or certificate number. Many patents are abstracted online at <www.glorecords.blm.gov> under "Search Land Patents."

It is important to note that federal patents were the first transfer of the land from the government to an individual. When that individual sold the land, the sale was not a federal transfer. Thus, it was recorded in the county deed books, as were all subsequent sales of that tract. (See chapter four.)

Several different laws provided for the sale of public land during the nineteenth century. As settlement spread west and the lands of Alabama, Mississippi, Louisiana, and Arkansas were available for purchase, many slaveholders moved their plantations to this new fertile soil. Many of them bought federal land for about $1.25 per acre as cash entries.

Some of the wealthier free persons of color may well have received patents in these states before the Civil War in spite of the general hostility of white planters to their presence. However, be cautious. If you find a person by your ancestor's name receiving a federal land patent in the South before or after the war, evaluate the person and the records thoroughly. Were they two people by the same name, one black and one white? Which one actually bought the land?

Notes

Note: Many moved to Texas and Tennessee as well, but these are not federal land states.

Sales of Western Land

The Homestead Act of 1862 took effect on the same day as the Emancipation Proclamation—1 January 1863—with the goal of encouraging settlement and agricultural development in the plains and prairies, especially west of the Mississippi River, and making land available at a reasonable cost to those who did not already own land. Homesteaders had to be citizens or immigrants who had begun the process of becoming citizens, over twenty-one years old or heads of families, and not already owners of more than 160 acres of land.

To get title to their land, they had to establish residency, cultivate and improve the land for five years, and pay filing fees. During the late nineteenth century, thousands of Americans moved west to take advantage of this opportunity. Homestead files at the National Archives are often valuable genealogical sources because they contain proof of citizenship and often proof of family.

Even patents that were later canceled can contain family information.

The Timber Culture Act of 1873 also allowed individuals and families to acquire 160 acres in return for planting trees on land that was naturally void of timber. The rules were similar to those for homesteaders, but without the residency requirement. The catch was keeping enough trees alive long enough to meet the requirements. Many applicants were unable to complete the requirements.

Figure 3-11, below, is the 1882 homestead application for Jerry Shores of Custer County, Nebraska, and provides the legal description of his 160 acres. The other documents in the file are mostly administrative, since he was a native-born citizen and did not have to prove his citizenship status. The file includes

- packet cover with final certificate number, application number, legal description of land, date of approval, and date of patent.
- receipt for fourteen dollars he paid at the time of application, 1882.
- final certificate entitling him to the patent, or title to the land, 1889.
- homestead affidavit swearing that he was head of a family, over twenty-one, and a citizen, 1882.
- homestead application, shown in Figure 3-11.
- final affidavit required of homestead claimants, 1889.

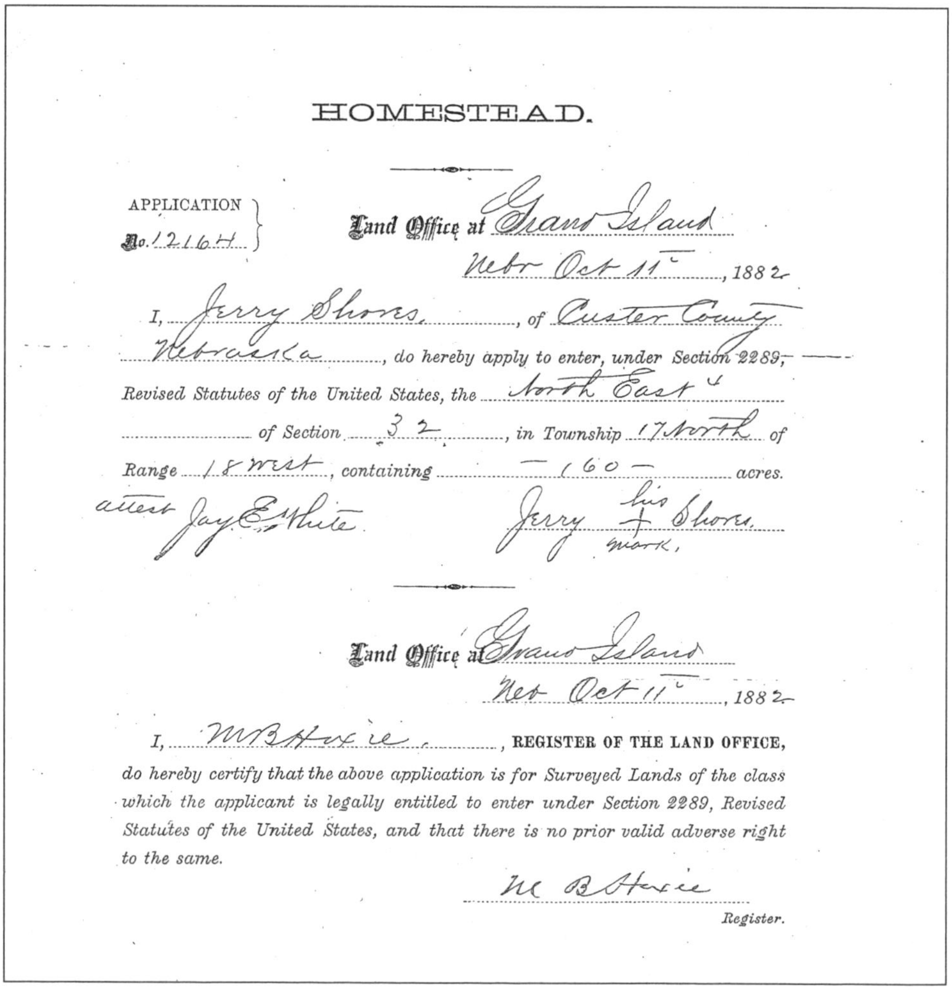

HOMESTEAD.

APPLICATION No. 12164

Land Office at Grand Island

Nebr Oct 11th, 1882

I, Jerry Shores, of Custer County Nebraska, do hereby apply to enter, under Section 2289, Revised Statutes of the United States, the North East 1/4 of Section 32, in Township 17 North of Range 18 West, containing 160 acres.

attest Jay E. White

Jerry his X mark Shores

Land Office at Grand Island

Neb Oct 11th, 1882

I, M B Hoxie, REGISTER OF THE LAND OFFICE, do hereby certify that the above application is for Surveyed Lands of the class which the applicant is legally entitled to enter under Section 2289, Revised Statutes of the United States, and that there is no prior valid adverse right to the same.

M B Hoxie

Register.

Figure 3-11 Homestead application of Jerry Shores, dated 11 October 1882, in land entry file for homestead Final Certificate 8483, patent date 1 November 1890, Grand Island land office, Nebraska, Records of the Bureau of Land Management, Record Group 49, National Archives.

- receipt for payment of four dollars balance due, 1889.
- newspaper notice published according to law for six weeks before his appearing in court to prove that he had met all the requirements in order to be granted his final certificate, 1889. This was done so that anyone who wished to protest or contest his proof would know to come to court to cross-examine his witnesses.
- acknowledgment of his appearing in court and presenting his "final proof" on his homestead entry, 1889.
- testimony of two witnesses, presented in court, as his final proof. Each witness filled out a form of twenty-nine questions about Shores's continuous residence on the land, his improvements to the land, and his cultivation of the land. For more details on his farm, see pages 63–64.
- testimony of Shores, answering forty-four questions, with much of the same information that the witnesses gave.

Some land files have more information; some have less. Much depends on the law under which the individual was applying for land. The most common types of patents were cash entries; credit sales from about 1800 to about 1820; homesteads from 1863 forward; timber culture from 1873; and donation lands in Florida, New Mexico, and Oregon and Washington Territories after 1850. Researchers need to exercise caution in evaluating the files since multiple claimants sometimes had the same name, and the records usually did not identify the claimants' race.

For More Info

For more information on land research, see Hone's *Land & Property Research in the United States,* and Hatcher's *Locating Your Roots: Discover Your Ancestors Using Land Records.*

NUCMC

The *National Union Catalog of Manuscript Collections* (called NUCMC, pronounced "nuck-muck") is a Library of Congress publication listing and describing collections of manuscript materials all over the country. These manuscripts include letters, documents, diaries, newspapers, church records, maps, and many others kinds of family, business, organization, and even government papers that have been deposited in an archive, library, or museum for preservation and/or study.

The ***Index to Personal Names in the National Union Catalog of Manuscript Collections, 1959–1984* is a valuable reference.** However, the topical index directs researchers to subjects such as Blacks, Afro-Americans, freedmen, slaves, and Bureau of Refugees, Freedmen, and Abandoned Lands. Under the subject heading for Blacks are topics such as churches, Civil War, genealogy, newspapers, and societies. The collection appears in NUCMC when the holding depository reports it. For example, an index item showing "77-1000" refers you to entry 1000 in the 1977 volume. The entry then describes the collection and tells which depository holds it. Since most of these materials are not microfilmed, you need to go to the depository to read the materials. However, if the collection is pertinent to your research, you may be able to obtain copies of key documents by mail. A reference librarian can help you learn to use this valuable finding aid.

Library/Archive Source

Internet Source

Post-1983 additions to NUCMC are available in electronic form in academic and large public libraries and online at <http://lcweb.loc.gov/coll/nucmc>. Search a variety of topics that pertain to your search, such as a surname or a county or town name. For example, an online search for "Afro-American churches" brought up a long list of churches, including those whose records are on microfilm at the Schomberg Center for Research in Black Culture of the New York Public Library. These churches included the First and Second African Baptist Churches of Savannah, Georgia, and Asbury United Methodist Church in Washington, DC. Records of these churches began in the nineteenth century, and the originals are reportedly still held by the churches. If your ancestors were members of these churches, or others on the list, you would have another potentially valuable source for research. The online NUCMC can tell you more about the records and the churches.

SOUTHERN CLAIMS COMMISSION

Beginning in 1871, the federal government set up a commission to examine claims of Southerners who asserted that they had been loyal to the U.S. during the Civil War and who lost or donated goods to the military during those years. A number of claimants were black. The microfilmed papers that deal with individuals are mostly letters. Roll thirteen of the series is a geographical list of claims by state, county, and the names of claimants. However, a published index, created from this roll, is available in many libraries: *Civil War Claims in the South: An Index of Civil War Damage Claims Filed Before the Southern Claims Commission, 1871–1880*, Gary B. Mills, compiler (Laguna Hills, Calif.: Aegean Park Press, 1980).

As you have seen in this chapter, federal records for research are numerous and are available in different forms and at many research locations. These are rich resources for genealogists and preserve valuable and interesting history.

FOUR

State, County, and Local Sources

S tate, county, and local sources for genealogists are both useful and plentiful. Not all the available records will provide information on all your ancestors, but chances are good that some of your ancestors' names will appear in some of the records, especially after 1900. Not knowing in advance which records will contain ancestral information, genealogists look at many different kinds of records.

As you research, consider that ancestors

* created records when they purchased land, paid taxes, got married, or served in the military
* were the subjects of records that others created, as in birth and death certificates, on tombstones, or in military pension applications that widows filed based on their husbands' service
* were mentioned in records of others, when they witnessed or performed a marriage, were named as a neighbor in a news story or land record, or purchased goods at a local store or estate sale

Idea Generator

STATE RECORDS

State archives and historical societies have numerous records of genealogical value, including early state government, county government, local, business, and individual family records. Many of these institutions have printed guides to their holdings and inventories of special collections. Serious researchers benefit from obtaining copies of the guides and inventories that pertain to their searches. Visit the state archives and historical society Web sites to learn more about specific holdings, as each state differs somewhat from others.

Sometimes private papers donated to the state archives pertain to African-American families, such as the James Boon papers (1829–1853) in the North Carolina Division of Archives and History. In addition, many state libraries and archives have genealogy collections that include microfilm of National

See Also

See Appendix C, page 211, for state archives addresses and Web sites.

Archives records pertaining to the individual state and its people, such as the Freedmen's Bureau records and census records.

The state sources highlighted in this chapter include the 1867 voter registration records, state adjutant general records, and state censuses. Other genealogical materials in state custody may include state court records, school censuses, petitions to the state legislature by individuals or on their behalf, governors' pardons, compilations on military servicemen from the state, newspapers from towns in the state, Bible records, and records of institutions in the state, including hospitals, prisons, or soldiers' homes.

1867 Voter Registrations

After the Civil War, the former Confederate states had to elect delegates to state constitutional conventions in order to construct new constitutions and be readmitted to the Union. A number of Southern states still have records of the voter registration effort. Male citizens over twenty-one, who had resided in the state for at least one year, had to swear or affirm that they had not been disfranchised for (1) participating in or supporting rebellion or civil war against the United States or (2) any felony conviction. They also had to swear to support the Constitution of the United States and agree to encourage others to do so.

Some registration forms were as simple as a list with each voter's signature or mark, his race, and the name of a witness. Others were more elaborate, requesting information on the length of residence in the county and state, birthplace, and whether each man was a naturalized citizen. In Panola County, Texas, for example, Charles Holland and John Darnell, both "colored" residents of Precinct Eight, affirmed they had been in the state, county, and precinct for twenty years. Holland gave Tennessee as his birthplace; Darnell said he was born in Georgia.[1]

State Adjutant General's Records

The adjutant general of each state oversees the administration of today's National Guard and records of state military units of the past. For the original thirteen states, the records of the adjutant general at the state archives contain muster rolls, pay rolls, and other documents pertaining to colonial militia and units raised for the American Revolution, the War of 1812, the Mexican War, and the Civil War. Early in the Civil War, units of free blacks were organized across the country, from Rhode Island and Pennsylvania to Michigan, Kansas, and Louisiana. Some of these units were later incorporated into the United States Colored Troops. Some units from Massachusetts, Connecticut, and Louisiana remained apart from the U.S.C.T.

State Censuses

Over the years, a number of states have conducted censuses, and some of these jurisdictions took censuses when they were colonies or territories. **Surviving records are usually found at the state archives and are available on microfilm there, in other research libraries, and at the Family History Library.** Check the Family History Library catalog or Heritage Quest catalog for those censuses you could rent for your state and county of interest. Check Web sites such as Ancestry.com

Sources

and USGenWeb <www.usgenweb.org> for state censuses that may be online.

Some of these state, territorial, and colonial censuses were statistical only and are of little value to genealogists. More useful for family history are those that (1) named heads of household and grouped family members by age and sex or (2) named each family member and gave individual details of age, birthplace, etc.

In 1885, Colorado, Dakota Territory (North and South Dakota), Florida, Nebraska, and New Mexico Territory accepted federal government help to conduct a census similar to the 1880 federal census. These schedules are available on microfilm, along with their agriculture, manufacturing, and mortality schedules. Indexes are available for some.

The Custer County, Nebraska, 1885 census lists Jerry Shores, his wife, and their daughter; sons James and William were not enumerated with the rest of the family.[2] Discrepancies exist with this census, as with others. For example, this family was black but was enumerated as white. Also, Jerry's wife and daughter were reported with a different surname: Rohbut or Rohbert. Could this be Robert(s)? Might this be a clue to Rachel's former surname, or was it just an error? These are further questions for the genealogist.

The mortality schedule for the county showed no deaths within the Shores family during the previous year. However, the agriculture schedule gave interesting details about the family's farm. Although not strictly genealogical, this kind of information is valuable in helping descendants learn about a family's life and work:

- 25 acres of tilled ground; 125 acres permanent pastures; no unimproved acreage.
- $1,800 value of farm land, fences, buildings; $25 value of farming implements, $250 value of livestock; $200 value of farm production for 1884.
- 4 horses; 1 milch cow, 50 pounds of butter made in 1884; 7 swine; 7 poultry, 50 eggs produced in 1884.
- 15 acres planted in Indian corn, 600 bushels of corn produced in 1884; 9 acres planted in oats, 100 bushels of oats produced in 1884; ½ acre planted in sweet potatoes, harvest seems to be 25 bushels; ½ acre planted in apple trees, no harvest reported.

Shores's 1885 agriculture census entry, combined with his 1889 testimony in support of his homestead patent, gives a much more complete picture of his home and farm.[3] Shores said he and his family moved to the farm in April 1883 and began improving it immediately. Figure 4-1 is a photograph of the Shores family in front of their house about 1887.

Shores built the family's home himself for a cost of $100. Typical of houses on the Great Plains, it was a sod house, eighteen feet by thirty-two feet, with a board and sod roof, a board floor, three doors, and four windows. For $100, he built his sod stable, twenty feet by fifty-four feet. His other outbuildings included a corn crib, hog pen, and hen house; he also had a cellar and a well that was thirty feet deep.

His land was prairie but not used for grazing. He had planted twenty fruit trees and five hundred forest trees; he had broken and plowed seventy acres for

Case Study

Notes

Milch cow was an old way of saying "milk cow." A sod house was built of grass-covered slabs of earth, stacked to form walls and sometimes laid on the roof.

Figure 4-1 Jerry Shores home and family, 1887, near Westerville, Nebraska. Left to right: daughter, Minerva Shores and infant; Albert Marks; wife, Rachel Shores; Jerry Shores; son, Jim Shores. *Nebraska Historical Society*

cultivation. In 1889, he had thirteen acres planted in wheat and four acres prepared for the next season. He felt his crops between 1883 and 1889 had been good ones but could not guess how many bushels he had raised each season.

Shores had made a conscientious effort to complete the requirements for his patent. After six years of hard work on his farm, he had achieved, with the help of his family, the ownership of a quarter section of land, something he may not have even dreamed about thirty years before as a North Carolina slave.

He lived sixty or more miles from the land office. Like numerous others, he lived much closer to his county courthouse—only about a day's travel. Thus, he was able to appear before the clerk of the district court at Broken Bow to complete his paper work for his patent.

COUNTY RECORDS

County records, normally housed at the county courthouse or the state archives, include birth, death, and marriage records; land and probate records; and court records. Every county courthouse holds other kinds of records as well.

Vital Registrations: Birth and Death Records

Among the most important county sources for African-American genealogy are registrations of births and deaths. Whether you find records from the nineteenth century or your ancestral state began registration in the twentieth century, your research often benefits from a search of these records.

Some states registered births and deaths in the nineteenth century. In the South, where the majority of African Americans lived, Virginia and Kentucky began such registries before the Civil War and continued afterward, with a few gaps in the records. Northern states such as Wisconsin and the New England states also recorded births and deaths before the Civil War.

To learn more about when your ancestral state began recording birth and deaths, consult one of these sources:

1. www.vitalrec.com
2. Thomas Jay Kemp, *International Vital Records Handbook.*
3. Alice Eichholz, ed., *Ancestry's Red Book.*
4. A book or article on research in the state. See the bibliography at the end of this chapter.

In these records, one of the most helpful pieces of information is parents' names. An early example comes from Botetourt County, Virginia. On 26 September 1855, Mary Elizabeth Wilson was born to free black parents, Cary and Susan Wilson.[4] **Prior to the Civil War, the child carried the legal status of the mother.** Since Susan Wilson was free, her daughter was born free.

Important

Sometimes, especially on death certificates, the informant did not know the parental information, and genealogists find *d.k.* ("don't know") where they had hoped for a research breakthrough. One page of a Virginia register of deaths listed four African Americans who died in 1867 at advanced ages between 82 and 102. Only entry one named a parent. Billy Goff, age eighty-six, had died in February 1867, probably of old age, although no cause of death was given. In reporting the event to the county clerk's office, Goff's wife, Lucy, named his father as Moses Goff.[5] Since Billy Goff had been born about 1780, the death record helps move his researcher a big step closer to the eighteenth century.

As shown in Figure 6-1, on page 109, the birth certificate may also give the parents' ages, address, and occupations at the time of the child's birth. This figure also shows a stamp across it reading "uncertified copy." For genealogical purposes, it is simply a photocopy of the record on file in the vital statistics office at the county courthouse, but it is not embossed with the official seal that would make it acceptable for legal use. The simple photocopy is much cheaper than the certified copy.

Some counties and states also have a short form of birth certificate that gives the bare facts of birth name, date, and place, and little else. What you want is the long or complete form that shows all information collected at the time of registration. Older certificates, such as the one in Figure 6-1, may be only a partial page in length but contain the complete information.

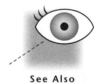

See Also

See the case study on pages 107–108, about using these records to evaluate the father's name.

Besides parents' names, death certificates may furnish additional information about the deceased: birth date and place, occupation, marital status, surviving spouse's name, cause of death, and burial information.

If you gather birth and death certificates for all the siblings of a family, you may be able to

- collect more evidence on the parents' names, birthplaces, or birth dates (figured from their ages), especially if their births were not recorded
- confirm or correct family tradition on the siblings' names, birth order, and vital statistics
- determine whether or when the family moved

- learn about cemeteries where family members were buried, especially family cemeteries, and funeral homes where more information may be on file
- gather medical history on causes of death

However, genealogists need to be cautious in using vital records, like any others.

1. The informant may not have been a family member or may not have been well informed.
2. Birth information on a death certificate is second-hand information and thus may not be accurate.
3. Some clerks made typographical or handwritten errors.
4. On most death certificates, the death date is correct. Discrepancies sometimes occur when the person died around midnight, and others present did not check the time or estimated differently about which side of midnight the person died.
5. The person's reported age at death may not match the birth date.

For More Info

For more on death records, cemeteries, and burial customs, see Carmack's *Your Guide to Cemetery Research.*

Warning

Figure 4-2, on page 67, is the death certificate of Nelson White of Adair County, Kentucky. It is a typical example, providing his death date, occupation, parents' names, cause of death, and burial site, as well as the name of the funeral home. Especially fortunate is the maiden name of his mother, for this is the only record of her maiden name that her researcher has found so far.

Note that the form asked for birthplace but requested no more than the name of the state or country. Thus, in this case, the certificate reports only that the ancestor was born in Kentucky. Sometimes the town or county of birth is given.

With this certificate, as with many others, several shortcomings appear. The most glaring is that Mr. White was black but was incorrectly registered as white, perhaps from a clerk's confusion caused by the surname. Secondly, the widow was the informant but was listed only as Mrs. Nelson White; genealogists would like her given name to be used as a double-check on the survivor's identity. She did not fill out the certificate but furnished the information to a clerk or funeral home staff member, who may not have asked for her given name.

The third problem with this death certificate is that the age at death does not match the birth date. This example is not far off; some are terribly wrong. You must check this information on the certificates you collect. In this case, the death date is recorded twice as 19 January 1955 and probably is correct. However, when you subtract the age at death from the death date, you find that the birth date would have been 3 September *1872*. The birth date reported was 3 September *1873*. Thus, the researcher has to determine which is correct.

This is a common problem on death certificates and tombstones. In this case, the informant must have believed, to the best of her knowledge, that Mr. White was born on 3 September 1873, as his descendants believe was his birthday. His reported age at death was eighty-two years, four months, and sixteen days. Whoever figured the age at death subtracted 3 (birth day) from 19 (death day) to get the sixteen days, then counted from his birthday in September to his death in January—four months.

The mistake probably occurred when the person subtracted 1873 (the birth

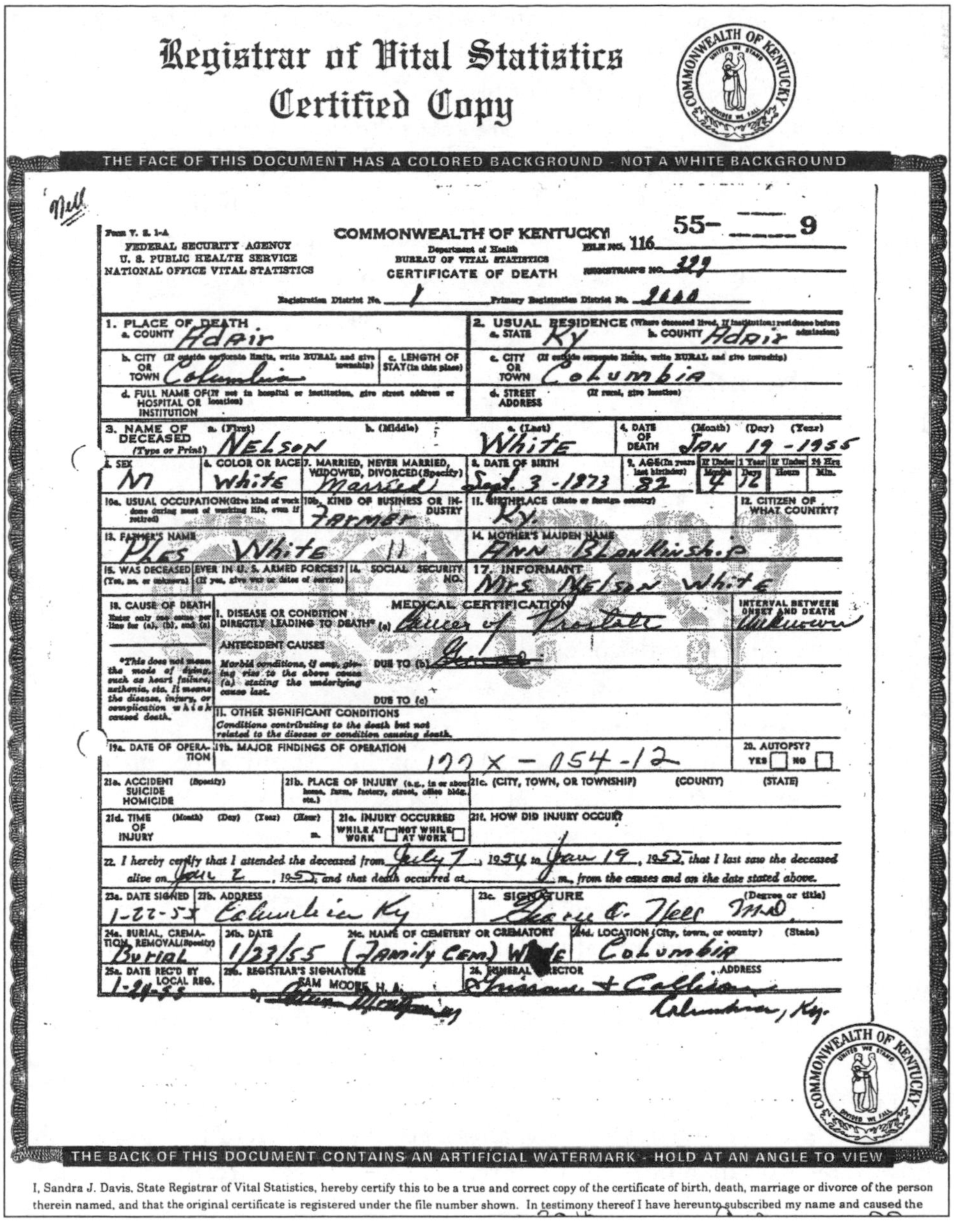

Registrar of Vital Statistics
Certified Copy

THE FACE OF THIS DOCUMENT HAS A COLORED BACKGROUND - NOT A WHITE BACKGROUND

COMMONWEALTH OF KENTUCKY
Department of Health
BUREAU OF VITAL STATISTICS
CERTIFICATE OF DEATH

Form V. S. 1-A
FEDERAL SECURITY AGENCY
U. S. PUBLIC HEALTH SERVICE
NATIONAL OFFICE VITAL STATISTICS

55- ___ 9
FILE NO. 116
REGISTRAR'S NO. 329
Registration District No. 1
Primary Registration District No. 2600

1. PLACE OF DEATH a. COUNTY Adair
b. CITY OR TOWN Columbia
c. LENGTH OF STAY (in this place)
d. FULL NAME OF HOSPITAL OR INSTITUTION

2. USUAL RESIDENCE a. STATE Ky b. COUNTY Adair
c. CITY OR TOWN Columbia
d. STREET ADDRESS

3. NAME OF DECEASED (Type or Print) a. (First) Nelson b. (Middle) c. (Last) White
4. DATE OF DEATH (Month) (Day) (Year) Jan 19 - 1955
5. SEX M
6. COLOR OR RACE White
7. MARRIED, NEVER MARRIED, WIDOWED, DIVORCED (Specify) Married
8. DATE OF BIRTH Sept. 3 - 1873
9. AGE (In years last birthday) 82 / If Under 1 Year: Months 4, Days 16 / If Under 24 Hrs: Hours, Min.
10a. USUAL OCCUPATION
10b. KIND OF BUSINESS OR INDUSTRY Farmer
11. BIRTHPLACE (State or foreign country) Ky.
12. CITIZEN OF WHAT COUNTRY?
13. FATHER'S NAME Ples White
14. MOTHER'S MAIDEN NAME Ann Blankinship
15. WAS DECEASED EVER IN U. S. ARMED FORCES?
16. SOCIAL SECURITY NO.
17. INFORMANT Mrs Nelson White

18. CAUSE OF DEATH — MEDICAL CERTIFICATION
I. DISEASE OR CONDITION DIRECTLY LEADING TO DEATH* (a) Cancer of Prostate
INTERVAL BETWEEN ONSET AND DEATH Unknown
ANTECEDENT CAUSES — DUE TO (b) — DUE TO (c)
II. OTHER SIGNIFICANT CONDITIONS
19a. DATE OF OPERATION
19b. MAJOR FINDINGS OF OPERATION 177X - 154 - 12
20. AUTOPSY? YES ☐ NO ☐
21a. ACCIDENT SUICIDE HOMICIDE (Specify)
21b. PLACE OF INJURY
21c. (CITY, TOWN, OR TOWNSHIP) (COUNTY) (STATE)
21d. TIME OF INJURY
21e. INJURY OCCURRED WHILE AT WORK ☐ NOT WHILE AT WORK ☐
21f. HOW DID INJURY OCCUR?

22. I hereby certify that I attended the deceased from July 7, 1954 to Jan 19, 1955 that I last saw the deceased alive on Jan 2, 1955 and that death occurred at ___ m., from the causes and on the date stated above.
23a. DATE SIGNED 1-22-55
23b. ADDRESS Columbia Ky
23c. SIGNATURE (Degree or title) George C. Hill M.D.
24a. BURIAL, CREMATION, REMOVAL (Specify) Burial
24b. DATE 1/23/55
24c. NAME OF CEMETERY OR CREMATORY (Family Cem) White
24d. LOCATION (City, town, or county) (State) Columbia
25a. DATE REC'D BY LOCAL REG. 1-24-55
25b. REGISTRAR'S SIGNATURE SAM MOORE H. A.
26. FUNERAL DIRECTOR Grissom + Collins
ADDRESS Columbia, Ky.

THE BACK OF THIS DOCUMENT CONTAINS AN ARTIFICIAL WATERMARK - HOLD AT AN ANGLE TO VIEW

I, Sandra J. Davis, State Registrar of Vital Statistics, hereby certify this to be a true and correct copy of the certificate of birth, death, marriage or divorce of the person therein named, and that the original certificate is registered under the file number shown. In testimony thereof I have hereunto subscribed my name and caused the

Figure 4-2 Death certificate of Nelson White of Columbia, Adair County, Kentucky, 19 January 1955, file 116, Office of the Registrar of Vital Statistics, Frankfort, Kentucky.

year) from 1955 (the death year) and got 82. However, if Mr. White was born in September 1873, he had celebrated his last birthday in September 1954. Subtracting 1873 from 1954 shows that he had lived eighty-one years, and his death occurred four months and sixteen days after his eighty-first birthday. He would have turned eighty-two on his next birthday. We could also say he died in his "82nd year," but that is not the same as "82 years old."

The problem could also occur if the informant knew the deceased was eighty-two years old and subtracted 82 from 1955 to get a birth year of 1873. The correct process, in such a case, would have been to subtract 82 from 1954 (the most recent birthday) to determine the man was born in 1872.

Various Web sites can calculate the birth date for you if you know the death date and the age at death. However, you must have correct information in order to get a correct birth date. The safe procedure would be to figure out an answer

Tip

yourself and check your answer on the Web calendar calculator. Do not blindly accept the response as an accurate birth date. You can access these Web sites from <www.cyndislist.com/calendar.htm>.

Most birth and death registrations are kept in the county courthouse, the town hall or health department, and/or the state bureau of vital statistics or its equivalent. Some early records are kept at the state archives. To obtain copies, try the county or town first, as getting copies is often cheaper or quicker than going to the state's designated office. Many such records have also been microfilmed and/or indexed. Some indexes are online.

Vital Registrations: Marriages

Marriage records vary from state to state and from time to time. The records may furnish not only the bride's and groom's names but their ages, birthplaces, occupations, and/or parents' names. After the Civil War, many counties in the South recorded freedmen's marriages in separate books from white marriages; in registers for all marriages, regardless of race, some reported a racial designation for all couples, or for none.

Many marriage records contain several dates—a date of the
- bond or license
- wedding
- return, when the clergyman or Justice of the Peace who performed the ceremony returned the license to the clerk's office
- filing of the license into the official record

Thus, in taking notes or recording the marriage date in your charts, double-check that you have the actual wedding date. If that date is not furnished, use the license or bond date, but label it for what it is. For the wedding date, you would have to record "on or after" the date of bond or license. Some couples did marry on the day they obtained their license; others married one to many days thereafter.

Figure 4-3, on page 69, shows the marriage bond and record of Robert White and Winny Workman of Adair County, Kentucky. With a relative or friend as surety, the groom had to swear before the clerk of court that he and the bride were of legal age to marry (over twenty-one years, in this state) and he knew of no legal cause that would prevent the marriage from taking place and being valid. Usually, the "no legal cause" meant that neither party was already married to someone else. Licenses gradually replaced bonds by the twentieth century in most places.

The page adjoining this marriage bond contains much helpful information. For example, the groom, a blacksmith, was thirty-eight years old and entering his second marriage. He and his parents were born in neighboring Green County, Kentucky. The bride, at twenty-two, was marrying for the first time. She and her father were natives of the county in which the bride and groom resided; her mother was born in Green County. Depending on the place, marriage records may provide more or less information.

Be aware that a marriage bond or license may appear in the marriage register, but the date of the wedding may be missing. You cannot assume that the mar-

Notes

The *surety* joined the groom in this guarantee and was jointly liable with him for the one hundred dollars (see Figure 4-3) if such a cause existed that would make the marriage illegal.

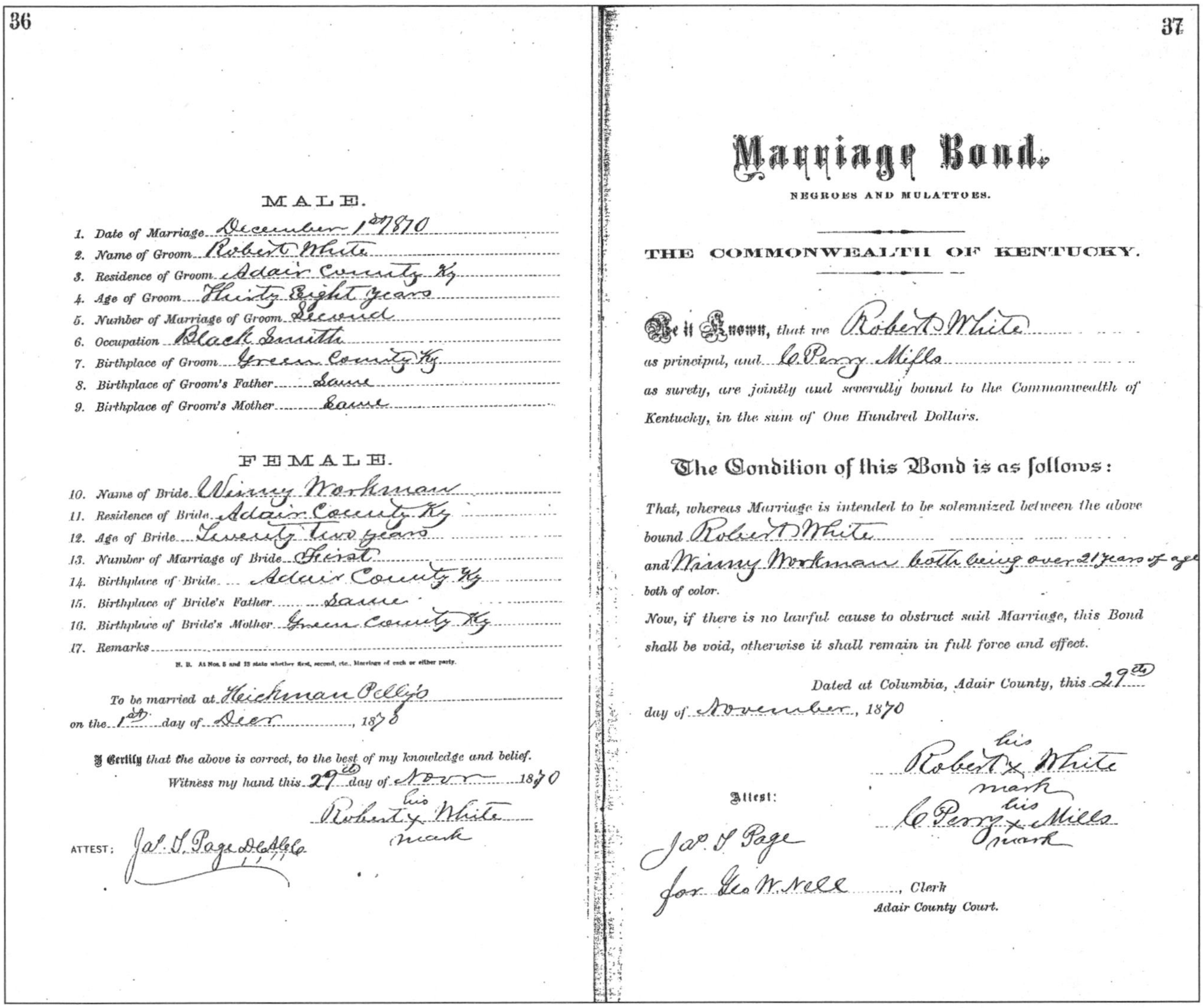

36

MALE.

1. Date of Marriage December 1st 1870
2. Name of Groom Robert White
3. Residence of Groom Adair County Ky
4. Age of Groom Thirty Eight years
5. Number of Marriage of Groom Second
6. Occupation Black Smith
7. Birthplace of Groom Green County Ky
8. Birthplace of Groom's Father Same
9. Birthplace of Groom's Mother Same

FEMALE.

10. Name of Bride Winny Workman
11. Residence of Bride Adair County Ky
12. Age of Bride Twenty two years
13. Number of Marriage of Bride First
14. Birthplace of Bride Adair County Ky
15. Birthplace of Bride's Father Same
16. Birthplace of Bride's Mother Green County Ky
17. Remarks

N. B. At Nos. 5 and 13 state whether first, second, etc., Marriage of each or either party.

To be married at Hickman Pelly's
on the 1st day of Decr, 1870

I Certify that the above is correct, to the best of my knowledge and belief.
Witness my hand this 29th day of Novr 1870

Robert his x mark White

ATTEST: Jas. S. Page DcAbC

37

Marriage Bond.

NEGROES AND MULATTOES.

THE COMMONWEALTH OF KENTUCKY.

Be it Known, that we Robert White as principal, and C. Perry Mills as surety, are jointly and severally bound to the Commonwealth of Kentucky, in the sum of One Hundred Dollars.

The Condition of this Bond is as follows:

That, whereas Marriage is intended to be solemnized between the above bound Robert White and Winny Workman both being over 21 years of age both of color.

Now, if there is no lawful cause to obstruct said Marriage, this Bond shall be void, otherwise it shall remain in full force and effect.

Dated at Columbia, Adair County, this 29th day of November, 1870

Robert his x mark White

C. Perry his x mark Mills

Attest:
Jas. S. Page
for Geo W. Nell, Clerk
Adair County Court.

Figure 4-3 Marriage record of Robert White and Winny Workman, 1870, Adair County, Kentucky, Colored Marriages, Book 2:36-37, County Clerk's Office, Courthouse, Columbia.

riage did not take place, although some did not; nor can you assume that the clergyman or justice of the peace simply failed to return the license to the clerk of court, as some did. You need to look for other confirmation of the marriage, for example, in a church record or in a census record that identifies the couple as husband and wife.

If the bride or groom was not yet of legal age to marry, a parent or guardian had to give permission for the underage person to marry. Figure 4-4, on page 70, shows such a note from 1884, in which Richard Massie of Cane Valley, Kentucky, gave permission for his eighteen-year-old daughter, Jennie Massie, to marry Frank Vaughn.

Marriage records, like the other vital records, are housed at the county courthouse or town hall, depending on the state. Early records may have been transferred to the state archives, and many have been microfilmed. Some states also began collecting marriage records at the vital records office in the capital city. You can locate many marriage records from microfilmed or printed indexes.

Figure 4-4 Parental permission of Richard Massie for Jennie Massie to marry, dated 28 February 1884, Adair County, Kentucky, Marriage Book 2:70, County Clerk's Office, Courthouse, Columbia.

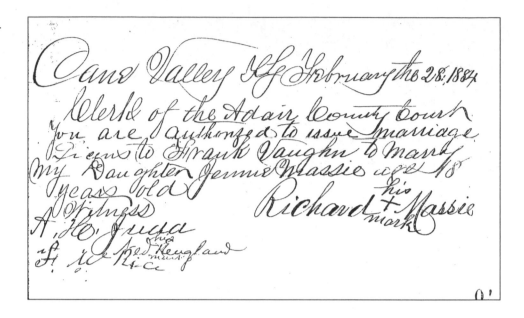

Gather these records for ancestors and their siblings for the same reasons you would gather birth and death records, and use them with the same cautions. For a variety of reasons, some of these events in the life of your ancestor or family members may not have been recorded, but your research is more thorough if you look for the records and get copies or make abstracts of the ones you locate.

Cohabitation Records

Before the Civil War, slaves were not allowed to be legally married. Yet, many couples married informally, some with large celebrations attended by slaves from neighboring properties. The slaveholder often presided over the ceremony and recognized the couple as husband and wife. In many locations, these weddings were for several couples at once and took place during the Christmas holidays.

After the Civil War, those couples who had married as slaves and wished to remain together as husband and wife had the opportunity to register and legalize their marriages at the county courthouse. These records vary in form and content. Many survive in the county courthouses and/or state archives, and a number have been microfilmed. Check with the state archives of your ancestral state, especially Kentucky, Virginia, and North Carolina, or at the county courthouse for specific information on the records held there.

In North Carolina, an 1866 law required the couples to register by the fall of 1866 and pay a twenty-five cent fee. Some cohabitation records for thirty-nine of the state's counties are known to survive. These have been abstracted and published in three volumes as *Somebody Knows My Name: Marriages of Freed People in North Carolina County By County*, Barnetta McGhee White, compiler (Athens, Ga.: Iberian Publishing Co., 1995). Many of these are also on microfilm.

As shown in Figure 4-5, on page 71, couples in Craven County, North Carolina, streamed into the courthouse in August 1866, before the September dead-

Definitions

Cohabitation meant that the couple had been living together as husband and wife and considered themselves married, even if their union was not legally recognized at the time.

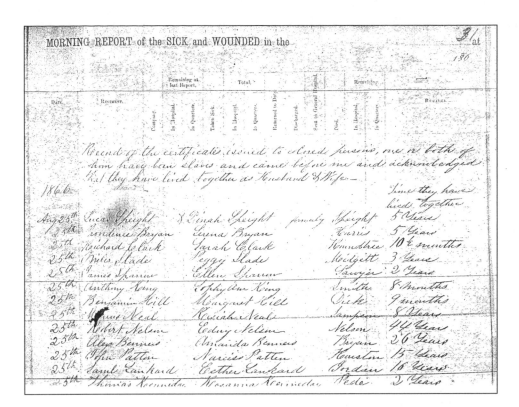

Figure 4-5 Cohabitation record, 1866, Craven County, North Carolina, Marriages 1865–1905, Vol. 2 (1865–1866):31, Family History Library microfilm 0288298.

line, to register their pre-existing cohabitation and obtain certificates of legal marriage. The columns record the date of the registration, the groom's name, the bride's name, the bride's former surname, and the time they had lived together. Notice that the shortest union recorded here was eight months; the longest, forty-four years. Two couples, the Speights and the Nelsons, may have lived on the same plantation before their marriage as suggested by the fact that the bride's former name was the same as her married name.

Note also that the county was not entirely prepared for this registration process and did not have a record book to dedicate to the purpose. Thus, the clerk used a blank army register printed for morning reports of the sick and wounded soldiers. This situation in itself is an interesting commentary on the scarcity of paper supplies both during and shortly after the war.

In neighboring Beaufort County, blank spaces and pages of another marriage record book became the cohabitation register. Figure 4-6, on page 72, is part of a page from the 1866 Beaufort County register, showing records of four couples who reported in different ways.

1. Dempsey Celia [*sic*], lately a slave of Elizabeth Macky, had been living with Ann Rowland, lately a slave of Mrs. Gregory. Knowing the former slaveholders' names is very helpful, but Celia didn't report how long he and his wife had been together.

2. Spencer Solomon Collins of Hyde County and Mary Jennett "had been living together as man and wife by mutual consent for one year and . . . desired so to remain the balance of their days." Helpful as it is to have Collins's residence and the length of time they had been together, no former slaveholder is mentioned.

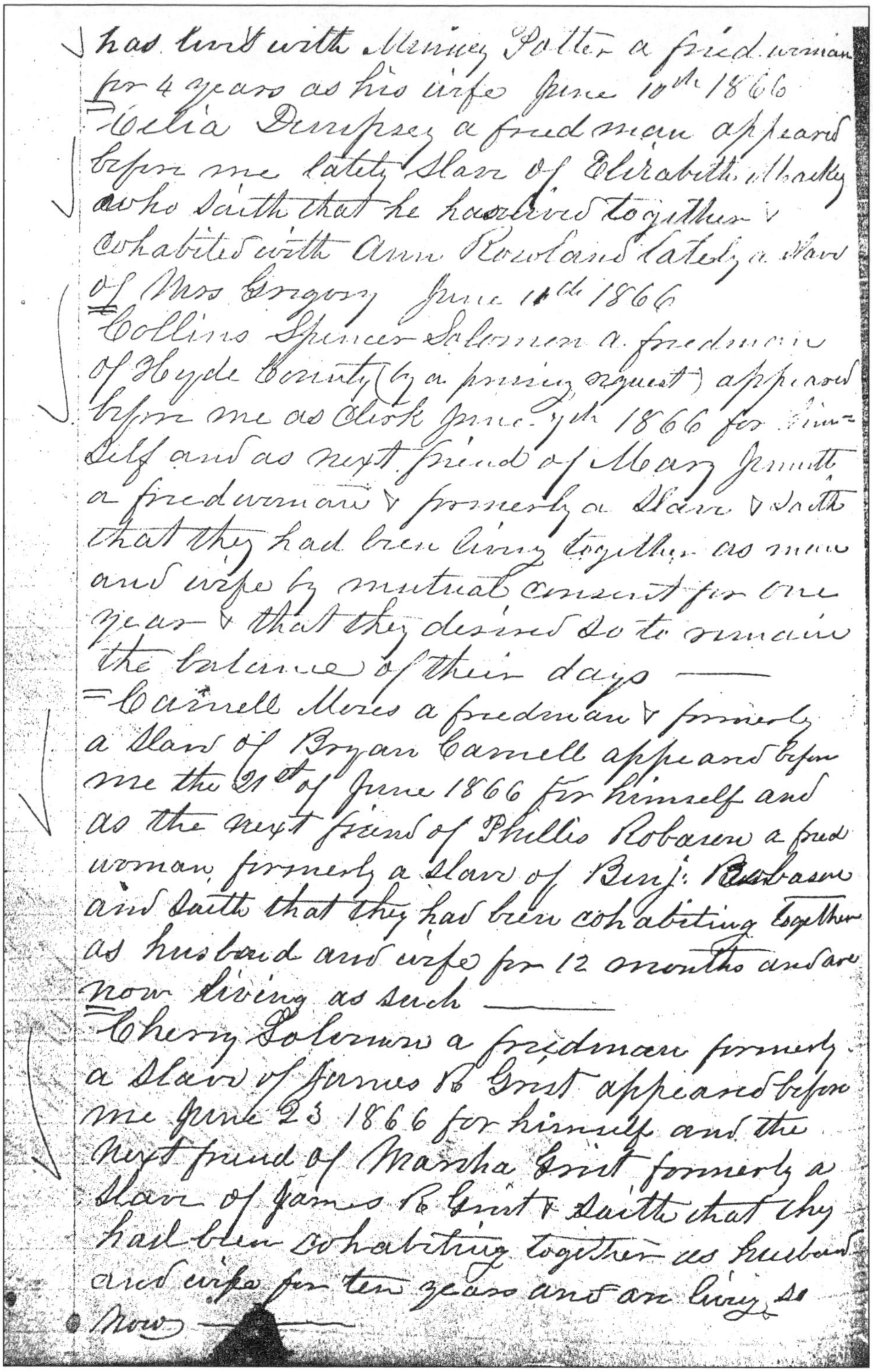
had lived with Minicy Potter a freedwoman
for 4 years as his wife June 10th 1866
Celia Dempsey a freedman appeared
before me lately Slave of Elizabeth Mackey
who saith that he has lived together &
cohabited with Ann Rowland lately a slave
of Mrs Gregory June 10th 1866
Collins Spencer Solomon a freedman
of Hyde County (by a previous request) appeared
before me as Clerk June 7th 1866 for himself and as next friend of Mary Jennett
a freedwoman & formerly a Slave & saith
that they had been living together as man
and wife by mutual consent for one
year & that they desired so to remain
the balance of their days ——
Carrell Moses a freedman & formerly
a Slave of Bryan Carrell appeared before
me the 21st of June 1866 for himself and
as the next friend of Phillis Robason a freed
woman formerly a Slave of Benj. Robason
and saith that they had been cohabiting together
as husband and wife for 12 months and are
now living as such ——
Cherry Solomon a freedman formerly
a Slave of James R Grist appeared before
me June 23 1866 for himself and the
next friend of Martha Grist formerly a
Slave of James R Grist & saith that they
had been cohabiting together as husband
and wife for ten years and are living so
now

Figure 4-6 Cohabitation records, 1866, Beaufort County, North Carolina, in Marriage Book 1851–1868, pages unnumbered but in rough alphabetical order by surname's initial letter, Family History Library microfilm 1689154, item 1.

3. Moses Carrell, formerly a slave of Bryan Carrell, and Phillis Robason, formerly a slave of Benjamin Robason, "had been cohabiting together as husband and wife for 12 months and are now living as such." This registry gives both former slaveholders and indicates that the couple married, as did the previous couple, just after the end of the war.

4. Solomon Cherry and Martha Grist, both formerly slaves of James R. Grist, had lived as husband and wife for ten years. They had been slaves of the same man, but Cherry now had, or had retained, a different surname, perhaps a clue to a former slaveholder.

Land and Property Records

Clues to whether your ancestor owned land may come from family tradition, family papers, and these census records:

- 1870 census—asked each head of household about the value of real estate owned
- 1900, 1910 censuses—asked whether the house or farm was owned or rented
- 1930 census—asked whether the home was owned or rented and its value or monthly rent

For More Info

See *Unpuzzling Your Past*, 4th edition, for a more comprehensive discussion of deed records. See also chapter nine.

If your ancestor owned land in the county, you will want to investigate the county deed records to learn the size of the property, when the ancestor purchased it, where it is located, what the purchase price was, and, sometimes, who the neighboring landowners were. If the ancestor sold the land, the deed should tell you when, to whom, and for what price he made the sale. Many deed records mention wives' names and show the names of witnesses, some of whom may have been relatives. Even if they give no further genealogical information, they show that the ancestor was alive and in that place at that time.

The county deed books are not the original documents but copies made by court clerks. Thus, the names at the end of each record are not the actual signatures of the parties involved. However, the copy will indicate whether the ancestor could sign his name or made his mark where someone else had written his name.

County deed records are indexed by the names of the buyers (grantees) and sellers (grantors). You need to look at both indexes so you can determine both purchases and sales your ancestors may have made. If your ancestor was not mentioned as a landowner, he or she could still be mentioned in the book in other capacities:

1. These are the same books that, prior to the Civil War, sometimes contained bills of sale for slaves. (See chapter nine.)
2. Deed records often named neighboring landowners, witnesses to the transaction, or former owners of the same land. Such people are not indexed.

Below is a transcription of part of a 1911 deed. The original shows both the purchase and the release of lien when the purchaser completed payment in 1912.[6] In this deed record, Nelson White, "of color," a resident of Penick, Marion County, Kentucky, was purchasing five acres from J. Edward Sullivan and his wife, Marion, for $110—$80 in cash and $30 credit at 6 percent interest, due in one year. The land was on a prong of Followells Creek known as Welch Branch, in Marion County. After describing the terms of the sale, the deed gave

Important

In a transcription, brackets indicate something the transcriber has added to make the meaning clear. A *pole* is a measurement equal in length to a rod or perch, 16.5 feet or 5.5 yards long. *Appurtenances* are rights or assets attached to the property: rights of way, fences, buildings.

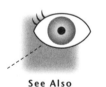

See Also

For more on tax records, see pages 94–96, 130–131, and 148; see Appendix C for information on state archives.

the legal description of the land and some history of its ownership. The legal description is typical of the metes and bounds survey system:

> Beginning at a maple and a buckeye tree on point of hill on east side of Welches Branch and County road, running from Riley to Bradfordsville Ky., then S[outh] 28.32 poles to a stone, near the County road, thence to two birch trees and black gum [West] 28.32 poles, thence [North] 28.32 poles in point of old patent known as John Mousers line, then with same E[ast] 28.32 poles to the beginning, containing five acres, more or less. Being the same land bought by Edward Sulivan party of [the] first part of Emmett Elison and wife, Ida Elison October 6th 1908, and recorded in Marion County Clerk's Office in Deed Book No. 31, Page 213.

This document is also a *warranty deed*, an instrument through which a seller guarantees to the buyer that he is getting a good and clear title to the land. The wording is typical; the key words are "will warrant [guarantee] the title."

> To have and to hold the same, together with all the appurtenances thereunto belon[g]ing unto the party of the second part [the buyer], his heirs and assigns forever, and the said party of the first part [the sellers] hereby covenants with the said party of the second part that they will warrant the title to the property hereby conveyed unto the said part of the second part, and his heirs and assigns forever.

If your ancestor bought land and later lost it for inability to pay the taxes on it or to make the installment payments of a mortgage, you may find the county sheriff selling the land at auction. This happened frequently in both black and white families in the late-nineteenth and early-twentieth centuries.

In some courthouses, you may find volumes dedicated to the registration of livestock marks and brands. Not only may such a book contain a drawing of an ancestor's registered brand, but also it may help you date the ancestor's arrival in the county.

Most states taxed land, cattle and horses, slaves (before 1865), and luxury items such as carriages, clocks and watches, and pianos. Property tax records that survive are usually found at the state archives or on microfilm at research libraries or from the Family History Library. You can check for existing tax records of your research county in the Family History Library catalog at <www.familysearch.org> and sometimes on the Web site of the state archives.

Probate Records

The court with probate jurisdiction handles matters involving estates, guardianships, persons judged incompetent to handle their own affairs, illegitimacy, adoption, orphans, and apprentices. Chapter nine, pages 148–155, includes an in-depth discussion of estate records created in and for the probate process. These include wills, inventories and appraisals, annual returns, estate sales, and final distributions or settlements of estates. Although chapter nine discusses these records in relation to the search for slave ancestors, the same kinds of records were created after the Civil War, sometimes by the same families who themselves had been slaves.

Another kind of estate record, an affidavit of descent, is transcribed below. In this case, the widower created the document before a Notary Public as a proof of the heirs of his deceased wife. Genealogists love to find this kind of record. The typewritten document was recorded in a Green County, Kentucky, deed book in 1942.[7] Notice that the death date was not given.

> Lucian Vaughn says that he is a resident of the State of Kentucky, and that he is widower of Eva Vaughn, who died intestate on or about the ____ day of _____ [sic], 1941, a resident of Greens [sic] County in the State of Kentucky, and that at the time of death of said Eva Vaughn, she was married, and left surviving he[r] the following persons as her husband and only heirs at law having an estate of inheritance in her land, to-wit [sic]:

Names	Ages	Addresses		Relationship	Int. Inherited
Lucian Vaughn	47	Coburg, Ky.		Husband	21.85%
Opal Vaughn	14	"	"	Daughter	¼ [sic]
Marvin Vaughn	10	"	"	Son	¼ "
Francis Vaughn	8	"	"	Daughter	¼ "
Inez Vaughn	6	"	"	Daughter	¼ "

> In testimony whereof he hereunto subscribe[d] his name this 16th. day of June, 1942.
>
> Attest: Vernon Shuffett
>
> his
>
> Lucian × Vaughn
>
> mark

> I, Vetnon [sic] Shuffett, a Notary Public in and for the state and County above shown hereby certify that the foregoing affidavit was subscribed and sworn to before me by Lucian Vaughn, this is the 16th. day of June, 1942. My Com[mission] expires 6th. day of February, 1944.

In addition to estate records, probate courts often hear testimony about insanity and determine whether a person should be sent to a state mental institution or hospital. They may place orphans in foster homes, approve guardians for orphans, finalize adoption papers, hear cases involving illegitimate children and one or both of their parents, and approve apprenticeships. **Depending on the nature of the cases, these records may or may not be open for public viewing.**

However, many nineteenth-century probate records, whether dockets or minutes, are available in the court clerk's office in the county courthouse. Many of these records are on microfilm. The genealogical importance of these documents is in the identification of family groups and relationships, especially parents and children.

Warning

Court Records

Civil court records reveal cases of many kinds. Probably the most important to genealogists are divorce and naturalization cases. Each state designates the court which is to handle divorce cases. Sometimes, separate indexes exist for divorce records. Depending on state law and the county, the actual files of the cases may be available for study.

Naturalization records are those proceedings by which a foreign-born person became a citizen of the United States. Often, but not always, these records too are in books dedicated to that kind of record. However, in older records, naturalizations can be sprinkled among all the other business handled by the various courts of record.

Especially for the late nineteenth and early twentieth century, researchers can browse through the minutes of the lower courts in a county and read about cases involving such issues as debt, assault and battery, liable or slander, gambling, liquor violations, petty theft, land being sold for taxes, or land being sold to satisfy a debt. The records often include lists of jurors. Finding an ancestor or family member named as a plaintiff or defendant or called as a juror or witness places that person in a given place at a given time. This can be an important clue for the genealogist.

In summary, county records are very important to genealogical research. Whether you find them as abstracts, transcriptions, microfilm of originals, official copies in a courthouse record book, or original document files, they often can advance your research. Since some of these records are not available elsewhere, your search may benefit by a trip to the courthouse.

LOCAL RECORDS

Resources available in ancestral communities may include cemeteries, church records, newspapers, education records, city directories, and city government records. Local libraries, museums, organizations, and businesses may also have materials useful in research.

Cemeteries and Churches

Many ancestral cemeteries lie adjacent to churches. If you know the church your ancestors attended, try to learn where the church records are and when the existing records began. Some of these records may pertain to the church's cemetery. Even if the ancestor's grave did not receive a tombstone, church records may give a burial date, usually one to three days after death.

Tombstones may give birth and death dates, maiden names of women, military service information, and parents' names, especially for children who died young. Tombstones may range from commercially produced marble or granite headstones to homemade concrete slabs, wooden crosses or slabs, and metal funeral home markers.

If a marked grave shows any indication of a funeral home name, ask in the local community about the location of that business. Many funeral directors and cemeteries will share their files with family members of the deceased. Figure 4-7, on page 77, is an example of a cemetery interment file, shared with a descendant of the deceased. The record gives not only vital statistics on the deceased but also the location of the grave within the cemetery.

Church registers vary greatly, depending on the record-keeping skills and desires of the pastors, elders, or members. Some churches have records that date well back into the nineteenth century; others are lucky to have records from the 1930s forward. Generally, Catholic churches have better records than the Methodists and Baptists. If an ancestral church was a small or independent congregation, any existing records probably are in the hands of long-time member families or descendants of various pastors. On the other hand, if the church was or is part of an organized circuit, conference, diocese, or other unit, records may be at the church itself, at a denominational archive, or held by member families. If the congregation is still active, ask the pastor or current members about the records.

The information in such records may include lists or chronological entries on membership, church officers, baptisms, confirmations, deaths and burials, removals, and transfers. Sometimes these lists include specific dates along with the names; sometimes they are lists by year—all baptisms for 1909 or all persons who joined in 1897. Nevertheless, finding an ancestor's name on such a list places the ancestor in that place at that time and gives you a little more information about the ancestor's life.

If you are seeking information about ancestors who lived in the twentieth century, you may well find church members, neighbors, or family friends who knew your relatives and would be glad to share information by telephone, mail, e-mail, or personal visit.

Newspapers

Not all ancestors subscribed to or got their names in the local newspaper, but newspapers provide many genealogists with good information, including such items as obituaries, birth or death notices, marriage licenses that were issued during a given time period, court case summaries, local news stories, local business advertisements, school news, and activities of local churches and organizations. Besides, local newspapers give researchers a good idea of what was happening in the ancestral community, what the weather was like, and what issues concerned the populace.

Obituaries are among the most common newspaper items that families keep. Figure 4-8, on page 78, is a 1980 obituary for Robert Lincoln White of Greens-

Figure 4-8 Obituary of Robert Lincoln White, 9 September 1980, found in a scrapbook of obituaries in the Columbia Public Library, Adair County, Kentucky.

Robert Lincoln White

9-9-80

Robert Lincoln White, age 72, of Route 1, Greensburg, passed away Tuesday, September 2, 1980 at Greensburg after a long illness.

He is the son of the late Nelson and Fannie Spalding White.

Mr. White is survived by five daughters, Ernestine Simmons, Elizabeth Newby, both of Louisville, Susie Barnett, Barbara Porter, and Martha Richardson, all of Greensburg; four sons, Ben White and Abra White, both of Greensburg, James White and Lincoln White, Jr., both of Indianapolis, Indiana; two brothers, John White, Louisville, and Nelson White, Indianapolis,

Indiana; five sisters, Nellie White and Beatrice McGill, both of Louisville, Marie Williams and Betty Washington, both of Lebanon, Kentucky, Josephine Smith, Campbellsville; 14 grandchildren; and one great-grandchild.

Funeral services were held Saturday, September 6th at 1:00 p.m. at the Pleasant Hill Church with Reverend George Johnson officiating. Burial was in the White Family Cemetery.

Grissom-Maupin-Heskamp and Morrison Funeral Home was in charge of funeral arrangements.

Internet Source

burg, Kentucky. It is especially useful for the genealogist because it names his parents, children, and siblings and their residences.

To learn about newspapers in your ancestral area, consult the United States Newspaper Program Web site at <www.neh.fed.us/projects/usnp.html>. This Web site provides links to your ancestral state(s)'s newspaper program site, where you can learn about newspapers in the state. The sites vary in content but can help you determine the names of newspapers in your ancestors' area during their lives. You can often borrow microfilm of these newspapers through the interlibrary loan department of your local public or academic library.

In most states, the archives or historical society has compiled a list of known newspapers published in the state and where existing copies may be found. Consult the state archives to learn whether you can purchase such a list. Some of these lists may also appear on the Internet.

Three published aids to finding newspaper titles, and sometimes existing copies, are below. You can consult these in libraries:

- Danky, James P., ed. *African-American Newspapers and Periodicals: A National Bibliography.* Cambridge, Mass.: Harvard University Press, 1998. Gives titles and publication dates, availability in microform and for what period of time, and libraries holding the title.
- Gregory, Winifred, ed. *American Newspapers, 1821–1936: A Union List of Files Available in the United States and Canada.* New York: H.W. Wilson, 1937, reprint by Kraus Reprint Corporation, New York, 1967. Organized by state, then city, then titles, indicating publication dates, known existing copies, and the holding library, as of the publication of this volume.
- *Newspapers in Microform.* 2 vols. Washington, D.C.: Library of Congress, 1984. Provides publications dates, known microfilm or other microform copies and where those were located at the publication of this volume.

Dedicated genealogists have abstracted and published data from a number of newspapers. Check the library catalogs of public and academic libraries or *Books in Print* in a library to learn whether such a book has been compiled for your research county.

If your ancestor's community did not have a newspaper, the residents may have read newspapers from the county seat or nearest large town. Even if your ancestors could not read and write, they could be mentioned in connection with events in their local communities.

If you know your ancestors' religious group or denomination, investigate whether there was a denominational newspaper. Ethnic newspapers in larger cities could also be pertinent to your research. In 1969–1970, the Negro Universities Press, which became part of Greenwood Publishing Group in Westport, Connecticut, reprinted a number of African-American newspapers from the nineteenth and early-twentieth centuries. These reprints are found in many academic libraries. Some of these publications carried marriage and death notices and other personal news items.

Education Records

When you learn from family sources, census records, obituaries, or newspaper articles that ancestors in a certain community attended school there, you may be able to get more details from records such as these:

- School yearbooks and newspapers in the school library, public library, or local museum
- Transcripts of an ancestor's school record from the school, school district, or college registrar
- County or town histories, with histories of education in the community or of specific educational institutions
- Information about schools, activities, graduates, and other bits of history from local newspapers at the time when the ancestor attended school
- School censuses, taken in some states, that may be housed in the school district office, county courthouse, or state archives

City Directories

City directories began as business directories for larger cities, usually in the early nineteenth century. Directories for smaller cities often appeared later in the century or in the early twentieth century. Each publisher established the format for the books he published, but most included names of individuals owning or working in businesses in the city, a business name and address for each person listed, and often a home address. Other information varied from city to city. Many directories included reference sections on city ordinances or state laws as well as city history, government, and organizations.

Usually, the older directories included a racial designation for non-whites and an indication of whether a woman was a widow. Sometimes entries mentioned genealogically pertinent details such as the number of people living in a household or the former residence of individuals. Some city directories may have a separate "colored" section. City directories also included advertisements from local businesses and thus give genealogists some details of ancestral occupations.

In 1866, the first Houston City Directory listed very basic information on residents who chose to be included: name, occupation, and place of employment. The following are examples of the African-American entries—identified as "col" (colored)—one year after the Civil War:

- Jno. Sessums, carpenter. The only other Sessums in town was A. Sessums, general commission merchant. A researcher would want to study the black carpenter and the white merchant to try to determine whether any slave-slaveholder relationship had existed between the two.
- Mary E. Warren, photograph printer. Listed above her was Robert Warren, a porter for the W.T. Austin company, cotton and wool factors. A researcher would want to study whether Mary and Robert were husband and wife, or other relatives, or no relation at all.
- Peter and Dennis Jackson and John Williams, all saddlers working for J.C. Wilson. These men worked together and formed a cluster of acquaintances, often helpful to study in research.
- Occupations of other black residents who were listed included laborer, cooper, tailor, barber, blacksmith, and telegraph repairer.

In a section on churches, the directory listed the Freedmen's Methodist Episcopal Church, connected with the Methodist Episcopal Church, North. The pastor was Rev. Elias Dibble, who "has long been known in our city, and enjoys the respect and confidence of our citizens."[8] After the white Methodist church building on the adjacent lot "fell down" one Sunday in 1860, the congregation rented the use of the "African church."

By tracing an ancestor or family members through several years of directories, you may learn

- whether and when the ancestor changed residences or places of employment
- approximately when a woman became a widow
- sometimes whether teenagers in the family were employed outside the home
- who worked for the same employer as your ancestor
- where the ancestor may be found in an unindexed census
- who lived at the same address

A person's absence from the directory may be due to
- removal to another location
- death after the preceding directory
- not choosing to pay the fee for inclusion, when a fee was necessary
- not being home when the canvassing agent came by
- being listed under a variant spelling or typographical misspelling of the surname

Telephone directories can serve a similar purpose for genealogists, depending on when the city got a telephone exchange and when the ancestors got telephones. Telephone directories can help researchers track ancestral residences but do not usually provide specific information about employment.

Many of these directories can be found at the local public or academic library, local museum, or state archives. Many city directories are available in research libraries on microfilm or microfiche. If your ancestors lived in a city, you need to look into this interesting and valuable source.

City Records

Large cities and small towns alike may have city government records that benefit research. Usually these records include minutes of the governing body and tax rolls. You may also be able to get copies of birth and death certificates from the local health department. Some cities have extensive archives available for detailed research.

Local Libraries

Many public libraries have genealogy and history collections that range from published family and local histories to microfilmed records and vertical files. Vertical files are folders of clippings and copies of documents that pertain to specific subjects or families in the community. Even if your ancestral community is not near your residence, you may be able to get copies of materials from these vertical files by mail. Even museums may have local history and genealogy collections, including photographs, maps, and artifacts. Sometimes, they allow researchers to use their materials.

Library/Archive Source

The *American Library Directory* volumes, available in many libraries, will help you identify public and academic libraries with genealogy collections or other special collections that could benefit your research. Library staff members cannot do research for you, but they can answer questions about their special collections, reference materials, and history collections. Your public library can help you with interlibrary loan of books and periodicals that could help you in your search. Genealogists often get titles of such publications by searching library catalogs online and reading the footnotes of pertinent history books and articles.

Local Organizations and Businesses

Fraternal and social organizations may have records of their membership and activities that may tell you more about your ancestors. If these groups have state or national offices or publications, consider contacting them for available information. For example, in a society periodical, you may learn that your great-grandmother held an office in the organization from 1930 to 1938. This one fact helps you know she was alive and in that place at the time, but it also gives you some interesting details about her life. You may be able to learn more about this part of her life in the newspaper or from people who knew her. Sometimes libraries or museums have materials related to local organizations.

Businesses that may contribute to your knowledge of ancestors include funeral homes, newspapers (discussed above), and stores. Funeral home records may or may not exist from the time when your ancestors lived in the area, but you can ask. These files may or may not add new information, but they can often help identify a death date and burial location. Merchants' ledger books and other records sometimes appear in local libraries, museums, or archives. They show who bought what from the merchant, when, what the price was, and sometimes whether the purchaser paid in cash or with credit. Again, this

Case Study

Quotes

Important

Please read the endnotes along with this case study; they will help answer questions that you may ask. Endnotes for this case study begin on page 229.

kind of information places your ancestor in that place at that time and may give you more interesting details about the ancestor's life.

COMBINING RECORDS
The Case of William Collins

Frederick Douglass explained a situation that many genealogists come to know in their research. He grew up in eastern Maryland in the 1820s and 1830s and could speak first-hand about his experiences there. However, his observation applies to many slaves nationwide:[9]

> I never met with a slave in that part of the country who could tell me with any certainty how old he was. Few at that time knew anything of the months of the year or of the days of the month. They measured the ages of their children by spring-time, winter-time, harvest-time, planting-time, and the like. Masters allowed no questions concerning their ages to be put to them by slaves. Such questions were regarded by the masters as evidence of an impudent curiosity.

A twentieth-century historian evaluated the issue with the advantage of extensive research and a broader regional perspective: "Douglass may have exaggerated the determination of the slaveholders as a class to suppress information and may have underestimated their carelessness and indifference, but most slaves in the South probably did not know their exact age."[10] Furthermore, slaveholders simply may have been ignorant of the ages of their slaves, especially those born elsewhere or acquired after childhood.

Genealogists find the reality of this observation as they study ancestors who were born into slavery or born into families who kept no written records of births and ages. A good example is one William Collins of North Carolina. So far, five documents have furnished age information about him:

1. A granddaughter recalls that her mother, Novella (Collins) Dixon, always said William claimed to be "a 64 slave."[11] Perhaps, he was suggesting he was born near the end of the Civil War, about 1864.
2. William's marriage record in 1912, reporting his age as thirty-nine, suggests his birth about 1873.[12]
3. His marriage record in 1915, giving his age as forty, suggests his birth about 1875.[13]
4. His 1920 census entry, listing William as sixty, suggests a birth year of about 1859.[14]
5. William's death certificate in March 1924, reporting his age as seventy-seven, suggests his birth in 1846–1847.[15]

Evaluating the Evidence

In evaluating such situations, genealogists must ask questions for which there are no answers. In this case, did William himself answer the age question on the marriage licenses? How accurate was the knowledge of the death certificate informant, who was also the undertaker and not a known relative? Who gave the information to the census taker? In the 1920 census, which reports the children's ages very precisely in years and months, perhaps their mother was the informant. According to her granddaughter, William's wife knew her husband was considerably older than she, but how could she know precisely how old he was if William himself did not know?

Thus, the available sources suggest for William Collins a range of possible birth years from 1846 to 1875, an amazing twenty-nine-year spread. What next? How is it possible to study this man further, not knowing whether he was child or adult in 1880, or young adult or middle-aged man in 1900? Without a more specific age range or other identifying information, how can a researcher know which William Collins in the 1900 and 1910 censuses is the subject William? Genealogists often study first the census records, in order, reaching back one at a time. In this case, it is necessary to study the age question first, as a tool for research.

Brothers or sisters could form a valuable cluster for research, but William's descendants do not know the names of his siblings, if he had any. The only other clues to a family cluster were the names of his parents, shown in his two known marriage records. The 1912 marriage record gives his parents as John and Jane Collins, both deceased by 1912. The 1915 record names his parents as Bert and Jane Clark, both deceased by 1915.

If the two marriage records were correct, they suggested that William's mother, Jane Collins, had married Bert Clark. Although no marriage record has been found for them, they became the target of research because few other options existed.

Working With the Evidence to Plan Further Research

Burton and Jane Clark were enumerated in the 1880 census in Pitt County, North Carolina, the county listed as William Collins's birthplace on his death certificate.[16] Burton's age was reported as fifty; Jane's, as forty-five. Their household included two daughters (at least, daughters of Burton, the head of household): Olley, age fifteen, and Judy, age nine. Not far away was a household of single young men, all farm laborers, among whom was Burton Clark, age twenty-two.[17]

Early the following year, Burton Clark Jr., age twenty-one, married Mary Clark, apparently the same young neighbor listed six households away from her groom in the 1880 census.[18] The license named the groom's parents as Burton Clark Sr. and Anniky Clark. Thus, it appears that Jane was not Burton Clark Sr.'s first wife.

The names of Burton Clark Jr. and Olley Clark help tie the 1880 census to the 1870 enumeration of Bert and Jane Clark in the same county.[19] Frederick Douglass's statement applies as well to the age discrepancies in the Clark family's census entry: Bert (twenty-eight), Jane (twenty-four), Susan (thirteen), Sarah (eleven), Bert (nine), Dave (seven), Ollie (five), and Olivia (three). At least the children Bert and Ollie were in the family in both censuses, and their ages were fairly consistent: Bert, age nine and twenty-two; Ollie/Olley, age five and fifteen.

No William, Collins or Clark, was listed in the household with his reported parents—or mother and stepfather—in either census. Burton Jr.'s mother, re-

Warning

Some freedmen used more than one surname during the post–Civil War years. One must ask whether William Collins did the same.

ported as Anniky, perhaps had died by 1870, but no marriage record has surfaced for Burton Clark Sr. and Jane Collins. Nevertheless, the parents' ages in the 1870 and 1880 censuses are strikingly different, almost doubling from one to the next. However, given the ages of the children in the 1870 census, Bert Clark was probably not twenty-eight in 1870 as reported, but older. Jane Clark's suggested birth years were 1845–1846 (from the 1870 census) and 1834–1835 (from the 1880 census).

The genealogist must think through this sea of data. If this Jane Clark really was William Collins's mother, as reported in his marriage records, and she was already married to Burton Clark by 1870, William probably was not born after 1870, as suggested in his marriage records, and he was not born a Clark. Nor would William and his mother have been born within a year or so of each other, about 1846. If Jane was born in the mid-1830s or early 1840s, she could have had a son, William Collins, in 1859 or 1864. Thus, eliminating the most unlikely birth years from the list of William's documents (1846–1847, 1873, and 1875) leaves two reasonable and possible birth years with which to study William further: 1859 and 1864.

An 1880 census index revealed five young black men named William Collins, born between 1855 and 1865 in North Carolina, who merit further study to determine if one may be the William in the records listed above.[20] In addition, the cautious genealogist must also consider studying an 1880 family whose head was Robert (Bert?) Clark, with wife Jane, son William (age eight), and daughter Jane (age six) in Beaufort County, neighboring Pitt County where the subject William was thought to have been born.[21]

However complex this study of five William Collinses and perhaps one William Clark may seem, it is considerably narrower than it first appeared to be. Approaching six candidates is much easier than trying to tackle the twenty-three William Collinses and forty-two William Clarks born over a thirty-year period in North Carolina, as indicated in the 1880 census.[22]

Part of the study will need to involve local and county records for several counties between 1880 and 1920 and the censuses of 1900 and 1910. Research will include the known children of Burton Clark and William Collins. The study of William prior to 1870 could take place, as discussed in later chapters of this book, based on what is learned in the planned phase of research, but it would be counterproductive to try to address the pre–Civil War period with only what is known at the present time.

If the study of the known Clark and Collins family members and the five candidates from the 1880 census does not lead to definitive information on the subject William, the researcher can develop another research plan and may conclude, based on the evidence found, that the subject William may have been missed in one or more censuses. Genealogists are usually optimists, and hope springs eternal in the human heart.

RESEARCH GUIDES TO THE STATES

Each state differs somewhat from the others in the records available for research and in the way records are created and stored at the state, county, and local jurisdictions. Serious genealogists benefit from knowing these specifics about their ancestral states. Published guides to research in many states are available to help you learn about their records and research facilities.

Some of these guides are articles published in the *National Genealogical Society Quarterly* and state genealogical society journals. Consult the Periodical Source Index (PERSI) for specific articles. The following are some of the books available, for sale and/or at libraries. For others, consult library catalogs, large libraries in the state, state archives or genealogical society, booksellers, and publishers catalogs.

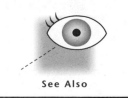

See Also

See page 133 for more on PERSI.

Printed Source

Multiple States—Stryker-Rodda, Kenn, ed. *Genealogical Research: Methods and Sources*. Rev. ed. Washington, D.C.: The American Society of Genealogists, 1983. Chapters on Alabama, Arkansas, Florida, Illinois, Indiana, Iowa, Kentucky, Louisiana, Michigan, Mississippi, Missouri, Ohio, Tennessee, Wisconsin.

Alabama—Barefield, Marilyn Davis. *Researching in Alabama: A Genealogical Guide*. Rev. ed. Birmingham: Birmingham Public Library, 1998.

Delaware—Doherty, Thomas P., ed. *Delaware Genealogical Research Guide*. Wilmington: Delaware Genealogical Society, 1997.

Georgia—Davis, Robert Scott, Jr., comp. *Research in Georgia*. Greenville, S.C.: Southern Historical Press, 1981.

Kentucky—Hogan, Roseann Reinemuth. *Kentucky Ancestry: A Guide to Genealogical and Historical Research*. Salt Lake City: Ancestry, 1992.

New England—Melnyk, Marcia D., ed. *Genealogist's Handbook for New England Research*. 4th ed. Boston: New England Historic Genealogical Society, 1999.

North Carolina—Leary, Helen F.M., ed. *North Carolina Research: Genealogy and Local History*. 2d ed. Raleigh: North Carolina Genealogical Society, 1996.

South Carolina—Holcomb, Brent Howard. *A Guide to South Carolina Genealogical Research and Records*. Columbia, S.C.: the author, 1998.

Texas—Ericson, Carolyn R., and Joe. E. Ericson. *A Guide to Texas Research*. Nacogdoches, Tex.: Ericson Books, 1993. Focuses on the kinds of records created in Texas.

Texas—Kennedy, Imogene Kinard, and J. Leon Kennedy. *Genealogical Records in Texas*. Baltimore: Genealogical Publishing Co., 1987. Focuses on county by county records availability and early Texas reference material.

Virginia—McGinnis, Carol. *Virginia Genealogy: Sources & Resources*. Baltimore: Genealogical Publishing Co., 1993.

General—Eichholz, Alice, ed. *Ancestry's Red Book: American State, County & Town Sources*, Rev. ed. Capsuled but very helpful guide to each state. (See bibliography, page 243.)

General—Prucha, Francis Paul. *Handbook for Research in American History: A Guide to Bibliographies and Other Reference Works*. 2d ed., rev. Lincoln: University of Nebraska Press, 1994.

FIVE

Special Situations

lthough the vast majority of African Americans in the United States before the Civil War were slaves in the South, and some in the North, thousands were born, or became, free. Many of these lived in cities and/or in the North or West, but even records of rural Southern counties identify some free blacks. A few others immigrated to this country as free persons, but mostly after 1865. Each situation has research considerations of its own.

Genealogists can imagine many events that may have affected ancestors and their records. What if one was a runaway who made a successful journey to a free state and changed both given name and surname? What if she came from Haiti or another Caribbean or Latin American location and was not born in the South after all? What if he was born in England, served in the Navy, and jumped ship in the United States? What if she went west and waited tables in a mining camp? What if a hard-to-find ancestor was really Native American? You can think of many reasons why you may have difficulty finding any given ancestor. However, don't worry about these possibilities until you have exhausted the more common scenarios.

This book focuses on these most common and most likely situations. If you try the records and techniques discussed in these chapters, you will have a good background with which to assess each ancestor individually. If your research suggests that a less common scenario may fit your ancestor, then address it with the same caution and thoroughness, and you may yet discover your ancestor's life story.

For freedmen before the Civil War and for African Americans after the war and well into the twentieth century, you will find that many records used a racial label: *free person of color*, *Negro*, and the like. Some counties had separate black and white marriage or birth registers. Although considered politically incorrect or socially unacceptable today, such labels help researchers, especially in the numerous cases where black and white residents of a county had the same name.

Notes

"FREE NEGROES" BEFORE THE CIVIL WAR

A significant number of African Americans in the United States before 1865 were free. Most were descendants of slaves, and many had begun life in bondage. Although many states attempted to limit manumissions, especially after 1830, slaveholders found ways to free slaves or allowed them to purchase their liberty, and other slaves ran to freedom.

Census numbers are not completely accurate but are our best indications of the nation's population. They show that free Negroes, as they were called then, though never more than 2½ percent of the national populace before 1860, were a little over 13 percent of the total black population between 1810 and 1840. By 1860, almost half a million strong, they were about 11 percent of the black population.[1]

Where did the 488,000 free blacks live in 1860?[2] Census figures show

- about 46 percent, a little over 226,000, scattered through the North and West—New England (Connecticut, Maine, Massachusetts, New Hampshire, Rhode Island, Vermont), Middle Atlantic states (New Jersey, New York, Pennsylvania), Ohio Valley (Illinois, Indiana, Michigan, Ohio, Wisconsin), Midwest (Iowa, Kansas Territory, Minnesota, Nebraska Territory), and the West (California, unorganized Dakota Territory, unorganized Indian Territory, New Mexico Territory, Oregon, Utah Territory, Washington Territory)
- about 46 percent, almost 225,000, in the Upper South—Delaware, District of Columbia, Kentucky, Maryland, Missouri, North Carolina, Tennessee, Virginia
- about 8 percent, almost 37,000, in the Lower South—Alabama, Arkansas, Florida, Georgia, Louisiana, Mississippi, South Carolina, Texas

Reminder

Research on free persons of color involves many of the sources and strategies discussed in the first four chapters. Some were wealthy and even owned slaves; these and the less wealthy may well have created land and probate records or paid taxes on their property. On the other hand, many more struggled to stay free in communities in both the North and the South where they were not entirely welcome. Eventually, if they or their ancestors were ever slaves in the American colonies or states, research will proceed in the same manner as discussed in the later chapters—trying to identify the slaveholder in order to identify previous generations of ancestors.

The following record groups apply particularly to free men and women before the Civil War. The point at which you search these records depends on the particulars of your research:

- If you identify free ancestors and therefore need to search for them in "free" records
- If you have a family tradition of pre-1865 free ancestors
- If your research into the period before 1870 leads you to suspect your ancestors may have been free before 1865
- If you are curious and simply want to study the possibility that certain ancestors were free

Notes

Manumit and *emancipate* both mean "to free." Both words were used prior to 1865 to mean freeing someone from the bonds of slavery.

Check the Family History Library catalog and guides to state archives holdings for the existence and location of these records in your areas of interest. Many such records survive, but not all are available for all locations.

MANUMISSION RECORDS

Many families were free for several generations before the Civil War, but at some time in the past individuals who were born slaves became free. When allowed by state law, some slaveholders freed slaves in their wills, in documents of manumission filed with county courts, or by petitions to state legislatures. Thus, manumission records are often found in county record books and state archives.

A number of manumissions were recorded in county and town deed books. For example, the town deed records of Petersburg, Virginia, contain a declaration from one George W. Harrison, dated May 1838, that he was freeing Rhoda Hamilton, whom he had bought from Robert H. Hackley. Rhoda was five feet six inches tall and would be thirty-five years old on 15 August 1838.[3]

A record in the Amelia County, Virginia, deed books was the instrument of Elizabeth Hudson, a [free] woman of color, who had been emancipated by Thomas Coverly's will. In the new document, Elizabeth was freeing her child, Albert Augustus, who had been willed to her by Francis Coverly. The document, written in October 1827, stated that the boy had turned two years of age in August of that year.[4] **If you find abstracted, published records such as this one, be sure to read or get a copy of the original, as a precaution for accuracy.**

Reminder

Legislative petitions and acts sometimes contain manumission records. In a petition to the Texas legislature, dated 1 November 1847 and signed by about eighty Houstonians, Mrs. Cynthia Ewing of that town asked permission for her slave Delilah to purchase her freedom with money she had earned. The records do not indicate what action, if any, the legislature took, but the petition contains many positive comments about Delilah's character and talents from citizens of Houston who supported her request.[5]

In 1862, during the Civil War, Congress abolished slavery in the District of Columbia, with compensation to the slaveholders. The records of the proceedings to implement the act are on National Archives microfilm: *Records of the Board of Commissioners for the Emancipation of Slaves in the District of Columbia, 1862–1863* (M520, six rolls). The emancipation papers created as a result of the act are on three rolls of film, along with manumission papers from earlier years: *Records of the United States District Court for the District of Columbia Relating to Slaves, 1851–1863* (M433).

FREE BLACK REGISTERS

In many states, especially from the 1830s forward, both northern and southern free blacks were required to register periodically at the town hall or county courthouse to document their residence and their free status. Showing the "free papers" they received upon manumission was especially important when they moved to new locations where they were not known.

The laws and their enforcement were more lax in some places than in others. Nevertheless, these registrations can be a great help to researchers. Families may be listed as a group, or individuals may be registered separately.

The following study demonstrates the combined use of the census and registers of free persons to document one family. The 1830 census of Jones County, Georgia, revealed Nathaniel Matthews as a "free colored" head of household, enumerated separately from any white household. Only two other free black heads of household were recorded in the county in that census. They were Free Anthony, head of a free family of three, and Free Milla, a free female head of household with three children. The other thirty-two free persons of color in the county were living with white households, five of which also had slaves and three of which did not.[6]

Reportedly, Nathaniel Matthews was older than fifty-five years; the female adult, of age to be his wife, was between thirty-six and fifty-five. A young female was between ten and twenty-four, and the two free boys were under the age of ten. Could this household be found in other county records?

Figure 5-1, on page 90, shows the 1818 registry of the apparent Nathaniel Mathews [*sic*] family in the records of the Jones County Inferior Court. The family registered six times—1818, 1820–1823, and 1826[7]. **Study of all six records was necessary to discover their full genealogical significance**, and the data they contain is quite remarkable.

1. In this family's case, their relationship as a family, though implied in the first three registrations, was not stated until the last three. Nathaniel's wife was Lear/Leah; Nancy was his daughter. Their ages were consistent with the 1830 census.

2. By occupation, Nathaniel was a farmer; his wife and daughter were spinners. Since so many women were listed with the occupation of spinner or "spinster," their researchers would want to learn about the milling industry in that county.

3. Nathaniel's age was given in the six records as 58, 59, 60, 56, 57, and 67 respectively. These suggest his birth between 1759 and 1766, especially 1759–1761. The first three registries claim Virginia as his birthplace; the last three give North Carolina. He came to Georgia, apparently to Jones County, between 1781 and 1789; most reports indicate between 1786 and 1789. In his registrations, his age and the number of years he had been in the state suggest his belief that he came to Georgia in his twenties, but he was apparently unsure of his age at the time of migration.

4. Lear's age was listed as 50, 51, 52, 50, 51, and 53 respectively, which suggest her birth between 1768 and 1773; by all reports, she was born in North Carolina. She came to Georgia, apparently to Jones County, between 1783 and 1788. She and her husband always reported a different number of years that each had been in the state. This suggests they did not come together as a couple but married in Georgia. Lear's reports consistently indicate she came to Georgia at age 15.

5. Nancy's age was reported as 10, 11, 12, 15, 16, and 17 respectively, which suggest her birth between 1807 and 1809; she was born in Georgia.

6. The young boy Hamlin Ooslam/Oslan/Ouslem apparently lived with the

Tip

When searching census or other indexes, check for those with no reported surname and those with the "surname" Free or Freed.

Research Tip

Figure 5-1 Came in to office Nathaniel Mathews a free man of coller born in virginia age fifty eight years old Resided in Gergia thirty one years by profesion a farmer

Came in to office Lear Mathewes a free woman of coller born in North carolina age fifty years Resided in Gergia thirty five yers by profesion a spiner

Nancy Mathews a free girl of coller Native of Gergia age twelve years by profesion a spiner

Hamlin ooslam a free boy of coller a Native of Georgia ten years old by [left blank]

Certificates Granted for the above persons

Registration of Nathaniel and Lear Mathews, 8 April 1818, Jones County, Georgia, Inferior Court Records, Book of Writs, 1818–1846, register of free persons of color, pages unnumbered but arranged chronologically, second page of register, Family History Library microfilm 0454256.

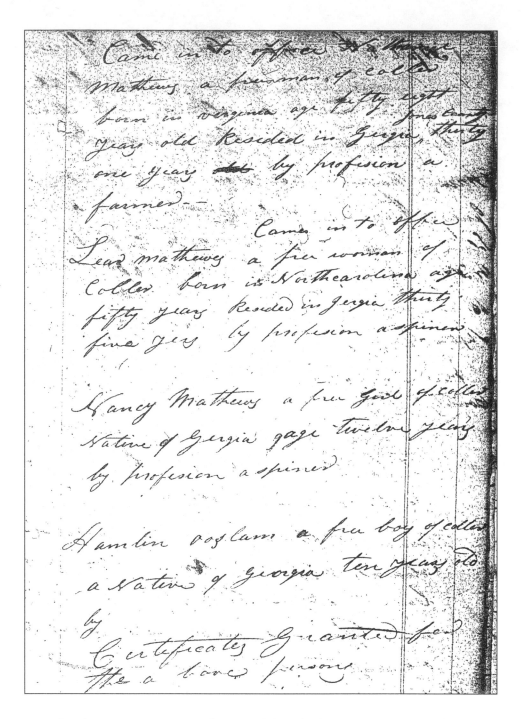

family in 1818, 1821, and 1826, although the register mentioned no relationship to them. A native Georgian, Hamlin was born about 1808–1809. Until 1826 and age 17, when he was listed as a farmer, his occupation was given as "ploy boy," apparently plow boy.

7. The registrations do not indicate how long Nathaniel and Lear had been free or whether Nancy was born free.

Since only heads of household were named in the 1830 census, the identity of the two young boys from the 1830 census remains a mystery. Hamlin Ooslam would have been about twenty-one or twenty-two years old in 1830. Only one free man of color of that age was reported in the county that year, and he lived with the white Daniel Nivin family.[8] Thus, the register of free persons provides good information and prompts further questions.

A number of these registers have been abstracted and published and are available in libraries all over the country. Others are available on microfilm through the Family History Library.

CENSUS RECORDS

The term "free persons of color" in the nineteenth century usually meant black or mulatto but could also include Indians, Chinese, Hispanics, or others with olive or brown skin. Granted, relatively few people of these other ethnicities lived in the South, and the majority of African Americans were in the South. However, genealogists must be cautious when reading early census records which, besides whites and slaves, show "all other free persons" (1790), "all other free persons except Indians not taxed" (1800–1810), and "free colored persons" (1820–1840).

As the 1830 census entry for the Nathaniel Mathews family (pages 89–90) indicates, some free persons of color were enumerated as families living on their own. Others were parts of white households and thus are more difficult to identify before 1850 since only the heads of household were named. (See Figure 5-2, line 3, below, the white household.) These pre-1850 census schedules in the South indicate that many free blacks lived in white households that also held slaves.

Before 1850, the census schedules often spread across two pages. Thus, the head of a free black household was named on the first page with the other heads of household, but was enumerated on the second page after slaves. Figure

Notes

1830 Census—Part 2

Local Community: Wayne County except Detroit   County: Wayne   State: Michigan   roll 69
Enumerator: Nathaniel Champ   Date Census Taken: 1830   Enumerator District # __   Supervisor District # __
[Official census day—1 June 1830]

Written Page No.	Printed Page No.	Name of Head of Family (from previous page)	Free Colored Males under 10	FC Males 10-24	FC Males 24-36	FC Females under 10	FC Females 10-24	FC Females 24-36	TOTAL
3	line 8	John Duggard	1			1	1		3
"	line 9	John Tylor	1	1		1			3
"	line 23	Gabriel Godfroy Sr. (white)	in household	1					
17	line 6	George Washington	1			1			2
28	line 23	Leonard Lenox	2	1	1	3	3		10
29	line 1	George Washington	1			1	1		3
"	line 2	William Charlton	2	1		2	1		6
"	line 3	Prime Johnson				1			1

Figure 5-2 Extract from 1830 Census, Wayne County, Michigan, 1830. Extraction forms for censuses 1790–1930 are in *Unpuzzling Your Past*, 4th ed.

5-2, on page 91, is an extract from the 1830 census of Wayne County, Michigan, on a convenient form, created from the original census forms. Notice the age categories and the numbers in each column. These represent the number of people in that household who were of the ages given at top of each column. For example, John Duggard was a free man of color and a head of household between thirty-six and fifty-five years of age, with a female of the same age bracket (possibly a wife) and a younger female between ten and twenty-four years of age (perhaps a daughter).

For 1850 and 1860, since the free schedules enumerated each free person, census marshals asked about race or color. The primary designations in their instructions were for black, mulatto, or white. Census takers may or may not have asked each family to describe themselves; some enumerators probably guessed by looking at family members. These enumerators may have done what later counterparts were instructed to do: use the term mulatto for persons with "some proportion or perceptible trace of negro blood."[9] (See pages 20–21, for details from the later censuses.)

For the census years 1850 and 1860, look also at the mortality schedules, which name both slave and free persons who died within the twelve months prior to the census. Not all families reported deaths to the census taker, but thorough researchers will look.

Reminder

Census records always are estimates of the population, for families and individuals were missed in every enumeration, for many reasons. One historian estimated that free blacks in the antebellum South were undercounted by at least twenty percent. As contributing factors, he pointed out the confusion in racial identification of this group, many of whom were racially mixed, as well as the reluctance of census takers to visit the "black alleys" in cities, where much of this population lived. In addition, many freemen "saw little reason to have themselves recorded in the census," and those who had started their free lives as runaway slaves and thus were not legally free "avoided enumerators at all cost."[10]

GUARDIANSHIP RECORDS

Manumission records, registrations of free blacks, and lawsuits by or against blacks are often found in county court records. One additional subject found in court minutes or files is guardianship records of free blacks in the states where such action was required, especially Georgia and Florida.

Case Study

Combining guardianship records with registrations provided insight into one free family in Jones County, Georgia. In December 1815, the court of ordinary appointed Harris Horn "guardian of the persons and Estates of Thomas Cozens, Patty Cozens, James Cozens, and Sally Cozens free persons of colour they having filed a petition and his consent in writing according on his giving security in the sum of $1,500."[11] The clerk of court was then ordered to grant letters of guardianship.

These four Cozens/Cousins residents and two children registered their free status in the county in 1820 although none of them were positively identified in the census that year. Although Tom, age twenty-seven, was a North Carolina-born farmer who reported being in Georgia for nineteen years, the other three adults—

Pat, James, and Saly [*sic*]—had been in Georgia seventeen years. Pat was born in Virginia forty-eight years before; James, in North Carolina, thirty-nine years before; Saly, in North Carolina, thirty-one years before. Listed after Saly were Russel, age eight, and Martha, age six. Pat and Saly were employed as spinners; James was a blacksmith. The following year, Thomas and James Cousins registered again, giving information that agreed with their previous statements.[12] The researcher must wonder whether the four adults were siblings in spite of a twenty-one year spread of their ages, whether Pat/Patty was the mother of Tom and Sally, whether any were husband and wife, or whether they were not related but had lived as slaves together and may have been living together in freedom.

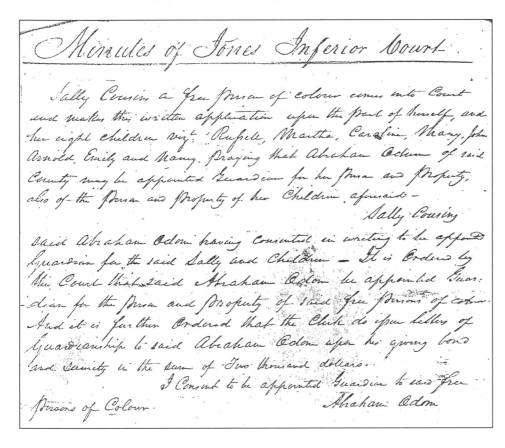

Figure 5-3 Court appointment of guardian for Sally Cousins, Jones County, Georgia, Minutes of the Inferior Court, volume and pages not numbered, facing page dated January term 1830, Family History Library microfilm 0454255.

On 11 June 1823, Sally Cousins, age thirty-five, registered herself and six children, apparently hers, although no relationship was stated: Russell, twelve; Martha, ten; Caroline, eight; Mary, six; John, four; and Arnold, two.[13] Finally, in January 1830, Sally petitioned the inferior court of Jones County to appoint Abraham Odom as guardian.[14] Figure 5-3, above, shows the court's action on her request:

> Sally Cousins a free person of colour comes into Court and makes this written application upon the part of herself and her eight children viz: Russell, Martha, Caroline, Mary, John, Arnold, Emily and Nancy, praying that Abraham Odum of said County may be appointed Guardian for her person and property, also of the person and property of her children aforesaid—Sally Cousins

> said Abraham Odom having consented in writing to be appointed Guardian for the said Sally and Children—It is Ordered by the Court that said Abraham Odom be appointed Guardian for the person and property of said free persons of colour And it is further ordered that the clerk do issue letters of Guardianship to said Abraham Odom upon his giving bond and security in the sum of Two thousand dollars.
> I consent to be appointed Guardian to said free persons of colour.
> Abraham Odom

The guardianship record confirmed the relationship between Sally and her children but offered no answers on any kinship with the other Cousins adults. At least the guardianship and registration entries in the court records provide some positive identification and clues on which to proceed with further research. These were probably not people of means; yet they were involved in the creation of some records. The legal requirements placed on them, although apparently not strictly enforced, become a research bonanza for descendants studying family history.

TAX ROLLS

Sources

Two kinds of taxes may survive for your ancestral county: the federal direct taxes of the 1860s and annual county-and-state property and "poll" taxes. Not all free ancestors are named in these records, but some of the records may show some of your ancestors. The majority of free African Americans in the antebellum period lived in the rural South or in towns, were poor, and worked as laborers. Due to their circumstances, their names do not always appear in records, except when paying the "poll" tax (or "head" tax) required of most adult men. However, if you find them in these or other records, you learn something more about them.

Internal Revenue Assessment Lists

To support the federal government and help pay for the Civil War, the Internal Revenue Act of 1862 provided for taxes on various forms of income, products, luxury items, and trades and occupations. Many of the surviving records, mostly for 1862–1866, are available on microfilm for thirty-three states and territories, including the South—*Internal Revenue Assessment Lists, 1862–1874.* Some free African Americans paid these taxes during the war. However, the 1865–1866 tax lists could help identify the whereabouts of freedmen shortly after the war, even those who had been slaves until 1865.

For example, Figure 5-4, on page 95, shows the 1865 annual tax list for Currituck County, North Carolina. Caleb Archer, of "colour," who lived at Guinea Mills, paid $2.50 tax for three months work as a cattle broker. The annual license fee for most trades and occupations was ten dollars. Note on this list that a physician, a lawyer, retailers, and fish peddlers were all paying taxes in this coastal county.

This entry raised the question of whether Archer was free before the war or was a recently freed slave. The war had ended officially on 9 April 1865, and

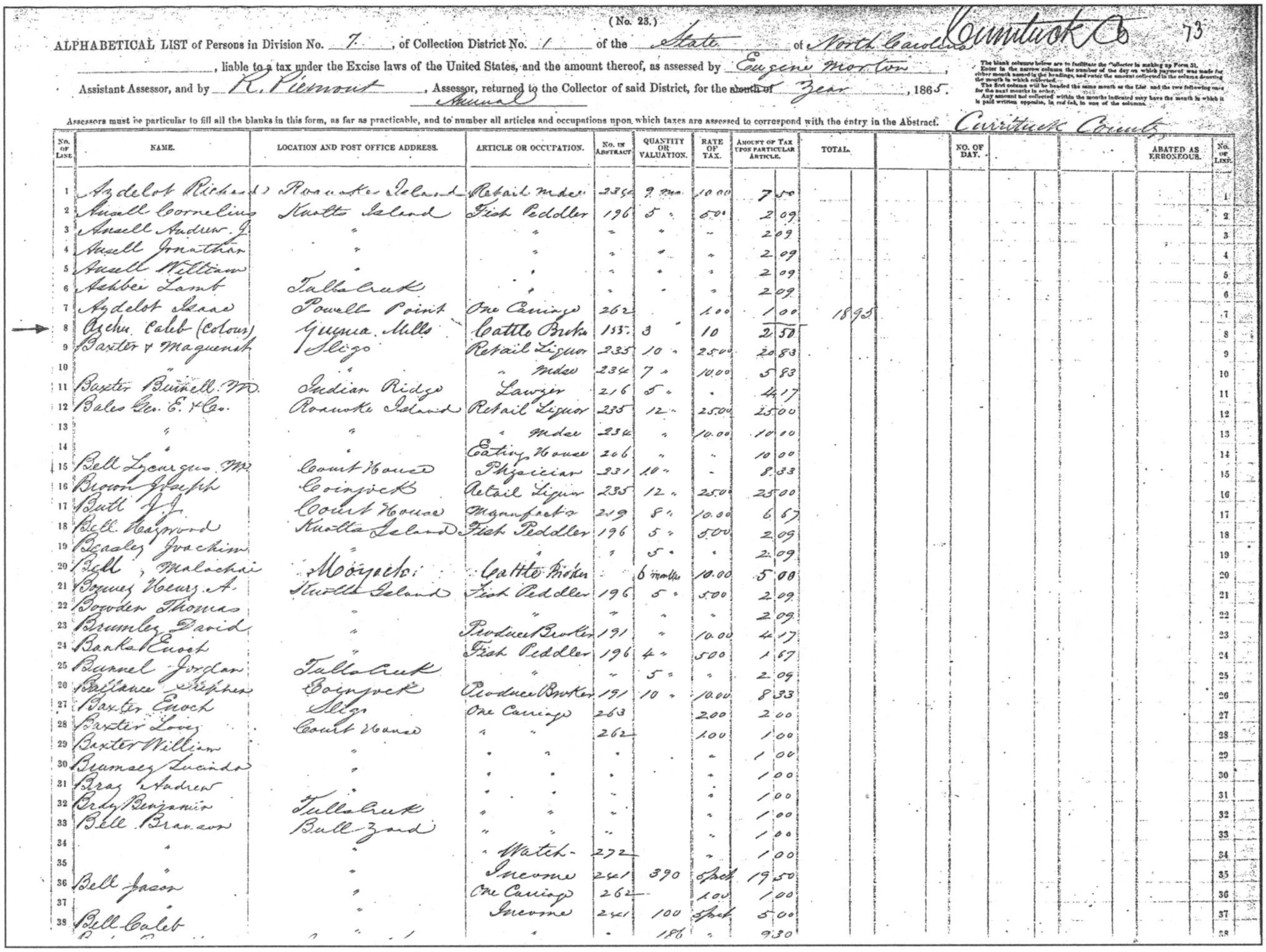

(No. 23.)

ALPHABETICAL LIST of Persons in Division No. 7, of Collection District No. 1 of the State of North Carolina Currituck Co 73

_______, liable to a tax under the Excise laws of the United States, and the amount thereof, as assessed by Eugene Morton, Assistant Assessor, and by R. Piemont, Assessor, returned to the Collector of said District, for the ~~month of~~ Annual Year, 1865.

Assessors must be particular to fill all the blanks in this form, as far as practicable, and to number all articles and occupations upon which taxes are assessed to correspond with the entry in the Abstract. Currituck County

No. of Line	Name	Location and Post Office Address	Article or Occupation	No. in Abstract	Quantity or Valuation	Rate of Tax	Amount of Tax upon Particular Article	Total	No. of Day	Abated as Erroneous	No. of Line
1	Ayzdelot Richard	Roanoke Island	Retail mdse	234	9 mo	10.00	7 50				1
2	Ansell Cornelius	Knotts Island	Fish Peddler	196	5 "	5.00	2 09				2
3	Ansell Andrew J	"	"	"	"	"	2 09				3
4	Ansell Jonathan	"	"	"	"	"	2 09				4
5	Ansell William	"	"	"	"	"	2 09				5
6	Ashbee Lamb	Tullscreek	"	"	"	"	2 09				6
7	Ayzdelot Isaac	Powell Point	One Carriage	262		1.00	1 00	1895			7
8	Archer Caleb (colour)	Guinea Mills	Cattle Broker	155	3	10	2 50				8
9	Baxter & Maguenah	Sligo	Retail Liquor	235	10 "	25.00	20 83				9
10	"	"	" mdse	234	7 "	10.00	5 83				10
11	Baxter Burrell M.	Indian Ridge	Lawyer	216	5 "	"	4 17				11
12	Bales Geo. E. & Co.	Roanoke Island	Retail Liquor	235	12 "	25.00	25 00				12
13	"	"	" mdse	234	"	10.00	10 00				13
14	"	"	Eating House	206	"	"	10 00				14
15	Bell Lycurgus M.	Court House	Physician	231	10 "	-	8 33				15
16	Brown Joseph	Coinjock	Retail Liquor	235	12 "	25.00	25 00				16
17	Butt J. J.	Court House	Manufacts	219	8 "	10.00	6 67				17
18	Bell Haywood	Knotts Island	Fish Peddler	196	5 "	5.00	2 09				18
19	Beasley Joachim	"	"	"	5 "	"	2 09				19
20	Bell, Malachai	Moyock	Cattle Broker		6 months	10.00	5 00				20
21	Bonney Henry A.	Knotts Island	Fish Peddler	196	5 "	5.00	2 09				21
22	Bowden Thomas	"	"	"	"	"	2 09				22
23	Brumley David	"	Produce Broker	191	"	10.00	4 17				23
24	Banks Enoch	"	Fish Peddler	196	4 "	5.00	1 67				24
25	Bunnel Jordan	Tullscreek	"	"	5 "	"	2 09				25
26	Ballance Stephen	Coinjock	Produce Broker	191	10 "	10.00	8 33				26
27	Baxter Enoch	Sligo	One Carriage	263		2.00	2 00				27
28	Baxter Lovey	Court House	" "	262		1.00	1 00				28
29	Baxter William	"	" "	"		"	1 00				29
30	Brumsey Lucinda	"	" "	"		"	1 00				30
31	Bray Andrew	"	" "	"		"	1 00				31
32	Brdy Benjamin	Tullscreek	" "	"		"	1 00				32
33	Bell Branson	Bull Yard	" "	"		"	1 00				33
34	"	"	" Watch	272		"	1 00				34
35	"	"	Income	241	390	5 pct	19 50				35
36	Bell Jason	"	One Carriage	262		1.00	1 00				36
37	"	"	Income	241	100	5 pct	5 00				37
38	Bell Caleb	"	"	"	186	"	9 30				38

Figure 5-4 Caleb Archer entry (marked with arrow), 1865 annual list, Currituck County, North Carolina, U.S. Internal Revenue Assessor's Office, Elizabeth City, District 1, volume for 1865, p. 73, Internal Revenue Assessment Lists, M784, roll 1, Family History Library microfilm 1578467.

slaves were emerging into freedom in the weeks and months thereafter.

The county's 1860 census in fact showed Caleb Archer and his family as free blacks in the household of William Etheridge, a white farmer:[15]

> Caleb Archer, age 25, black male, born in North Carolina, occupation—farm labor
> Lovey Archer, age 25, black female, born in North Carolina
> Thadeus Archer, age 3, black female [*sic*], born in North Carolina
> Caleb Archer, age 2, black male, born in North Carolina

The tax and census records together give a cameo picture of Archer's life and family. His researcher can use these details to search for him in other records.

State Taxes

Annual state taxes collected by the counties sometimes list free blacks. Figure 5-5, on page 96, illustrates the Georgia law that required free blacks to have guardians, as would orphans or persons judged incompetent to handle their

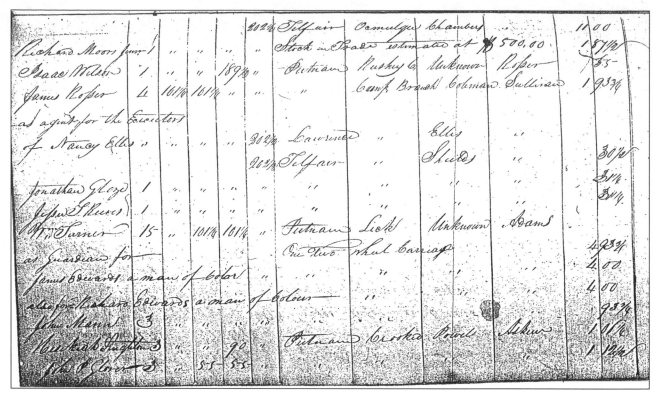

Figure 5-5 Turner and Edwards entries, 1820 tax digest, Capt. William Evans's district, Putnam County, Georgia, Family History Library microfilm 401836.

own affairs. In this instance, William Turner (abbreviated Wm) was paying the 1820 tax as guardian for James Edwards and Richard Edwards, each a free "man of colour." William Turner's tax entry indicated that he owned 202.5 acres of land on Lick Creek in Putnam County and a taxable two-wheel carriage. He was apparently a slaveholder, as he was paying tax on fifteen polls, or taxable heads, including himself.

In fact, the 1820 census identified Turner as a young white man, apparently with a young wife and daughter, as well as fourteen slaves.[16] He and the slaves would account for the fifteen polls reported on the tax list. However, his census entry showed no free persons of color in his household, nor were James and Richard Edwards named as heads of household.

The county's 1820 tax roll named four free men of color, and the census enumerated (not by name) seven free black men of varying age brackets, living in six white households. No free women of color lived in those six households. This observation suggests that the men did not have free families at that time; perhaps some had slave wives and children. Further research is necessary to determine the ages and residences of the Edwards men and whether they had families.

Research Tip

At least **the tax and census records place the men in a specific county at a specific time, and research on them would continue there.** The other records discussed in this chapter and records of neighboring counties would be other sources in which to search for them.

STATE RECORDS

State archives usually hold a variety of records from the antebellum period that include free African Americans, including petitions for manumission as mentioned earlier. Acts of the state legislatures also dealt with requests from free persons, sometimes based on their petitions. In libraries of law schools and, sometimes, county courthouses, compiled acts and resolutions are available in books or on microfiche. Personal names may be indexed, and sometimes the private acts, dealing with individuals and thus different from public acts, are listed separately.

The Congress of the Republic of Texas took action in 1840 in support of several families of free blacks. The petitioners—William, Abner, David, and Aaron Ainsworth (or Ashworth, as both names were used in the published record) and Elisha Thomas—declared that they and their families were in Texas when Texas declared its independence from Mexico on 2 March 1836. They requested and were granted permission to remain in the republic and to be exempt from the act of 5 February 1840.[17] That act had tried to require free blacks to leave Texas by 1 January 1842 but was later superseded by a presidential proclamation, allowing them to stay until February 1845. Apparently, the second deadline was not enforced.

LAND RECORDS

While the majority of rural free persons of color rented land, worked as employees of other landowners, or moved onto unoccupied land, some free blacks owned land before 1865. County deed book indexes should help identify these, especially those whose 1850 or 1860 census entries state a value of real estate owned. Their land records would be the same as those discussed in chapter four.

Historian John Hope Franklin identified in the North Carolina census more than thirteen hundred free Negro farmers who owned land in 1860 and named 233 free blacks who owned slaves.[18] Their reasons for holding slaves and their relationship to any of the slaves cannot be discerned from census records. Nevertheless, these facts are clues for descendants to use in research to try to learn more. Each state had similar free persons of color who were well enough established to own and bequeath or sell property.

Some of the earliest land records in Texas are found in Stephen F. Austin's Register of Families, housed at the Texas General Land Office. The Mexican government required such registration of colonists if they were to receive land. Two of the early families were free blacks:[19]

- Jesse Wilson, age thirty-nine, took the required oath of allegiance to the Mexican government in May 1830. He was a farmer and reported that he and his wife, Jane, age twenty-four, previously resided in Louisiana.
- Levi B. Jones, age fifty, took the oath in December 1829. He was a farmer, married to Sarah, age thirty-five. They had three children and had formerly lived in Mississippi. Jones requested one-half sitio of land on Fish Pond Creek, adjoining J.E. Groce's eastern boundary.

Notes

A *sitio* was the same as a league of land, 4428.4 acres.

URBAN FREE BLACKS BEFORE 1865

In the South, the smallest numbers of free blacks lived in Arkansas, Florida, Mississippi, and Texas, which were also predominantly rural states. The largest free population in the region lived in North Carolina, Virginia, and Maryland, where considerable numbers resided in towns. One historian estimated that, by 1860, about one-third of the free blacks in the South lived in towns and cities, especially Baltimore, New Orleans, Memphis, Natchez, Vicksburg, Mobile, Charleston, Savannah, Richmond, and even St. Louis.[20] A few free blacks lived in western towns such as San Francisco and Sacramento. Northern cities with large free black populations included Boston, New York, Philadelphia, and Cincinnati.

Urban Life

Urban free blacks in the North and the South lived similar lives. "Most lived in the poorer neighborhoods located on the outskirts of cities or in the low-lying areas around rivers and railroad yards."[21] Even if houses in these areas were crowded, oppressive, and unhealthy shanties, families often needed the low rent. However, many needed to live near their work and thus scattered into neighborhoods throughout the cities, even if their addresses were back alleys. On the other hand, free blacks of some means owned homes, even in the better parts of town.

Writing about northern cities, though applicable to the South as well, one historian explained: "Although some Negroes could be found in the skilled trades and professions, most of them continued to labor in the service and menial occupations."[22] In their efforts to move up the economic ladder, urban free men and women sometimes found themselves competing and clashing with poor, newly arrived immigrants, especially Irish in the East and Chinese in the West.

Among the urban blacks, churches and schools provided spiritual and practical support and relief from the drudgery of everyday life. Often churches and schools were closely connected or, in reality, the same institution. Fraternal and benevolent societies developed in most cities, and ethnic newspapers survived in some.

City Directories

Besides the other sources mentioned in this chapter and the occasional discovery of organizational and church records, city directories are useful for studying free persons in urban areas. Not all households were included in these compilations, but **if you had free urban ancestors before 1865, you should look at the existing city directories**. Many are available on microfiche and microfilm in research libraries; some have been reprinted or abridged and published. Others are available in their original form in state, academic, or large public libraries.

The Charleston, South Carolina, directories are examples of the changing scene. As page 80 pointed out, a directory alone cannot tell genealogists why a person is listed only one or two years. In addition, the editor of the reprinted directories of Charleston warned that because many of the houses had no num-

Research Tip

bers, the agents gathering the directory information assigned them numbers. This arbitrary system could mean that Sarah Johnson, listed below, remained in the same house for several years, and only the numbers changed. The following are several entries from early Charleston directories for "free persons of color," all noted "F.P.C." at the end of each entry. Most entries showed the name, occupation, and residence.[23]

- John Bazil, Fruit Store, [at] 27 Tradd St. (directories of 1830–1831 and 1835–1836).
- Robert Howard, a lumber dealer [on] Williams Wharf, residence 80 Anson St. (1835–1836); listed as a wood factor, 80 Anson St. (1837–1838) and wood factor [on] Williams Wharf, residence 80 Anson St. (1840–1841).
- Flora Johnson, [at] 18 Pinckney St. (1830–1831); listed as a seamstress [at] 72 Anson St. (1835–1836).
- Sarah Johnson, a mantuamaker [at] 95 Wentworth St. (1830–1831); listed as a seamstress, 72 Anson St. (1835–1836, the same address as Flora Johnson. Were they relatives?); Sally Johnson, a pastry cook, 87 Wentworth St. (1837–1838); Sally Johnson, no occupation reported, 91 Wentworth St. (1840–1841). (Sally is a common nickname for Sarah. Because of the similarity of three of these addresses and the fact that no other person of the same name was listed, it is likely that Sarah and Sally were the same person.)

Like Flora and Sarah Johnson in 1835–1836, other people by the same surname lived at the same address and provide the researcher clues for further study into the possibility of relationships—parent and child, spouses, siblings, or cousins. In 1830–1831 at different addresses, Jehu Jones operated a boarding house and Jehu Jones Jr. was a tailor, but Ann Humphreys, a mantuamaker, and Joseph Humphreys, a tailor, lived together at 110 Queen Street. Charlotte Lee, a mantuamaker, and Edward Lee, a barber, lived at 55 Broad Street in 1840–1841.[24]

Notes

At this time, a *mantua-maker* was a dressmaker, comparable to a men's tailor. The term was apparently carried over from an earlier period when a mantua was a style of gown (dress) for ladies. Perhaps there was a local distinction between seamstress, dressmaker, and mantuamaker, for all three terms are used in the city directories. A *factor* was an agent, broker, or dealer who bought or sold goods on behalf of others, for a commission.

NATIVE AMERICAN CONNECTIONS

Many Americans today have a tradition of Native American ancestry, although relatively few can confirm the tradition. Thus, the first task of the genealogist is to work back in time, confirming one generation at a time, to the person(s) the family believes to have been Indian. The second task is to study the candidate(s) individually and thoroughly to try to determine what the true origin may have been. In some cases, the "American Indian" actually was white or Hispanic, in a time or community where families felt that having Indian ancestry was more acceptable than the reality. The same deceptive tradition appears in white families.

If it seems likely that an ancestor truly was Native American, confirming the lineage may well depend on when and where the person lived. Numerous records exist for Indians who remained associated with their tribes and be-

For More Info

For more on Native American research, see *The Genealogist's Companion & Sourcebook* and *A Genealogist's Guide to Discovering Your Immigrant & Ethnic Ancestors*.

came residents of government reservations. This category includes especially the Five Civilized Tribes (Cherokee, Choctaw, Chickasaw, Creek, and Seminole) and others who settled in Indian Territory, now included in Oklahoma.

Five Civilized Tribes

Some records of the Five Civilized Tribes remain in the southeastern states, where the tribes lived before being moved west. A number have been published; others are at the various state archives and the East Point, Georgia, branch of the National Archives. The largest collections of records after the tribes' removal to Indian Territory are at the National Archives; its Fort Worth, Texas, branch; the Oklahoma Historical Society in Oklahoma City; and the Western History Collection at the University of Oklahoma in Norman.

Microfilm Source

Numerous National Archives records for these tribes and others throughout the country are available on microfilm. Resources include enrollment cards, tribal census rolls, allotment records, trading post records, Indian agency reports and correspondence, and military service records.

Among the most useful in establishing ancestry are the enrollment cards prepared by the Dawes Commission between 1898 and 1914. The commission enrolled as tribal members a number of freed slaves, formerly held by these Indians. The enrollment cards on National Archives microfilm identify Cherokee Freedmen, Choctaw Freedmen, Chickasaw Freedmen, Creek Freedmen, and Seminole Freedmen. Some claimants were rejected, but their records are included in the microfilm.

Census Records

Notes

The first time *Indian* was a color or race category in the federal census was in 1870. However, scattered census entries across the country in earlier years labeled Native Americans as "Indian" and enumerated them as free persons of color. In 1860 and likely in 1850, some individuals' birthplaces were recorded as "in the Cherokee Nation, North Carolina." People identified in some way as Native American in all these censuses used English names (often a white father's surname), or Indian names, or apparent English translations of Indian names, such as Jim Wood Pecker. However, name changes or mobility make it difficult to track some families from one census to the next.

In 1860, whites and a few free blacks living in the unorganized Indian Territory were enumerated on the federal census as living in the "Indian lands west of Arkansas." Indians were not enumerated. These schedules appear in the microfilm at the end of the Arkansas schedules. However, the slave schedule for the same census names the many Indian slaveholders and thus creates a partial Indian census.

For certain tribes in Washington, Oregon, California, and Dakota Territory, a special census was taken in 1880 and is available on microfilm. The 1900 and 1910 censuses included, nationwide, a scehecule for families composed primarily of Indians—on reservations, in a tribal relationship, or in counties with large Indian populations. These schedules are found at the end of the county or enumeration district. Indians living in predominantly black or white households were to included with the general population. However, ancestors of Native American lineage who had blended into black or white families may or may not have identified themselves as Indians in any of the late-nineteenth- or early-twentieth-century censuses.

The Challenge

State archives and historical societies hold records for many eastern and western Indian tribes and bands, as do the special collections departments of academic and large public libraries around the country. The challenge is connecting a specific person to a specific Indian identity. History and reference books on the individual states and their native inhabitants may help.

However, researchers must be very cautious not to claim a tribal association for an ancestor based only on where that ancestor was born. What if the Indians someone claimed as ancestors had been gone from the area for generations? What if the claimed tribe had never lived in the ancestral state or region? Research is the key; wishful thinking and jumping to conclusions are traps, as well as bad genealogy.

It is well known that runaway slaves often sought refuge near or among Indians in remote mountains, forests, swamps, or other hard-to-penetrate landscapes. Black communities formed in some of these isolated areas. The extent to which the two races mixed in these situations is a matter of study and debate among scholars. However, genealogists would be hard-pressed to prove lineages in such circumstances.

Numerous Native Americans blended into black and white society and became disconnected from any band or tribe. Research on these ancestors must proceed the same as on any other person in the white-based record system. However, it is very difficult to confirm any prior tribal connection for most of these ancestors. Sometimes, the best result is making an educated, research-based guess at a tribal connection and studying the life and history of that group, without claiming a definitive kinship with them.

For Further Reference

It is beyond the scope of this book to discuss in depth how to research in Native American records. Below are listed some of the published works that can guide researchers in such a search.

American Indians: A Select Catalog of National Archives Microfilm Publications. Rev. ed. Washington, D.C.: National Archives Trust Fund Board, 1998.

Danky, James P. *Native American Periodicals and Newspapers, 1828–1982.* Westport, Conn.: Greenwood Press, 1984.

Forbes, Jack D. *Africans and Native Americans: The Language of Race and the Evolution of Red-Black Peoples.* Urbana, Ill.: University of Illinois Press, 1993.

Hill, Edward E., comp. *Guide to Records in the National Archives of the United States Relating to American Indians.* Washington, D.C.: National Archives and Records Administration, 1982.

Library/Archive Source

Printed Source

Katz, William Loren. *Black Indians: A Hidden Heritage*. New York: Aladdin Paperbacks, 1997.

Kirkham, E. Kay. *Our Native Americans and Their Records of Genealogical Value*. 2 vols. Logan, Utah: Everton Publishers, 1980.

Parker, Jimmy B. "American Indian Records and Research." Chapter 7 in *Ethnic Genealogy: A Research Guide*, Jessie Carney Smith, ed. Westport, Conn.: Greenwood Press, 1983.

Spindel, Donna. *Introductory Guide to Indian-Related Records, to 1876, in the North Carolina State Archives*. Raleigh: North Carolina Division of Archives and History, 1977.

Walton-Raji, Angela Y. *Black Indian Genealogy Research*. Bowie, Md.: Heritage Books, 1993. Especially for ancestors among the Five Civilized Tribes in Oklahoma. See also <www.african/nativeamerican.com/>.

Witcher, Curt B., and George J. Nixon. "Tracking Native American Family History." In *The Source: A Guidebook of American Genealogy*, Loretto Dennis Szucs and Sandra Hargreaves Luebking, eds. Rev. ed. Salt Lake City: Ancestry, 1997.

IMMIGRANTS

Blacks who immigrated to the United States as free persons prior to the Civil War were relatively few in number, but the several thousand who came generally originated in the West Indies or Caribbean region and often entered the United States along the Gulf coast. Most of these came because of political and racial unrest in their native islands.

Other free blacks were already living in Louisiana or Florida or along the Mississippi-Alabama coast before the United States acquired those regions. They made up a sizable portion of the New Orleans population in 1803, the year of the Louisiana Purchase, and many were mulattos.

If your research suggests that some of these people may have been your ancestors, you would research them in the government and church records of Louisiana, the territorial records of the United States, and the colonial and territorial records of the states now in that region. The process is similar to research on free persons in later eras, but the records would be somewhat different. They are also often written in French or Spanish; church records are often in Latin. The strategy still involves

- using the records that are available for the specific time and place
- reading history of the particular area where the ancestor lived
- learning about research in the area and its records
- studying the ancestor and his or her cluster of relatives and associates in the records
- being as thorough and careful as possible in research and evaluation
- documenting every piece of information
- consulting with experts in the use of the foreign-language records
- perhaps hiring an experienced researcher familiar with the records

FOR FURTHER READING
Free Persons of Color Before 1865

Genealogists are interested in learning about the history of their ancestral community, county, and state because that history involved and affected their ancestors. Although a published history may not name your ancestral family, it may give pertinent information on an ancestor's occupation, religion, and other aspects of daily life as the ancestor probably experienced it at a specific time and place.

Reading such histories helps genealogists understand why they find or do not find certain things in the records. For example, you would not expect to find a telephone directory for many communities in the rural South until after World War II because both blacks and whites in many such places had neither telephone nor electricity until the late 1940s or after.

To find additional titles of history books and articles, consult the *Journal of Negro History*, historical journals in the states, the Periodical Source Index (PERSI), and the bibliographies and footnotes of the works listed below. Usually found in academic and large public libraries, the index *America: History and Life* will alert you to articles and doctoral dissertations about free blacks and many related subjects.

Tip

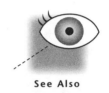

See Also

See page 133 for information on PERSI.

Berlin, Ira. *Slaves Without Masters: The Free Negro in the Antebellum South.* New York: Random House, 1974. See also his Appendix 2: Manuscript Sources Consulted, 404–410.

Bogger, Tommy L. *Free Blacks in Norfolk, Virginia, 1790–1860: The Darker Side of Freedom.* Charlottesville: University Press of Virginia, 1997.

Brown, Letitia Woods. *Free Negroes in the District of Columbia, 1790–1846.* New York: Oxford University Press, 1972.

Curry, Leonard P. *The Free Black in Urban America 1800–1850: The Shadow of the Dream.* Chicago: University of Chicago Press, 1981. See also his Note on Sources, 275–279.

Everett, Donald E. "Free Persons of Color in Colonial Louisiana." *Louisiana History* VII (1966): 29–40, 46–47.

Fields, Barbara Jeanne. *Slavery and Freedom on the Middle Ground: Maryland During the Nineteenth Century.* New Haven, Conn.: Yale University Press, 1985.

Finkelman, Paul, ed. *Free Blacks in a Slave Society.* New York: Garland Publishing, 1989.

Franklin, John Hope. *The Free Negro in North Carolina, 1790–1860.* Chapel Hill: University of North Carolina Press, 1943.

Franklin, John Hope, and Loren Schweninger. *Runaway Slaves: Rebels on the Plantation.* New York: Oxford University Press, 1999.

Frazier, E. Franklin. *The Negro Family in the United States.* Chicago: University of Chicago, 1939.

Freeman, Rhoda Golden. *The Free Negro In New York City in the Era Before the Civil War.* New York: Garland Publishing, 1994.

Genovese, Eugene D. *Roll, Jordan, Roll: The World the Slaves Made.* New York: Vintage Books, 1976.

Glasrud, Bruce A. *African Americans in the West: A Bibliography of Secondary Sources.* Alpine, Tex.: Sul Ross State University, Center for Big Bend Studies, 1998.

Ham, Debra Newman. *List of Free Black Heads of Families in the First Census of the United States.* Washington, D.C.: National Archives and Records Service, General Services Administration, 1973.

Hogan, William Ransom, and Edwin Adams Davis, eds. *William Johnson's Natchez: The Ante-Bellum Diary of a Free Negro.* Baton Rouge: Louisiana State University Press, 1951.

Horton, James Oliver. *In Hope of Liberty: Culture, Community, and Protest Among Northern Free Blacks, 1700–1860.* New York: Oxford University Press, 1997.

Jackson, Luther Porter. "Free Negroes of Petersburg, Virginia." *Journal of Negro History* XII (1927): 365–388.

———. *Free Negro Labor and Property Holding in Virginia, 1830–1860.* Reprint of 1942 original. New York: Russell & Russell, 1971.

———. "The Virginia Free Negro Farmer and Property Owner, 1830–1860." *Journal of Negro History* XXIV (1939): 390–439.

Katz, William Loren. *The Black West: A Documentary and Pictorial History of the African American Role in the Westward Expansion of the United States.* New York: Simon & Schuster, 1996.

Lebsock, Suzanne. *Free Women of Petersburg: Status and Culture in a Southern Town, 1784–1860.* New York: Norton, 1984.

Litwack, Leon F. *North of Slavery: The Negro in the Free States, 1790–1860.* Chicago: University of Chicago Press, 1961. See his bibliographical essay, 280–303.

McConnell, Roland C. *Negro Troops of Antebellum Louisiana: A History of the Battalion of Free Men of Color.* Baton Rouge: Louisiana State University Press, 1968.

Mills, Gary B. "Tracing Free People of Color in the Antebellum South: Methods, Sources and Perspectives." *National Genealogical Society Quarterly* 78 (December 1990): 262–278.

Muir, Andrew Forest. "The Free Negro in Jefferson and Orange Counties, Texas." *Journal of Negro History* 35 (July 1950): 183–206.

Nash, Gary B. *Forging Freedom: The Formation of Philadelphia's Black Community, 1720–1840.* Cambridge, Mass.: Harvard University Press, 1988.

Peskin, Allan, ed. *North into Freedom: The Autobiography of John Malvin, Free Negro, 1795–1880.* Cleveland, Ohio: Press of Western Reserve University, 1966.

Pierson, William D. *Black Yankees: The Development of an Afro-American Subculture in Eighteenth-Century New England.* Amherst, Mass.: University of Massachusetts Press, 1988.

Russell, John Henderson. *The Free Negro in Virginia, 1619–1865.* Reprint of 1913 original. New York: Dover Publications, 1969.

Schweninger, Loren. *Black Property Owners in the South, 1790–1815.* Urbana: University of Illinois Press, 1997.

Sterkx, Herbert E. *The Free Negro in Ante-Bellum Louisiana.* Rutherford, N.J.: Fairleigh Dickinson University, 1972.

Voegeli, V. Jacque. *Free But Not Equal: The Midwest and the Negro During the Civil War.* Chicago: University of Chicago Press, 1967.

Wikramanayake, Marina. *A World in Shadow: The Free Black in Antebellum South Carolina.* Columbia: University of South Carolina Press, 1973.

Winston, James E. "Free Negro in New Orleans, 1803–1860." *Louisiana Historical Quarterly* XXI (1938): 175–185.

Witcher, Curt Bryan. *African American Genealogy: A Bibliography and Guide to Sources.* Fort Wayne, Ind.: Round Tower Books, 2000.

Woodson, Carter G. *The Education of the Negro Prior to 1861.* Reprint of 1919 2d ed. New York: Arno Press, 1968.

———. "Freedom and Slavery in Appalachian America." *Journal of Negro History* I (1916): 132–150.

———. *Free Negro Heads of Families in the United States in 1830.* Washington, D.C.: Association for the Study of Negro Life and History, Inc., 1925.

———. *Free Negro Owners of Slaves in the United States in 1830.* Reprint of 1924 original. Westport, Conn.: Negro Universities Press, 1968.

Woolfolk, George R. *The Free Negro in Texas, 1800–1860: A Study in Cultural Compromise.* Ann Arbor, Mich.: University Microfilms International for the Journal of Mexican American History, 1976.

Wright, James M. *The Free Negro in Maryland, 1634–1860.* Reprint of 1921 original. New York: Octagon Books, 1971.

SIX

What's in a Name?

G enealogical lineages depend on linking names into family relationships. Researchers use other tools, such as dates and places, to confirm the names in each family in each generation. Successful genealogists, therefore, pay close attention to both given names and surnames within the family and the community, to variant spellings of names, and to evaluation of names in documents.

GIVEN NAMES

Until the end of the Civil War, most slaves were identified publicly by only a given name. Slaves on the same plantation with the same given names were distinguished by the slaveholder based on the slave's age, size, or color: old Jim or young Jim; big Moses or little Moses; yellow Sam, copper Sam, or black Sam. However, this practice does not mean that slaves limited themselves to the names given them. **Within their families and communities, they followed their own naming practices by the use of nicknames, which remains a common practice in the African-American community today.**

The slaves' discretion to name their children varied from slaveholder to slaveholder. Slaveholders with many slaves were more likely involved in naming newborns than those with few slaves, perhaps to prevent confusion that could result from overuse of the same names. Repeated use of given names was likely to be found in family groups. However, if the parents chose a name, they probably did so only after the slaveholder approved.

Because of the restrictions imposed by slavery and the lack of documentation on slave culture, proof of naming practices during slavery is difficult to identify or confirm. However, scholars have speculated that naming patterns existed to the extent possible to identify kinship or maintain family ties. If your research has taken you back several generations into slavery, watch for the repeated use of given names, especially if they are unique and, as always, compare those names with names of post–Civil War family members.

Studying Given Names

Both before and after the Civil War, a person's given name sometimes varied from one record to the next, as illustrated in the census example, Figure 2-2, on page 23. The differences may have resulted from the way

- the family reported the name—Matilda, Tildy, or Tillie.
- the family pronounced the name and, thus, the way each clerk or census taker heard it—Marian, Marin, or Maron; Celia, Selah, Siller, or Cilly; and Harriett, Haritt, or even Harry. One 1880 census taker recorded almost every female named Emily as Emley. Especially when you see the names Anner (Anna), Emer (Emma), Eaver, Ider, Eller, Marrietter, and Dannel in the records, you can almost hear the community, black and white, speaking.
- the recorder chose to spell the name—Louisa, Luisa, Luesia, or Leweser; Eunice or Unus; Lindsey or Linzy; Phyllis or Fillis; Ezekiel or Ezecal; Rufus or Ruphes. Three women in one county obviously had the same name, but the 1870 census listed them with three different spellings: Cindarella, Cyndarilla, and Syndrilla.

Occasionally, families used nicknames in public records. Many male nicknames are well known—Bob for Robert, Bill for William, Hank and Harry for Henry, and Sam for Samuel. Some female nicknames are not as widely used today as they were fifty or a hundred years ago and therefore may stump descendants. Although some females were originally named Betsy, Mamie, Sadie, or Patsy, such names can also be nicknames. These are a few of the female nicknames you may find during research:

For More Info

You may want to look at *Black Names in America: Origins and Usage,* collected by Newbell Niles Puckett, edited by Murray Heller (Boston: G.K. Hall, 1975).

GIVEN NAME	NICKNAMES AND DIMINUTIVES
Elizabeth	Beth, Betsy, Betty, Liz, Liza, Lizzie
Margaret	Daisy, Maggie, Meg, Midge, Peg, Peggy
Martha	Mattie, Patsy, Patty
Mary	Mamie, Minnie, Molly, Polly
Sarah	Sallie, Sadie

Case Study: Teat Dixon's Given Name

You are likely to find some given names spelled various ways in the records. At these times, you need to use a combination of records to determine the name. **The key in research is not what the "real" name or "correct" spelling was but what the family considered and thus reported the name to be.** The more documents you find, the more variations you may encounter. However, these variations help you

Case Study

Research Tip

- know what to expect as you look for the person in other records
- determine when you have records on the correct family even though the spelling is inconsistent

An example is the unique name of a North Carolina man—Teat Dixon. The first two reports of his name showed it as *Tea*. Was this a nickname for Theodore or something else, or was this his actual name?

The first documents found on the Dixon family furnished enough versions of Teat's name to send up red flags of caution. Such discrepancies are important to note, especially when, as in this case, another black man named Peter Dixon lived in the same county. Yet, the 1920 census had reported the list of Teat's children, and family letters had named Tea and Teat, his first wife and children, and the spouses of his children James and Velma—enough information to verify the correct family members in the records.[1]

The following eight documents generated the questions about his given name. They are listed in the order they were found and with the spelling of his name that appeared in each one:

1. His son James's memory of his name, in a letter, 2001—Tea Dixon
2. The family's 1920 census entry—Tea Dixon
3. His son James's marriage record, 1939—Pete Dixon
4. His son Ernest's marriage record, 1928—Tete Dixon
5. His own marriage record, 1928—Teat Dixon
6. His daughter Jessie's marriage record, 1940—Peter Dixon
7. His daughter Bell's marriage record, 1935—Pete Dixon
8. His daughter Velma's marriage record, 1925—Teate Dixon

In such cases, genealogists must (1) think about how the name must have been pronounced and how the clerk must have heard it and (2) try to find other records to help clarify the name. The following documents supported the family's knowledge and three of the previous records.[2]

1. His 1900 census entry—Teat Dixon
2. His 1880 census entry—Teap Dixon
3. His 1910 census entry—not yet found
4. His son Gentry's birth certificate, 1918—Teat Dixon (See Figure 6-1, page 109.)
5. His daughter Coatnie's marriage record, 1923—Teat Dixon
6. His death certificate, 1937—Feate Dixon

This additional evidence supports a conclusion that he and the family considered his name to be Teat, regardless of how it was spelled in the records. The spelling is not critical—not all the clerks and recorders heard the name the same way. At least enough heard it in approximately the same way for the genealogist to find a consensus and to understand how *Pete* and *Peter* crept into the list. The important results are the confirmation of what the family called him and the awareness of discrepancies that might be found in future research.

SURNAMES

A common and often erroneous presumption is that most freed slaves took the surname of the most recent slaveholder. **In fact, the surname may have belonged to a prior slaveholder—the first, the favorite, or the longest—or the slaveholder of a parent or grandparent.** Even in the eighteenth century, many slaves had surnames and carried them from owner to owner, although few slaveholders knew, acknowledged, or used these names. One example of the public use of a slave's

Research Tip

The genealogist's goal is correct lineages, produced by careful research in multiple sources. It is easy to jump to conclusions or make giant leaps of faith, but quick judgments can be hazardous to accuracy.

Important

surname was in a 1746 report from the governor's council in New Hampshire. This body awarded slaveholder Theodore Atkinson money to replace a gun used in military service by his slave, John Gloster.[3]

According to historian Eugene Genovese, the "percentage of slaves with surnames is unknown, but they did appear in all parts of the South."[4] Especially after attaining freedom, former slaves needed surnames, either choosing a name for the first time or publicly recording the one they had been using privately—in some families, for several generations.

Historian William D. Piersen observed, especially for eighteenth-century New England: "The adoption of a master's name, although relatively common in the New World, was as symbolic of the connection between master and servant as it was useful for purposes of identification."[5] On the other hand, former slaves had a "significant reason for going back in time to take the name of the first master they had ever had, or perhaps of the first whom they could remember as having been a decent man: by so doing, they recaptured, as best they could, their own history."[6] Stepping back at least one generation, a number of slaves and freedmen preserved a father's given name or surname for future generations, as did Paul Cuffee[7] and Jacob Branch, whose father was sold away when the son was very young.[8]

Taking this idea further, historian Herbert Gutman found considerable evidence that a "surname often symbolized the close tie between an immediate slave family and its family of origin . . . ."[9] As part of his extensive evidence, this scholar quoted the 1865 diary of Eliza Frances Andrews, a slaveholder's

daughter in Georgia, who observed: **"I notice that the negroes seldom or never take the names of the present owners in adopting their 'entitles' as they call their own surnames, but always that of some former master, and they go back as far as possible."**[10]

Of course, some families chose surnames with no apparent connection to former slaveholders. Some individuals or families chose

1. The surname of a locally prominent family, such as Pinckney in South Carolina, or a famous American—Washington or Lincoln.

2. A name identifying a personal characteristic—Long, Strong, Brown, Freeman, or African. Remember, however, that many such names were also common English surnames, as were many names of occupational sound, and thus could have been names of former slaveholders or names of choice.

3. Perhaps a name with an occupational link to the bearer—Mason or Carpenter.

4. Perhaps a given name of choice combined with a given name by which the person was known (or the name of a parent)—James Caesar or John Caleb.

5. A surname with a possible geographic connection, such as these shown in the 1870 census: Arkansas, Boston, Carolina, California, Georgia, or Tennessee. The Georgetown County, South Carolina, 1870 census enumerated several black residents with the surname Blackriver. Since that county has a Black River, it is possible that these residents derived their surname from a plantation name or the part of the county in which they lived. However, we cannot assume that all those who bore such names ever lived in or were born in these places. Although a name such as Canada or Canida may have had geographic or symbolic significance for the bearer, the name could also have been a variant spelling of Cannady or Kennedy. Also, names such as Boston, Carolina, and others could have been parents' names.

6. A name with perhaps a religious or symbolic significance. We cannot assume that the names Canaan, Calvary, Freeman, Jordan, or Justice had such a significance, although the possibility exists. Even the surname Preacher could be a variant rendering of Pritchard.

7. A name "for no apparent reason other than the pleasure of the author," including such names as Prince, Dukes, Captain, or Governor.[11]

8. Different surnames. For example, Will Oats of Mercer County, Kentucky, reported to an interviewer that his brothers were Jim and Lige (Elijah) Coffey. Their masters had been Lewis Oats and his sister. Apparently, one brother chose to use the Oats name; two brothers made a different choice.[12]

9. Different surnames at different times. This was true for Pinkney Hollis of Claiborne County, Mississippi. The 1870 census listed him as eleven-year-old Pickney Tannyhill in the home of his half-brother, Henry Dotson. By 1880, the census showed him with no reported surname, living with his mother, Winny, as a separate family in the Henry Dotson household. Although listed as Jones elsewhere, Winny in 1880 was enumerated with the surname Dotson, possibly an error by the census taker or informant.

Pinkney married in 1888, using the surname Hollis, which he used thereafter. The reason for his choice remains a mystery, especially since there were no Hollis surnames, black or white, in Claiborne County or the surrounding counties in 1870.

The ancestor's surname may be the clue that opens the door to your family's pre–Civil War history. For some families, the reason behind a choice of a surname is already known. For others, the reason may be discovered during research. For many, the reason may never be known. If you already know the history behind your family's choice of a surname, you may be able to eliminate years of tedious and often frustrating research.

A CASE STUDY
One Crossley Family

Case Study

The importance of the given name in African-American genealogical research is exemplified in the history of the Thomas and Lucy Crossley family from Amite and Lincoln counties, Mississippi. Over a period of nearly thirty years, a group of names appeared in documents that suggested and confirmed kinship. Such a group of names alerts the cautious researcher to pay attention and study further. **Sometimes, researchers need to work backward and forward in time as new evidence is found and new questions arise.**

Pre-1865 Estate Records

Research Tip

The 1844 inventory and appraisal of Lodwick L. Weathersby's estate listed yellow man Tom, yellow man Andy, yellow man Sylvester, yellow woman Lucy, yellow girl Matilda, yellow girl Dicy, and yellow man David. The listing by color indicated a common denominator that might indicate a potential family relationship. The remaining slaves, identified by gender only, did not suggest any grouping according to family.[13]

Further research of the Lodwick L. Weathersby estate revealed that Tom and Lucy were a couple and the parents of Andy, Sylvester, Matilda, and Dicy. The family was willed to Lodwick Weathersby in 1843 by his father, Lewis Weathersby, who died before Lodwick.[14] Lewis Weathersby's will left specific instructions regarding the status and care of this family. Tom and Lucy were to be allowed to live as free, and their children were to be allowed to purchase their freedom.

In 1846, after Lodwick Weathersby's death, several heirs of Lewis Weathersby filed a lawsuit against the administrators of Lodwick L. Weathersby's estate. The suit alleged that the freedom clause was an attempt to contravene the Mississippi law requiring legislative approval before a slaveholder could free his slaves. The heirs argued that, in effect, Lewis had freed the family without legislature approval; thus, the provision was void and the slaves should be sold and proceeds distributed among the heirs.[15] Apparently, the case was resolved in favor of the Lodwick Weathersby estate, the defendants, since the six slaves were named in the division of Lodwick's estate in 1853.[16] Although they were not sold and remained a part of Lodwick's estate, it is unclear whether, after the deaths of

Lewis and Lodwick, they were allowed to live as free persons as prescribed in Lewis Weathersby's will.

The lawsuit was featured in a doctoral dissertation about slavery in Amite County.[17] However, there was no reference to the family after slavery, no indication that they had been identified or their whereabouts determined.

Post-1865 Records

As part of a separate project, L.L. Weathersby, son of Lodwick L. Weathersby, became a research subject. In 1870, L.L. Weathersby resided in Lincoln County, Mississippi, as a single head of household.[18] In the neighborhood were four households with given names remarkably similar to the family who had been the subject of the Weathersby legal fight. The early estate documents were created about twenty-six years before the 1870 census. By 1870, three of the children—Andy, Sylvester, and Dicy—were adults in separate, but neighboring, households.[19]

Household 7	*Andy* Crossley	40, mulatto
	Jane Crossley	25, black
	Lena Crossley	4, black
	Adolphus Crossley	2, black
Household 11	N. H. Sims	42, white, physician
	Elizabeth Flowers	21, mulatto
	Dicy Weathersby	43, mulatto
	Leland Anderson	20, mulatto
Household 12	*Thomas* Crossley	78, mulatto
	Harriett Crossley	30, mulatto
	Sidney Crossley	10, female, black
	Harrison Crossley	11, black
	Wilson Crossley	8, black
	Van Crossley	3, black
	Nepolean Crossley	1, black
Household 13	*S.* Crossley	45, mulatto
	Louisa Crossley	40, black
	Andrew Crossley	14, mulatto

The given names Thomas (Tom), Andy, Dicy, and S[ylvester] and the designation *mulatto* matched four of the six family members from the lawsuit. The fifth, Tom's wife, Lucy, may have died before 1870, and Harriett may have been a second wife. Matilda, the sixth family member, may have been married and living elsewhere. S. Crossley and his apparent wife, Louise, in the census may have been the same couple listed in 1853 in Missouri (Weathersby) Godbold's share of the division of the Lodwick Weathersby estate.[20]

The reason for the use of the surname Crossley is not clear although there were white Crossleys in the area for many years. However, records of the Freedmen's Bureau confirmed the identity of at least some of these black Crossleys in an 1865 list of the freedmen on the plantation of James. R. Godbold, husband of Missouri (Weathersby) Godbold.[21] Heading the list were Sylvester Crossley (two-thirds white [*sic*], age forty-seven), Louise Crossley (black, age forty-six), and Andrew Crossley (one-half white, age eleven). This was undoubtedly the same Sylvester and Louise who were listed in Missouri Godbold's share of Lodwick Weathersby's estate and the same S., Louise, and Andrew Crossley in household thirteen in the 1870 census of Lincoln County. The given names in the cluster in the 1870 census ultimately led to their identity, which the Freedmen's Bureau records confirmed.

THE NEXT STEPS

Research Tip

As you prepare to reach into pre–Civil War family history, update and review a family group sheet or similar list of the members of the family on which you want to focus your research. A list of their given names and their ages in 1870 is a necessary tool for the next step: (1) determining which family members may have been born as slaves and (2) trying to determine the slaveholder.

The name of the slaveholding family is essential to moving your research to the next level. Those who already know this information can start researching that family. If this information was lost with your ancestors, you will need to identify the slaveholder. You can start with the presumption that your ancestral family kept their former or most recent slaveholder's surname, but be alert for clues that point to other possibilities.

Working Back From the 1870 Census

Step By Step

1. Using the list of your ancestral family members from the 1870 census, subtract ten years from their 1870 ages to estimate their ages in 1860. Isolate the names and ages of those who were living in 1860 for reference in the steps below.

2. Look at the neighborhood where your ancestors lived in 1870 for white families with the same surname. (See also chapter seven.) Make your search countywide, or even statewide if your ancestors' surname was unique. Create a list of same-surname candidates for the slaveholding family. Include possible spelling variations of the surname—for example, Harget(t), Hargit(t), Horgett, Hargot, Horgatt, Herget, and possibly Haggett or Haggart, one of which could have been the name from which the others derived. Consider going as far back as the 1850 census to look for white families of that surname. The marriage and deed records in your research county may also suggest possible slaveholder candidates.

3. Work with your list of white families. Determine which of these families owned slaves in 1860 by looking at the 1860 slave schedule for that county. You may be able to mark off your list those white families whose names do not appear in the 1860 slave schedule, but wait until step six below.

Figure 6-2, on page 114, illustrates an 1860 slave schedule. Notice that the slaves were enumerated under the name of the slaveholder, by gender, age, and color, but not by name, except those one hundred years old or older. Sometimes, special skills or trades were reported, as were various disabilities. Some slaves were listed in apparent family groups; the number of slave houses reported may help you determine such family groups.

Figure 6-2 U.S. Census of 1860, Slave Schedule, roll 428, Claiborne Parish, Louisiana, p. 41.

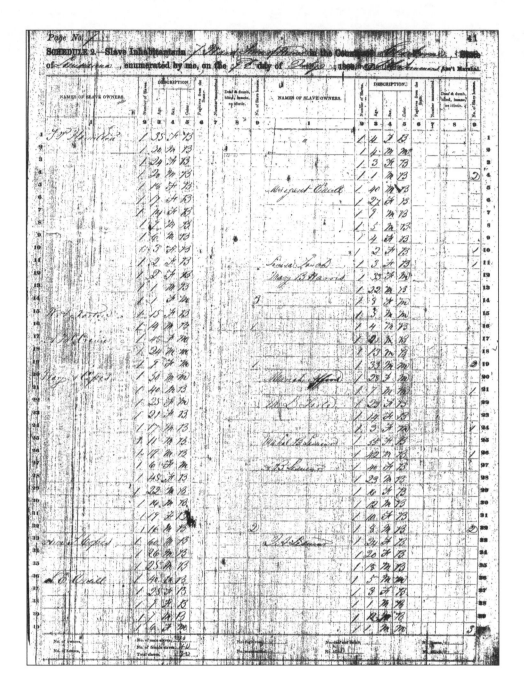

The 1850 and 1860 slave schedules are rarely indexed. Since the schedules named only the slaveholders, only they would be indexed. Any indexes would appear in journals of genealogical societies, in books about the county, or on county Web pages on USGenWeb <www.usgenweb.org>. The schedules are National Archives microfilm, available in libraries and on loan from the Family History Library, Heritage Quest, and the National Archives Census Microfilm Rental Program. Most are online at the Ancestry.com subscription site. See "Slave Schedules in the Federal Census Records," on page 115, for more information on the slave schedules.

4. Compare the ages of your ancestor's family group in 1860 with the ages of slaves in households in the slave schedule. Does a group of slaves in any

---

SLAVE SCHEDULES IN THE FEDERAL CENSUS RECORDS

1850 and 1860 Slave Schedules:

Alabama	Kentucky	New Jersey (1850 only)
Arkansas	Louisiana	South Carolina
Delaware*	Maryland	Tennessee
District of Columbia⁺	Mississippi	Texas
Florida	Missouri	Virginia
Georgia	North Carolina	Indian Lands west of Arkansas**

*Delaware's 1850 slave schedule appears after the Sussex County census on roll 55 of the free schedule.

⁺The district's 1850 slave schedule appears at the end of the free schedule, roll 57.

**The Indian lands eventually became Oklahoma. No 1850 census was taken in the area. The 1860 slave schedule appears at the end of the Arkansas slave schedule, roll 52.

Censuses 1850–1860 listed slaves under the name of the slaveholder and by age, sex, and color, rarely by name.

Censuses 1830–1840 listed for each household the number of slaves, male or female, in age groups: under 10, 10–under 24, 24–under 36, 36–under 55, 55–under 100, 100 and older.

Census of 1820 listed for each household the number of slaves, male or female, in age groups: under 14, 14–under 26, 26–under 45, 45 and older.

Censuses 1790–1810 listed only the number of slaves in a household.

---

household match the list of your family members' genders and ages? Remember that the slaves were grouped under the name of the slaveholder and were identified by sex, color, and age, but rarely by name. The process would be easier with names, but genealogists work with what is available.

This step should help narrow the list of slaveholder candidates by eliminating (a) those who did not own slaves and (b) those whose slaves' ages did not correspond to your ancestral family. Although your ancestors may have been a family prior to the war, the parents may have lived apart, on neighboring farms or plantations. Therefore, search for the mother and children together.

5. Prioritize the candidates according to what you find in the slave schedules; this evaluation will either strengthen a possible connection or eliminate unlikely candidates.

- Likely slaveholder candidates: The ages of your ancestral family members fit within the ages listed in their 1860 slave schedules.
- Less likely slaveholder candidates: The ages of your ancestral family members and those listed on the 1860 schedule do not appear to coincide.
- Least likely candidates: Those candidates not listed in either the 1860 or 1850 slave schedule. As with any census, some slaveholders may have been omitted, but the schedules are probably the most complete pool of slaves and slaveholders available.

6. Repeat this step for the 1850 slave schedule, especially if the ages of your ancestors indicate they were a family before 1850. This step will help you

Notes

You may find your ancestral family named in 1850 if they lived in Bowie County, Texas, one of the rare instances where slaves' names were reported. See Figure 6-3, page 117.

compare your list of same-name slaveholder candidates with the reported slaveholders. Sometimes, people were accidentally omitted from both general population and slave schedules. A slaveholder candidate may have been enumerated in 1850 and missed in 1860.

7. If your search based upon the surname approach produces enough evidence to suggest further investigation of a particular candidate, start researching that white family. Study the leading candidate(s) in the county records to try to determine whether your family was mentioned or suggested in records of the white family. See chapters eight and nine and the case studies in chapters ten and twelve.

8. If you do not find slaveholder candidates of the same surname as your family, consider slaveholders from the 1860 slave schedules who lived near your family in 1870. (See chapter seven.) Review those who owned slaves in your focus county in 1860. Your ancestors may have lived on a plantation near the same-surname white family.

9. Do not get stuck trying to make your ancestor fit into what is obviously an unlikely match. If these steps do not produce the name of a slaveholder, consider these options:

- Your family may have moved from their 1860 home county after the war to a neighboring county or into a town in the region. Although some freed men and women moved miles away from their pre-war homes during or at the close of the war, most stayed relatively near, at least for a few years. Many remained on the same land and in the same houses for many years.
- The slaveholding family may have moved away after the war, but pre-war county records may reveal their identity.
- **Use a reference book such as Eichholtz's** *Ancestry's Red Book* **or Everton's** *The Handy Book for Genealogists,* **or visit the Family History Library Web site** at <www.familysearch.org>, to determine the availability of land and probate records for the county. The records you need may have been destroyed in a fire or other natural disaster or during the war. In this case, you may not find the evidence you need there. However, these reference books will tell you the name of the county from which your county was created (the parent county) and when your county was formed. The formation date of your county may mean that key records may be available in the parent county.

Sources

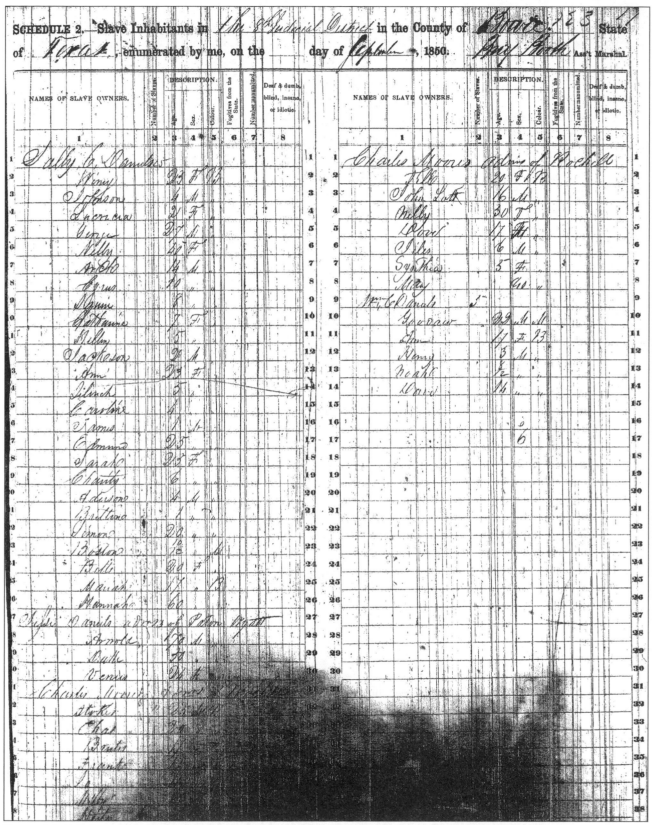

Figure 6-3 U.S. Census of 1850, Slave Schedule, roll 917, Bowie County, Texas, p. 17, showing slaves by name.

Location, Location, Location

Research Tip

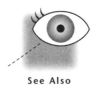

See Also

See Appendix A, on page 201, Free and Slaveholding States and Territories in 1861.

As chapter six emphasized, not all freed slaves took the name of the most recent slaveholder or, for that matter, any former slaveholder. If your search for a slaveholding family based on the same surname failed, not all is lost. **You may still identify the slaveholder by looking in and around your ancestor's 1870 neighborhood.**

For a variety of reasons, many newly freed slaves remained in or near their pre–Civil War homes. Established family ties, limited resources and opportunity, and the challenge of making the transition from slavery to freedom not only limited their movement but left many unsure of what to do next. Many of those who moved away often did so to reunite with family from whom they had been separated by force. Finding or reuniting with family was the reason most freedmen gave when requesting travel assistance from the Freedmen's Bureau.

From 1790 to 1900, about 90 percent of the African-American population lived in the South. The black population remained primarily rural after the war and until the Great Migration in the early twentieth century. After the war, the South was an economic wasteland where former slaves and slaveholders alike faced desperate conditions. More out of mutual need than any strong sense of allegiance, many former slaves and slaveholders remained near each other. If your ancestors lived in a rural Southern community in 1870 and were not landowners, it is possible they were living on land owned by a former slaveholder or in the same neighborhood as a former slaveholder. This chapter will help guide your search through the neighborhood and identify those factors you should consider to determine which white families may have been your ancestors' slaveholders.

1870 FAMILIES IN THE NORTH AND WEST

First, did any of your ancestors live in northern states or western states and territories in 1870? If so, pay close attention to the birthplaces reported in their census

118

entries. If birthplaces indicate the family was in free states or territories before 1865, your study will have a different strategy. You will need to review chapter five, look for your ancestors in the 1860 census, and plan your strategy accordingly.

If your family was in the north or west in 1870, were any individuals born in slaveholding states before 1865? If so, the family probably migrated north during or after the war. Thus, your pre-1865 research will probably take place in the South, according to the strategies outlined in chapters six through nine.

The challenge is identifying the county or area where the family resided within the southern state. One or more of the following suggestions may help you narrow the search for a location in which to focus your next research:

Technique

1. Check the 1860 census index of the southern state for (a) your family in case they were free or (b) white families of the same surname, especially if the name is found in only a few counties in 1860.

2. Look for other black families near yours in 1870 with similar birthplace or migration patterns. Try suggestion number one for them. They are part of your family's cluster of neighbors in 1870; thus, they may have been relatives or pre-1865 neighbors.

3. Try to find black families of your family's surname in the 1870 census in the southern state. Especially if the surname is not a common one, these black families could have been your family's relatives or pre-1865 neighbors.

4. Gather everything you can on all the members of your 1870 family. Look for death certificates, marriage records, newspaper obituaries, funeral programs, church and military records, and others to try to find the pre-1865 county or district name mentioned. (Review chapters three and four for ideas on additional sources to try.)

5. Consult indexes to other pre-1865 records in the southern state, including the 1850 and earlier censuses and indexes to wills, to look for your family's surname. A number of statewide indexes exist for such records. In some states, the 1867 voter registration records have been compiled and may point you to a location where people by your family's surname lived. This strategy could also include querying surname forums online to see if someone else is researching the same surname in the same southern state.

6. Let the search rest while you work on a different family. Sometimes new materials and indexes become available, and new records become available online. Besides, in working on another family, you may learn more about the "resting" family.

7. As a last resort, you could make an alphabetical or regional list of counties in the southern state and begin working your way through county records looking for slave families with the given names in your family. This process is very time-consuming and may be counterproductive. The choice is yours.

Remember, the focus of these suggestions is to identify a pre-1865 residence of your family in order to search for a slaveholder family. You could actually find the slaveholder family and your slave ancestors while looking for the location. Every family was different, and every search will be somewhat unique. In the end, in all black and white families, each lineage comes to a halt before genealo-

Reminder

gists want it to end. Thus, you may not be able to trace an 1870 family further, especially if the pre-1865 county records burned, if the family changed its surname after 1865, if the family chose a surname that had no connection to pre-1865 relatives, or if the surname was a very common one, such as Jones, Smith, Davis, Clark, or others.

1870 FAMILIES IN THE SOUTH

If similarity of surname does not produce likely slaveholder candidates, examine your ancestors' neighborhood as shown in the 1870 census. Many census pages show the township, town, district, or nearest post office at the top of the page. Usually, residents enumerated with the same page heading lived in the same general area. Thus, as you read the 1870 census, list white families living in the neighborhood for five or more pages on either side of your ancestors, especially within the same district. Note the value of the real estate these white families owned. If they owned no real estate in 1870, it is possible they did not own land before the war and thus are less likely to have had slaves.

Look for other clues to connect your family to a former slaveholder.

Idea Generator

- If your adult ancestors were middle-aged or elderly and were born in another state, look for white neighbors who were born in that state.
- Look at the migration pattern of your family as shown in the birthplaces reported in the 1870 census for individuals in your family. If different birthplaces were reported for different family members, make a timeline showing where the family was when each person was born. Does a neighboring white family mirror that migration pattern?

If your ancestors lived in a southern town or city in 1870, they also may have been there before the war. In this case, begin with the same process described above and realize that urban slaveholders generally had only a few slaves. Some of these remained in the white households as domestic servants after the war, as did some in rural areas.

1860 CENSUS SCHEDULES

Using your list of possible slaveholder candidates from the 1870 census, look for those heads of household in the 1860 slave schedule. Look also at the names of several neighboring slaveholders on either side of a possible slaveholder candidate in the slave schedule. Since only the slaveholding population is listed in these schedules, you get a fairly detailed view of the slave community as it may have existed before the Civil War. If your ancestors and their family members were not with the suspected candidate(s), they may have been held by a neighboring slaveholder.

Tip

Tip: In reading the slave schedules, pay close attention to the township or district name at the top of each page and to page numbers. When the pages were assembled either for binding or for microfilming, many of them were re-arranged, not in numerical order. Thus, identifying neighbors requires cautious reading. It may be easier to photocopy the pertinent pages as you find them and reassemble them in numerical order to get a better idea of the neighborhood. The process may require close comparison of the 1860 free and slave schedules.

In reading the 1860 slave schedules, record the number of slave houses each slaveholder reported in column nine. Many of the houses where your ancestors lived in 1870 were probably there in 1860.

Look at the 1860 free population census to determine what the community looked like prior to the war. If your search reveals that much of the free population in 1870 was there in 1860, the community may not have changed significantly after the war.

The 1850 and 1860 free schedules asked questions similar to the 1870 census, and none showed the relationship of household members to the head of the household—wife, son, daughter, etc. These three censuses requested such information as

- the name, age, sex, color, birthplace, and occupation of each free person in each free household
- the value of real estate the head of household, or other individual, owned
- the value of personal estate the head of household, or other individual, owned in 1860 and 1870
- which couples married within the census year
- which young people attended school within the census year
- which persons could not read and write

USING LAND RECORDS

Another approach in looking for a former slaveholder is to use records that identify or describe land ownership. Land plat books, land tax records, and county deed records denote land ownership and help identify neighborhoods. These records may help you determine where your ancestors lived before the war based on who owned the land they lived on in 1870.

In federal land states, where land is identified by township, range, and section, farms can be precisely located on a county map. Pre-war slaveholding states and territories that were also federal land states were Alabama, Arkansas, Florida, Louisiana, Mississippi, and Missouri. If your ancestors lived in these states, it is generally easy to plot their neighborhoods on a map or grid. Federal tract books, plat books, and county land records may help identify the white families in the ancestral neighborhood before the war.

Legal descriptions of land are not as precise in the state land states using metes and bounds land descriptions. The slaveholding states that were also state land states were Georgia, Kentucky, Maryland, North Carolina, South Carolina, Tennessee, Texas, and Virginia/West Virginia. Although more difficult to pinpoint on a map, the descriptions you find in plat books or in deed records might be helpful when combined with census records and slave schedules.

If land tax records, plat books, or county deed records are available, look at them for landowners near your family in the 1870 census. These records may be in the county courthouse or state archives. They may be available on microfilm at a public or academic library or available for rent from the Family History Library.

Research Tip

MISCELLANEOUS RECORDS

A number of other records in courthouses and archives may help identify the slaveholder. Three unrelated types of sources that may provide clues are slave manifests, marriage records shortly after the Civil War, and slave narratives.

Slave Manifests

Settlement spread rather rapidly to the southwest after 1800 into former Indian lands in western Georgia, Alabama, Mississippi, and Arkansas, into the Louisiana Purchase, and by the 1820s into Texas. Many planters moved their operations from the worn-out soil on the east coast to the rich and fertile ground in the newly opened areas. Some moved their slaves overland; others sent them by ship to gulf ports.

In the new territories, the demand for labor grew, especially after the importation of slaves from abroad was banned in 1808. Eastern slaveholders, especially in Maryland, Virginia, and North Carolina, sold slaves to traders, who in turn sold them in the growing cotton country along the Mississippi River and Gulf coast. Most of these laborers journeyed by ship.

The ships' masters were required to make a list, or manifest, of their slave passengers to turn in to the Collector of Customs when the ships reached their destinations. Surviving records are now in the National Archives. These slave manifests for New Orleans have been microfilmed, for enslaved passengers coming in and going out of that port. Many slaves "inward bound" into New Orleans were coming from Baltimore, Richmond, Petersburg, Mobile, Savannah, Charleston, and ports in Florida. The manifests named the ship and its master, the slave owner or trader, the ports of departure and arrival, and, sometimes, the slaves.

The lists that named individuals frequently reported only a given name, but a number of records from Virginia and Maryland included surnames. The manifest also reported each individual's gender, age, height, and "color." One ship, the brig *John A. Lancaster*, for example, left Richmond for New Orleans about 27 December 1849 with a number of slave passengers. Two on the list of owner or consignee John Hagan of New Orleans were Cornelius Brown—age nineteen, five feet eight inches tall, and of black complexion—and Ann Madison—age sixteen, five feet three and one-half inches tall, also of black complexion.[1]

This is very little information with which to confirm the discovery of an ancestor. The genealogist cannot know who assigned and reported the surnames, whether the slaves ever considered those names as their own, and whether they used those names thereafter. It may be possible if you have very strong clues that a plantation owner moved his operation to Louisiana or Mississippi, for example, at a particular time. If you had developed a list of names for an ancestor's cluster of fellow slaves and your research suggested Virginia or another eastern birthplace for them, you could read the manifests, looking for the group of names and other clues. However, the process is very time-consuming and requires great caution before you conclude that you have found your ancestor.

Dedicated volunteers are creating an index to the ships, the owners' or shippers' names, and the slaves with surnames for the Web site <www.afrigeneas.com>. At this writing, several of the sixty-three rolls of microfilm have been abstracted for the database.

Marriage Records

Continuing an older practice, some Southern states after the Civil War still required grooms to sign a bond before they could marry. In most of the bonds, the grooms affirmed that they knew of no legal reason that would prevent the marriage from taking place—neither bride nor groom was already married to someone else and neither was below the minimum age. A relative or friend often acted as surety on the bond. In the first years after the Civil War, it is at least possible that a surety, or bondsman, was the former slaveholder of the bride or groom.

For example, the 1880 census listed Thornton and Lizzie Alexander in Fayette County, Tennessee, along with a son, John (age ten), and Thornton's stepdaughter (thus, possibly Lizzie's daughter), Addie (age fifteen). Thornton was reportedly forty-five years old and a black native of Georgia; Lizzie was fifty and a mulatto native of Tennessee.[2] The 1870 census showed Thornton, age forty-four [*sic*, not thirty-four], living there alone.[3] Where was Lizzie?

The marriage record for Thornton and Lizzie was located in neighboring Hardeman County, where Thornton married Lizzie Blaylock on 12 April 1868, having completed his marriage bond the previous day. The other bondsman was Jessee [*sic*] Blalock.[4]

The 1870 census, supported by other censuses, revealed that J[esse] Blaylock was a white farmer with a sizable family.[5] His household in 1870 included, among others, a female named only as L. Alexander (age thirty-seven, born in Tennessee, reported as white) and a one-year-old black boy, J. Alexander. These two appear to be Lizzie and her son John, from the 1880 census. Besides the white nuclear family and L. and J. Alexander, seven other young people were in the household. Two young girls, reportedly white but probably not, were M. and A. Blaylock, ages nine and five, respectively. Could five-year-old A. Blaylock be the fifteen-year-old Addie Alexander of the 1880 census? Could Lizzie be the mother of others in the household?

The 1860 slave schedule for Hardeman County showed Jesse Blaylock with three male slaves—ages thirty-five, thirty-three, and ten—and five female slaves—ages twenty-eight, twenty-six, eight, seven, and one.[6] Lizzie could have been one of the adult women. In 1850, Blalock reported five slaves—young men of twenty-four and twenty-two years (apparently the same two who were there in 1860), a five-year-old boy (the one reported as ten in 1860?), and two females, age twenty-one and seventeen.[7] The younger female matched Lizzie's age of thirty-seven in the 1870 census; she was mulatto, as Lizzie was reported in 1880. Even in 1840, the Blalock household reported, in addition to four male slaves, two females—one under ten (as Lizzie would have been) and one between ten and twenty-four.[8]

These records alone do not confirm that Jesse Blalock had been Lizzie's slaveholder but offer strong evidence for the possibility. Lizzie's researcher must also study one other woman in the marriage records whose name before mar-

Case Study

Notes

Spelling of names often varies from record to record; they are reported here as each record reported them.

riage was Blaylock, other records of Jesse Blalock, and a Blalock family living in neighboring Fayette County in 1860. Nevertheless, the name of the bondsman on the marriage record became the first clue for this avenue of study.

Slave Narratives

Oral History

One writer suggests that about six thousand autobiographical narratives of former African-American slaves have been published.[9] In library catalogs, these may be found under such subject headings as Afro-American, African-American, and Slave and often under the subheading "biography." **Probably the largest collection is the forty-one volumes of over two thousand published interviews conducted in the 1930s by the Writers Project of the Works Progress Administration (WPA).** This set, *The American Slave*, is available in many academic and large public libraries. These interviews are also available on microfilm in libraries and on CD-ROM from Ancestry.com or Ancestry at (800) 262-3787.

At least three indexes have been compiled:

- Potts, Howard E. *A Comprehensive Name Index for The American Slave*. Westport, Conn.: Greenwood Press, 1997.
- Terry, Brenda. *Slaves II: A Deeper Look into the WPA Slave Narrative*. Dallas, Tex.: OneBorn, 1998. Includes abstracts of narratives, but does not cover all volumes.
- <http://memory.loc.gov/ammem/snhtml/snhome.html> on the Library of Congress Web site. The texts of the narratives are also available on the site.

The interviewees were elderly African Americans who lived in twenty-five states and the District of Columbia in the 1930s. These states were not necessarily their homes before the Civil War or even before 1920, but the narratives were conducted and published by state. Thus, the account of a person interviewed in Ohio about life as a slave in Tennessee will be in the volume that includes Ohio narratives.

The former slaves answered questions about many aspects of their pre-war and post-war lives, including family history. Some gave the names of slaveholders; many named their parents, siblings, and even grandparents. As you can imagine, this information is valuable for family history. The following are genealogical abstracts of two 1937 interviews.

1. Charles H. Anderson was interviewed at age ninety-one at his home in Cincinnati, Ohio, where he had lived for fifty-three years.[10] He was born 23 December 1845 in Richmond, Virginia, a slave of J.L. Woodson, a grocer and a good man. With his parents and thirteen brothers and sisters, Anderson spent his childhood at the Woodson home. He enlisted in the army in April 1865 and served in Texas; in 1937, he was receiving a monthly pension of six dollars. He married Helen (Cruitt) Comer, a widow with four children, fifty-three years before (about 1884). They had two sons: Charles (forty-seven) and Samuel (forty-three), both bachelors in 1937. His wife died about 1927, but his two sons and a stepdaughter were living with him.

   Anderson apparently had no grandchildren, but he had siblings and stepchildren, some of whom undoubtedly had children. Although he named only his wife and sons, his interview would be of interest to descendants of the other family members, as well as descendants of the Woodsons.

2. When Mrs. Hannah Davidson was interviewed in 1937 in Toledo, Ohio, she related a very different childhood experience and a life of hard work.[11] She was born in Ballard County, Kentucky, in 1852, on the plantation of Emmett and Susan Meriwether. Her parents were Isaac and Nancy Meriwether; her brothers were Major and George Meriwether; and she had sisters Adeline, Dorah, Alice, and Lizzie. She related that the master kept her and her sister Mary, perhaps one of the four sisters listed above, for years after they were supposed to be free and did not pay them a penny. She married William L. Davidson when she was thirty-two years old and apparently had children, though she did not name them. Her one living granddaughter was Willa May Reynolds, who had taught school in Grove, Tennessee, before she married.

Mrs. Davidson told some of the same things twice, but with slightly different facts. However, she and Charles Anderson and the other twenty-three hundred interviewees made an important contribution to U.S. oral history and genealogy.

ON LOCATION
A Study of Thomas Bowen

Case Study

This case study applies the strategies discussed in this chapter: using clues in the ancestor's 1870 location to try to determine the identity of the slaveholder. Although the identity of the slaveholder of Thomas Bowen of the Brandy Wine District of Claiborne County, Mississippi, is not confirmed, two primary candidates have been identified.

The 1870 census listed Thomas Bowen as fifty years old and born in Virginia. He arrived in Mississippi no later than 1858, since the oldest child in his household, twelve years old in 1870, was born in Mississippi.[12] Ned Bowen, age forty-four and born in North Carolina, lived one household away. Since the oldest child in Ned's home in 1870 was fourteen and born in Mississippi, Ned and his family were probably in Mississippi by about 1856.

It is possible that Thomas and Ned were brothers, but a relationship has not been confirmed. No other evidence of a cluster was evident in the 1870 schedule. Post–Civil War research and family history added no further clues. A same-surname search was also unsuccessful in identifying relatives or a slaveholder. Studying the location or nearness of residence was the only hope of making a connection to a slaveholder.

Strategy 1: Study the 1870 Community

Step By Step

The 1870 census suggested two, maybe three, possible slaveholder candidates:[13]
- C.H. Barland, age 60, closest to Bowen, household 337, real estate valued at $5,000
- Evan S. Jefferies Jr., listed as a head of household for the first time, household 331, real estate valued at $2,500
- Evan S. Jefferies Sr., age 57, household 313, real estate valued at $21,750

Why record the number of slave houses? If, in 1870, your family was listed only three houses from a white family who, in 1860, owned a hundred slaves and had fifteen slave houses, your family may have been living in one of the slave houses that was there before the war. The process would be easier with names, but genealogists work with what is available.

Strategy 2: Check the Slave Schedules

The 1860 slave schedule revealed more information about the candidates:[14]

- C.H. Barland with 25 slaves and 6 slave houses
- E.S. Jefferies, Homeplace, next to Barland in the schedule, with 100 slaves, number of slave houses not reported
- E.S. Jefferies, Greenwood, next to the Jefferies Homeplace in the schedule, with 102 slaves, number of slave houses not reported

The age ranges of both Thomas Bowen's and Ned Bowen's families made C.H. Barland a possible match but suggested either of the E.S. Jefferies' plantations as a more likely match. Although it is possible that Thomas Bowen and his wife could have lived on adjoining plantations, they may have been on the same plantation, as their reported ages coincide with some of the Jefferies slaves.

In the 1850 slave schedule, E.S. Jefferies reported 100 slaves, but C.H. Barland did not appear in the schedule.[15] Between 1850 and 1860, E.S. Jefferies added a plantation and over 100 slaves to his holdings. It is possible that Thomas and Ned Bowen were among the additional slaves Jefferies acquired. Since both Bowens were over thirty years of age when they started their families in the 1850s, they may have arrived in Mississippi after 1850.

Strategy 3: Study the White Community in 1850 and 1860

The 1860 census enumerated both E.S. Jefferies Sr. and C.H. Barland.[16] Although Jefferies was in the county in 1850, C.H. Barland was not.[17]

The white community remained much the same from 1860 to 1870. Although other Barlands were in the area, C.H. Barland was not enumerated in their households. Since Barland did not appear in either the 1850 census or slave schedule, he may have arrived in Claiborne County after 1850. It is possible that he brought Thomas and Ned Bowen with him.

Strategy 4: Check the 1866 State Census

In most former slave states, a post–Civil War census was conducted in 1866. This census was authorized and, in many instances, conducted by federal agents. Most of these censuses did not survive. The census for Claiborne County did survive but, unfortunately, named only a few former slaves. Instead, it listed mostly landowners or white families and the number of freedmen (listed only by age and sex) living on their property or for whom they were responsible.

Five freedmen were reported with Barland, probably the five listed as laborers or servants in his household in 1870. Although E.S. Jefferies Sr. was not listed, E.S. Jefferies Jr. was listed with forty-four freedmen; William T. Jefferies, another son of the senior Jefferies, reported thirty-seven freedmen. The E.S. Jefferies Plantation reported sixty-nine freedmen.[18]

This census provides further evidence that Jefferies may well have been the Bowens' slaveholder. The fourteen white families listed between E.S. Jefferies Jr. and the Jefferies Plantation included Barland and William T. Jefferies. Of the remainder, only two other families were enumerated with two freedmen each; the others reported none. Thus, only the Jefferies properties showed

If you are researching in Alabama, note that the Alabama Department of Archives and History holds the 1866 census for most of its counties; the microfilm is available from the Family History Library.

enough freedmen to accommodate the Thomas Bowen family—both parents and three children.

Strategy 5: Consider Land Ownership in 1866

The land tax roll for 1866 listed the landowners and a description of the property each owned in that year.[19] Since Mississippi is a federal land state, the land in Claiborne County can be plotted on a grid to show the 1866 neighborhood (see Figure 7-1 below). Such a map could help determine the property where Thomas Bowen lived in 1870. Likewise, if Bowen was in about the same location before the war, the map could help determine where he lived before the war and who the slaveholder may have been.

In this case, the 1866 tax roll provided land descriptions. In other locations, the source of land descriptions could be plat books, federal tract books, or county deed records. For this particular investigation, the closer the records are to 1865, the better.

The nearest landowner to Thomas Bowen in the 1870 census was C.H. Barland, who owned land in sections three and four of Township 10, Range 4 East, as shown in Figure 7-1, below. Thus, the grid provides a visual representation of the landowners on whose land Thomas Bowen may have lived in 1866. Notice that C.H. Barland's land adjoined the E.S. Jefferies property.

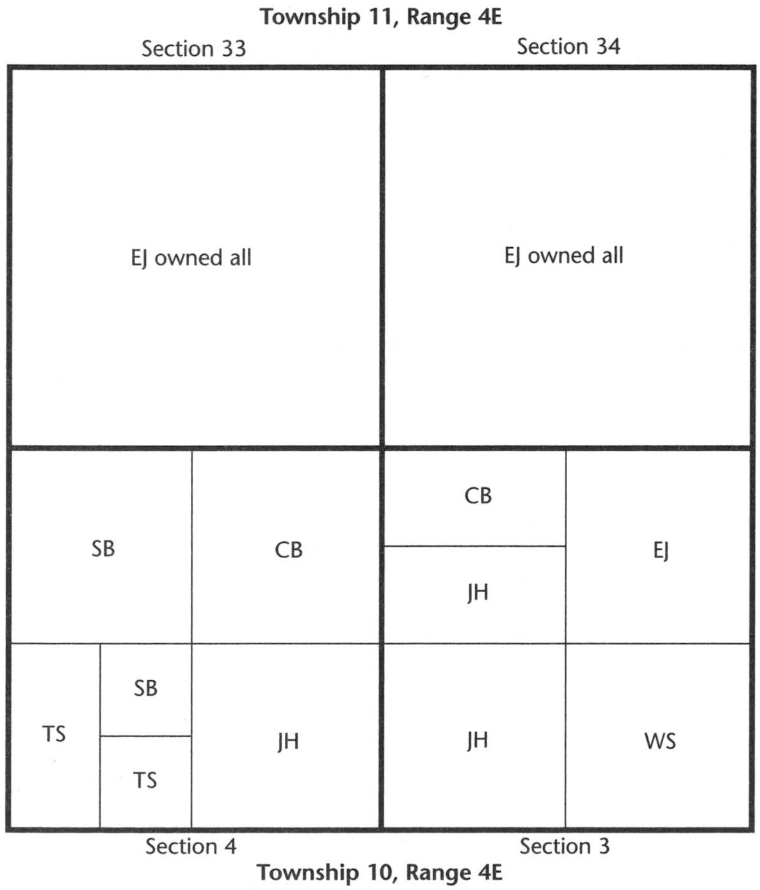

Township 11, Range 4E

Section 33 · Section 34

Section 4 · Section 3

Township 10, Range 4E

Figure 7-1 Thomas Bowen's neighborhood as developed from the land tax roll, 1866, Claiborne County, Mississippi, Chancery Clerk's Office, Courthouse, Port Gibson. The two largest squares each represent one section or 640 acres, which cover one square mile of land. The quarter-section squares represent 160 acres, such as Barland's northeast quarter of Section 4, Township 10. Range 4 East.

Key:

CB = C.H. Barland

EJ = E.S. Jefferies Sr.

JH = John Heath

SB = Sarah Buck

WS = William L.J. Shannon

TS = T.G. Spindle

Given Bowen's location in the 1870 census, it is highly possible that Bowen would have lived on land owned by Barland or Jefferies in 1866. If Bowen did not move before 1870, he could have been on the same land before the war. Although it is not certain that either Barland or Jefferies was the slaveholder, the combined circumstantial evidence suggests they are the primary candidates, worthy of further investigation.

The resources used in steps one through three are widely available to researchers—the free and slave census schedules for 1850 and 1860 and the population schedules for 1870. The sources used for steps four and five are available for Mississippi but not necessarily for the other former slave states. **The key is to look for whatever materials do exist for your ancestral county and state to help you develop a picture of the neighborhood as it existed in 1870 and perhaps before the war.**

Reminder

EIGHT

The Other Family

W hile the objective of your research is looking for slaves, the next focus is learning more information about each slaveholder candidate once you have narrowed the list of possibilities. Chapters six and seven focused on confirming that each candidate was a slaveholder and that your ancestors may have been among the slaves of specific candidates, especially in 1860. **Next, it is necessary to learn about each candidate's family and that family's history as slaveholders.** Your planning and research will depend on the public records available for the location.

STUDYING THE SLAVEHOLDER CANDIDATE

From census and tax records, you may have learned the number of slaves a particular candidate held in 1850 and 1860 and their ages. You may also have estimated how long your ancestors were a family based on the ages of the children in the household in 1870.

Census returns and existing tax records may provide information for a time-line showing where and how long each family held slaves. Creating this timeline provides insight into several pertinent questions:

1. When or how the slaveholder may have first acquired slaves. For example, a twenty-year-old man's first appearance in census records with slaves would suggest that the slaves may have been a gift or an inheritance from family or a wife's family.
2. When the slaveholder first appeared as a head of household.
3. When a slaveholder arrived in or left an area.
4. Whether an increase in the number of slaves reported may have resulted from an event other than births.

Censuses

Study each slaveholder candidate in federal census records, as well as any state or territorial censuses that exist. How far back your search extends will depend

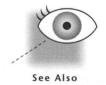

Step By Step

See Also

See the table on page 115, for information on how each census reported slaves.

on the age and birthplace of the slaveholder candidate. For example, a fifty-year-old man in 1870 (born in 1820) would not likely appear as a head of household until after 1840.

Before 1850, federal census records named only free heads of household. Family and other household members were grouped according to gender and age, although the age brackets were not the same in every census. Slaves were reported along with white and free black persons between 1790 and 1840. Only the 1850 and 1860 censuses had separate slave schedules.

Check the mortality schedules that accompany the 1850 and 1860 censuses. If slaveholders reported deaths within their own families and among their slaves, the names of the deceased should appear together on that schedule. Slaves usually were not reported with a surname, but the name of a white deceased person above or below a slave's name could be a clue to the slaveholding family. Also, the family number given on the mortality schedule was supposed to match the family number in the free schedule. Sometimes errors occurred, but checking the free schedule for the reporting family number may provide a clue to the identity of the slaveholder.

Carefully review the slaveholder candidate's neighborhood in the censuses. The composition of the neighborhood could be as important to this phase of your research as it was when searching the post–Civil War neighborhoods of your ancestors. The technique of cluster genealogy applies here; ask yourself questions such as these:

- What was the makeup of the candidate's household?
- Who were the neighbors?
- Were the same or similar surnames shown in nearby households?
- Did the neighbors remain the same from census to census?
- Does it appear that the candidate family moved at some time?

Research Tip

A piece of information discovered at this stage could fill a gap or confirm a hunch and thereby extend your search. **The more you know about the candidate family, the more likely you are to find your ancestors or at least limit their whereabouts to a specific area or neighborhood.** If they were not where you suspected they were, they may have been as close as the neighboring farm or plantation.

Tax Records

When they exist, tax records can help fill the gaps between censuses and help determine

- when slaveholder candidates held slaves
- whether the number and ages of slaves suggest that your family may have been present in a particular household
- whether a particular slaveholder candidate is worthy of further research as you search for your family

Since, by law, slaves were taxable property, they were reported annually on the slaveholders' tax record. Taxes were usually authorized by the state legislature but collected at the county level, often by militia district or other division. Thus, neighbors were often reported in the same district on the tax rolls.

Usually, only slaves of a certain age range were taxed, and taxable age varied from time to time and state to state. Sometimes, only a total number was reported; at other times, slaves were reported in age groups, such as under sixteen and over sixteen. When the tax form had only one column for taxable "polls," or individuals, the number included slaves and any men of taxable age in the white household. Taxable age for the white men varied: sixteen, eighteen, or twenty-one. Thus, a total number of polls given for a household did not always specify how many were slaves and how many were members of the white family.

You may find that the numbers of slaves reported in these tax records do not coincide with census numbers. Why?

- Each state legislature determined the age at which slaves would be taxed. In Mississippi, for example, only slaves over five and under sixty were taxable.
- Just as some taxpayers today under-report their income or property, taxpayers of earlier eras sometimes misrepresented the number of slaves they held in order to reduce their tax liability.

Which states have pre–Civil War tax records? Check in any state where your ancestors may have lived as slaves, even where slavery was abolished before 1865. A number of states or colonies had eighteenth-century tax lists, but at first, you need to be concerned about the nineteenth century. Some states, such as Georgia, Kentucky, Mississippi, Texas, and Virginia, have many surviving tax records; others, such as Louisiana, have relatively few. (Appendix A, on pages 201–207, shows the areas which still held slaves in 1861.) To locate tax records, check the following:

- the Family History Library (FHL) catalog to learn whether county tax rolls have been microfilmed so that you can rent the film through a Family History Center.
- the state archives, to learn which tax rolls they have and which are on microfilm. (See Appendix C, pages 211–217, for information on state archives.)
- genealogical journals for the county or state, as some individual county lists have been published. See the discussion of PERSI on page 133 later in this chapter.
- the tax assessment office or county clerk's office at the county or parish courthouse.
- the National Archives Record Group 351 and microfilm publication M605, *Records of the City of Georgetown (D.C.), 1800–1879*, for the District of Columbia.

Sources

THE OTHER FAMILY: A FAMILY PROFILE

Knowledge of the slaveholder's family is essential if you expect to conduct a successful search for your ancestors during the pre–Civil War years. Locating your ancestors could depend on how much you know about the slaveholder's family history. In addition, identifying earlier generations of the slaveholding family could lead to the identity of earlier generations of your ancestors. Some slaves remained

Important

in the same white family over several generations. In many families, the sale of slaves was considered a last resort and was usually the result of financial problems.

The need to research the slaveholder's family history makes your search different from that of other ethnic groups. Although unique, this research method can be mastered and should not discourage descendants of slaves from pursuing the history of their slave ancestors.

Internet Sources

Unfortunately, many beginning genealogists feel that they need look no further than the Internet for answers to their genealogy questions. Without a doubt, the Internet has become a valuable resource for disseminating information and bringing together those with common research objectives. However, you should judge the reliability of the information you find there according to the source and the setting in which it appears. In other words, the information is only as reliable as the person or organization placing it there and the quality of their research. Sites that provide documentation for their sources will probably be more reliable. Although increasing in number all the time, relatively few good sites and resources exist at this time to assist African-American researchers. It is likely that most of the information available online at this time comes from post–Civil War records.

Nevertheless, a quick and easy way to start your search for information on slaveholder candidates is on the Internet. Helpful information may appear on genealogy Web sites, message boards, surname lists, family pages, and even county pages. Your objective is to create a pedigree chart for the slaveholder candidate and his wife. Among the helpful Internet sites are these:

- <www.ancestry.com>, the paid subscription site or the message boards at <http://boards.ancestry.com>
- <www.genealogy.com>; surname forums that allow those researching the same surname to exchange information, at <http://genforum.genealogy.com>
- <www.usgenweb.org>, especially the state and county Web pages
- <www.rootsweb.com>, through its Rootsweb Surname List <http://rsl.rootsweb.com>
- <www.surnameweb.org>
- <www.familysearch.org>, the Family History Library Web site that allows you to search for published genealogies in their library catalog or search for names in their database
- search engines, such as Yahoo, Hotbot, and Google
- <www.cyndislist.com> with links to many family history sites

Published Family Histories

Information you find in census records, legal documents, or business and personal records may provide the clues you need to identify the slaveholder's parents, siblings, and children as well as his wife's family. However, if you are lucky, much of the legwork may have been done for you. White Americans

Warning

Don't get bogged down in the details of the slave-holding candidate's pedigree chart. Your effort can go hand in hand with a search of records in chapter nine.

Internet Source

have been hard at work researching their families far longer than the African-American population.

Many have compiled and published family histories. In books, in articles, or on Web pages, you may learn about the slaveholding family: names, dates, places, and relationships. You may learn about their personal and business records and where researchers can find and use them. Genealogists must be cautious in accepting as fact every detail published in such works, unless the compiler documents the sources that confirm the information. However, from the published works, you may get enough information to lead you to the original records that contain the proof of slave ancestors.

To learn about the existence of published family histories and where you might find them, use sources and indexes such as these:

Sources

1. Periodical Source Index (PERSI). Available online through the Ancestry .com subscription site, in book form at many research libraries, and on CD-ROM, this index is a product of the Allen County Public Library in Fort Wayne, Indiana. It is not an every-name index but does index names, places, and topics in the titles of articles in numerous journals. If you would like a copy of an article mentioned in PERSI and your local library does not have the periodical, you can request a copy for a small fee from the Allen County library. For ordering information, see <www.acpl.lib.in .us/database/graphics/order_form.html>. Phone: (219) 421-1200.

2. *Virginia Historical Index*, popularly called the Swem Index, after its editor, Earl Gregg Swem (reprint of 1934 original, Magnolia, Mass.: Peter Smith, 1965). Available on CD-ROM and in book form in many research libraries, the index includes hundreds of personal and place names and historical topics in several important Virginia publications up to about 1930.

3. *America: History and Life*, Eric H. Boehm, ed. (Santa Clara, Calif.: American Bibliographic Center, 1964–) is an index to topics, people, and places that are subjects of published articles, books, and dissertations. These volumes are often found in academic and research libraries and now are available in electronic format.

4. *A Bibliography of American County Histories* by P. William Filby (Baltimore: Genealogical Publishing Co., 1985). Many more county histories have been published since this volume was released; county histories often include biographical sketches of the county's nineteenth-century residents.

5. *Genealogies in the Library of Congress: A Bibliography*, 2 vols., with two supplements and *A Complement to Genealogies in the Library of Congress* (1981), Marion J. Kaminkow, ed. (Washington, D.C.: Library of Congress, 1972, 1977, 1987; reprint, Baltimore: Genealogical Publishing Company, 2001).

6. *Guide to Local and Family History at the Newberry Library*, by Peggy Tuck Sinko (Salt Lake City: Ancestry, 1987). The Newberry Library is in Chicago.

7. Articles about prominent or notable Americans published in biographical dictionaries, often found in academic and large public libraries. One finding aid is the *Biography and Genealogy Master Index* (Detroit: Gale Research, 1975–), also available on CD-ROM.

8. Family history collections at major genealogy libraries, such as Clayton Library in Houston, Texas, and Allen County Public Library in Fort Wayne, Indiana.

9. *National Union Catalog Pre-1956 Imprints* (Washington: Library of Congress) in academic and large public libraries. Arranged alphabetically by author, these volumes can help you determine whether a person of a particular surname wrote a book about that family's history.

10. The catalog of the Family History Library in Salt Lake City, on microfiche or CD-ROM at Family History Centers or at <www.familysearch.org>.

11. Public libraries, museums, and state archives and historical societies in the states or counties where the white families lived.

If you find a family history title that sounds promising, request it through interlibrary loan at your local library. Family histories are not always available on interlibrary loan, but you might be lucky. Some of these works are also available on microfilm.

Family Papers

Hidden Treasures

Just as families today save a variety of certificates, clippings, photographs, letters, and memorabilia, **some slaveholding families also preserved letters, diaries, plantation and business records, and other papers that reveal family and personal history.** The following sources are helpful in identifying papers of a slaveholder's family that might also aid in your research:

1. *African American Genealogy: A Bibliography and Guide to Sources*, by Curt Bryan Witcher (Fort Wayne, Ind.: Round Tower Books, 2000).

2. *National Union Catalog of Manuscript Collections* (NUCMC, published by the Library of Congress) and *Index to Personal Names in the National Union Catalog of Manuscript Collections, 1959–1984* (Alexandria, Va.: Chadwyck-Healey, 1988). Additions to NUCMC after 1993 are available in electronic form and online at <http://lcweb.loc.gov/coll/nucmc>. This series identifies family papers and other archival materials held by the reporting libraries and museums. Ask a reference librarian at a public or academic library to show you how to use NUCMC. (See also pages 59–60.)

3. Publications and Web sites of state archives and state historical societies. An example is *A Guide to the Business Records in the Virginia State Library and Archives* (Richmond: Virginia State Library and Archives, 1994).

4. Bibliographies in scholarly books or journal articles on African-American history.

5. University and historical society special collections, especially the extensive collections at Louisiana State University, Tulane University, Duke University, the University of North Carolina, the University of Texas, the Virginia Historical Society, and the University of Virginia.

6. *Records of Ante-Bellum Southern Plantations from the Revolution through the Civil War*, Kenneth M. Stampp, editor (now, Bethesda, Md.: University Publications of America). More than 1,500 rolls of microfilm include materials from the collections of the institutions mentioned in

source number five above. Brief descriptions of the contents of Series A–N are available at <www.lexisnexis.com/academic/2upa/Ash/AnteBellumSo uthernPlantations.htm>. Another UPA microfilm series, *Slavery in Ante-Bellum Southern Industries*, includes materials from Duke University, the Virginia Historical Society, and the University of Virginia. Because these collections are expensive, they would likely be at an academic or large public library. See descriptions of this collection at <www.lexisnexis.com/academic/2upa/Aaas/Ante-BellumSouthernIndustries.htm>.

7. *Records of Ante-Bellum Southern Plantations From Emancipation to the Great Migration*, also by University Publications of America, contains many plantation records after about 1860 and some evidence of post-war renters and sharecroppers. This microfilm collection is found mostly in academic libraries. See the U.P.A. Web site for more information: <www.le xisnexis.com/academic/2upa/Ash/plantMig.htm>.

Microfilm Source

CASE STUDY
Caldonia (Short) Hilson

Case Study

Finding a published genealogy on a slaveholder's family could reveal unexpected surprises about your ancestors. Such was the case for the family of Caldonia Short Hilson. Research on this family was challenging because both counties under investigation had suffered courthouse fires that destroyed most documents that would have named slaves.

In the Beginning: What Was Known?

1. According to the 1900 census, Caldonia was born in December 1864.[1]
2. She married James W. Hilson in Lincoln County, Mississippi, before 1883. A date of marriage could not be confirmed because Lincoln County's marriage records were destroyed in a courthouse fire in 1883.
3. She died before 1910; Mississippi did not register deaths until after 1912.
4. All the children born to Caldonia and James W. Hilson died before 1980.
5. Caldonia had a brother, Robert (Rob) Short, and a sister, Easter (Short) Nelson.

Family members had kept a program from a family reunion of Caldonia's descendants in the mid-1990s. This document noted that Caldonia's father was Bob Short, a Cherokee Indian; it did not mention her mother. Reportedly, Bob Short had been run off his property by "whitecappers" (Ku Klux Klan) after the Civil War, but there was no mention of where he may have gone. To date, Bob Short has not been located or confirmed as Caldonia's father; her mother remains unidentified.

Caldonia Short's Early Years

Five-year-old Caldonia Short was in the household of Perry Cotton and his wife in the 1870 census.[2] The household included

* Perry Cotton, age 46, mulatto, born in Mississippi
* Ferma [*sic*] Cotton, age 45, black, born in North Carolina

- Caldonia Short, age 5, mulatto, born in Mississippi
- Perry Black, age 15, mulatto, ditto
- Warren Wood, age 12, mulatto, ditto
- Isabell Cotton, age 45, mulatto, ditto
- Via Jones, age 13, black female, born in Louisiana
- H. Miles, age 3, mulatto female, ditto
- James Cotton, age 70, mulatto, born in South Carolina
- Betsy Cotton, 78, black, born in Maryland

At age fifteen, Caldonia was still in the Cotton household in 1880, along with the following:[3]

- Perry Cotton, age 60, born in Mississippi, father born in South Carolina, mother born in Maryland
- Tamer Cotton, age 55, wife, born in North Carolina, as were her parents
- Ruben Wells, age 17, no relationship given, born in Mississippi, as were his parents
- Caldonia Short, age 15, no relationship given, born in Mississippi, as were her parents
- Stephen Wells, age 11, no relationship given, born in Mississippi, as were his parents
- Betsy Cotton, age 96, mother, born in Maryland, as were her parents
- Isabella Cotton, age 52, daughter [probably of Betsy], born in Mississippi, father born in Maryland, mother born in North Carolina
- Harriett Cotton, age 12, daughter [perhaps of Isabella], born in Mississippi, father born in Maryland, mother born in North Carolina [sic]
- Harriett Cotton, Sen[ior], age 66, daughter [of Betsy?], born in Mississippi, father born in South Carolina, mother born in Maryland

The census information had yielded no new clues to Caldonia's parents and had not clarified her relationship, if any, to Perry Cotton's family. Would a search for her brother, Robert Short, and sister, Easter Short, provide additional clues?

Robert Short, in 1880, was an eighteen-year-old single head of household.[4] Easter, at age nineteen, was the wife of Richard Nelson, with three children, the oldest of whom was age four.[5] Based on the ages reported in 1880, Robert and Easter should have been in their parents' household in 1870. However, neither was listed that year in a Short household or household of any other surname in Lincoln or surrounding counties. Furthermore, census reports for Robert and Easter through 1920 yielded no further clues to help identify their parents. Research on these siblings continues.

The Perry Cotton Household in Two Censuses

Though not identifying Caldonia's parents, census records revealed that the Cotton family probably filled the role of her parents. At least from the age of five until her marriage to James W. Hilson, Caldonia was part of the Perry Cotton household. Although they were not her natural parents, they may have been the only parents she knew. For that reason alone, they were worthy of

Notes

Tamer and *Ferma* are other examples of spelling variations of a given name. Spelling is not the critical issue; using the available evidence to identify the correct person is what matters.

investigation. In addition, a closer look at the Cotton family could lead to additional information about Caldonia, her relationship, if any, to the Cottons, the identity of her parents, or clues to where they were or what had happened to her family.

Comparison of the 1870 and 1880 census entries for Perry Cotton's household indicated quite an extended family. In 1880, Perry's entry stated that his parents were born in South Carolina and Maryland. In the 1870 household, James Cotton, age seventy, was reportedly born in South Carolina, and Betsy Cotton, age seventy-eight, in Maryland. Although James was not listed in the 1880 household, Betsy was then named as Perry's mother, who had aged eighteen years between censuses. The two entries together had apparently identified Perry's parents.

Also in the 1870 household was forty-five-year-old Isabell Cotton, who was listed as the fifty-two-year-old Isabella in 1880. She was probably a daughter of Betsy since she was listed after Betsy. This designation suggests she was, therefore, Perry's sister, in spite of the differences in the reported birthplaces of their parents. After all, informants and census takers did make mistakes.

In addition, it is unlikely that the parents of twelve-year-old Harriett Cotton were born in the same states as Isabella Cotton's parents, as reported in 1880. Harriett Cotton may be the same H. Miles, three-year-old female in the 1870 household. In both censuses, she was listed in a way that suggests she may have been Isabella's daughter even though the child's birthplace differs—Louisiana in 1870 and Mississippi in 1880. (Later evidence showed that Harriett was the given name of H. Miles.)

Sixty-six-year-old Harriett Cotton Sen[ior] appeared in the household for the first time in 1880, and she has not been located in 1870. Her parents' birthplaces—South Carolina and Maryland—were the same as the birthplaces of James and Betsy Cotton in the 1870 household. In 1880, this Harriett was reported as a daughter, presumably of Betsy Cotton.

Three of the children in the 1870 household had left the home by 1880: Perry Black, Warren Wood, and Via Jones, possibly Isabell's daughter. Two additions to the household by 1880 were Ruben and Stephen Wells, whose relationship to the head of household was not reported. It is unclear whether Perry Cotton's wife was related to any children in the household. The only information given was that she was born in North Carolina, as were her parents.

None of the Cottons in these two census entries were enumerated in any census after 1880. A follow-up of the other children in the household yielded no further clues of connection to the Cottons or to Caldonia. Furthermore, there were no other African-American Cottons in the area.

The Cotton Family and Other Post–Civil War Records

The Freedmen's Bureau records for the Brookhaven, Mississippi, sub-district office contained a register of complaints. With these complaints was a list of discharges of colored soldiers from the Union Army.[6] The list named Perry Cotton of Company B, 6th U.S. Colored Heavy Artillery. Cotton's service record showed that he enlisted in Natchez in March 1864 and was mustered out of the service there in May 1866.[7]

Important

This case study exemplifies the cluster genealogy approach: studying family members and neighbors for clues in both black and white families.

See Also

For more information on pension records and getting copies, see pages 37–42.

Research Tip

Always check the people swearing affidavits, to determine if they were veterans and filed for pensions, especially if they stated they knew the applicant before the war or since childhood.

Technique

Although such "burned counties" are a fact of research in the South, some have records that survived the fire. Check also for local, state, and federal records as discussed in previous chapters.

This list led to the discovery of an application for a widow's pension by Perry's wife, Tamer Cotton, dated 9 March 1889.[8] The application revealed that Perry Cotton had died on 1 October 1881, apparently before applying for his pension. To confirm that Tamer was Perry's widow, she had attached a copy of their marriage certificate showing her name as Tamer Williams and dated 7 July 1865. Page Tyler, minister of the African Methodist Episcopal (A.M.E.) Church in nearby Natchez, Mississippi, had performed the ceremony. Witnessing Tamer's application was Harriett Miles, the same H. Miles from the Cotton household in 1870.

Tamer reported in her affidavit that neither she nor Perry had children prior to or during their marriage. Fifty-six-year-old Mann (Manuel) Middleton and fifty-seven-year-old Moses Hunter swore affidavits in support of the pension application in 1892. Both were residents of Lincoln County. Mann Middleton stated that he became acquainted with Tamer Cotton in 1850 and had known both Perry and Tamer twelve to fifteen years before the war and before their marriage. Moses Hunter said he was acquainted with Tamer before the war, while she was a maid, had known both before their marriage, and had known Perry since childhood. No final action was taken on the application. Tamer may have died before a decision was made, and she was not enumerated in the 1900 census.

Although the affidavits did not mention Perry or Tamer's slaveholder, they suggested that Mann Middleton and Moses Hunter may have been on the same plantation with Perry and his wife. A search of service and pension records revealed that Moses Hunter was also a Civil War veteran and filed a pension. Since he had known Perry since childhood, it was possible that they were on the same plantation. His pension records may identify a slaveholder who could be Perry Cotton's slaveholder as well.

The Search for the Slaveholder: Cotton Families

While the post–Civil War research continues for clues about the Short and Cotton families, enough information was available to begin research on their pre–Civil War lives. Lincoln County, where the Cottons lived in 1870 and 1880 and which lost records in the 1883 courthouse fire, had been created in 1870 from parts of Franklin, Copiah, Amite, Pike, and Lawrence counties. The censuses suggested that Perry Cotton and his family lived in the section of Lincoln County that was once part of Franklin County. Indeed, Perry was listed in that parent county's 1867 personal tax records.[9] Thus, a search for Perry and his family prior to 1870 would begin there.

However, pre–Civil War research in Franklin County was almost impossible because a courthouse fire in 1877 had destroyed all but a few of the records needed for this stage of the research. It was questionable whether the slaveholder family could be found, given the absence of county records. However, research could turn to census records for white families with the Cotton and Short surnames.

Perry Cotton's nearest neighbor in the 1870 census was P.M. Smith.[10] In his household lived Matilda Cotton, a seventy-year-old white female, born in Georgia. The 1880 census identified her as Smith's mother-in-law and thus mother of his wife, Emiline.[11] In 1860, Matilda was living in the household of another apparent daughter and her husband, John Ruples, in neighboring Lawrence County. Neither the Smith nor Ruples households were listed as slaveholders in the 1850 or 1860 slave schedules.

Neither Matilda nor Emiline, who married after 1850, was found in Mississippi or any neighboring state in the 1850 census, the first to name all members of free households. The identity of Matilda's husband remains a mystery. Although several Cotton slaveholders were named in the Franklin County slave schedules, no connection appeared likely between them and Matilda Cotton. Likewise, no connection could be established or seemed likely with the Cotton families in the surrounding counties of Amite, Lawrence, and Copiah. Thus, it was time to study the Short surname.

The Search for the Slaveholder: Short Families

Other than Caldonia Short, the only person with the surname Short in Lincoln County in 1870 was S.F. Short, a fourteen-year-old white female, living in the home of W. [sic] Calcote, age twenty-six.[12] They lived close enough to the Perry Cotton household to warrant consideration.

In 1860, three households with the surname Short were enumerated in Lincoln County. However, only Thomas R. Short reported slaves in the 1860 slave schedule.[13] This household was worthy of further investigation, not only because they had slaves but because they seemed to reside in the same area as the Perry Cotton family in 1870 and were large landholders.

The 1860 household included the following members, all with the surname Short:

- Thomas R. Short, age 27, born in Mississippi, farmer, $3,300 real estate, $8,300 personal estate
- Matilda, age 19, domestic [meaning "keeping house," likely the wife], born in Mississippi
- Sarah, age 4, born in Mississippi
- Martha, age 2, ditto
- James, age 9/12, ditto
- Demsey, age 45, female, domestic ["keeping house"], born in South Carolina, $320 real estate, $9,000 personal estate
- Willis, age 17, born in Mississippi
- William, age 15, ditto
- Lee, age 13, ditto
- Cade, age 8, ditto

The ages of the children in the census suggested that Thomas and Matilda married about 1855. The census also implied that Demsey was Thomas's mother. The corresponding slave schedule showed Thomas Short with seven slaves and five heirs with forty-one slaves. Neither Thomas nor Demsey was found in the 1870 census.

However, the 1850 census listed T.R. Short, age eighteen, in the D.C. Short household in neighboring Amite County:[14]

- D.C. Short, age 43, white male, born in Tennessee
- Nancy Short, age 37, born in North Carolina

- T.R. Short, age 18, male, born in Amite County
- Sarah E. Short, age 16, born in Amite County
- G.B.P. Short, age 14, male, born in Amite County
- Eliza N.C. Short, age 12, born in Amite County
- J.G.W. Hughes, age 18, male, born in Amite County

This entry made it evident that Thomas's mother was not Demsey Short, as suggested in the 1870 census. Could Demsey have been his mother-in-law? A marriage record confirmed the union of Thomas R. Short and Mahala Calcote in 1855.[15] Mahala was living in the home of her parents in Franklin County in 1850:[16]

- Willis M. Calcote, age 41, born in Mississippi
- Demsey Calcote, age 36, born in South Carolina
- Mahala Calcote, age 9, born in Mississippi
- Willis Calcote, age 7, ditto
- William Calcote, age 5, ditto
- Lee Calcote, age 3, ditto
- Martha Riley, age 19, ditto

Notes

A widow was entitled to one-third of her husband's property, called a widow's *dower*.

Reminder

The "cluster" approach to research and the process of elimination brought the search to this point.

Willis M. Calcote died after 1850. Thomas Short married Mahala Calcote and assumed the role of head of household for the Willis Calcote family. The several years of surviving probate court minutes from Franklin County indicate that Thomas Short served as administrator of Willis Calcote's estate.[17] Thomas R. Short died by 1866, and Mahala Calcote remarried before 1870, according to probate minutes from neighboring Amite County.[18] Thomas Short owned land in Amite County on which Mahala applied for a widow's dower in 1866.[19]

The inventories and appraisals of Franklin County residents did not survive the courthouse fire. Thomas Short's father, D.C. Short, disappeared from the records after 1850, and no record was found for him in Amite or neighboring counties. However, D.C. Short reported nine slaves in the 1850 slave schedule.[20] This entry may account for some of the seven slaves held by Thomas Short in 1860, although the ages did not suggest a match.

Further investigation of the T.R. Short family revealed no significant connection to Caldonia Short or the Perry Cotton family. However, the Willis M. Calcote family seemed to have both the slaves and the land to accommodate a possible connection.

The Search for the Slaveholder: Calcote Families

If the white Calcote and black Cotton families had a connection before the war, it was possible they were still living in close proximity to each other after the war. A search of the 1870 Cotton neighborhood could provide additional clues.

After T.R. Short died, Mahala married William Howard in October 1865.[21] However, no William Howard household or Howard household with a Mahala was found in Franklin or surrounding counties in 1870. Nor was Mahala's mother, Demsey Calcote, found.

In Perry Cotton's 1870 neighborhood was a twenty-six-year-old white male, M. or W. Calcote; in his home lived S.F. Short, a fourteen-year-old white female.[22] The names and ages were clues that this Calcote was probably the same as seven-year-old Willis in the Willis Calcote household in 1850 and seventeen-year-old Willis, apparent son of Demsey, in the Thomas R. Short household in 1860. (See preceding pages 139–140.) Likewise, the fourteen-year-old S.F. Short was probably the four-year-old Sarah Short from the 1860 Thomas R. Short household. The only other member of the Demsey Calcote family enumerated with Thomas R. Short in 1860 who was found in 1870 as a head of household was Lee Calcote.[23]

The proximity of the Calcote and Cotton families in 1870 necessitated a search for them in 1880. The results were positive. Caldonia Short's brother, Robert Short, known from family tradition, was enumerated in 1880 within one household of Lee Calcote.[24] Next to Robert and within three houses of Lee Calcote was Mann (Manuel) Middleton, apparently the same who filed an affidavit in support of Tamer Cotton's pension application. The 1880 census was the first to list Robert Short or Mann Middleton.

The circumstantial evidence connecting the Cotton, Short, and Calcote families was growing. Another clue was the appearance of Robert Short, age sixteen, on a Franklin County list of educable children, made in 1878. Robert was named next to Lee Calcote's children but was identified as white; no head of household was listed.[25]

The Search for the Slaveholder Narrows

The 1877 courthouse fire in Franklin County destroyed any public records that might provide more information on the Perry Cotton household during slavery. If there was a connection between these families, it would have to be established from Calcote personal, family, or business records. A good place to begin was the Internet.

A message posted to the Calcote surname forum on Genealogy.com mentioned a published family history for the Calcote family, including the Mississippi Calcotes.[26] Fortunately, Clayton Library in Houston had the book, which contained an exciting find.

One section was devoted to James Calcote, father of Willis M. Calcote and grandfather of Mahala (Calcote) Short.[27] It shared an excerpt from the diary of Alexandra Kocsis Anderson, granddaughter of James Calcote and first cousin of Mahala Short. Alexandra spoke of James Calcote's arrival in Mississippi from South Carolina and identified the first two slaves he purchased from Mr. Middleton, his father-in-law, as Jim and Betsy Cotton. James Calcote supposedly told Betsy that if she had twenty children, he would free her. According to Alexandra Anderson, Betsy had nineteen children and was freed before Calcote's death in 1838. Reportedly, she gave birth to the twentieth child the year Calcote died and lived to be 109 years old. Alexandra Anderson also stated that Jim and Betsy Cotton's daughter, Mammy Easter, nursed the children of John Calcote, youngest son of James.

The book documented the sale of John's slaves, including Esther (Easter), to his brother James L. Calcote in 1849. Record of the sale had survived the courthouse fire because it was recorded in neighboring Adams County, where James L. Calcote resided. In addition to Esther, the bill of sale mentioned a

Internet Source

Many surname forums are available at <www.genforum.genealogy.com>.

female slave named Isabell. Was this perhaps the same Isabell who was in Perry Cotton's household in 1870 and 1880? (See page 136.) Could Caldonia's sister Easter have been named for this Easter?

Could the Jim and Betsy Cotton in Alexandra Anderson's writings be the same James and Betsy Cotton in Perry Cotton's home in 1870? In the censuses, Betsy aged eighteen years between 1870 and 1880, with reported ages of seventy-eight and ninety-six. These ages suggested she was born between 1784 and 1792. Of the adults in the Cotton household for these two censuses, only Tamer Cotton's age of fifty-five in 1880 was consistent with the reported age of forty-five in 1870. She was likely present when the census was taken or reported information on the family members. It was probable that Jim was older than the seventy years reported in 1870 but younger than Betsy.

A section of the WPA history of Lincoln County highlighted the county's black population. Included was an abstract from the *Brookhaven Times*, a local newspaper—an abstract of an obituary for Betsy Cotton.[28] It reported that Betsy Cotton, known as Betsy Calcote during slavery times, died in Lincoln County near the Franklin County line; she was 110 years old. She had belonged to James Calcote and left survivors in four generations. She was born in Richmond, Virginia, at the close of the Revolutionary War and was brought to Mississippi where she was purchased by James Calcote. She married one of his slaves. James Calcote freed Betsy before his death, sixty years ago. Neither her date of death nor the date of the article was given, and the search for a copy of the original newspaper is still underway, but the article probably appeared between 1894 and 1898. Interestingly, no census before 1870 listed a free person of color named Betsy Cotton (or Jim Cotton). Besides, the Franklin County courthouse fire destroyed any manumission records.

Although not confirmed, it is possible that Jim and Betsy Cotton were Caldonia Short's grandparents or great-grandparents, since a sixty-year-old surviving great-granddaughter was named in the *Brookhaven Times* article. If so, such a relationship could explain her presence in the Cotton home. Could her mother have been one of Betsy's children or grandchildren? With so many siblings, Perry Cotton could have raised some of his nieces or nephews or their offspring.

James Calcote's History During Slavery

The following facts were now known about James Calcote and his wife:[29]
- James Calcote was born in South Carolina, the son of John Calcote and an unidentified mother.
- James migrated with his parents and siblings from Marion County, South Carolina, to Mississippi before 1808.
- He married Martha "Patsy" Middleton on 31 March 1808, in Adams County, Mississippi Territory. Patsy, the daughter of John Willis Middleton and Martha Mote, was born in South Carolina and died in Franklin County, Mississippi, about 1844.
- James and Martha Calcote had these children: Willis, Stephen M. Cade, Delilah, James Lee, William Siguer, Levi Gibson, Mahala Buckles, and John James.
- James died in 1838 in Franklin County, Mississippi.

Notes

Mississippi became a state in 1817.

The census taker recorded James Calcote for the first time as a head of household in 1810 in Franklin County, Mississippi Territory. The following list summarizes James's entries in Mississippi census and tax lists:[30]

1810 Franklin County, territorial census. Slaves reported: 1

1813 Amite County property tax list. Slaves reported: 2

1816 Amite County, territorial census. Slaves reported: 1

1817 Amite County property tax list. Slaves reported: 1

1820 Franklin County, federal census. Slaves reported: 12 (4 males, 8 females)

    Males: 2 slaves under 14 years, 1 slave 14–26 years, 1 slave 26–45 years

    Females: 4 slaves under 14 years, 3 slaves 14–26 years, 1 slave 25–45 years

1830 Franklin County, federal census. Slaves reported: 33 (13 males, 20 females)

    Males: 7 slaves under 10 years, 2 slaves 10–24 years, 2 slaves 24–36 years, 2 slaves 36–55 years.

    Females: 9 slaves under 10 years, 7 slaves 10–24 years, 2 slaves 24–36 years, 2 slaves 36–55 years.

The 1820 census, the first to report slaves in gender and age categories, seems to confirm the story of Jim and Betsy Cotton. The ages of the reported slaves suggest the presence of a family: both parents and their ten children. The increase to thirty-three slaves by 1830 indicates additions to the slave population from sources other than natural increase. By 1830, Jim and Betsy were in the thirty-six to fifty-five age brackets.

By the 1840 census, James Calcote had died, and all his children, except John James and William Siguer Calcote, were enumerated in Franklin County as heads of household with slaves. James's widow and son John James Calcote appeared to be in the household of James L. Calcote. It is likely that each of the Calcote children received some of the Cotton family as part of their share of James Calcote's estate. In 1840, James L. Calcote reported one male slave age fifty-five to one hundred and one female slave of the same age bracket. These two could have been Jim and Betsy Cotton.

The major question arising from this profile is the whereabouts of the Cotton family before 1820. Only in 1813 did James Calcote report two slaves. Perhaps in the previous years, his one slave was Jim Cotton, and Betsy and the children may have been on a neighboring plantation. Calcote could then have purchased of other family members to unite the family. Perhaps Betsy was not purchased from Willis Middleton, who died in 1808, but may have belonged to another member of the Middleton family or a neighbor of James Calcote. These possibilities present new avenues for investigation.

Summary

Although it was a long journey from Caldonia (Short) Hilson to Jim and Betsy Cotton's probable slaveholder, this kind of research is rewarding as you begin to learn about your ancestors, their lives, their neighbors, and their relatives. Even if names are never found for Caldonia's parents, the family in which she grew up surely shaped her life in positive ways. This extended Cotton family was not an unusual one in the years before and after the Civil War. Families often took care of extended family members—siblings, cousins, nieces, nephews, orphans, the elderly, and the infirm. Perry and Tamer Cotton must have

Idea Generator

Successful genealogists remain alert for new clues and ideas for research. Write down these ideas as you think of them.

had big hearts and a strong sense of family, especially if the children for whom they provided a home were related to them. Theirs was not an easy life, and the many mouths to feed and young lives to foster must have required constant and diligent effort.

The Cottons are but an example of ancestors or foster-ancestors all over the country whom genealogists are trying to find. Even when the searching seems endless or fruitless, you can rest assured that your ancestors were real people. Getting as close to them as possible in the available records is worth the effort.

NINE

The Search for Ancestors in Slaveholder Documents

P ublic and private slaveholder records help locate individual slaves in specific households. Public sources include such legal proceedings as deeds, probate documents, and civil court records. Slaveholder business and personal records may also confirm the whereabouts of slave ancestors. Vital records, church records, and newspapers may also reveal the presence of slaves.

THE SLAVE AS CHATTEL PROPERTY

The institution of slavery has existed in many cultures around the world from the earliest times known to man. Some of the earliest recorded references to slavery are found in the Bible. While slavery in any form in any place at any time was and remains unacceptable and morally wrong, the institution varied in its degree and application, depending on when and where it was found.

Whether voluntary or forced, indentured servitude was the first form of slavery in the American colonies, other than a comparatively few efforts to enslave Indians. Indenture afforded many poor Europeans, largely from the British Isles, the opportunity to seek a new life they otherwise would have been unable to attain. While the experience was often fraught with hardship and/or abuse, these servants could hold on to the hope that the experience would end and they could find a better life. Although their lives were restricted in many ways, often including the prohibition of marriage and denial of the right to vote, indentured servants maintained some basic human and legal rights, such as limited property ownership, the right to sue and be sued, and the right to petition a court when personally abused.

Indentured servitude lasted throughout the colonial era and into the nineteenth century, but its numbers diminished as African slavery grew. European slave traders and colonial purchasers considered Africans racially, culturally, and intellectually inferior. Thus, as the institution of slavery developed in the

Notes

colonies, enslaved Africans were denied not only their personal liberty for life and for that of their offspring, but also most other human and legal rights.

Both European indentured servants and African slaves became, by law, the personal property of their purchasers, or chattel property. By definition, chattel property is tangible, moveable personal property, different from real property—real estate or land. However, like land, chattel property could be bought, sold, taxed, mortgaged, and bequeathed in a will.

THE RECORDS

As your research reaches the stage of using slaveholder documents, your search becomes one for an individual's property, and the records and documents that identify that property. What you find in these documents is, by its very nature, dehumanizing and likely to send you on a roller-coaster of emotions that range, at their worst, from anger and frustration to, at their best, a great sense of pride and a renewed sense of self. The key is not to allow the anger and frustration to overwhelm and discourage you. Your objective should be greater than you or your emotions. It should be to recognize and honor those who came before you and to tell their stories.

Most documents that name slaves fit into two classes: legal and public records or business and personal records. Some, such as church records and newspapers, do not fit easily into either category. However, structuring your search according to this breakdown will help you organize and focus your efforts, save time, and eliminate unwarranted frustration.

Legal or public documents, by far the most important, include deed and property records, wills, probate records, guardianship records, manumission records, and civil court records. Because they became part of the public record, they are far easier to locate. The personal or business sources include plantation and business records, Bible records, diaries, letters, and other personal papers. These documents, created and kept by the family, are less likely to have survived and harder to locate.

LEGAL AND PUBLIC DOMAIN RECORDS

Because these records were filed in county courthouses, and many are still found there, knowing when your county was created and the identity of the parent county or counties is essential. If the slaveholder was in the area before your county was created, records may be in the parent county's courthouse. If possible, visit the county courthouse at least once. If a visit is impossible, you may find many of the records on microfilm at a large genealogy library or available for a nominal fee through your local Family History Center. (See page 19.) A number of states have collected early county record books at the state archives; thus, original or microfilm copies may be found there.

For More Info

Two good sources of county creation and parent county information are Eichholz's *Ancestry's Red Book* and Everton's *The Handy Book for Genealogists.*

DEEDS AND PROPERTY RECORDS

Deeds transfer title to or ownership of real (land) or chattel (personal) property. Thus, before 1865, the transfer of title to slaves was sometimes recorded in deed books. Finding ancestors named in a slaveholder's deed means they were likely the subject of a sale, gift, or trust, or were collateral for a mortgage. In some jurisdictions, manumission papers, surety bonds for free persons, and slave bills of sale were also filed with deeds. An example of the latter is an October 1860 record of one A.S. Coleman acknowledging that he had received from Austin Miller $1,450 as full payment for two Negro boys—Burley, age nine, and Willis, age seven.[1]

The frequency of the recordings varies from jurisdiction to jurisdiction. Researchers may be surprised that such documents were not recorded more consistently, considering that the value of a plantation owner's slaves many times exceeded the value of the real estate. In addition to naming your ancestors, these documents could provide information about the slaveholding family that is needed to broaden your search.

Deeds were recorded at the county courthouse. Contact the county courthouse in your ancestral county to determine which office holds deed records and which years the existing deeds cover. For example, if a county suffered a devastating courthouse fire in 1877, they may have no surviving deed records before that date.

Notes

In Louisiana, land records are called conveyances; estate records are called succession records; and counties are called parishes.

Search both the grantor (direct) and grantee (reverse) index for each slaveholder candidate. Start with about 1870 and search back as far as you feel necessary. Since the index is arranged alphabetically, note variant spellings and surnames similar to the ones you are researching, especially if the research name is somewhat unique or is found infrequently in that area. For each entry you find, write down the names of the grantor and grantee, the dates given in the index, and the volume and page number where the deed record may be found. The date given may be the date the deed was written or the date it was filed with the clerk. In some counties, both dates were recorded in the index.

Next, locate and search the records themselves. In addition to the grantor and grantee, note other people named in the document, any relationships that are mentioned, any witnesses, the names of any plantations given, land descriptions, and any references to where the people may have lived prior to residence in the county. **In other words, be alert to any information that could help provide answers to how, from where, or when slaveholders may have acquired their slaves.** If slaves are named in the document, copy their names and compare them to your known ancestors and their neighbors.

Research Tip

Tip: Read each document carefully. Buried in a land transaction may be the names of slaves included in the sale or other valuable information.

Deeds of Trust and Gift

Slaveholders sometimes used slaves as collateral or security, as shown in deeds of trust and mortgages. For example, in May 1842, Thomas Patton of Fayette County, Tennessee, bought a slave woman, Mary, and her child, Sarah Jane, from Jesse Day for $320 and immediately gave them to H.B. Buckley to secure a debt of $198. By the agreement, if Patton was unable to pay the debt by Christmas of 1842, Buckley could sell the mother and child, called Sarah this time, at public auction to satisfy the debt.[2] Apparently, Patton managed to pay the debt and keep the slaves.

The following year, when his son-in-law, John L. Day, was in debt for $110, Patton sold Mary and her child, Jane, to James W. McCaully for five dollars to secure the debt. Day seems to have paid the debt by the Christmas 1843 deadline.[3] Not only did these documents illustrate the use of the slaves as chattel property, but they identified the mother-daughter relationship that is not always easy to confirm. Furthermore, the 1843 deed of trust gave Mary's age as about thirty years and Jane's age as two and one-half years. These details help place Mary's birth at about 1813 and Jane's at about 1840 to early 1841.

Then in January 1845, Patton executed a deed of gift to his daughter Sarah Jane Day, wife of John L. Day. The gift was the Negro woman Mary, about forty years old [*sic*], and her children Penny (age fourteen), Jane (age five), and Leanna (age three), along with a bureau, a clothes press, a folding table, and a bed and bedstead.[4] The document reveals the apparent lack of knowledge on the part of the slaveholder about Mary's actual age since her birth range now appeared to be between 1805 and 1813; Jane's birth date was pushed back to early 1840 or late 1839. Despite these discrepancies, the records provide important information on relationships and ages as well as a slaveholder history for Mary and her family.

Property Taxes

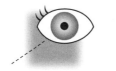

See Also

See pages 130–131, for more on using tax rolls.

Despite their shortcomings and a serious lack of records in some locations, tax records can aid in your search for slaves in a candidate's household. For example, some Virginia tax lists between 1782 and the early 1800s named the slaves who were taxed. For the 1783 tax lists of Cumberland County, Virginia, William Coleman reported, among his thirteen slaves, Charles, Sid, Mary, and Mourning, who were over sixteen years of age, and Dick, Nial, and Randol, under sixteen. Twenty-one years later, in 1804, Charles, Sid, Mary, Mourning, "Mial," and Randolph were still in the household, all over sixteen. After Coleman died in 1811 and his executors reported to the court about the property and business of the estate, they noted that the slave Nial was already with Coleman's son Henry. Figure 9-1, on page 149, shows the 1804 tax roll described here.

In addition, tax records help researchers estimate when a taxpayer died and thus narrow the search for probate records. The records may show a person paying tax year by year, and then the same property appears under "the estate of John Harris, dec'd" or "Samuel Harris, executor of John Harris." The words *estate* and *dec[ease]d* (dec'd) indicate that John had died; *executor* means he left a will, which Samuel Harris was handling and which the researcher needs to read.

ESTATE DOCUMENTS

Estate or probate records were created for large and small slaveholders alike and will likely provide the best chance of finding your ancestors during the years of slavery. The level of research success usually depends on how frequently members of the slaveholding family died. For example, one line of ancestors could be traced continuously from 1802 to 1842 because three generations of the same slavehold-

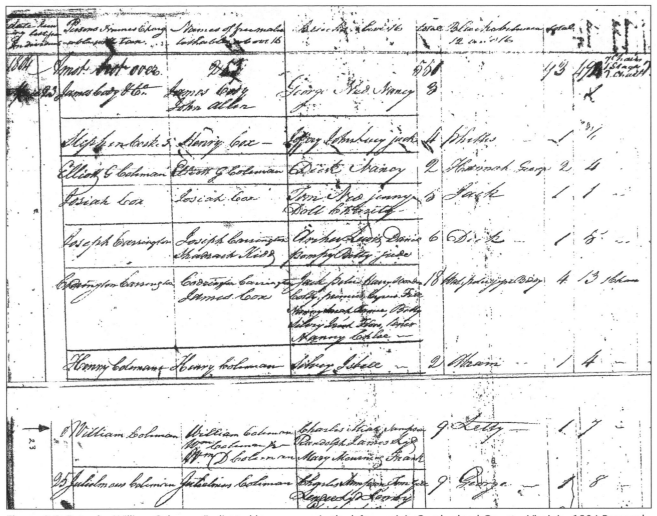

Figure 9-1 Entry for William Coleman (indicated by an arrow in the left margin), Cumberland County, Virginia, 1804 Personal Property Tax List, p. 23, showing slaves' names, Library of Virginia, microfilm.

ing family died within that time, and the family apparently left no other records that named their slaves.

The Probate System

An understanding of the probate system can make your search somewhat easier. When an individual died and left sufficient property, a court proceeding was initiated to pay off any outstanding debts and distribute the property of the deceased. How the property was distributed depended on whether the individual executed a will before death. **An individual with a will was considered to have died *testate*.** In testate cases, the terms of the will determine how the property is distributed. Testate proceedings require less court intervention and supervision because they are guided by the terms of the will.

However, if the individual died without a will, the probate court, through the state's laws of heirship, determined who received the property of the deceased. **This *intestate* (without a will) proceeding required greater court supervision and involvement and, thus, often meant the creation of more documents that can help genealogists.**

\di'fin\ *vb*

Definitions

Important

149

You can distinguish testate from intestate cases by the title of the individual responsible for managing estate business. The executor (male) or executrix (female) was named in the will as the person to handle settlement of estate business. If you find the name of an executor or executrix, you know there was a will. On the other hand, if the person responsible for settling the estate business is called an administrator (male) or administratrix (female), you know there was no will. The court appointed the administrator to oversee the estate.

The existence or lack of a will could significantly impact the amount of information you find on your ancestors. Intestate cases often took longer to probate than those in which there was a will, so the quantity, if not the quality, of the information was sometimes greater. The more information you find, the better chance you have that some of it will relate to your ancestors. The administrator in an intestate proceeding had to seek court authorization or approval for all decisions affecting the estate. The executor, on the other hand, was guided by the terms of the will and did not have to seek court approval. The administrator's records will likely be more thorough and more detailed than that of an executor.

Large estates and those with minor children required a longer time and more records for settlement, especially if the deceased left no will. Intestate cases with minor children often remained under the probate court's supervision until the youngest heir reached the age of adulthood or married. The longer the case was in probate, the better your chances of learning more about your ancestors. The law also prescribed more steps in settling an intestate estate than one with a will. The requirement of more documentation and the added steps in intestate cases make it more likely you will find ancestral information.

Using Probate Records

Once you have determined the office where the records are filed in your ancestral county, you are ready to begin your research. Since you are unlikely to find slaves named in estate records after 1865, start your search with that year and work back. If your slaveholder candidate was alive in 1870, you know there were no probate records for that person in 1865. This means

1. you are unlikely to find former slaves mentioned in his probate records when he died.
2. you must look for probate records of the slaveholder's family—parents, siblings, children, or other relatives—who died before 1865. In this case, knowledge of the candidate's family history is very helpful.

If the slaveholder candidate died before 1865, you would be searching for that individual's records. In both instances, it is important to consider the wife's family in your search. A daughter's inheritance was often slaves; land usually went to sons.

You probably will find some or all of the following estate records in the clerk's office or on microfilm:

- Will books and indexes
- Probate record books
- Probate minutes

- Probate packets or files of loose papers, although not all states kept these papers
- Guardianship or orphan records

Wills

Wills distributed slaves and any other property that belonged to slaveholders at the time of death. A slaveholder could also provide for the distribution of any slaves born after the will was written or after his death.

The quantity of information varied from will to will. In their wills, some slaveholders freed slaves, provided for lifetime maintenance of slaves, or authorized the sale of slaves. Other wills contain

- nothing more than a reference to "my property," without specifying slaves
- only a general reference to "all my slaves"
- a list of given names and an occasional full name
- suggestions of slave family units or descriptions of families
- information on how or from where the slaveholder acquired the slaves
- the identity and location of slaves who had been loaned or hired out or for other reasons were not in the possession of the slaveholder

Important

The will often helps identify the slaveholder's family and relatives. Make note of the names and relationships mentioned in the document, the names of witnesses, property descriptions, places of birth or former residence, and any other information that might expand the search for your ancestors.

An example is the will of John Wright, written 9 December 1852 in Yadkin County, North Carolina.[5] This will implied that the testator (the one creating the will) had no wife or children and thus left his estate to other relatives. He willed his "negro woman Annis" and his "negro woman Fanny and her two children Matty and Nicholas" to his niece Mary Foote, daughter of Henry Foote, during her lifetime, then to her children. To Henry Foote, his brother-in-law, Wright left "my boy Armistead." He also mentioned his nephew James Wright, son of his brother Williams Wright of Wilkes County, North Carolina. In a less common gesture, another testator, A.P. Woodruff, in 1851 designated that at the death of his wife, Celia Woodruff, his "negro boy John" was to be emancipated.[6]

In most states, wills were filed in a county courthouse. Check with your ancestral county to determine which office holds them. In some counties, early wills and deeds were copied into the same record books. Other counties have separate will books into which wills were copied in the order of their filing. The filing date is usually the date the probate proceedings were initiated. In some locations, the original wills were filed with the other probate papers under the name of the deceased and may be available for researchers. Check the Family History Library catalog and the state archives to learn which records have been microfilmed.

If you find a will and it does not identify or bequeath slaves, search for the inventory and appraisal. Search the probate indexes for names of the slaveholder candidate, his known relatives, his wife's family, and similar surnames. Even if you do not find a will, continue your search of other probate records.

Idea Generator

Probate Records

The clerk of the probate court kept a record of estate business that was heard in court, along with supporting documentation. In some jurisdictions, the transcribed documents were recorded in bound probate record books. In other places, all you may find are probate minutes in which the clerk recorded the type of matter presented before the court, the date of the proceeding, and the ruling of the court. Some courts created both kinds of records.

Because they contain detailed information, the records themselves are far more informative than the minutes. The minute books can provide proof of what actions were taken and when; even this information can help narrow and direct your search. In addition to the records and minutes, you may also find packets of loose papers. These files may contain actual documents and other supporting information.

Research Tip

If you are lucky, the volumes have indexes. **If there is no index, you need to search page by page**. As with wills, search the index or probate record books for the slaveholder candidate, spouse, known relatives, and neighbors. Read each document thoroughly and make note of the type of document you read, its volume and page number, or the identification number of the probate file. This finding information not only helps you document your research and show where you got each piece of information, but it also helps you find the information again if you need to refer to the document at a later date.

Although you should review each probate document pertaining to a specific slaveholder candidate, some of these records are especially informative. The most important are the

- inventory and appraisal
- annual accountings
- return of sale (report of estate sale)
- final settlement or decree of distribution

Inventories and Appraisals. The first major action the court took in a probate proceeding was appointing several men to inventory and place a value on the personal property of the deceased. Slaves owned at the time of death would be listed, usually by first names, with their appraised values. This document will likely exist whether the person died with or without a will.

Inventories can contain a wealth of information, but some give sparse details on slaves. Appraisers sometimes reported slaves in family units or valued them separately but in a sequence that inferred a family relationship. Ages, color, and other physical descriptions may also be included. Figure 9-2, on page 153, is an example of such groupings in an inventory, dated 28 May 1856. Note that the appraisers included the ages and relationships for one family group.

Study such reports in detail and compare them with other information you have found in order to develop the most complete picture possible on the slaves of that estate.

Returns of Sales. The executor or administrator filed a return with the court when he sold estate assets at public auction. Returns often listed slaves who were sold in addition to livestock, crops, farming implements, furniture, and

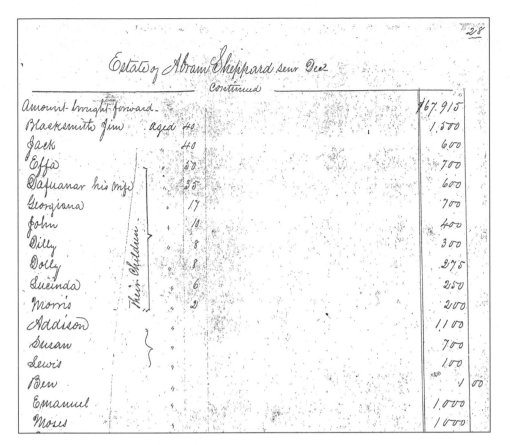

Figure 9-2 Appraisal of Abram Sheppard's estate, 1856, Matagorda County, Texas, Inventory Record Book C:28, County Clerk's Office, Courthouse, Bay City.

Case Study

household items. Many reports also list the purchaser and the purchase price of each slave or item. The description of the slaves could be as general as "one lot sold" or "Alfred and family" or as specific as naming the individual and his or her age.

Some estates sold slaves as late as 1864. One such sale gave encouraging clues toward identifying a slaveholder candidate for one Lewis Poindexter of Yadkin County, North Carolina. Lewis, his wife, Mary, and their children lived in East Bend township of that county in 1870 and 1880.[7] Their neighbors included few black families but a number of white Poindexter families, who warranted study because of the same surname.

Indeed, the 1860 census showed numerous Poindexter families, but the slave schedule showed only three as slaveholders. Two of these each had one adult male slave, but John G. Poindexter's male slave was closer to the age Lewis would have been in 1860, about forty to forty-seven.[8] This Poindexter also reported a woman, age forty-nine, and young woman of similar age to Lewis's wife, Mary, but no children to match the two who would have been alive in 1860, figured from the 1870 and 1880 censuses.

County probate records reported the sale of John G. Poindexter's estate in January 1864. The estate sold four slaves: for $3,000, the girl Amelia and her child, apparently the same as the nineteen-year-old female from the slave schedule, with a child born after 1860; for $56 [*sic*], the woman Hannah, possibly the forty-nine-year-old female from the slave schedule; and for $2,400, the man named Lewis, reported as forty in 1860.[9] Although A[ndrew] Webb apparently purchased both Hannah and Lewis, it is not clear whether they were related, nor has a post-war marriage record been found for Lewis and Mary. The low purchase price for Hannah suggests she was perhaps older than forty-nine or was disabled. Nevertheless, the estate sale record justifies further research on John G. Poindexter as the likely slaveholder of Lewis Poindexter, if not his wife and children.

Annual Accountings. The administrator or executor had to file annual reports detailing the income and expenditures of the estate as long as the case was under the authority of the probate court. Many of the reports accounted for the births, deaths, sales, and purchases of slaves, as well as expenditures for food and clothing of both slaves and the slaveholder's family. Reports of income included the sale of crops and products, income from rental of property, and income from hiring out slaves. Sometimes, the individual slave who was hired out was named, along with the amount of money the estate received for those services and the job the slave was hired to do. See Figure 12-3, on page 199, as an example. Meticulous administrators named newborns and their mothers; less detailed reports simply listed births and deaths by numbers, with their appraised value. Large purchases of shoes, cloth, or food were usually for the slaves. In addition, medical bills for slaves receiving medical care could be included in the expense reports.

Final Settlement and Decree of Distribution. A final settlement was filed once all estate business was resolved. The report included an itemized statement of estate assets and disbursements and the type and amount of assets remaining for distribution to heirs.

The decree of distribution or division determined each heir's share of remaining assets. In some cases, the final settlement and decree of distribution were combined. Slave sales, purchases, births, deaths, and names of those hired out sometimes were recorded in the settlement. In the distribution, slaves sometimes were grouped into families. Names gathered from these records should be compared with other pre-1865 and post-1865 records.

The Cumberland County, Virginia, estate division of William Daniel in 1813 listed each heir and named the slaves each received. The widow, Martha Daniel, received her dower—one-third of the estate—which included land and the slaves named Squire, Jenny, Moses, Betty, and Barber. Martha's daughter Obedience and her husband, William Thompson, received the slaves Cate, Hannah, Milly, Jack, and Jimboy. Daughter Polly and her husband, Henry Woodson, received Mary, Rubin, Sarah, Phil, Joice, and Ned. The record names all eight of the Daniel sons and daughters, these along with their husbands, since married women normally could not inherit property in their own names. In addition, a monetary value was given for each slave. This information sometimes is useful in estimating whether the slave was a child or an adult.[10]

Such records are especially helpful if your ancestor, hypothetically, was named Joyce Daniel and your research pointed to an 1850s slaveholder named Woodson. Studying the Woodson family, including the females, could help explain why your ancestor had the surname Daniel and how she came into the Woodson family.

Guardianship or Orphans Court Records

Look for guardianship or orphans court records if minor children survived one or both parents. These records are more likely to exist in intestate cases or after both parents had died. The court with jurisdiction over probate matters often has jurisdiction over orphans. Because minors could not legally manage their own affairs, the court appointed a guardian to oversee their property. **The names of slaves the minor inherited may be in these records as well as information on the birth, death, sale, and rental of the slaves and the cost of their maintenance.** The court required these records to be kept and reported until minors reached adult age, or until they married, if they married before the age of adulthood.

For example, a guardian's return provides a follow-up to the will of William Doss, executed in Surry County, North Carolina, in January 1841. In his will, Doss had left to his daughter, Sarah Ann, a "negro girl Martha Paulina." Doss died between 1841 and 1846, apparently in the part of Surry that became Yadkin County in 1850. His executor, Isaac Jarratt, was also guardian for the daughter, Sarah Ann. The guardian's return for 1846–1851, filed in Yadkin County, mentions the slave girl, Lina, several times.[11]

According to the return, Lina was hired out to William C. Kelly for about a year and then to her mistress's brother, John P. Doss, for about a year. Although the nature of her work was unspecified, she earned the estate $18.00 from Kelly and $14.31 from Doss. In October 1850, the guardian purchased shoes for Lina at a cost of $1.50. The rest of the return details Sarah Ann's schooling, clothing, and travels. Besides giving a small glimpse into Lina's life, the documents together give her formal name and the name she was called. Even these details can be helpful in further research.

Important

COURT RECORDS

Because slaves were property, they were subjects of disputes that often ended in litigation. It is unlikely that you will find blacks named as parties in any court action unless they were free. Thus, your search would be for cases in which the slaveholder was a plaintiff or a defendant. Such cases often involved family members suing other relatives. Disputes involved collection of money for slaves sold, misappropriation or theft of slaves, and injury to slaves. An owner might also be sued for damages caused by slaves.

Figure 9-3, on page 156, is a page from the Jones County, Georgia, inferior court minutes for January 1829. A lawsuit had caused a sale of Samuel Bond's property, and the sheriff was being told to pay Bond's creditors from the proceeds. Six slaves had been sold, among them a possible family group—Negro Dick, Jude, and her two children Jude and Dick.

Many court minute books, which summarize civil cases, have been microfilmed. Any surviving papers that provide the details of the cases may be in the court clerk's office or in storage at another location. Check the county courthouse to determine which office holds these records.

In Putnam County, Georgia, slaves were rarely mentioned in court records, but one issue involving a slave was brought before a grand jury there in September 1833.[12] A white resident named William Arnold was charged with illegally

Microfilm Source

Figure 9-3 Creditors of Samuel Bond vs. the sheriff, January 1829, Jones County, Georgia, Inferior Court Minutes, pages not numbered, Family History Library microfilm 0454255.

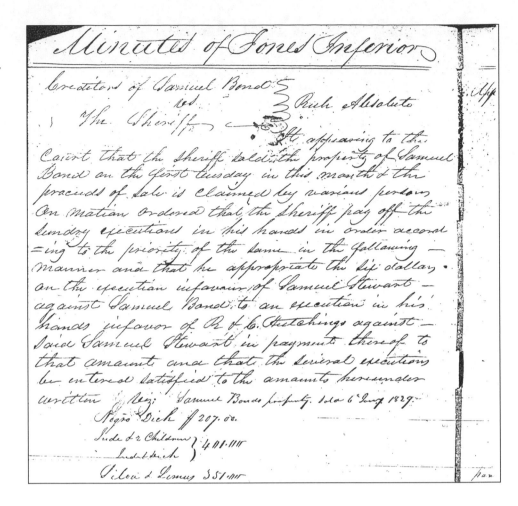

trading with a slave at night. According to the court minutes, on August 13 after nine o'clock at night, at or near his own house near Lamar's Cross Roads, Arnold had unlawfully purchased or received a bushel of wheat, worth one dollar, from Jack, a slave of Mason Tiller. The minutes did not mention a curfew, nor did they suggest that Jack had stolen the bushel of wheat that he sold. The jurymen discussed at length what they considered the "great injury sustained by the community from having the negroes traffic and carry on business for themselves" but took no action against either man or the slaveholder.

If Jack were your ancestor, this court record could motivate you to

- find out about curfews or other regulations limiting Jack's life in rural Georgia in the 1830s
- learn about Mason Tiller as Jack's slaveholder, in hopes of learning more about Jack, his family, and their lives

BUSINESS AND PERSONAL RECORDS

Locating business or plantation records will present a serious challenge for those whose ancestors were held by average or small slaveholders. Those whose ancestors lived on large plantations with hundreds of slaves stand a better chance of locating business records that named slaves.

Surviving documents from the average or small slaveholder probably are personal records such as Bible records, diaries, or letters. Because business and personal records were made and kept by the family, surviving records may still be in the family's possession. If you are lucky, the family donated them to a university library, state archive, or historical society.

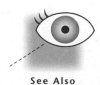

See Also

See the list on pages 134–135, for information on finding business and family records that have been donated to a library or archive.

Business and Plantation Records

The most thorough and complete records kept on slaves were the plantation or business records of slaveholders. As with any business, detailed records were essential to a profitable enterprise. Since slaves were likely a slaveholder's most valuable asset, as a group often more valuable than his land, large slaveholders kept records of slave purchases, sales, births, deaths, marriages, family makeup, skills, work assignments, medical treatment, food and clothing distributed, runaways, and punishments.

The quantity and quality of records you might find probably depend on the size of the slave population on the plantation, the size and/or longevity of the business, and whether the slaveholding family preserved any of their records. The average slaveholder held fewer than ten slaves, and few records survive from these family farms and small plantations. Only a small percentage of slaveholders held more than one hundred slaves; their records are usually the most comprehensive and the most likely to have survived.

Many archives and libraries have printed or online guides to these special collections to help researchers identify potentially helpful records. Ask about such guides or inventories at the research facilities or consult their Web sites. One example of surviving business records, reported in *A Guide to the Business Records in the Virginia State Library and Archives* (Richmond: Virginia State Library and Archives, 1994), is the ledger book of William Gatewood, who operated a grist mill in Essex County, Virginia. Several pages at the front of Gatewood's book list the births of 123 slaves between 1773 and 1861.

Personal and Private Records

The family Bible has long been the place to record vital statistics and store important documents. In addition to their own family information, some slaveholders recorded in the family Bible the births and deaths, and perhaps marriages, of their slaves. Such records are more likely associated with smaller slaveholders than huge plantations. As with other private records, locating surviving records presents a serious challenge.

Figure 9-4, on page 158, is a page from one slaveholder's family Bible, documenting slave births. Some of the births occurred after the publication date of this Bible (1855) and thus may have been recorded close to the birth date. Other entries, however, recorded births between 1808 and 1854. These were obviously entered some years after the events. The person who recorded them in the Bible may have had another written record from which to take the dates or may have created the entries from memory. They may be accurate, or they may be approximate. The researcher would need to study other records of these persons and the white family to evaluate the accuracy of the entries.

Figure 9-4 Register of Births, showing slave births, p. 3 of Family Register, in family Bible of William Lackey Jr. (1807–1895) of Tennessee, Georgia, Louisiana, and Texas, Bible published in 1855, original in possession of Mrs. Jane S. Blanks, Houston, Texas.

FAMILY REGISTER.

Births.	Births.
Bella Lacky was born 8th November 1855	Nachael Wos Born 20 July 1817
Emma Lena Lackey was born 17th July 1858	Willis Wos Born 5 Sept 1808
Mary Frances was born 12 August 1859	Benn Wos Born 10 Oct 1828
Stepney Bounsers child was born 24 May 1862	Nole Wos Born 13 Febrary 1834
These are Slaves	
Dick Nancys child was born 12 Decbr 1859	Beckey Nachels Child Wos Born Jun 5. 1844
Mary Nancys child was born 15 Oct 1861	Loyesa Mary ann childe was born 10th of May 1846
Moses was born 12th June 1854	
Beckey Ann's child was born July 20th 1857	Permealy anns Childs Wos Born 21 Dec 1851
Thomas Penn's child was born June 11th 1859	Mar the Roses child was borne 16th of march 1852
Claribel Veal was born July 15 1890 in San Marcos Bella's only child. (white child)	Cicero Moses Boy May 15, 1854
Mary Rona's child was born July the 21st 1859 Slave	Moses anns child 6 of June, 1854

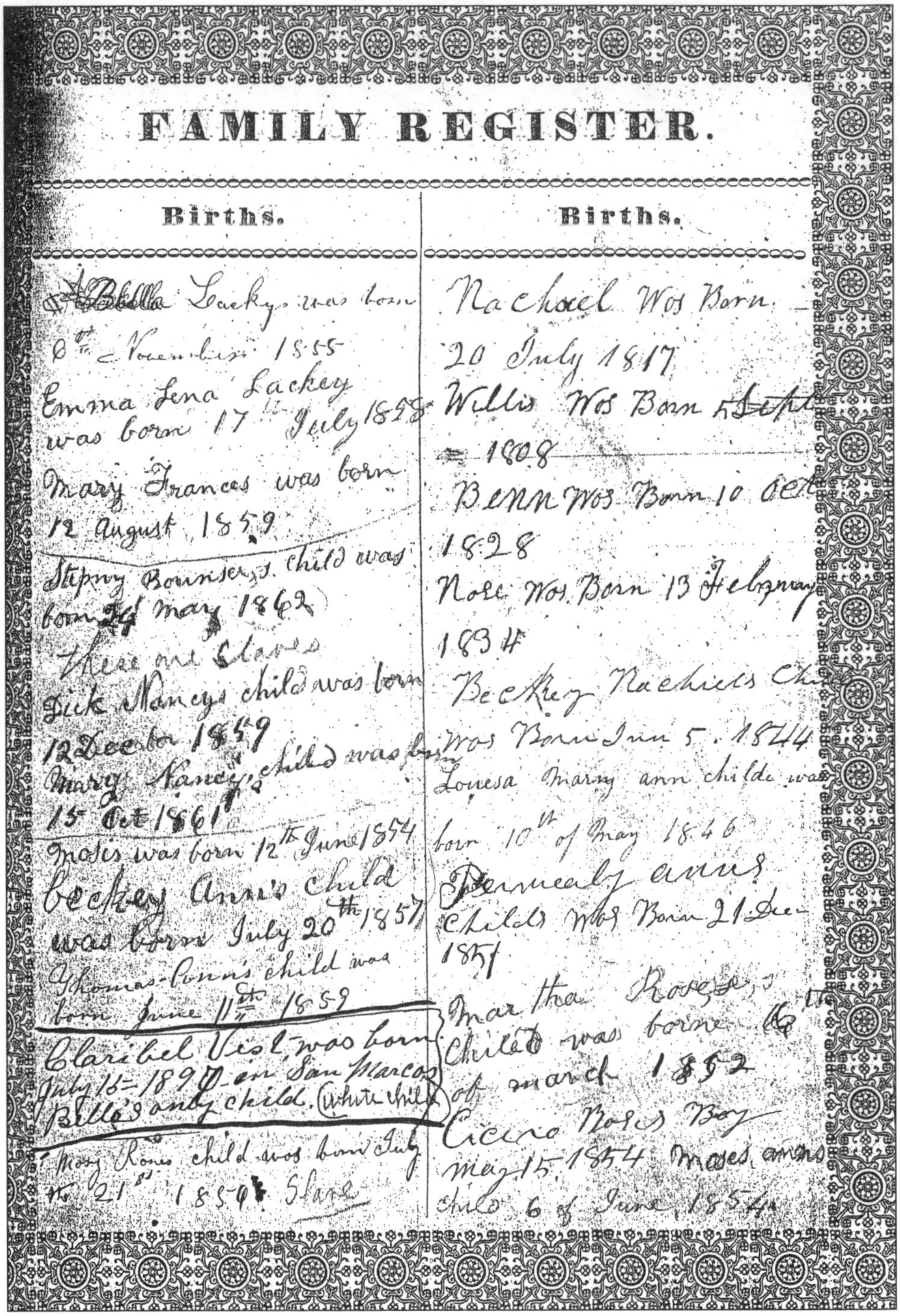

Hidden Treasures

Other personal records that might name slaves are diaries and letters, many of which have been published but may or may not be indexed. At least three bibliographies of published diaries may be found in research libraries:

- Arksey, Laura, et al., comp. *American Diaries*. Detroit: Gale Research Company, 1983–1986.
- Matthews, William, comp. *American Diaries: An Annotated Bibliography of American Diaries Written Prior to the Year 1861*. Berkeley, Calif.: University of California Press, 1945.

- Pate-Havlice, Patricia. *And So to Bed: A Bibliography of Diaries Published in English*. Metuchen, N.J.: Scarecrow Press, 1987.

More recent publications may be found through booksellers and library catalogs, or consult *Books in Print* at a library. In addition, consult NUCMC and other finding aids listed on pages 134–135 to locate family letters and diaries in manuscript collections in libraries and archives.

Diaries probably are more useful than letters, whose mention of slaves is often casual and limited. For example, E.G. Coleman of Bolivar, Tennessee, wrote to his father in Cumberland County, Virginia, in September 1855. After reporting on his family, health, and business activities, he added:

> We are more than obliged to you for sending us Sarah   she answers our purpose very well   verry obedient and faithfull and Catherine [his wife] joines me in ten[d]ering thanks to you for her   tell her mother not to be distressed   I will take good care of her and when I come to Va I will bring her with us. I can't say when I shall come to see you[,] that is set any time[,] except when the Memphis & Charleston RR is completed . . . [13]

Thus, the letter identifies and characterizes one of his father's slaves, Sarah, but does not name her mother or give other useful clues for the researcher. This may well be the only mention of Sarah by name, as she has not been positively identified in earlier or later documents. Because the senior Coleman died after the war, in 1867, little opportunity exists for confirming the identity of his slaves, other than in family letters and the probate records of his relatives.

OTHER RESOURCES

Other records connect slaves to the slaveholders. No universal registration existed, but a number of slaves are identified in church records, vital registrations, and newspapers. Check in your research county and state for the existence of these and other records, as they vary with time and place.

Church Records

Church records show American slaveholders as a study in contradictions. While they took steps to ensure that slaves had no legal, human, or civil rights, they did encourage salvation for these lost souls. Some slaveholders believed the Christian slave was more docile and easier to control than the unsaved slave. While other slaveholders had more genuine motivations for bringing slaves into the religious community, the message was clear: Submit thyself, be the good servant, and honor thy master.

Some slaveholders sponsored or allowed their slaves to become members of churches to which the white families belonged. Slaves attended services with the whites, although usually seated in balconies or separate sections of the sanctuary. Church records from northern as well as southern states sometimes provide information on the slaves who joined: the slaveholder, the date of baptism or admission, slave family members, and dates of marriage or death.

One example appeared in the register of the Presbyterian Church of Bolivar,

Tennessee.[14] The register listed Rose, a servant of E.G. Coleman, who was baptized and admitted to membership by examination on 21 November 1858; in the last column of her membership record was later added "dead," without a date. Rose's four children were baptized on 19 June 1859: Moses Elijah, Lewis Pleasant, Joe Stevens, and Thomas Henry.

The 1870 census identified Rose and her husband, Pleasant Coleman, with children Thomas, Lewis, Moses, Elvira, and Adaline (age ten). The 1860 slave schedule, though quite faded and difficult to read, showed E.G. Coleman and his mother-in-law, C.E. Patton, with enough slaves of the appropriate ages to accommodate Rose and all her family, including the youngest, for a four-month-old female was listed.[15] The church record had confirmed the relationships that were not recorded in the 1870 census and had identified the slaveholder, whose surname Rose and her family adopted after emancipation.

The extent of slave involvement in the church depended on the slaveholder, the individual church, and the denomination. Large slaveholders may have prescribed the terms on which their slaves could receive religious instruction on the plantation, without allowing them to attend the white churches. The exception would have been the slaves working in the big house. Slaveholders with only a few slaves may have allowed their slaves to become church members.

The slaveholder's denomination was also a factor. If your ancestors were slaves in Louisiana and the slaveholder was Catholic, you are more likely to find your family in church records. Small rural Protestant churches across the South often kept poor records of their white members, and many of these records no longer exist.

If you determine the slaveholder's religious affiliation, try to identify the congregation with which he or she was associated, likely near the residence. Contact the church or congregation, neighboring church, or denomination headquarters to determine if records exist. Check PERSI, library catalogs, and other finding aids to learn whether the records have been published. Ask the reference librarian at your local public library for assistance in finding published records. When searching these finding aids, try looking for the name of the individual church or congregation, the town or county, and the subject heading "church records." (See also pages 59–60.)

Vital Records: Births and Deaths

Few states outside of New England registered births and deaths before the Civil War. However, Virginia—including West Virginia—and Kentucky recorded these events for both blacks and whites from 1853 and 1852, respectively, until the late-nineteenth or early-twentieth century, depending on the town or county. Many of these registers survive, in the county courthouses and/or in the state archives. Most have been microfilmed, and some have been abstracted and published. Remember, not all births and deaths were reported.

When entering the births of slave children, clerks recorded the name of the owner but not always the mother and rarely the father. Nor did the slaveholder always report the child's name. The most helpful records, of course, name the child and the mother. The following are two examples:

- Silus, a male slave, born 3 June 1858, in Ballard County, Kentucky, son of Martha, a slave of G.G. Brown.[16]
- Harriet Jane Saunders, a female slave, born 15 September 1853 in Botetourt County, Virginia; slaveholder John W. Robinson; mother not named. Note that the child was reported with a surname.[17]

Likewise, the registers show slave deaths. For example, Rachel, a sixty-year-old female slave of Robert Duff, died of "fitts" on 28 May 1855 at Wallen's Creek, Lee County, Virginia; her parents' names were not reported.[18] At that period of time, infant mortality was high, and these registers are crowded with the deaths of young children.

Check with the state archives of your research state and consult the Family History Library catalog to determine whether such records were made, which still exist, and whether they are accessible to researchers. Some localities made records even if the state as a whole did not. Recording of slave births and deaths was probably more sporadic than that of whites, but as the examples above show, the records are worth checking. Besides *Ancestry's Red Book*, consult the Web site <www.vitalrec.com> for addresses and information.

Library/Archive Source

Newspapers

As is true with other pre-1865 records, your search for newspaper records is in the name of the slaveholder, unless your ancestors were free. Some African-American newspapers were published before the Civil War, but most were located in free states.

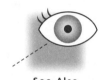

See Also

See pages 77–79, for information on finding newspapers.

Many newspapers, especially in the South and the border states, carried announcements by slave brokers and traders. However, these advertisements are unlikely to assist your search since they do not identify the slaveholder. The kinds of newspaper notices that might benefit your search include

- slaveholder announcements of slave sales, if they identify the slaves by name.
- announcements of estate sales, which often named and provided ages of the slaves.
- notices of estate hearings for divisions of estates, widow's dower, or final settlements. Although such notices may not name the slaves, they could help focus and narrow the search for the records that do identify slaves.
- court-ordered sales of slaveholder property to satisfy judgments for unpaid debts, which could include slaves.
- advertisements for the capture and return of runaway slaves.

If you identify a newspaper published in the area you are researching and covering the time period of interest, you probably will need to read the extant issues on microfilm. You may be able to visit a library that holds the microfilm copies. Otherwise, try to borrow the microfilm on interlibrary loan. The interlibrary loan librarian at your local library can assist you in making the request.

When you begin reading the newspaper issues, write in your notes the exact title of the paper, in what city it was published, the date of the issue from which you make notes, and the page number on which your information appeared.

Familiarize yourself with the layout of the paper and carefully review the sections that contained legal notices and advertisements of sales.

An example of family information found in a pre–Civil War newspaper appeared in the 28 May 1848 issue of the *Port Gibson (Mississippi) Correspondent*. The administrators of the estate of Duncan H. McIntyre had published a Notice of Administrator's Sale. The announcement indicated that a public auction was to be held on 10 July 1848 at the courthouse. The sale was to include land and slaves. The slaves to be sold were identified as Mary, a Negro woman aged about thirty years, and her four children: Littleton, a boy about ten years old; Martha, a girl about six; Ferdinand, a boy about four; and Wilson, a boy about two. (See chapter twelve for more about this family.)

As shown in this chapter, the search for slave ancestors must concentrate on documents created essentially for and about the slaveholder, especially property, estate, court, business, and personal records. Persistent genealogists can often cull facts and clues from the mass of written materials generated prior to 1865.

TEN

Case Study: The Issue of Mixed Race

If asked to identify an issue on which the United States has struggled from its beginning until the present, many would undoubtedly rank the issue of black-white race relations at or near the top. From the time the first Africans were brought to Jamestown in 1619, America has struggled with how and where the black American fit within the fabric of American life.

The signers of the Declaration of Independence struggled with how or whether that document should deal with the issue of slavery and the rights of blacks; they chose to maintain the status quo. The debate continued to escalate and eventually erupted in a war that divided and nearly destroyed the United States. Although it was hoped a resolution would come with the end of slavery, the struggle was far from over. Racial segregation became the law of the land. After a long and hard-fought struggle, right and reason prevailed; and the African American, in theory if not in practice, became an equal participant in American society.

One aspect of race relations that historically, and even in today's world, has caused consternation and anger is the issue of miscegenation. By definition, miscegenation is the mixing of races, especially marriage or cohabitation between a white person and a member of another race. Coined in the mid-nineteenth century, **the word comes from two Latin words:** *miscere,* **"to mix,"** and *genus,* **"race."** However, many seventeenth-century American colonists considered the concept inherently unnatural. Beginning in Maryland in 1663, colonial governments banned multiracial marriages and relationships. In effect, the laws banned whites from marrying someone of a different race, primarily black or Indian.

The move to prohibit interracial mixing was law even before the institution of slavery was firmly established in law. This legislative response can be attributed in part to a prevailing belief that the African was racially and culturally inferior and incapable of intellectual and social equality. Eventually, some worried that mixing the races would blur the lines of racial distinction and thereby weaken the system of slavery, a system firmly entrenched in racial identity.

However, laws alone were not enough to prohibit the slaveholder from exer-

\di'fin\ *vb*

Definitions

163

cising what he considered his proprietary right over his female chattel in any manner desired, or the genuine attraction of two individuals of different races. As a result, with each new generation, the skin color of the slave and free black populations continued to change. New racial terms were created to ensure that no matter how light the skin, those descending from slaves or free blacks remained legally black. A mulatto was considered half black; a quadroon, one-fourth black; and an octoroon, one-eighth black. The lines were continually redrawn as the racial divide blurred even further.

After the Civil War, the free movement of the black population afforded many the opportunity for a new life and, for those who appeared white, to start that new life as white. Because skin color alone was no longer enough to determine racial identity, legislatures and courts chose a broader definition. As a result, anyone with at least one drop of black blood or one black ancestor was, by law, black. The "one-drop rule," as it was known, and laws against miscegenation remained on the books until the last half of the twentieth century. America's palette of colors fades even more as we move into the twenty-first century, yet we are still faced with the same question of racial identity—what it means to be Black/African American.

Case Study

THE SEARCH FOR HENRY DOTSON

The case study on Henry Dotson not only exemplifies the same-surname search strategy covered in chapter six but also the role that race plays in researching African-American ancestors. Henry Dotson was the offspring of a white slave-holder father and mulatto slave mother; by definition, he was a quadroon. He was by no means unique and represents the paradox facing many who are researching similar ancestors, especially those born during slavery—whether one should research slavery-era white ancestors, many of whom, along with their descendants, even today would categorically deny these common blood lines. In addition, that period represented a time in our ancestors' lives that many found disturbing and just hoped to forget. Ultimately, the response is an individual one. However, we must remember that we have a responsibility to tell the whole story, even if we would prefer to forget or ignore certain chapters.

In the Beginning: What Was Known

Research Tip

Your research must begin with what you know, as this case study did.

1. Henry Dotson was born in Claiborne County, Mississippi, during slavery, about 1853, according to the family.
2. His father, William Dotson, was white and his mother, whose name was unknown, was said to be Indian.
3. Henry married Angeline, whose maiden name was thought to be Frazier, and raised twelve children.
4. He had a known sister, Sarah (Dotson) Campbell.
5. He owned and farmed a large parcel of land in the Willows Community, which was thought to have been an inheritance from his father.
6. He died 31 August 1918 in Claiborne County and was buried in the Campbell Chapel Church Cemetery in the Willows Community. (His death date is recorded on his headstone, but no date of birth is given.)

THE POST–CIVIL WAR SEARCH

Research Tip

Since Henry's death date was known, ordering his death certificate seemed a good place to start. According to the certificate, Henry (recorded as Dodson) was born in Claiborne County and died in district three of the county at age seventy. The age given on the certificate suggested a birth date of about 1848. The document listed his father as William Dodson, of unknown birthplace, and his mother as Winnie Jones, born in Virginia. The informant was not a family member but the white funeral director, H. Marx.[1]

What additional or confirming information might be found in Henry's census entries? Since Henry died in 1918, the last census in which he would be listed was 1910. That year, in Claiborne County, Henry was head of a household of five persons:[2]

- Henry Dotson, age 58, mulatto
- his wife, Angeline, age 60
- son Lemuel, age 25
- son Burnet, age 18
- daughter Maggie, age 20

Henry and Angeline reported being married forty years, since about 1870; Angeline had borne thirteen children, twelve of whom were then living. Claiborne County marriage records confirmed that Henry Dotson married Angeline Walters on 28 February 1870.[3]

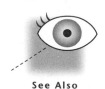

See Also

In the 1900 census, Henry was listed as a farm owner, forty-nine years old, and born in August 1850.[4] In the household were his wife, Angeline (fifty-one), and nine children. In addition to the children named in 1910, the household included

- Ella, age 24
- Isaac, age 20
- William, age 19
- Katie, age 18
- Elias, age 13
- Sarah, age 12

Figure 10-1, on page 166, is a photograph of Henry, taken about 1900.

More importantly, in the household was Henry's mother, Winnie Jones, age seventy, a widow who had borne ten children, of whom six were living. She was reportedly born in 1830—the month was unknown—in Virginia, as were her parents.

The 1880 enumerator found thirty-year-old Henry and his twenty-five-year-old wife, Angeline. This census named three more children: daughter George [*sic*] Ann (age eight), John (age seven), and Albert (age six).[5] These three apparently completed the list of Angeline's twelve surviving children mentioned in 1910.

Listed as a separate family in the same dwelling were four additional relatives, reported as Henry's mother, brother, sister, and child Winny, daughter of Fanny:[6]

- Winny Dotson, age 45, born in Virginia
- Pickney [*sic*, no last name given], age 22
- Fanny Rives, age 20
- Winny, age 1

Figure 10-1 Henry Dotson, about 1900.

The earliest of the post-war censuses, 1870, enumerated Henry Dodson [*sic*] in Claiborne County as a farm laborer, age twenty. He was head of a household that included six other young people, all born in Mississippi:[7]

- his known sister, S. A. Campbell, age 19
- twins Jacob and Isaac Reaves, age 14
- his brother, Pinkney Tannyhill, age 11, known from the 1880 census
- Rose A. Bean, age 10
- Wm. Thos. Rundell, age 1

Since the relationship to the head of household was not given in 1870, Henry's relationship to some in his household was unclear. However, living next door was Winnie Jones, age forty; in her household was twenty-one-year-old Westly Hinds. Neither Henry nor his mother was a head of household in a census prior to 1870.

Claiborne County deed records revealed that Henry Dotson was the grantee (purchaser) of land on three occasions. By 1900, he owned 751 acres of land.

1. Henry and his mother, Winnie, purchased 200 acres on 1 January 1870.[8]
2. The second tract was 153 acres, purchased in 1888, not from William's estate.[9]
3. The third purchase was for 398 acres in 1898, not from William's estate.[10]

Summary of Post–Civil War Research

1. According to census records, Henry was born about 1850 in Claiborne County, Mississippi.
2. Henry married Angeline Walters on 28 February 1870.

3. His mother was Winnie Jones, a mulatto, born in Virginia about 1830, as were her parents. Winnie died between 1900 and 1910, before Mississippi began recording deaths in 1912.

4. In addition to a sister, Sarah Ann Campbell, Henry had a brother, Pickney Tannyhill, and possibly a sister, Fanny Rives. From information reported about Winnie in the 1900 census, Henry had two other unidentified, living siblings.

5. Henry owned 751 acres of land which he purchased between 1870 and 1898.

THE PRE–CIVIL WAR SEARCH

Although it was confirmed that Henry was born during slavery and that his father, William Dotson, was white, the nature and extent of their relationship was unclear. Was theirs the typical one in which the slaveholder fathered children by his slave, never acknowledging them or providing for their futures, or was there something more? The fact that the family still possesses William's portrait and Bible implies something beyond the usual scenario that defined these relationships. In addition, family oral tradition that Henry received his substantial land holdings from his father suggests that the family was led to believe that Henry was acknowledged by his father. The answers to these questions would have to come from clues in pre–Civil War records.

The search proceeded as it would for any former slave. The difference in this case was that researching the likely slaveholder would involve researching an ancestor. Fortunately, the family's oral history, which suggested the likely slaveholder, saved research time and resources. However, even without the family's oral tradition, the same-surname research strategy could have led to William's identity as the slaveholder, if not as Henry's father. Because William was the only slaveholding Dotson mentioned in Claiborne County's pre–Civil War records, he would have been a prime candidate for study.

According to William's Bible, into which someone else recorded the information, he died in New Orleans in 1858; his body was returned to Claiborne County and buried in the William Clark Cemetery.[11] Knowledge of the date of death helped narrow the search for probate records.

Claiborne County probate records contained a copy of William Dotson's will, dated 21 January 1858 and filed for probate in May 1858.[12] Item three of the will named twenty-eight slaves who were to be equally divided between William's brother, Asa Dotson of Georgia, and his sisters Elizabeth Smith and Susan Free of Alabama. In item four, Dotson left to his heirs *in fee simple* the following: fourteen additional slaves, unnamed; two plantations totaling about 1,450 acres; and all the remainder of his estate. Item six appointed as executor, Lemuel N. Baldwin, described as "my friend."

Since Henry, his mother, Winnie, his sister, Sarah, and his brother, Pinkney, were not among the twenty-eight slaves named in the will, were they among the fourteen unnamed slaves? Finding an inventory and appraisal of William's estate might identify these fourteen.

The executor filed an inventory and appraisal with the probate court on 29

May 1858.[13] The first twenty-eight slaves named in the inventory were the same twenty-eight named in item three of the will. The document named twelve additional slaves, not fourteen as stated in the will. An estate accounting reported the death of an old woman, possibly the thirteenth of the unnamed group, stating she had not been appraised due to her old age. The identity of the fourteenth is still unknown.

Brothers and Sisters

Listed on the inventory were Winny [*sic*], Henry, Sarah Ann, and Pinckney [*sic*]. Named among these were Wesley, Isaac, and Jacob, who were in Henry's or Winnie's household in 1870. Although the seven were not identified as a family in the inventory, it is assumed that the other three boys also were Winnie's children. Winnie may have been the mother also of William and Maria, since they and the other known children were listed after Winny in the inventory. Figure 10-2, on page 169, shows the portion of the inventory that names Winny and the children.

Others listed in the inventory, but not in the will, were Spencer, Jacob (a second one), and Amanda. Later estate documents indicated that Spencer and Jacob were old; their age explained their appraised values of only one hundred dollars each. Amanda and Winny, each appraised at twelve hundred dollars, were probably about the same age. No family ties of any of the named slaves could be confirmed from this document.

Annual accountings filed by the executor confirmed Winnie as the mother of Wesley and William, both of whom ran away with Union soldiers during the war. Estate records also identified the birth of two additional children of Winnie— Susan in 1859 and Rose in 1861.[14] Rose was likely the Rose A. Bean listed as a member of Henry's household in 1870; Susan may have died during childhood.

Maria, of the 1858 inventory, was later identified as Maria Taylor who married Major Barnes. Maria was identified when it was discovered that she was the wife of Major Barnes, who acted as surety on the marriage bond of Henry Dotson and Angeline Walters in 1870. Maria was confirmed as Henry's sister by a descendant of their sister Sarah Ann (Dotson) Campbell.[15]

Census enumerations and William Dotson's estate records led to the identity of Winnie's ten children and the likely surviving six reported in the 1900 census.

1. William — oldest, born before 1847
2. Maria Taylor — born about 1847 (alive in 1900)
3. Wesley Hinds — born about 1849 (alive in 1900)
4. Henry Dotson — born about 1850 (alive in 1900)
5. Sarah Ann Dotson — born about 1851 (alive in 1900)
6. Jacob Reaves — born about 1856 (alive in 1900)
7. Isaac Reaves — born about 1856 (died by 1880, husband of the widow, Fanny Reaves, in Henry's household in 1880, confirmed by marriage records)
8. Pickney Tannyhill — born about 1858 (alive in 1900, changed his name to Pinkney Hollis after 1880)
9. Susan — born about 1859 (probably died before 1870)
10. Rose A. Bean — born about 1861 (possibly died 1870–1880)

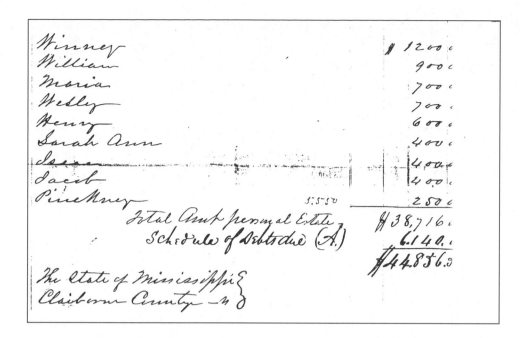

Figure 10-2 Portion of William Dotson's estate inventory showing Winny and children, May 1858, Claiborne County, Mississippi.

Maria, Henry, Sarah Ann, and Jacob raised families and spent the remainder of their lives in Claiborne County. After 1900, Wesley and Pinkney moved to north Mississippi—the Mississippi delta—where they were still residing in 1920.

Winnie Jones, the Mother

Although William Dotson's probate records proved valuable in uncovering the identity of Henry's brothers and sisters, they were no help in identifying Winnie's parents or any of her relatives. She may have had a connection to the other slaves retained as part of the Dotson estate—Jacob, Spencer, Amanda—or the old, unnamed woman, but no evidence supporting such a conclusion has been found.

The similarity of given names may suggest a connection to the couple Billy and Maria listed in the estate records. It may have been more than mere coincidence that she named her first two children William, formal for Billy, and Maria. Estate records also suggested that Billy, Maria, Winnie, and her children, with the exception of William and Wesley, were among the fifteen slaves remaining on the plantation when invading Union forces overran it in May 1863.[16] Beyond those listed in the will and probate records, no other family ties have been confirmed. Nor have any of the other slaves listed in estate records been identified in the post-war period.

Another possible clue to Winnie's identity surfaced during research on William Dotson. He was appointed administrator of the estate of George Tannyhill, who died in 1837, and guardian of George's sons Pickney [sic] Tannyhill and George Tannyhill Jr. Further investigation produced another link between Dotson and Tannyhill: Their wives were related. George's second wife, who predeceased him, appeared to be the mother or sister of William's wife, Mary Jane Bryce, who died before 1840. At this point in the search, the purpose of studying the Tannyhills was not to identify the specific relationship between the Bryce women but to locate records that might mention Winnie.

Listed in the inventory of George's estate were nine slaves, among them, a girl Winny, age eight.[17] Based on Winnie's estimated 1830 year of birth, from the 1870 and 1900 censuses, she could have been seven or eight years old in 1837. Three women and two men were listed in the inventory, but it is unclear if they were connected in any way. The girl Winny was listed between the man Bob and the woman Philis.

Tannyhill's personal estate, including slaves, was sold at public auction on 6 January 1838.[18] The return of sale indicates the slaves were sold in lots, but neither the names nor the total number sold was reported. William Dotson was not a purchaser. No reference to Winnie was found in Tannyhill's estate records beyond the inventory.

According to Orphans Court records, Pickney Tannyhill died in 1846 and George Jr., before 1850.[19] This eliminates the possibility of either being the father of Winnie's son Pinkney Tannyhill. Although no connection of Winnie to the Tannyhill family can be established with certainty, surely there is an explanation for Winnie's having a child named Pinkney Tannyhill.

Family folklore claims Winnie was an Indian. Since she was described as mulatto in two of the three censuses in which she appeared, she was probably very light, probably descended from black and white ancestors, and was unlikely an Indian. Most Indians had been removed from Virginia by 1830, her estimated year of birth. Possibly, Winnie was separated from her family at an early age by sale and was shipped to Mississippi. Descendants have been unable to identify any possible family she may have had in Mississippi. The search for her family and how and when she became part of the William Dotson household is ongoing.

Reminder

Review pages 20–21 and 91–92 for the race/color designations in federal census records.

WILLIAM DOTSON, THE SLAVEHOLDER

Would research into William's history as a slaveholder and his family history provide clues about when and how Winnie Jones came to the Dotson plantation? Even if her exact arrival could not be determined, was it possible to narrow the time period in which the search should be focused?

History as a Slaveholder

The following timeline shows the Mississippi documents that identify William Dotson as a slaveholder and the number of slaves reported in each one.[20]

DOCUMENT	NUMBER OF SLAVES REPORTED
1824–1829 Claiborne County tax roll	one or two slaves
1830 Adams County, Mississippi, census	sixty-eight slaves
1834 Adams County tax toll	two slaves
1836 Claiborne County tax roll	nine slaves
1837 Claiborne County tax roll	eight slaves
1838 Claiborne County tax roll	one slave
1839 Claiborne County tax roll	five slaves
1840 Claiborne County census	nineteen slaves
1841–1842 Claiborne County tax roll	twenty-one slaves

1844 Claiborne County tax roll	seven slaves
1845 Claiborne County tax roll	nine slaves
1846 Claiborne County tax roll	twenty-three slaves
1847 Claiborne County tax roll	sixteen slaves
1849 Claiborne County tax roll	twenty-seven slaves
1850 Claiborne County slave schedule	thirty-one slaves

William Dotson appeared for the first time on the Claiborne County tax roll in 1824 with one slave. Between 1824 and 1829, he was taxed for one or two slaves. He disappeared from the Claiborne County roll after 1829 but was found in nearby Adams County in 1830. The census reported sixty-eight slaves, one white male, and one white female in the household.[21] The white female was Mary Jane Bryce, whom he married in Claiborne County in 1822. The marriage record was the earliest evidence of him in Claiborne County records.[22]

Since the Adams County tax roll in 1834 listed him with only two slaves, which is consistent with the number he held before leaving Claiborne County, it remains unclear how he came to possess sixty-eight in 1830. By 1836, William had returned to Claiborne County and was taxed for nine slaves, but he reported only one slave in 1838. That year, William purchased seven slaves from the estate of William Harmon, for whom he served as co-executor.[23]

William reported nineteen slaves at the time of the 1840 census. In his household were one white male and two minor white males but no white female.[24] The two minor white males were the Tannyhill orphans, for whom he was appointed guardian in 1838. The absence of a female in the household suggests his wife may have died.

Note that the number of slaves dropped from twenty-one in 1842 to seven in 1844 and nine in 1845 before returning to twenty-three in 1846. **To determine which years' reports were probably more accurate, look at the numbers reported over a certain time period.** For the ten years between 1840 and 1850, the higher range of numbers appeared more consistent. In addition, a slaveholder was more likely to under-report and pay lower taxes than to over-report and be charged a higher tax. Therefore, the higher numbers reported are likely to be more accurate than the lower figures.

Research Tip

The 1850 slave schedule reported William Dotson with thirty-one slaves.[25] Since Henry Dotson's estimated year of birth was about 1850, Winnie probably was on the Dotson plantation by that year. She was likely one of the two twenty-five-year-old mulatto females reported in the 1850 slave schedule.

The number of slaves reported in the above timeline and Winnie's estimated birth in 1830 in Virginia suggest that she came to the Dotson plantation between 1836 and 1849. She came probably no earlier than 1836 because Dotson consistently reported only one or two slaves in tax returns prior to the nine reported in 1836. Winnie arrived probably no later than 1849 since Henry was born in August of 1850, according to the 1900 census. Further research is underway into William Dotson's presence in Adams County, Mississippi, from 1830 to at least 1834. Could he have acquired the seven additional slaves reported in tax returns between 1834 and 1836 while he was in Adams County?

Technique

The Dotson Family History

Would William's family provide additional clues to unlock the mystery surrounding the appearance of Winnie in William's slave records? William had married Mary Jane Bryce in 1822. Although not yet confirmed, she may have been the daughter of Thomas Bryce, who was listed as a resident of Claiborne County in the 1810 Mississippi territorial census.[26] He was the only Bryce in the area to have three daughters, and it was known that Mary had two sisters.[27]

Thomas Bryce did not report owning slaves in 1810 and was not enumerated in a census after 1810. Because Mary's family was in Mississippi prior to 1810, and she and William married there in 1822, it is unlikely—though not impossible—that she was connected to Winnie, who was born in Virginia about 1830. Mary disappeared from William's household after 1830. Since she was not in the household in 1850 to report a birthplace, this information remains unknown. Research continues on the identity of Mary's family and their previous residences.

By 1850, William Dotson was a sole head of household, a fifty-five-year-old planter, born in South Carolina.[28] According to his will, he wished to be buried next to his father in the burying ground of his friend William Clarke. Listed in Clarke Cemetery records was the headstone for William Dotson, born 3 September 1794, died 2 May 1858.[29] Buried beside William was Esau Dotson, whose headstone bears no dates, only the inscription "Erected by his son William Dotson." A search for probate records in his name in Claiborne County was unsuccessful; nor were any filed in Fairfield County, South Carolina, his previous residence.

Printed Source

A published history of the Dodson/Dotson family contains a biographical sketch of Esau Dodson.[30] He was born about 1754, the son of Lambert Dodson, and was a veteran of the Revolutionary War. His name appeared on the 1790 census of Burke County, North Carolina, with one white male and one white female in the household and no slaves. According to the family history, he was not mentioned in any other records until he appeared in Claiborne County in 1832, when he applied for a military pension at age seventy-eight. No descendants had been traced, and no other record was found for him in Claiborne County.

Actually, Esau was listed in the 1810 and 1820 censuses in Fairfield County, South Carolina. In 1810, he was listed as Esau Godson.[31] He was not a slaveholder at the time of these censuses, and no records in Fairfield County reflect slave ownership. Esau died probably between 1832 and 1840, since he was not listed in 1840 census records. Apparently, he died in Claiborne County, where he was buried.

William Dotson appeared only once in Fairfield County records as the purchaser of a tract of land in 1817.[32] He was not listed in the 1820 South Carolina census as a head of household nor was he indicated as a member of his father's household. Thus, he migrated to Mississippi probably between 1817 and 1822. Research on the brother and two sisters mentioned in his will revealed that none owned slaves. William's mother's identity is unknown. The evidence so far indicates William's slaves were not likely an inheritance or gift from his family or his wife's family since records indicate that neither owned slaves.

WILLIAM DOTSON, THE FATHER

It would be difficult to determine the exact nature of the relationship between William Dotson and his slave-born children. Since no written documentation of his acknowledgment of paternity exists, we are left to interpret the circumstances of his life and the documents created in anticipation of and after his death.

William Dotson died in 1858 before the Civil War. Above all else, any relationship he may have had with his children would have been limited by (1) the social constraints imposed by slavery and the white community and (2) the legal constraints in place in the state. In Mississippi, those constraints would have been severe. While it was fairly common for slaveholders to father children by their slaves, it was uncommon to acknowledge or provide for them in any significant way. If preference was shown, it was usually through lighter work assignments, such as work in the big house as opposed to field labor. Most faced the same risk of being sold as other slaves. Occasionally, a slaveholder attempted to free his slave-born children, but these attempts were rare and extremely difficult to carry out.

First, consider the circumstances surrounding William's life. Although he married in 1822, it appears from census records that his wife may have died between 1830 and 1840. No white female was present in his household after 1830, and no evidence suggests that he remarried. His will and census records indicate the couple had no children, or none who survived. The two minor children listed in his household in 1840 were the minor Tannyhill boys for whom he was guardian.

In addition, it appears that his closest relatives were living in Alabama and Georgia at the time of his will in 1858. At fifty-six, William would have been considered up in years when Henry was born. At such a late age and with no wife, children, or family near him, it is reasonable to assume that he could develop, if not a paternal bond, at least an emotional attachment to his slave-born children.

Just as important, the absence of a wife, children, or family nearby may have eliminated many of the problems that slaveholders in those situations would have encountered. Finally, Henry and his sister Sarah Ann looked more white than black. Regardless of what William thought of his children, legally they were black.

The relationship between William and Winnie may have been no different from that of other slaveholders who used their position and power to have their way with what belonged to them. If there was an attachment, it may not have extended beyond the children.

Actions Taken in Anticipation of His Death

Next, consider the actions William took in anticipation of his death—the terms and conditions of his will. The terms and conditions of the will are paraphrased as follows:

1. William stated that he was in feeble health and executed his will in anticipation of his death. He died less than four months later.
2. In item three, he left to his brother and two sisters, or their children if either brother or sister had died, the twenty-eight named slaves.
3. In item four, he left to his heirs the remainder of his estate, in fee simple. This estate included fourteen slaves and personal and real property, which included his two plantations.
4. **Item five was a no-contest clause.** William stated that he deliberately gave his brother and sisters and their descendants the twenty-eight slaves and their increase. The remaining real and personal estate was left in the hands of his friend and executor, L.N. Baldwin. William stipulated that if any of his legatees or devisees (his brother and sisters and their heirs) were dissatisfied with the will and attempted to embarrass the settlement by litigation, their share was to be withheld at the time of division of the estate, and the cost to his estate in defending such action was to be deducted and retained from the challengers' share of the estate.
5. In item six, William named his friend Lemuel N. Baldwin as sole executor with entire discretion in the management of the estate.

Important

William Dotson's will was anything but clear. The major question left unanswered was to whom he intended to leave the bulk of his estate. In the will, he stated that he left to his heirs the remainder of his property, without condition. Since he had no wife or children who could legally inherit his property, his unnamed heirs would be his heirs at law—his brother, two sisters, and possibly their children. Yet, he made it clear by including the no-contest clause that he intended that they receive no more than the twenty-eight slaves named in item three. This provision eliminates his family as the heirs to which he refers. If not his family, then who? Why not name them, since it appears he knew he might not live much longer?

If anyone knew the answers to these questions, it was probably the executor, Lemuel N. Baldwin. As expected, William's brother-in-law Richard G. Smith, husband of his sister Elizabeth Smith, filed suit on behalf of the family against Baldwin, the executor, in 1859, alleging fraud. Although the original complaint has not been found, the case continued through the war years and finally was dismissed in favor of the executor, Lemuel N. Baldwin, in 1867. The plaintiffs received nothing. Thus, could the unnamed heirs be the minor children of his slave Winnie? This would surely explain why he was apprehensive about naming his heirs in the will.

William Dotson had firsthand knowledge of the obstacles facing someone attempting to leave such a large estate to slaves. In 1838, William Harmon named his brother, Stephen Harmon, and William Dotson as co-executors of his estate. Harmon left half his estate to his niece and the other half to a female slave, Maria, and her children, Winslow, Anderson, Sarah Ann, and Eliza. The will directed that Maria and her children be taken to Ohio and freed and that the children receive an education or trade.[33] Since neither Maria nor her children were listed in the inventory and appraisal of Harmon's estate, it is possible they were freed. However, no evidence was found that she and her children received half the estate as called for in the will.

The final distribution of Dotson's estate should resolve the unanswered question of the identity of the unnamed heirs in the will. As mentioned earlier, the suit brought on behalf of William's sisters in Alabama was dismissed in favor of executor, Lemuel N. Baldwin. In addition, a settlement document in Dotson's probate file stated that in 1862, Sarah C. Moore and her husband, James M. Moore, of Harris County, Georgia, released to L.N. Baldwin their interest in the estate of William Dotson for four thousand dollars. Sarah was the daughter of Asa Dotson, William's deceased brother.

After Dotson's family's interest in the estate was terminated, Baldwin was free to distribute the estate. On 1 January 1870, L.N. Baldwin deeded to J.I.B. Rundell fourteen hundred acres of land, the two Dotson plantations, for ten thousand dollars.[34] According to Dotson estate records, Rundell had served as overseer of the Dotson plantation after William's death. On the same day as the Rundell deed, Rundell deeded to Henry Dotson and Winnie Jones two hundred acres for five hundred dollars cash, which was paid by L.N. Baldwin.[35] In 1874, Rundell deeded to William Campbell, husband of Sarah (Dotson) Campbell, approximately two hundred acres.[36] Baldwin, in 1878, repurchased the remaining property, approximately one thousand acres, from Rundell for ten thousand dollars, the original purchase price.[37]

Were Henry and Sarah the Unnamed Heirs Referred to in the Will?

The circumstantial evidence, though not conclusive, seems to point to Henry and his sister Sarah Ann as the heirs to whom Dotson intended to leave the remainder of his estate. **While each piece of evidence alone may not suggest such a premise, the combination of evidence suggests strong support for this conclusion:**

Technique

1. Winnie's family was the only family retained by the will as part of the estate.
2. William was probably aware that naming slaves as heirs would not survive a legal challenge by his family. This fact was a good reason not to name them as heirs.
3. William's family was eliminated as the heirs by the specific bequest of slaves and inclusion of the no-contest clause.
4. Winnie and Henry were deeded two hundred acres of the estate land, paid for in full by the executor, Lemuel N. Baldwin.
5. The estate records named no one else as heirs in relation to this part of the will.
6. Henry's descendants have a portrait of William and his personal Bible. Figure 10-3, on page 176, is the portrait of William, dating from about the late 1840s or early 1850s.

Because Henry and Sarah were quite young when William died, they did not know him long, and it is impossible to evaluate their personal relationship with him. However, ample evidence exists to support the conclusion that it was his

Figure 10-3 William Dotson (1794–1858).

intent to keep the family together, at least in the short term, following his death. Whatever his good intentions toward his slave children, William Dotson still was a holder and trader of slaves. As this case study exemplifies, even when a slaveholder such as William Dotson attempted to do what was right and responsible, legal and human obstacles intervened to thwart those good intentions.

ELEVEN

Case Study: A Story of Triumph and Tragedy

T he search for Sarenthia (Hilson) Smith's ancestors is a good example of how to research an individual born shortly before 1900 and for whom little or no information was available. For some of your ancestral lines, you may already know the names of ancestors born during slavery. The post–Civil War research of these ancestors will involve confirming what is known and collecting additional information.

For other lines, you may have only the name of an ancestor born several generations out of slavery, or shortly before or after 1900. In these cases, the search involves finding new clues that will guide you back step by step, generation by generation. Though both kinds of searches should be approached with equal determination and diligence, the search for the absolute unknown may require more effort and time. Such was the case of Sarenthia (Hilson) Smith.

This case study will reach back to 1870 and, from there, into the pre–Civil War and slavery era. **The research strategy that led to the identity of the slaveholder was a combination of the same-surname approach of chapter six and the location approach of chapter seven.** In the 1870 census, the former slave and the prospective slaveholder lived within one house of each other. Although the heads of the households had different surnames, members of both households shared a common surname. The relationship of the individuals with the different surname to the head of household was unclear since no relationship to the head of household was reported in the 1870 census. The objective was to determine, if possible, how each was related to the head of household and how that relationship might explain any connection between the households.

Technique

In the Beginning: What was Known

Sarenthia Hilson was born and spent her early years in Lincoln County, Mississippi. She met and married Willis Smith in Lincoln County and moved to Claiborne County, Mississippi, where she remained until her death. Her exact date of birth and death had been forgotten. Little was known about her early years in Lincoln County or exactly when or why she moved to Claiborne County. Her only surviving child was unable to provide any additional information.

Sarenthia and Willis had nine known children: Cary, Walter, Willie M., Geneva, Sammy, Robert Lee, Charlie, Jimmy, and Pearlie Mae.[1] Contact with Sarenthia's extended family had been lost over the years and would not be reestablished until the late stages of the research. Research of census and other public records provided the information needed to reconstruct Sarenthia Hilson's family history.

Step By Step

THE FIRST STEPS
Tracking Back to 1870

Since it was known that Sarenthia died after 1940 in Claiborne County, a search of the 1920 census was the place to start. In 1920, thirty-eight-year-old Serintha [*sic*] and her thirty-nine-year-old husband, Willis Smith, lived in Claiborne County, Mississippi.[2] In the household were

- son Cara, age 17
- son Walter, age 14
- stepson James H. Hilson, age 14 (actually Sarenthia's brother, James W. Hilson Jr.)
- daughter Janie, age 8
- daughter Willie M., age 6
- son Robert E., age 5
- son Samie, age 4
- son Charlie, age 3
- son Jimmie, age 11/12

Also in 1910, Sarenthia and Willis Smith were in Claiborne County.[3] In the household were

- Willis, age 35
- Sara [*sic*], age 32
- son Cary, age 6
- son Walter, age 4
- brother John W., age 4 (actually Sarenthia's brother, listed as James H. Hilson in 1920)

The age of the oldest child in this census record suggested that the couple married about 1903 and moved to Claiborne County prior to 1910. Lincoln County marriage records confirmed that Willis Smith married Sarenthia Hilson on 3 August 1902.[4]

Because the couple married after 1900, they were probably living with their childhood families in 1900. As expected, the 1900 census did not show a Willis Smith as head of household with a wife, Sarenthia. The Hilson surname was unique and rarely found outside Lincoln County before 1900. Thus, a search of the 1900 Soundex quickly located Sarenthia.

In the household of thirty-nine-year-old James W. Hilson and his thirty-five-year-old wife, Caldonia Hilson, was fourteen-year-old Surrintha [*sic*], born in

March 1886.[5] Both James and Caldonia were born in Mississippi. James's parents were reportedly born in Virginia, and Caldonia's in Mississippi. The couple had been married for nineteen years. Caldonia had given birth to nine children, seven of whom had survived. In the household, in addition to Surrintha [sic], were the other six children: daughter Genavor (age eighteen), son Robert (age nine), son Other (age seven), daughter Argustava (age five), daughter Ratta (age three), and son Ferrius (age one). Neither James W. Hilson nor Caldonia was enumerated in a census after 1900. It was known that Caldonia died before 1910; this fact explained why Sarenthia was raising her brother, James W. Hilson Jr. Later research confirmed that Genavor (Hilson) Cain, her oldest sister, raised the other siblings.

Because these Hilson parents had been married nineteen years and the oldest child was reported as eighteen in 1900, James and Caldonia probably married after 1880. Therefore, the search for James and Caldonia in 1880 and prior years would center on finding them as members of their childhood families.

At this point, Caldonia's maiden name was unknown. The earliest marriage records available for Lincoln County dated from 1893; a courthouse fire in 1893 had destroyed all previous records. With no direct source available for determining her maiden name, research on her would wait. First, the search would focus on the Hilson line.

The Search for James W. Hilson's Family

As expected, the 1880 Soundex did not list James W. Hilson as a head of household. Although several Hilson households were in Lincoln County in 1880, neither James W. nor anyone of his approximate age was in them.

James W. was not discovered in the 1880 census until the release of the 1880 census on CD-ROM in 2001. This index and abstract led quickly to finding his entry on the census microfilm. He was identified as twenty-year-old Walter Hillson [sic] in the household of a white family headed by George W. Smith; Hillson [sic] was working on the farm.[6]

Nevertheless, before the 1880 census entry was discovered, research continued. In 1870, only two Hilsons were listed in Lincoln County: one, as head of household; the other, as a member of another household. James W. Hilson was not listed in either of these households. However, in the household of Eli Hilson was nine-year-old Watt Hilson.[7] At age nine, Watt was about the same age that James W. would have been in 1870, based on James W.'s age and date of birth reported in the 1900 census. *Watt* could have been the enumerator's hearing of *Walt*, short for Walter. The 1870 and 1880 censuses suggested that Walter is the name the initial "W" likely represented.

The lack of other possible candidates and the similarity of the ages made Watt Hilson worthy of further investigation. Evidence confirming Watt and James W. as the same person came from several sources:

1. A recently identified and contacted descendant of James W. Hilson said the initial *W* stood for Walter.[8] She said James W. was known by the nickname Wady; this may have been the name given the census taker in 1870 and recorded as Watt.

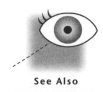

See Also

See pages 135–144 for more on the search for Caldonia.

CD Source

The Church of Jesus Christ of Latter-day Saints produced the set of fifty-five discs of index and abstracts, which are available at many libraries.

2. The 1878 census of educable children in Lincoln County, Mississippi, listed eighteen-year-old Wady Hilson, along with Jacob and Ely Hilson, the other children in Eli Hilson's household in 1870.[9]

3. James W.'s son Other Hilson named Wardy Hilson as his father on his SS-5 application for a Social Security card.[10]

Studying Eli Hilson in Census Records, 1870–1900

The Eli Hilson household in 1870 showed the following:[11]

- Eli, age 50, born in North Carolina
- Elizabeth Hilson, apparently his wife, age 46, born in Mississippi
- Gen. [sic] W. Hilson (male), age 15, born in Mississippi, as were the other children
- Jacob Hilson, age 11
- Watt Hilson, age 9
- Eli Hilson, age 7
- Henry America, age 4
- Nicy Weathersby, age 65, born in North Carolina

The relationship of Nicy Weathersby and Henry America to the head of household could not be determined from the 1870 census.

The Eli Hilson family was one of the three Hilson households found in the 1880 census. This time his household was smaller:[12]

- Eli Hilson, age 62, born in North Carolina as were his parents
- his wife, Elizabeth, age 58, born in Mississippi; her parents, born in North Carolina
- son, Eli Hilson Jr., age 16
- servants Vess Crosby, age 16; John Maiten [sic], age 12; and Payson Watts, age 8

Nicy Weathersby was no longer in the household nor was she listed elsewhere in the 1880 census; she probably had died by then. Since the mothers of Eli and Elizabeth were born in North Carolina, as reported in 1880, Nicy may have been the mother of either spouse. However, if her age as reported in 1870 was correct, it is more likely that she was Elizabeth's mother.

Eli Hilson, at age seventy-seven, was part of the 1900 household of Abram Brown and his wife, Sylvia.[13] Eli was listed as father-in-law of the head of household. Sylvia Brown may have been Abram's second wife, since they reported being married for nine years as of 1900; she apparently was not Eli's daughter.

However, Abram's wife in 1880 was named Louise.[14] Also in their household were stepson Henry America (age fourteen), who had been in Eli's household in 1870; Nancy Brown (age six); and Eli Brown (age three). Perhaps Louise was a daughter of Eli Hilson.

In 1900, Eli Hilson's birth date was reported as March 1823; he was a widower, reportedly born in North Carolina. He disappeared from the records after 1900. Based on ages reported in census records, Eli was born between 1818 and 1823 and his wife, Elizabeth, between 1822 and 1824.

The Results of the Post–Civil War Search

The following information resulted from the post–Civil War research of Sarenthia (Hilson) Smith.

1. Sarenthia was born in or about March 1886.
2. Her parents were James W. Hilson, born about 1860, and Caldonia Hilson, born about 1865, both natives of Mississippi.
3. Her siblings were sisters Geneva, Argustava, and Ratta; brothers Robert, Other, and Ferrius.
4. She married Willis Smith on 3 August 1902 in Lincoln County, Mississippi.
5. Her paternal grandparents were Eli and Elizabeth Hilson. Eli was born between 1818 and 1823 in North Carolina, as were his parents. Elizabeth was born between 1822 and 1824 in Mississippi, to parents who were born in North Carolina.
6. A possible great-grandmother, Nicy Weathersby, probably the mother of Elizabeth Hilson, was born about 1805 in North Carolina.

Research Tip

Notice that the research moved back and forth between the 1870 and later censuses and other records in order to learn more about the people who could have significant roles in the unfolding story. This strategy would continue as long as necessary.

THE SEARCH FOR A CLUSTER IN 1870

The research focus then turned to studying Eli Hilson in 1870 and gathering information that could lead to information on the Hilson family during slavery. Based on the ages of the family, it was clear that Eli and Elizabeth were born as slaves, along with all their children born prior to 1865. The age of the oldest child in the household in 1870, fifteen-year-old Gen. [*sic*] W. Hilson, indicated they were a family prior to 1855. If Eli and Elizabeth were not slaves on the same plantation, they were probably on adjoining plantations.

Would examining their 1870 neighborhood reveal additional details or clues about the family? The Hilson surname appeared only one other time in the neighborhood. A twenty-one-year-old, Mississippi-born mulatto, Jack Hilson, was listed in the household of Anson Runnels.[15]

The 1880 census enumerated thirty-year-old mulatto Jack Hilson as a head of household. His birthplace was given as Mississippi, and that of both parents, as North Carolina.[16] This entry placed Jack's birth about 1850 in Mississippi. Also in Jack's 1880 household was his five-year-old son, Eli Hilson. This circumstantial evidence suggested that Jack was the elder Eli Hilson's son. This information was later confirmed in Jack Hilson's death certificate, which named Eli Hilson as his father; his mother was unknown to the informant.[17]

The censuses had placed Jack's birth about 1850 in Mississippi. This additional evidence suggested that Eli came to Mississippi after 1818, his earliest suggested date of birth, and before 1850, the year Jack was born. It could not yet be determined whether Elizabeth was Jack's mother. No other obvious connections linked the Hilsons to any other African-American families in the neighborhood. A cluster could not be established based upon surname or any other noticeable characteristics in the community.

THE SEARCH FOR THE SLAVEHOLDER

The pre-1865 phase of the research could prove to be very difficult. Lincoln County was created in 1870 from Franklin, Lawrence, Copiah, Pike, and Amite counties. If Eli Hilson resided in the part of Lincoln that was previously part of Franklin and Lawrence counties, the search could be near impossible. A courthouse fire in 1877 destroyed most of Franklin County's pertinent records, and many of Lawrence County's probate and deed records had also been lost or destroyed.

A general survey of the neighborhood did not identify the county of which his neighborhood may have been a part prior to formation of Lincoln County in 1870. However, it appeared likely that it may have been Franklin County since most of the white 1870 neighbors appeared to live there in 1860. If this indication was correct, finding pre–Civil War documentation would be nearly impossible.

The Franklin County personal tax roll of 1868 was the only countywide document found that listed former slaves before the 1870 census.[18] The microfilm was arranged alphabetically, listing white taxpayers first, then black taxpayers. Eli Hilson was not listed; perhaps he was in one of the surrounding counties.

The Same Surname: A "Fishing" Expedition

The first stage of the search for Eli in the pre–Civil War era would utilize the same- or similar-surname strategy. However, a search of the 1870 and earlier census records recorded no white Hilsons living in Eli's neighborhood or any surrounding county. The one Hilson in Mississippi prior to the war had been there since shortly after 1800. The available records indicated he was never a slaveholder.

Research on the Hilson surname revealed that most families of the name resided in Alabama and Georgia prior to the Civil War. Two Hilsons were found in census records in North Carolina, Eli's birthplace, between 1800 and 1830, the years before and shortly after Eli's birth. However, no records were found to indicate that these had ever owned slaves. In addition, the deed and marriage records that were reconstructed for Franklin County, Mississippi, and the surrounding counties failed to produce any reference to a Hilson. The same-surname approach yielded no candidates that might lead to the identity of Eli's slaveholder.

At this point, the Weathersby name in both black and white families made it the clue to research.

The Location Search

The next step was to search the "location" or local community in which Eli lived in 1870. The starting point was all the white families listed five pages on either side of Eli in that census. A review of the surrounding households suggested a connection, though indirect, in the household of John Martin who lived only two households from Eli.[19]

As noted earlier, Nicy Weathersby was a member of Eli Hilson's household in 1870. At the same time, in the John Martin household was M. Weathersby, a twenty-five-year-old white female, and three Weathersby children: seven-year-old Robert, four-year-old Frank, and two-year-old Willie. Since no relationship to the head of household was reported in the 1870 census, further investigation was necessary to determine any relationship of M. Weathersby and the minor Weathersby children to the John Martin household.

The presence of Nicy Weathersby in Eli's household and the Weathersbys in John Martin's household was a significant find, especially since no other factors appeared to connect Eli to other white families in the community. A search of the Weathersby surname revealed numerous white families inhabiting Amite, Franklin, and Lawrence counties, all of which contributed to the formation of Lincoln County. However, before undertaking a multi-county search of Weathersbys, the Martin-Weathersby connection would be explored further.

Reaching Back: A Prime Candidate Emerges

In addition to the Weathersbys, the 1870 Martin household included the following:[20]

- John Martin, age 56, a farmer, born in South Carolina
- E.O. Martin, a female, age 60, also born in South Carolina
- John O. Martin, age 25, born in Mississippi
- Nancy Maegaha, age 16, born in Louisiana

If the Weathersbys were still in John Martin's household in 1880, a relationship to head of household would be given. However, in 1880, John O. Martin was head of the household in which the senior John Martin resided; neither M. Weathersby nor the minor Weathersbys were living with them.[21] In addition, Eli Hilson no longer lived nearby.

Perhaps a search for the John Martin family prior to 1870 would provide information that the 1870 and later censuses did not. The John Martin household was found in Amite County, Mississippi, in 1860.[22] In the household were

- John Martin, age 47
- E. Martin, female, age 51, apparently John's wife
- John Martin, age 13
- Solomon Weathersby, age 17, born in Mississippi
- Nicy McCudry, age 5, born in Louisiana

Although neither M. Weathersby (later identified as Mary) nor a female of her approximate age was in the household, the presence of Solomon Weathersby established an additional Weathersby connection. Living nearby were William J. Weathersby and L.L. Weathersby. Because the relationship to the head of household was not reported until 1880, the Martin-Weathersby connection was still undetermined.

Before research continued on the Martin family, the 1860 slave schedule was checked to determine whether the family owned slaves. The answer would either strengthen or eliminate this family as possible candidates. In fact, listed in succession in the 1860 Amite County slave schedule were John Martin with seven slaves, E. Martin with sixteen slaves, Solomon Weathersby with eleven, William J. Weathersby with seventeen, and L.L. Weathersby with thirteen slaves.[23]

This information only strengthened the connection between these families

Notes

The 1850 census of Amite County, in naming Amite County as a birthplace, was another example of the census taker providing more specific information than what the form requested and thus helping today's researchers.

and identified additional Weathersbys who might assist in defining that connection. Would a search of the 1850 census provide additional information? So far, each step back in time had yielded additional information that might link these families.

The John Martin household in 1850, still in Amite County, consisted of eight individuals:[24]

- John, age 37, born in South Carolina
- Elphany Martin, apparently his wife, age 40, born in South Carolina
- Lewis L. Weathersby, age 18 (Census reported all these children born in Amite County)
- Missouri A. Weathersby, age 16
- William J. Weathersby, age 14
- Virginia A. Weathersby, age 11
- Solomon C. Weathersby, age 8
- John O. Martin, age 3

The Weathersbys were apparently related to either John Martin or his wife; the question was how. Since all the children in the household were born in Amite County, would Amite County marriage records provide additional clues?

In fact, Elphany Obier married Lodwick L. Weathersby on 14 November 1831.[25] The connection was finally established. John Martin probably had married the widow of Lodwick L. Weathersby, although no marriage record was found. It appeared from the 1860 census that the M. Weathersby in John Martin's household in 1870 was the wife, Mary, of L.L. Weathersby, a son of Elphany Weathersby Martin and Lodwick L. Weathersby.[26]

Step By Step

FOCUS ON PRE–CIVIL WAR DOCUMENTS

With the Weathersby-Martin connection now established, research on Lodwick L. Weathersby was the next step. John Martin was not a subject of the search at this stage because the connection being sought was one between Nicy Weathersby and the Weathersby family. If this strategy failed, the search would continue on Elphany and then on John Martin.

If Lodwick L. Weathersby had died in Amite County, probate records there might reveal when he died. Amite County probate records indeed indicated that an administration was granted on the estate of Lodwick L. Weathersby on 27 November 1843; Elphany Weathersby and William A. Obier, Elphany's brother, were appointed administrators.[27]

Clues From Inventory, Appraisal, and Annual Returns

Lodwick L. Weathersby died intestate, leaving no will. However, Amite County probate records showed that an inventory and appraisal of the estate of Lodwick L. Weathersby was returned on 2 February 1844.[28] The inventory named thirty-three slaves. Among them was a man Eli, appraised at $700; a woman Betsy and child (child's name unreadable), appraised at $650; and Nicy, an old woman, appraised at $200. No family connections could be determined from the inventory, other than various mothers being listed and appraised with their young children. However, the appearance of Eli, Betsy, and Nicy—names of members of Eli Hilson's household in 1870—seemed very promising and warranted further investigation.

A further search of Lodwick L. Weathersby's estate records provided additional information. Estate records indicated that, when he died, Lodwick Weathersby had five minor heirs under the age of ten. His estate was large enough that a long-term administration was likely until the minor children were of age or married. The guardian, probably their mother, would be required to file with the court yearly accountings of estate income and expenditures. These accounts perhaps would identify the births and deaths of slaves.

Although annual reports were filed with the probate court, they identified no slave births or deaths by name, only the number of slaves who were born or who died and their appraised value. The next step in the probate process would involve the division of the estate on request of the heirs or the administrator. If found, the division might provide additional insight into the Eli Hilson Family.

Estate Division

The division of the estate of Lodwick L. Weathersby provided the information that confirmed the identity of the Eli Hilson family. Amite County probate records revealed that, on request, the probate court ordered a division of the estate of Lodwick L. Weathersby. On 18 February 1853, a division was recorded.[29] The estate was divided into six equal lots; the five children and widow of Lodwick Weathersby each drew a lot. Lot three, pulled by William J. Weathersby, included the following and their appraised value: Negro man Eli, $1,100; Negro man Moses, $1,100; Negro woman Betsy and child Ellison, $1,200; Negro girl Elvira, $400; Negro boy James, $600; and Negro boy Jack, $350. The division seems to have been made along family lines to some extent. Figure 11-1, below, is a portion of this estate division, showing this family.

The appearance of the names Eli, Betsy (Elizabeth), and Jack in the same lot confirms what was suspected from the inventory and appraisal—that they were in fact the Eli Hilson family that was the subject of this search. Although no

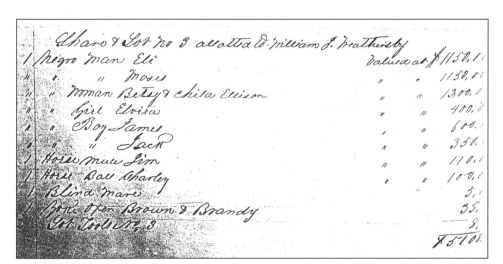

Figure 11-1 Lodwick Weathersby's estate division, 1853, showing Eli, Betsy, and Jack.

ages were given in the probate records, estimates from census records indicated that Jack Hilson was born about 1850 and would be the right age to be the Negro boy Jack, valued at $350. The grouping in the lot suggested with relative certainty the Elizabeth was Jack's mother.

The woman Nicy, now appraised at $400, was listed in Lot five, drawn by Solomon C. Weathersby. Nicy's relationship to Eli and Elizabeth was not clarified in the estate records. Elvira may have been the same as Louise, the wife of Abram Brown and believed to be a daughter of Eli Hilson. The boys James and Ellison would have been too old in 1853 to be James W. and Eli (Jr.) Hilson, who were born about 1860 and 1863. Although not confirmed, it is possible that Eli, Elizabeth, and Nicy were in some way related to some of the other slaves listed in Lodwick Weathersby's estate.

Earlier History

Lodwick Weathersby was the son of Lewis Weathersby. Lewis was allegedly born in North Carolina and migrated with his family to Amite County, Mississippi, from the Barnwell District of South Carolina about 1820.[30] He first appeared in Amite County records in the 1820 U.S. census with eleven slaves. Lodwick first appeared as a head of household on the Amite County Personal Tax Rolls in 1824 with four slaves. Research is still underway on Lodwick's family and that of his wife, Elphany Obier, to determine how and when Eli, Elizabeth, and Nicy may have become slaves of Lodwick Weathersby.

EPILOGUE

The search for the ancestors of Sarenthia (Hilson) Smith led to the identity of her parents, grandparents, and a possible great-grandmother. In addition, identifying the slaveholding family opened an entirely new avenue for research and extended the search back through two additional states—South Carolina and North Carolina. By any standard, this was a successful research effort.

However, along with great triumphs, we occasionally come face-to-face with unimaginable tragedy. Such was the case during research on the Hilson family. While Eli and his family managed to survive the unspeakable horrors of slavery, the family would face a heinous and deadly tragedy after the war. Apparently, Eli Hilson Jr. became a landowner and a successful farmer, much too independent for a black man during that time. He was told to leave town by a white supremacist group known as the whitecaps, a warning he failed to heed. In November of 1903, shots were fired into his home. He still did not leave. On the evening of 23 December 1903, while he was on his way home from town, he was shot and killed in his buggy. The horse returned the buggy with Eli's lifeless body home to his wife, Hanna, and their ten children.[31]

TWELVE

Case Study: All in the Neighborhood

T he search for the ancestors of Archie Davis Sr. and his wife, Martha (Humphreys) Davis, exemplifies the search strategy covered in chapter seven. The assumption that former slaves took the surname of the most recent slaveholder is a long-held fallacy encountered by African-American researchers. This case study refutes this assumption and demonstrates how the slaveholder can be identified when there are no apparent surname connections.

The research began with the presumption of a surname connection, but it became apparent that the same-surname strategy would not lead to the identity of the slaveholder. Any hope of finding the Davis and Humphreys slaveholder(s) would require a change of course.

Knowing when to change course is an integral part of developing and implementing a successful search strategy. If the Davis and Humphreys family did not take the name of their most recent slaveholder, maybe they still lived in the same community as the slaveholder or on land owned by the former slaveholder. The composition of the community provided important clues that helped identify the former slaveholder. Moreover, this case study is a good example of the value and use of cluster genealogy.

In the Beginning: What Was Known

1. Archie Davis Sr. was born a slave.
2. Archie Davis Sr. raised a family in the Willows community in Claiborne County, Mississippi, and had these known children: Amanda, Henderson, Harriett, Archie Jr., and Lenora.
3. He farmed about one hundred acres of land he owned in the Willows community.
4. He was a founding member of the Campbell Chapel Missionary Baptist Church in the Willows community about 1907.
5. He died 7 September 1923 at age eighty-four and was buried in the Willows Cemetery. His death certificate did not name his parents.[1]

Case Study

Step By Step

Reminder

Remember, you cannot know who reported the information to the census taker and how accurate their knowledge was. Comparing ages from all the census entries helps you evaluate the information for each member of the household.

POST–CIVIL WAR RESEARCH
Identifying Archie's Family

The first step in this research effort was a study of Archie Davis Sr. in the five post–Civil War census records from 1920 back to 1870. The 1920 census enumerated "Arch" Davis Sr. as eighty-one years old and head of a household that included Arch Davis Jr.; his wife, Alice; his mother-in-law, Dina Clark; and a seventy-year-old widow, Ann Blackstone, whose relationship was reported as sister.[2] Although the reported relationship was supposed to be the relationship to the head of household, later research found no evidence that Archie Sr. had a sister named Ann. Was she perhaps Dina's sister? That answer has not yet been found.

The 1910 census taker found Arch Davis Sr., a sixty-eight-year-old farmer, heading a household that included his son Elias, daughter-in-law Virginia, and young grandson Fred. The next household was that of Archie Davis Jr., his wife, and his mother-in-law.[3] As reported to the census taker, Archie Sr. had aged thirteen years between the 1910 and 1920, from sixty-eight years to eighty-one. His wife was yet to be identified.

Archie was a widower also in 1900.[4] This was the year when the census asked each person for a month and year of birth. Archie was fifty-eight years old with a reported birth year of 1842, consistent with the 1910 census. In the household were these relatives:

- daughter Amanda, age 34
- stepdaughter Estella Brown, age 25
- son Archie Jr., age 22
- son Elias, age 19
- son John, age 16
- daughter Lenora, age 14
- son Shelly, age 11

The presence of a stepdaughter younger than his oldest child suggested that Archie may have married twice and the stepdaughter was the child of his second wife. Confirmation was found in a marriage record for Archie Davis and Harriett Brown, dated 11 January 1887.[5] Shelly Davis's reported birth date of September 1888 suggests that he was probably a child of Harriett and thus a half-sibling to the others.

The makeup of the household in 1880 had to come mostly from the family's Soundex entry since the microfilmed page of the census was very faded and thus difficult to read.[6] This time, Archie's reported age of forty suggested a birth year of about 1840. His wife, Martha, was thirty-eight. Information discovered to this point suggested that she must have died between the birth of the daughter Lenora, about August 1884, and 1886, since Archie remarried in January 1887.

The 1880 household listed seven children, the oldest of whom was Amanda (sixteen) and the youngest, Archie Jr. (two). However, the surprise was finding the name of an additional family member: Archie's mother, Nellie Davis, age eighty.

The available index for the 1870 census did not show Archie but did list *Nella* Davis in the Grand Gulf precinct of Claiborne County.[7] She was a black, female head of household, reportedly eighty years of age—the same as in 1880. Four others were in her household: Harriett Woods (age forty-one), Jane Green (age thirty-five), Betsy Woods (age thirteen), and Matthew Green (age ten months), all born in Mississippi, as was Nellie. Where was Archie?

A page-by-page search of the county was the advisable approach since he was not listed in the index. Actually, he and his family were enumerated close to Nellie Davis, only one quite faded page away.[8] Studied with extra caution, the page contained a list of Archie's household: his wife, Martha, age twenty-six, and four children, six and under. For the fifth time, Archie's birthplace was given as Mississippi. Within the birth-year range suggested in the later censuses, Archie's reported age of twenty-nine placed his birth about 1840–1841.

Nellie's age of eighty years in 1880 (birth date about 1800) appeared more reasonable than the eighty years in her 1870 census entry. Archie's suggested birth range of about 1838 to 1842 corresponded reasonably to Nellie's birth around 1800. Together these records suggested he was born when his mother was about forty, a more likely age for bearing a child than near fifty, which the 1870 census suggested.

Because Harriett and Jane were single women in Nellie Davis's 1880 household, apparently with their children, perhaps they were Nellie's daughters and, therefore, Archie's sisters. Their ages fit this suggestion: Harriett, born about 1828–1829, and Jane, about 1834–1835. One fact in support of this proposition was that Archie acted as surety on the marriage bond of Richard Wallace to marry Harriett Woods, 8 October 1876.[9] The Wallaces lived near Archie until the 1900 census, after which they have not been located.

Finding Jane and Matthew Green in Nellie's household in 1870 led to a search for them in a later record. In 1880, the census taker listed Jane Alexander (age forty-five) and Matthew Smith (age eleven) next to Archie Davis. Their names and ages suggested they were the same as Jane and Matthew Green in Nellie Davis's home in 1870.[10] These entries were first discovered on the CD-ROM set of the *1880 United States Census and National Index*, released in 2001. **These discs are a valuable finding aid but do not replace the microfilm records.** In this instance, a combination of the CD-ROM, the badly faded microfilm, and a digitized version of the original on Ancestry.com helped determine the identity of these neighbors, who were not on the Soundex because Matthew was older than ten years.

At this point, attention to detail was important, focusing on Nellie Davis and Archie's family cluster. For example, Nellie's household reported her birthplace as Mississippi in the 1870 and 1880 censuses, and Archie's household reported the same birthplace for her, as Archie's mother, in 1880, 1910, and 1920. However, in 1900, the households of both Archie Davis and Harriett Wallace reported their mother's birthplace as Tennessee. (This suggestion will be a clue for future research into earlier generations.)

Research Tip

See pages 22 and 24 for reasons some people are not listed in an index.

Important

Summary of New Information About the Family of Archie Davis Sr.

1. Archie Davis Sr. was born probably between 1838 and 1842 in Mississippi.
2. His mother, Nellie Davis, was born about 1800 in Mississippi or maybe Tennessee.
3. Two probable sisters were Harriett (born 1828–1829) and Jane (born 1834–1835).
4. Archie and his wife, Martha, had at least ten children, as identified in censuses: Amanda, Robin (a son), Henderson, Mary Ann, George? (a son), Harriett, Archie Jr., Elias, John, and Lenora.
5. Martha Davis, Archie's first wife, was born about 1842–1844 and died between 1884 and 1886.
6. Archie married Harriett Brown in January 1887; they had one son Shelly, born in 1888.
7. The family lived in Claiborne County, Mississippi, at least from 1870 forward.

THE 1870 COMMUNITY

Research into many lineages, especially those of former slaves, benefits from the use of cluster genealogy. Although many people today live away from their birthplaces and relatives, ancestors often grew up and lived their lives among relatives, extended family, and neighbors—a cluster of people who knew each other. Studying this cluster for your ancestors includes paying attention to the neighbors around your family in census records, especially in 1870, the first census after emancipation. This strategy was important in the research on Archie Davis.

In 1870, one family listed next to Archie Davis Sr. was that of Jesse Humphreys, with his wife, Caroline, and four children. Two entries away, but next to Nellie Davis, were James Humphreys, his wife, Eliza, and their children.[11] Were these four families connected in any way? Were they relatives?

Attempt to Study Archie's Wife, Martha

These questions could not be answered from census records alone. Any relationship between the Humphreys and Davis families would have to come from other sources. What about a marriage record for Archie and Martha? Such a record might provide Martha's maiden name.

Censuses had suggested that their first child, Amanda, had been born between mid-1863 and September 1865; thus, the family probably existed as a family unit before emancipation. If so, did Archie and Martha report and legalize their marriage after the war, as many former slave couples did?

No record of their marriage has been found in the county marriage records, in the records of the Mississippi field office of the Bureau of Refugees, Freedmen, and Abandoned Lands, or in the index, "Marriage Records Prior to 1926," compiled by the Works Progress Administration in the 1930s from records at the Mississippi state board of health and available on microfilm. All that was known about Martha Davis, therefore, came from census records. She died when her

Notes

In rural areas, it is difficult to determine the census taker's exact route. Often, the family listed next to yours in the census lived on the same land in a separate house, or next door, or across the road, but they usually were close neighbors.

children were young, and they had all died by the time this research began. Thus, no family members or others who had known her could be interviewed.

Clues from Oral Tradition

Oral History

Fortunately, some oral tradition survived. Two family members found a photograph of an elderly lady seated in a chair (see Figure 12-1 below) and identified her as Aunt Cindy Haywood. Was she really an aunt? Of whom? Or was she a close friend of an earlier generation whom they called "aunt," even if she was not related? The ladies provided three tidbits of information, besides the Aunt Cindy's name, that turned out to be valuable:[12]

1. Aunt Cindy's husband had fought in "the war," which in the South meant the Civil War for generations after the conflict.
2. They thought Aunt Cindy was related to their grandfather, Henderson Davis, a son of Archie Davis Sr.
3. They thought Aunt Cindy, in her later years, had lived with Henderson Davis's sister, Harriett.

Researching the Clues

Harriett Davis's oldest living grandchild remembered that Aunt Cindy Haywood was Harriet's aunt, and thus Henderson Davis's aunt. In fact, she said Aunt Cindy was their mother's sister—Martha Davis's sister, not Archie's.[13] If Cindy's marriage record could be found, then her maiden name and that of her

Figure 12-1 Lucinda (Humphreys) Haywood, about early 1930s, Claiborne County, Mississippi.

proposed sister, Martha, might be identified. Indeed, the Claiborne County marriage records verified the marriage of Lucinda Humphreys to Jordan Haywood on 12 October 1870.[14]

Since the family tradition connected Lucinda (Aunt Cindy), rather than her husband, to the Davis family, and her marriage record gave her maiden name as Humphreys, perhaps the Humphreys neighbors in the 1870 census were related to her and thus to Martha Davis, her sister. One way to begin to find an answer was to consult the 1870 census for other Humphreys families, since Lucinda was not named in the James or Jesse Humphreys households and did not marry until after the census was taken.

In the same district as James and Jesse Humphreys and Archie and Nellie Davis lived Willoughby Humphreys and his family, which included twenty-two-year-old Lucinda.[15] Willoughby was a fifty-five-year-old black native of Mississippi; his wife, Mary, was fifty-six and a native of Missouri. This census implied that Willoughby and Mary were Lucinda's parents.

The fact that Archie Davis's mother was not Mary, but Nellie, who was a head of her own household in 1870, supported the tradition that Lucinda and Martha were sisters, now believed to be children of Willoughby and possibly of his wife, Mary. If Lucinda was a daughter of Willoughby, then Martha should have been as well. Willoughby was reportedly the same age as James Humphreys, Nellie Davis's neighbor; perhaps the two men were brothers. The forty-year-old Jesse Humphreys, Archie's neighbor, was in between Martha (age twenty-six in 1870) and Willoughby and James (age fifty-five). His relationship was difficult to guess without more evidence.

PRE–CIVIL WAR RESEARCH
Identifying the Slaveholder(s)

Important

Extended family clusters are often important in identifying slaveholders and slave family groups. **Like many white and free black families, many former slave families remained near friends and relatives for a number of years after the war.** The cluster of Davis and Humphreys households in 1870 and the proposed relationship between Lucinda (Humphreys) Haywood and Martha (Humphreys) Davis meant that research on Archie Davis's pre-war life would include both Davis and Humphreys families. Although Archie was an adult before the war was over, his mother, Nellie Davis, was also a primary focus of research.

Researching the family in the pre-war years would, by necessity, involve finding a slaveholder and researching his or her records, since slaves had little public or official identity of their own. Thus, the next step was to search for the slaveholder(s).

Same-Surname Approach

Census records had suggested that Nellie Davis was born about 1800, either in Mississippi Territory, created in 1798, or in east or central Tennessee, since much of West Tennessee was still Indian land. However, research could not begin with Nellie's birthplace. It had to begin with Mississippi as her residence, and the fact that Archie and his implied sisters, Harriett Woods Wallace and

Jane Green Alexander, reported Mississippi as their birthplaces. **Research must progress from what is known to find what is not yet known.**

Thus, were there Davis and Humphreys white families in Claiborne County between 1840 and 1870? Where they slaveholders before 1865? County land, probate, and tax records before 1865 and the 1850 and 1860 censuses did not suggest any obvious connections between the black families of Archie and Nellie Davis and any white Davis families in the area.

By the late 1790s, a white man named George Wilson Humphreys had come to the Claiborne County area. During the early nineteenth century, he accumulated large land holdings and many slaves; he died in 1843. Probate records of his estate and of other Humphreys decedents did not reveal among their slaves the names of Nellie or Archie or the other members of the two-family cluster, except for one: the name of Willoughby.

A civil court action that George Wilson Humphreys brought against his mother, Agnes Humphreys Burnett, in 1800 contained the name of a young boy named Willoughby. This boy would have been too old to be the Willoughby Humphreys in the 1870 census, the probable father of Lucinda and Martha; the 1870 Willoughby was born closer to 1815, not the 1780s or 1790s. However, the earlier Willoughby would have been of an age to be his father. This possibility is still under investigation.

The absence of the black Davis-Humphreys cluster from white Davis and Humphreys records was *negative evidence*, the absence of evidence, which can be important in research. How? In this case, it meant that same-surname research had not identified a slaveholder family, and research would turn to the "location" approach.

The Location Approach

This same-surname investigation took much time and effort but did not yield answers to the research questions. **When one approach does not produce results, re-evaluate the known and develop another strategy to change or broaden the search.** It is important not to give up without trying another approach.

In the Davis case, many scenarios could hamper the search. A slaveholder may have died before 1870 or may have left the area during or after the Civil War. A slaveholder may have held the Davis family members and died after the war; in such a case, his probate records would not reflect slaves. Other situations were possible as well. However, **research has to begin somewhere, has to have a plan, and should deal with the most likely, typical, or reasonable scenarios first.** Other strategies could be developed later, if necessary.

Since the Davis and Humphreys families were in Claiborne County in 1870 and may well have been there earlier, a reasonable strategy was to study white families who were also in the county in 1870 and who had surnames other than Davis and Humphreys. Thus, the next approach in the Archie Davis research involved white families who met three criteria: those who

1. lived in the same part of Claiborne County as the Davis family cluster in 1870
2. owned property, especially real estate, as shown in the 1870 census
3. had held slaves, as shown in the 1850 and/or 1860 census slave schedules

Reminder

\di'fin\ *vb*

Definitions

A *decedent* is one who is deceased.

Research Tip

Important

About a dozen families met the criteria for study. For some, records were not available; for others, records did not indicate a connection with the Davis-Humphreys family members who were living before 1865. Through a process of elimination, the candidate list dwindled to a thirty-three-year-old farmer named John P. McIntyre, who owned four thousand dollars worth of real estate. The 1870 census showed him within five households of Archie Davis Sr. and two households from Nellie Davis; in 1880, he was listed next to Archie Davis Sr.[16] Also in 1880, the James Humphreys and now-widower Willoughby Humphreys households were still nearby.[17] In fact, the census taker visited all these households on the same day—19 June 1880.

One more element necessary for McIntyre to remain in the search was slave ownership before the war. Although he was only twenty-two years old and single in 1860 and lived with a probable brother, D. McIntyre (age nineteen), and a Dr. E. Pollard (age thirty-one), McIntyre owned thirty-four slaves.[18] Ten years earlier, in 1850, he lived with his mother, A.C. McIntyre, and siblings Duncan H. (nine) and Louisa (fourteen).[19] John T. [*sic*] McIntyre was thirteen; his mother, identified as such in his 1880 household, was thirty-eight years old and owned thirty-four slaves. Mrs. McIntyre's name was given as Adeline C. in John's 1870 household.

A CANDIDATE FAMILY TO STUDY

This McIntyre family had met all the criteria for study, and the research continued back to the 1840 census. This census and Claiborne County probate records revealed that Adeline was the widow of Duncan H. McIntyre, also a slaveholder, who had come from Franklin County, Mississippi, to Claiborne County in the 1830s.[20]

When he died in 1842, D.H. McIntyre owned two plantations, called Caledonia and Beeches, and 102 slaves. The inventory and appraisal of the Beeches Plantation listed a girl Mary and her child and children named Margaret and Littleton. Later, an 1848 sale of slaves to an unidentified purchaser mentioned Mary, age thirty, and her children Littleton (ten), Martha (six), Ferdinand (four), and Wilson (two).[21]

Strong circumstantial evidence had accumulated to suggest that this Mary was the one who married Willoughby Humphreys, and six-year-old Martha was their daughter, who later married Archie Davis Sr. In 1870, Mary Humphreys was reported as fifty-six years old, with an estimated birth year of about 1814, not too different from the 1818 estimated birth year of the thirty-year-old Mary in the 1848 sale. Censuses suggested that Martha Davis was born between 1842 and 1844, virtually matching the 1842 birth year of the six-year-old Martha in the 1848 sale. Furthermore, the Wilson Humphreys in the Claiborne County census of 1900 reported his mother's birthplace as Missouri, the birthplace of Mary Humphreys as reported in the 1870 census.[22] **Another piece of evidence in support of this scenario was the fact that this same group of names and appropriate ages had not surfaced in other slaveholding households in the area.**

Notes

Was There More?

With a strong circumstantial link already made to the McIntyre family, showing Mary, Martha, and Wilson among the slaves of Duncan H. McIntyre, and the proximity of the Davis, Humphreys, and McIntyre families after the war, perhaps the McIntyre family warranted further study. They probably were not the slaveholders of the Davis family or the Humphreys men, but maybe, somehow, their other records would be helpful.

The 1830 and 1840 censuses had shown that Duncan H. McIntyre came to Claiborne County in the 1830s. An older man, Peter McIntyre, apparently made the same move from Franklin County to Claiborne between 1830 and 1840. He was of the age to be Duncan McIntyre's father (twenty to thirty years older) and he, too, was a slaveholder.[23] Additional evidence that they may have been father and son came from an 1841 land transaction. Peter McIntyre deeded all his property to D.H. McIntyre, including the plantation Caledonia, which was part of Duncan's estate in 1842.[24]

In 1833, Josiah B. Sugg of Claiborne County had married Elizabeth McIntyre, daughter of Peter McIntyre and, thus, apparently a sister of Duncan.[25] Five years later, Duncan H. McIntyre and Peter McIntyre both purchased land from Josiah B. Sugg.[26] Then, in 1844, Duncan and Adeline C. McIntyre's daughter, and John P. McIntyre's sister, Mary A. McIntyre, married William Robert Sugg, a nephew of Josiah B. Sugg.[27] An additional connection between the two families was that they were adjoining landowners, as shown in the 1848 tax roll. Josiah B. Sugg owned section 16 of Township 12, Range 3 East; Duncan McIntyre's estate owned section 17 of the same township and range.[28]

The McIntyre estate records had strongly suggested that Mary Humphreys and her children had been slaves of Duncan H. McIntyre but had not shown any evidence of the other members of the Davis-Humphreys cluster. Would the Sugg family, so closely connected to the McIntyres, play a role in finding them?

William Robert Sugg was the only child and minor orphan of William Sugg, who died in 1824. William Sugg and Josiah B. Sugg were brothers, and Josiah acted as his brother's executor. William Sugg's estate records mentioned eight slaves in December 1824 and twelve in August 1829.[29] The 1830 census of widow Margaret Sugg's household showed fourteen slaves, in addition to the young widow (age twenty to thirty), her son (age five to ten), and another male (age fifteen to twenty).[30] According to the same census, her brother-in-law, Josiah B. Sugg, was a young man (age twenty to thirty) with a female (age sixty to seventy), possibly his mother, in the household; they too were slaveholders.[31]

Margaret Sugg died in 1831, and Josiah B. Sugg became guardian of the boy, William R. Sugg. Both the inventory and appraisal of Margaret's estate, dated 25 March 1831, and the guardian's inventory of his ward's property in January 1832 listed sixteen slaves.[32] Because the 1832 document also reported their ages, eleven of them could be grouped into two suggested families, based on the ages and names from post-war censuses of the Davis and Humphreys families:

- woman Nelly, age 25–28
- her infant, Eliza (1831) or Elisha (1832), age 12 months, who died in 1832
- girl Harriett, age 8 or 9

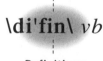

\di'fin\ vb

Definitions

A *minor* is a person under the age of adulthood, usually twenty-one in the nineteenth century; an *orphan* is a child who has lost one parent or both parents.

- girl Caroline, age 5 or 6
- girl Jenny/Jane, age 4 or 5

- woman Celia, age 38–40
- boy Willoby, age 13 or 14
- boy James, age 12 or 13
- boy Sampson, age 8 or 9
- boy Jess, age 5 or 6
- infant John, age 18 months

The first group, of course, appeared to be Nellie Davis; her two implied daughters, Harriett and Jane, from the 1870 and 1880 censuses; and another suggested daughter, Caroline, perhaps the Caroline who later married Jesse Humphreys. Archie Davis had not yet been born.

The second family unit was of the right names and ages to be Willoughby, James, and Jesse Humphreys, with a woman of age to be their mother, Celia, and her infant, apparently the toddler, John, of the 1832 list. The boy Sampson seemed to fit into this group, especially since James Humphreys later had a son named Sampson.

The remaining five slaves in the Sugg inventories did not have immediately apparent connections to the others and are still under investigation.

- woman Till, age 18–20
- her child, age 2 or 3, perhaps Albert of a later list
- girl Mary, age 4 or 5, perhaps Till's child or Celia's
- man Moses, age 26–28
- man Abram, age 26–28

The women and children, except for the infants, had all matched the slaves enumerated in the Margaret Sugg household in the 1830 census. The two men, it appeared, came to the plantation after June 1830.

The Connecting Piece of the Puzzle

Josiah B. Sugg moved to Louisiana about 1837–1838, and Duncan McIntyre became William R. Sugg's guardian. The 1840 census showed W.R. Sugg living alone, a single young man, age fifteen to twenty, with twenty-one slaves.[33] These, too, matched the 1832 inventory, with the addition of six boys under ten, one girl under ten, and one girl age ten to twenty-four.

When Duncan McIntyre died in 1842, another Peter McIntyre was appointed W.R. Sugg's guardian.[34] His inventory of his ward's estate named eighteen slaves, along with their ages. Two boys, Sparks (age five) and George (age two), accounted for two of the young boys added in the 1840 census. The other newcomers from 1840 were not listed, except for one: a three-year-old boy named Arche [sic]. This was the only pre-war record that named Nellie and Archie together. Figures 12-2A and B, on page 197, show this important inventory document and its transcription.

This succession of probate documents of the William and Margaret Sugg's estates revealed the history of ownership of the Davis and Humphreys families. Probably

Brick Wall Buster

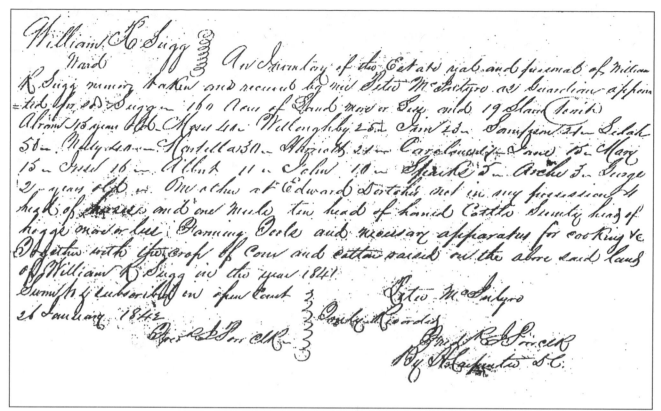

Figure 12-2A Peter McIntyre's Inventory of William R. Sugg's Estate, 1842

William R. Sugg

  Ward   An inventory of the Estate real and personal of William R Sugg minor taken and recused by me Peter McIntyre as Guardian appointed for sd Sugg~160 Acres of Land more or Less and 19 Slaves to wit Abram 45 years old~Moses 40~Willoughby 25~Jim 23~Sampson 21~Selah 50~Nelly 40~Martella 30~Harriett 21~Caroline 17~Jane 15~Mary 15~Jesse 16~Albert 11~John 10~Sparks 5~Arche 3~George 2 years old~One other at Edward Dortche's not in my possession--4 head of horses and one mule ten head of horned Cattle Seventy head of hoggs more or less Farming Tools and necessary apparatus for cooking &c Together with the crop of corn and cotton raised on the above said land of William R Sugg in the year 1841

Sworn to & subscribed in open Court   Peter McIntyre

26 January 1842   Truly Recorded

  Fred RJ Poor Clk~   Fred RJ Poor Clk

              By H Carpenter D.C.

Figure 12-2B Transcription of Above Document

the families and other Sugg slaves were hired out between 1831 and W.R. Sugg's marriage in 1844. As a boy, he would not have been farming on his own. After his marriage, when he was barely twenty-one, or perhaps as early as the 1840 census, he may have farmed his land, using some of his slaves as labor. Nevertheless, in 1860, as he apparently prepared to move to Louisiana, he sold his property to his wife's brother, John P. McIntyre.[35] Although documents have not shown the whereabouts of the Davis and Humphreys families between 1842 and 1865, they apparently remained in Claiborne County on the land of John P. McIntyre. This supposition would help explain why the three families were living in close proximity in 1870 and 1880.

THE PARENT GENERATIONS

Archie Davis's wife, Martha Humphreys, her siblings, and her mother, Mary, had lived on Duncan McIntyre's plantation at least until 1848. After that, apparently, they remained in the same vicinity. Mary Humphreys' early years are still under investigation.

Martha's probable father, Willoughby Humphreys, his siblings, and his mother, Celia, had been Sugg slaves before the group was transferred to neighbor and relative, John P. McIntyre in 1860. A close neighbor of the Suggs was Agnes Humphreys Burnett, mentioned earlier. In 1800, she had transferred to her son, George Wilson Humphreys, the slave boy named Willoughby, who would have been near Celia's age. On the same day, George transferred Willoughby back to Agnes for the remainder of her life.

A receipt found in Duncan H. McIntyre's estate file reflected a payment to Willoughby Humphreys in 1850 for blacksmith's work done in 1849. This paper proves that Willoughby was using the surname Humphreys before the Civil War. (See Figure 12-3 on page 199.) In addition, Celia's other children appeared with the Humphreys surname after the war. These two facts only strengthen the idea of a possible connection to the Willoughby on the Humphreys-Burnett plantation, whether he was Celia's husband or his relative. Furthermore, the Sugg estate papers suggested that the two men, Abram and Moses, probably did not father Celia's children. Thus, the possible Humphreys-Burnett connection is another focus for research.

Celia

The Sugg inventories of 1832 and 1842 indicated that Celia (Selah in the 1842 inventory) was born about 1792 to 1794. Even if she lived long enough to experience emancipation, she apparently died before 1870.

Continuing research on the Sugg family showed a transfer of slaves in Claiborne County in 1804. Josiah Bryan Sugg, who later moved to Louisiana, and his brother, the William Sugg who died in 1824, each were given three slaves from the estate of their grandfather, Britton Bryan. The gift was from Bryan's widow, Elizabeth, and their mother, Nancy (Bryan) Sugg, widow of their father, Josiah Sugg.[36] The 1804 inventory and appraisal of Britton Bryan's estate reported Selah as about eleven years old.[37] The inventory was consistent with the Sugg inventories in suggesting her birth about 1793.

Notes

The names Celia and Selah are further examples of given names spelled as the recorder heard them. All other aspects of the records indicate this was one person, not two.

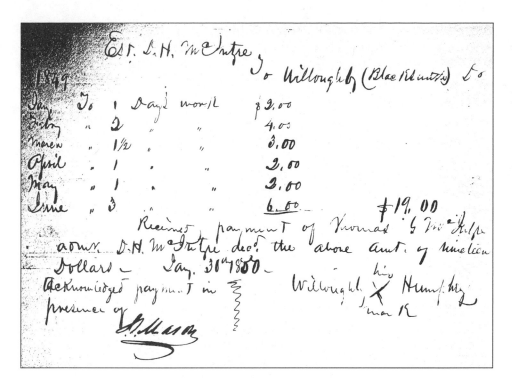

Figure 12-3 Receipt of payment from D.H. McIntyre estate to Willoughby Humphreys for blacksmith work, dated 1850, probate file M-9 (D.H. McIntyre), Claiborne County, Mississippi, Chancery Clerk's Office, Port Gibson.

The 1804 inventory did not group the Bryan slaves into families but listed them by age. The women on the list included Molly, forty-five, of the age to be Celia's mother. Research into the Bryan estate continues in the effort to identify Celia's childhood family. Britton Bryan has not been identified in the 1800 census but may be the Britain Bryant enumerated in 1790 in Edgecombe County, Halifax District, North Carolina.[38] The research will turn to him next.

Nellie

Finding ancestors of Martha (Humphreys) Davis solved only part of the puzzle of the Davis-Humphreys cluster. Archie Davis Sr., his siblings, and his mother, Nellie, had been on the William Sugg and John P. McIntyre plantations along with Celia and her children. Celia had come into the household by way of Sugg's maternal grandfather Bryan. How and when did Nellie come into this household? She had not been part of the Bryan estate.

Nellie was younger than Celia, but post-war censuses and Sugg estate inventories suggested she was born about 1800 to 1807, with emphasis on the 1800-1804 period. Since early Sugg records did not mention Nellie, as they had Celia, a candidate for research was William Sugg's wife, Margaret Daniel, whom Sugg had married in Claiborne County in 1822.[39]

Margaret was the daughter of William Daniel and Ann (Erwin) Daniel, who moved to Claiborne County before 1810.[40] Ann Daniel wrote a will in July 1830 and died not long thereafter.[41] From her mother's estate, Margaret (Daniel) Sugg received a Negro boy Abraham, probably the same as Abram named in Margaret Sugg's estate about a year later. The Ann Daniel estate revealed no additional clues about Nellie.

However, Margaret Sugg's father, William Daniel, had died in 1815. His inventory and appraisal listed eight slaves, including a woman Nelly.[42] Nellie

Davis would have been about eleven to fifteen years old in 1815, more a girl than a woman. Nevertheless, the inventory first named three men, then five women, but did not list their ages. The document did not indicate whether the eight were a family group. Based on their appraised values, the two who seemed to be older than the others were named Anthony and Lucy. Since no young children were indicated on the list, it is possible that Anthony and Lucy were the parents of some or all of the others, including Nelly.

In 1821, the widow Ann Daniel petitioned the probate court for a division of the assets of William Daniel's estate. In lot three of the division, Margaret (Daniel) Sugg received the Negro Nelly, valued at six hundred dollars.[43] This division answered the question of how and when Nellie came into the Sugg family. Thus, research continues on the Daniel family.

Conclusion

In the long run, both the same-surname and location approaches to research may identify more ancestors for Archie and Martha Davis's descendants. However, the proximity of the 1870 and 1880 residences of the Davis, Humphreys, and McIntyre families was the key to discovering the childhood families of both Archie and his wife, as well as her father. Studying the cluster of the Davis and Humphreys families, as well as the slaveholder families, in several generations, was an essential technique for success so far and will be necessary as research reaches into the eighteenth century.

Free and Slaveholding States and Territories in 1861

I mportant factors in successful research are the availability of records in ancestral jurisdictions and the researcher's knowledge of history in these areas. When searching for African-American ancestors before 1865, genealogists need background on the existence and abolition of slavery to help determine what kinds of records may assist in research. This appendix capsules abolition history for U.S. states and territories.

The legal history of slavery and freedom is complex. Colonial, state, territorial, and national governments regulated the lives of both slaves and free blacks, some laws reaching into the early seventeenth century. These laws not only affected the lives of ancestors but also may have generated records of use to genealogists and historians. In studying ancestors' lives and records, researchers should investigate the social, political, economic, and legal history of ancestral jurisdictions. Pertinent reference materials may include publications on American history and culture, history of specific areas, and African-American history in general and in ancestral locations. Such works and the laws of the states are often available in university, special, and law libraries.

Free States

In the 1790 and 1800 censuses, slaves were enumerated in all the original thirteen states except Massachusetts. The Ordinance of 1787 had prohibited slavery in the Northwest Territory (north of the Ohio River and east of the Mississippi River), but slaves did live in some of these areas as well.

The following states were considered free of slavery when the Civil War began:

For More Info

See *A Century of Population Growth, 1790–1900*, in the source list on page 206, for more statistics on blacks in the censuses.

California—admitted as a free state by the Compromise of 1850.[‡]

Connecticut—original state; in 1784, state legislature enacted gradual abolition of slavery, with provisions for all blacks born after 1 March 1784 to be free at age twenty-five; legislature enacted several other laws, the last one in 1797, providing that black children born in the state would be slaves only until the age of twenty-one; slaves were enumerated in the state, 1790–1840; in 1848, state legislature abolished slavery.

Illinois—slavery prohibited by the Ordinance of 1787 and by its constitution at the time of statehood, 1818; became a territory, 1809; slaves enumerated, 1800–1840.

Indiana—slavery prohibited by the Ordinance of 1787 and by its constitution at the time of statehood, 1816; became a territory, 1800; slaves enumerated, 1800–1840.

Iowa—slavery prohibited by Missouri Compromise,[+] 1820; became a territory, 1838; sixteen slaves enumerated, 1840; admitted as a free state, 1846.

Kansas—originally considered free by the Missouri Compromise[+]; given the right of popular sovereignty[*] when it was organized as a territory by the Kansas-Nebraska Act, 1854; two slaves enumerated in 1860; admitted as free state, January 1861.

Maine—free by virtue of being part of Massachusetts in 1780; admitted as free state, 1820.

Massachusetts—original state; slavery virtually gone by the end of 1776; state's Chief Judge William Cushing, 1783, made a statement (at the end of a case but not as a judicial decision) that the state constitution of 1780 had abolished slavery by granting rights and privileges incompatible with the existence of slavery; state constitution's bill of rights declares "all men are born free and equal" and "every subject is entitled to liberty"; one slave enumerated in 1830, no others enumerated from 1790 to 1860.

Michigan—slavery prohibited by the Ordinance of 1787; became a territory, 1805; slaves enumerated in 1810 and 1830 (in 1830, most of these were reported in the Wisconsin census); admitted as a free state, 1837.

Minnesota—area east of Mississippi River implied free by Ordinance of 1787 and the rest, considered free by the Missouri Compromise, 1820[+]; became a territory, 1849; admitted as a free state, 1858.

New Hampshire—original state; common interpretation of the bill of rights of the state constitution of 1784 was that the clause "All men are born equally free and independent" meant just that; some in the state inferred that all born after the constitution went into effect were free, and slaves born before it would remain slaves (see Belknap, Skinner, and Supreme Court of New Hampshire in source list on pages 206–207); 157 slaves enumerated in 1790, eight in 1800, three in 1830, one in 1840; no legislative act or judicial decision initiated abolition of slavery in the state, and no specific date marks freedom of slaves in the state.

New Jersey—original state; legislative act of 1804 declared all persons born of slave parents in the state after 4 July 1804 to be free, males upon reaching age twenty-five, females at age twenty-one; gradual abolition enacted, 1846, with all slaves made apprentices for life and their children being free at birth; slaves enumerated in censuses, 1790–1860, with eighteen "apprentices for life" listed in 1860; thirteenth amendment[**] to the U.S. constitution, 1865, freed any remaining slaves.

New York—original state; 1788 state law provided for freedom for all slaves illegally imported into the state; gradual abolition enacted 1799, whereby children born of slave parents after 4 July 1799 were to be freed, males upon reaching age twenty-eight, females upon reaching age twenty-five; by legislative act, 1817, all Negroes born before 4 July 1799 would be free as of 4 July 1827 and those born between 1799 and 1827 would be indentured servants until reaching the ages specified in the 1799 law; slaves enumerated, 1790–1840.

Ohio—slavery prohibited by the Ordinance of 1787 and by state constitution, 1802, prior to statehood in 1803; six slaves enumerated in 1830, three in 1840.

Oregon—organized as free territory, 1848; admitted as a free state, 1859.

Pennsylvania—original state; gradual abolition enacted, March 1780, with (1) children born of slave mothers in Pennsylvania after enactment of the law to be free at age twenty-eight and (2) persons already held as slaves at the time of the law would continue to be slaves; slaves enumerated, 1790–1840.

Rhode Island—original state; gradual abolition enacted, 1784, whereby (1) all children born of slave mothers after 1 May 1784 would be free and (2) to defray cost of supporting these children, they could be bound out, males to the age of twenty-one, females to the age of eighteen; law changed in 1785: instead of their hometown supporting them, this responsibility shifted to the mother's master; slaves enumerated, 1790–1840.

Vermont—slavery abolished in state constitution, 1777, when Vermont declared itself independent and separate from England, New York, and New Hampshire; in 1786, state legislature reiterated that all former slaves had been liberated by the state constitution; no slaves enumerated in federal censuses; statehood, 1791.

Wisconsin—slavery prohibited by Ordinance of 1787; some slaves enumerated, 1830 and 1840; admitted as free state, 1848.

Territories

Congress enacted abolition of slavery in the territories, without compensation to slaveholders, in June 1862.

Colorado Territory—created as a free territory, February 1861; no slaves enumerated in 1860; statehood, 1876.

Dakota Territory—created in March 1861; no slaves enumerated in 1860; statehood as North Dakota and South Dakota, 1889.

Nebraska Territory—slavery prohibited by Missouri Compromise,[+] 1820; created as a territory, 1854, by the Kansas-Nebraska Act, with the right of popular sovereignty[*]; fifteen slaves enumerated in 1860; statehood, 1867.

Nevada Territory—created, March 1861; no slaves enumerated in 1860; statehood, October 1864.

New Mexico Territory—created, September 1850, with no restriction on slavery[‡]; no slaves enumerated in 1860; statehood, 1912.

Oklahoma/Indian Territory—unorganized Indian territory in 1861; 1860 slave schedule is found at the end of the Arkansas slave schedule under Indian Lands West of Arkansas; territory created, 1890; statehood, 1907.

Utah Territory—created, September 1850, with no restriction on slavery[‡]; slaves reported in 1850 (26) and 1860 (29); statehood, 1896.

Washington Territory—territory created, 1853; no slaves enumerated, 1860; statehood, 1889.

Territories created during the Civil War included Arizona (1863), Idaho (1863), and Montana (1864). Other future western states were included in the territories listed above. Alaska and Hawaii were not U.S. territory in 1861.

Slaveholding Areas

Following South Carolina's lead in December 1860, ten other slave states seceded from the United States in the first half of 1861 to form the Confederate States of America. War broke out at Fort Sumter, South Carolina, on 12 April 1861.

President Abraham Lincoln's Emancipation Proclamation of 1 January 1863 declared all slaves free in regions still in rebellion—the Confederate states—with the exception of the areas occupied by Union military forces: Tennessee and portions of Virginia and Louisiana. In effect, the U.S. government could not immediately enforce the proclamation because it applied only to the areas over which the government had no control.

However, word of the proclamation eventually spread throughout the Confederacy. Anniversary celebrations in some areas occurred on January 1 of succeeding years. In other areas, freedmen celebrated the anniversary of the day the proclamation was announced, such as 19 June 1865 in Texas. The proclamation did not affect the slaveholding states in the Union: Delaware, Kentucky, Maryland, Missouri, and New Jersey.

Technically, slavery ended in the South with the ratification of the thirteenth amendment to the Constitution in December 1865.

When the war broke out, the following were slaveholding jurisdictions:

Alabama—territory organized, 1817; slaves enumerated from 1800 (as Washington County, Mississippi) through 1860; statehood, 1819.

Arkansas—territory organized, 1819, with no restriction on slavery; slaves enumerated from 1810 (in the unorganized area called Louisiana territory) through 1860; admitted as a slave state, 1836.

Delaware—original state; slaves enumerated, 1790–1860; remained in the Union during the Civil War; did not ratify the thirteenth amendment** but slavery there was abolished when the amendment was declared ratified in December 1865.

District of Columbia—created out of Maryland, in use as seat of government by late 1800; slaves enumerated, 1800–1860; Congress abolished slavery in the district, with compensation to owners, in April 1862.

Florida—acquired in 1819; territory organized, 1822; slaves enumerated, 1830–1860; admitted as slave state, 1846.

Georgia—original state; slaves enumerated 1790–1860.

Kentucky—admitted as state, 1792; slaves enumerated, 1790–1860; considered a border state in the Civil War; remained in the Union; did not ratify thirteenth amendment** but slavery there was abolished when the amendment went into effect, December 1865.

Louisiana—acquired in Louisiana Purchase, 1803; organized as Orleans Territory, 1804; statehood, 1812; slaves enumerated 1800–1860.

Maryland—original state; slaves enumerated, 1790–1860; considered a border state during the Civil War; remained in the Union; the state's constitutional convention of 1864 changed an article of the state's Bill of Rights to abolish slavery; new constitution narrowly approved by voters in October and went into effect, 1 November 1864.

Mississippi—territory organized, 1798; statehood, 1817; slaves enumerated, 1800–1860.

Missouri—territory organized, 1812; admitted as slave state, 1821, as result of the Missouri Compromise⁺ of 1820; considered a border state during Civil War; remained in the Union; an ordinance of a state convention, 11 January 1865, provided immediate emancipation.

North Carolina—original state; slaves enumerated, 1790–1860.

South Carolina—original state; slaves enumerated, 1790–1860.

Tennessee—statehood, 1796; slaves enumerated, 1790–1860.

Texas—Spanish and Mexican territory until 1836; republic, 1836–1845; admitted as slave state, 1845; slaves enumerated in censuses, 1850–1860.

Virginia—original state; slaves enumerated, 1790–1860.

West Virginia—part of Virginia before being admitted as free state, 1863; state constitution of 1863 provided for gradual emancipation, one requirement for admission as a new state.

Notes

⁺ The Missouri Compromise, 1820, banned slavery in the lands of the Louisiana Purchase that lay north of 36° 30′ latitude, the northern boundary of Arkansas. Louisiana was already a slave state, and Arkansas Territory had been organized in 1819 with no restriction on slavery. The compromise allowed Missouri to enter the Union as a slave state and Maine, as a free state. The Kansas-Nebraska Act of 1854, in effect, repealed the Missouri Compromise by allowing the practice of popular sovereignty* in the territories.

‡ Compromise of 1850—five measures Congress enacted in September 1850 after months of debate and compromise: (1) admitting California as a free state; (2) Texas relinquishing claim to New Mexico, and Congress establishing New Mexico Territory with no restriction on slavery and allowing for popular sovereignty there (see below) on the issue of slavery; (3) organizing Utah Territory with the same provisions concerning slavery; (4) abolishing the slave trade in the District of Columbia as of 1851; and (5) tightening the federal fugitive slave law.

*Popular sovereignty—the idea that the people of the territory should decide by popular vote whether the territory should be free or allow slavery; incorporated in the Compromise of 1850 and the Kansas-Nebraska Act of 1854.

**Thirteenth amendment to the U.S. Constitution—prohibited slavery in the United States; proposed 1 February 1865; declared in force 18 December 1865. The following former Confederate states ratified the amendment as a requirement to readmission into the Union but were counted as legitimate and active states in the ratification process, prior to their readmission: Alabama, Arkansas, Georgia, Louisiana, North Carolina, South Carolina, Tennessee, Virginia. The remaining Southern states—Florida, Mississippi, Texas—ratified the amendment later as a prerequisite to readmission.

Sources

A Century of Population Growth: From the First Census of the United States to the Twelfth, 1790–1900. Washington, D.C.: Government Printing Office, 1909. Reprint, Orting, Wash.: Heritage Quest Press, 1989. Especially pp. 132–133 (slave population in each state, 1790–1860), 274–275.

Arnold, Samuel Greene. *History of the State of Rhode Island and Providence Plantations.* 2 vols. New York: D. Appleton & Co., 1860. 2:503, 506.

Belknap, Jeremy. *The History of New Hampshire.* 3 vols. Reprint of 1792 edition. New York: Arno Press, 1972. III:280–282.

Cunningham, Valerie. "The First Blacks of Portsmouth." Part 2. *Historical New Hampshire* 44 (winter, 1989). Reprinted online. SeacoastNH.com. 1997. <www.seacoastnh.com/blackhistory/blacks2.html>. Accessed 30 November 2001.

Daniell, Jere R. *Experiment in Republicanism: New Hampshire Politics and the American Revolution, 1741–1794.* Page 179.

Dodson, Howard, Christopher Moore, and Roberta Yancy. *The Black New Yorkers.* New York: John Wiley and Sons, 2000. Especially pp. 52, 56–57.

Ellis, David M., James A. Frost, Harold C. Syrett, and Harry J. Carman. *A History of New York State.* Rev. ed. Ithaca, N.Y.: Cornell University Press, 1967. Especially p. 186.

Flick, Alexander C., ed. *History of the State of New York.* 10 vols. Empire State Historical Publication XVIII, 1934. Port Washington, Long Island, N.Y.: Ira J. Friedman, Inc., 1962. Especially p. 328.

Futhey, J. Smith, and Gilbert Cope. *History of Chester County, Pennsylvania.* Philadelphia: Louis H. Everts, 1881. Facsimile reprint. Chester County Historical Society, 1996. Especially pp. 423–427; also describes the slave registration process set out in two 1780 laws and applicable records of Chester County.

Hodges, Graham Russell. *Slavery and Freedom in the Rural North: African-Americans in Monmouth County, New Jersey, 1665–1865.* Madison, N.J.: Madison House, 1997. Especially pp. 129, 134, 149, 175.

King, David Thomas. "The End of Slavery in Massachusetts." In *Historic U.S. Court Cases 1690–1990: An Encyclopedia* edited by John W. Johnson. New York: Garland Publishing Co., 1992. Pages 339–341. King asserts, p. 341, that the failure of the slaveholder, Jennison, in the several cases against Quock Walker "discouraged other owners from contesting legal efforts of slaves to gain freedom and thus in effect signaled the end of slavery in Massachusetts."

Litwack, Leon F. *North of Slavery: The Negro in the Free States, 1790–1860.* Chicago: The University of Chicago Press. Especially pp. 3, 7, 9.

Long, Luman H., ed. *1970 Edition: The World Almanac and Book of Facts.* New York: Newspaper Enterprise Association, 1969. Chronological List of Territories, p. 32.

Ludlum, David M. *Social Ferment in Vermont, 1791–1850.* New York: AMS Press, 1939; reprint, 1966. Especially pp. 4, 6, 134.

March, David D. *The History of Missouri.* 4 vols. New York: Lewis Historical Publishing Co., 1967. Especially pp. 950–961, 998–1000.

Morris, Richard B., and Henry Steele Commager, eds. *Encyclopedia of American History*. Updated and revised ed. New York: Harper & Row, 1965. Especially pp. 211, 543–545.

Morse, Jarvis Means. *A Neglected Period of Connecticut's History, 1818–1850*. New Haven: Yale University Press, 1933. Especially pp. 193, 203.

Pennsylvania Act of 1 March 1780 for Gradual Abolition of Slavery. Online. <www. yale.edu/lawweb/avalon/states/statutes/pennst01.htm>. Accessed 30 November 2001.

Randall, J.G., and David Donald. *The Civil War and Reconstruction*. 2d ed. Boston: D.C. Heath and Co., 1961. Especially pp. 4–5 (created from 1850 and 1860 census statistics), 372–373, 380–381, 385, 395.

Roth, David M. *Connecticut: A Bicentennial History*. New York: W.W. Norton & Co., 1979. Especially p. 126.

Scharf, J. Thomas. *History of Maryland from the Earliest Period to the Present Day*. 3 vols. Reprint of 1879 original. Hatboro, Penn.: Tradition Press, 1967. 3:583, 596–597.

Skinner, Harland C. "Slavery and Abolition in New Hampshire." Master's thesis, University of New Hampshire, 1948. The date of abolition of slavery in New Hampshire is difficult to determine. "[S]lavery gradually ceased to exist in New Hampshire and what references are given in the New Hampshire laws are merely an official confirmation of this fact. The Revolution had a greater influence in freeing the slaves than the constitution of 1784." (pp. 74–75)

Supreme Court of New Hampshire. "Opinion of the Justices of the Supreme Judicial Court." 41 N.H. 553. 1861. *Lexis-Nexis Academic Universe*. 1 December 2001. On 26 June 1861, the state legislature asked the state supreme court for an opinion on the constitutionality of an act passed 26 June 1857, "to secure freedom and the rights of citizenship to persons in this State." The court felt the constitutionality of the act had never been questioned, nor did it change existing law or conflict with U.S. law or constitution. The third section of the law made it a felony to hold any person as a slave in the state; the exception was an officer of the U.S. or other person acting in the execution of a legal process—i.e., dealing with fugitive slaves. The 1857 law did not initiate abolition of slavery in the state, as some sources report, but it and the court affirmed what was already in practice.

Federal Census, 1790–1930

Which Census Reports . . . ?

age, sex, race of each individual in free household	1850 forward
agricultural schedules	1850–1880
attendance in school	1850 forward
months attending school	1900
birth date (month/year) of each person	1900
month of birth if born within the year	1870, 1880
birthplace of each person	1850 forward
citizenship, see *male . . . ; naturalized citizen . . .*	
convict	1850, 1860, 1890
crippled, maimed, deformed	1890
deaf, dumb, or blind	1850–1890, 1910
defective, dependent, delinquent schedules (DDD)	1880
disabled: crippled, maimed, bedridden, or other disability	1880
employer, self-employed, or wage earner	1910–1930
months unemployed	1880–1900
whether person worked yesterday	1930
home or farm as residence	1890–1910, 1930
home owned or rented	1890–1930
home owned free of mortgage	1890–1920
farm owned or rented	1890
farm owned free of mortgage	1890
value of home or monthly rent	1930
homeless child	1890
illness, current, or temporary disability	1880
chronic or acute illness, length of time afflicted	1890
immigration year	1900–1930
number of years in United States	1890, 1900
industry/manufacturing schedules	1820, 1850–1880
insane, idiot	1850–1880
defective in mind	1890
language, native	1890, 1910–1930
native language of parents	1920
speaks English	1890–1930
male, eligible/not eligible to vote	1870
marital status	1880 forward

age at first marriage	1930
married within the census year	1850–1890
month of marriage, within census year	1870
number of years of present marriage	1900, 1910
mortality schedules	1850–1880
mother of how many children, number living	1890–1910
name of each individual in free household	1850 forward
name of head of household only	1790–1840
naturalized citizen "Na" or first papers "Pa"	1890–1930
year of naturalization	1920
occupation	1850 forward
parents, whether foreign born	1870
birthplace of parents	1880 forward
pauper	1850, 1860, 1890
prisoner	1890
radio set in home	1930
reading and writing, whether able to read or write	1890–1930
persons unable to read and/or write	1850–1880
relationship to head of household	1880 forward
slaves by age and sex	1820–1860
number of slaves in household	1790–1860
social statistics schedules	1850–1880
Soundex (see chapter ten)	beginning 1880
street address of family	1880 forward
value of real estate owned	1850–1870
value of home or monthly rent	1930
value of personal estate	1860–1870
veterans: pensioners	1840
Union veterans and widows, special schedule	1890
Civil War veteran or widow, Union or Confederate	1890
Civil War veteran, Union or Confederate	1910
veteran of U.S. military or naval forces, which war	1930

First Federal Census Available for Each State*

Alabama	1830	Idaho	1870
Alaska	1900	Illinois	1810
Arizona	1850	Indiana	1820
Arkansas	1830	Iowa	1840
California	1850	Kansas	1860
Colorado	1860	Kentucky	1810+
Connecticut	1790	Louisiana	1810
Delaware	1800+	Maine	1790
District of Columbia	1800	Maryland	1790
Florida	1830	Massachusetts	1790
Georgia	1820+	Michigan	1820
Hawaii	1900	Minnesota	1850

Mississippi	1820	Pennsylvania	1790
Missouri	1830	Rhode Island	1790
Montana	1860	South Carolina	1790
Nebraska	1860	South Dakota	1860
Nevada	1870	Tennessee	1820 (1810 partial)
New Hampshire	1790		
New Jersey	1830+	Texas	1850
New Mexico	1850	Utah	1850
New York	1790	Vermont	1790
North Carolina	1790	Virginia	1810+
North Dakota	1860	Washington	1860
Ohio	1820	West Virginia	1870+
Oklahoma	1860** 1900	(part of Virginia until 1863)	
		Wisconsin	1820
Oregon	1850	Wyoming	1870

+Published substitutes exist for the 1790 census, created from other records. For other states or counties missing from the 1790 schedules, see town or county courthouse records of the period—original, published, or microform.

*Censuses may be missing for several reasons:
  1. State or territory not yet organized, or enumerated with parent territory.
  2. Census was taken but schedule misplaced, not turned in, ruined, lost, destroyed.

**Free, non-Indian residents of Oklahoma area are enumerated at the end of roll 52 (Arkansas) under Indian Lands.

State Archives

The Web sites for the state archives may contain descriptions of their collections, online indexes, searchable databases, and information about research in the state. These sites often include the address of the facility, the hours when it is open for research, and the rules that researchers are asked to follow. The staff of some state archives and historical societies will answer short queries by mail; some will not. If you visit in person, they may answer questions about the records and may help you in using the records. They cannot research for you but often can assist you in requesting copies of specific records that they hold.

The following lists the state archives or historical societies, their physical addresses and phone numbers, and the Web sites that were available at this writing. If a Web site changes, the older address may lead you to the new one. Another way of finding a new Web address for the archives is to consult <www.coshrc.org/arc/states/htm>, the Web site of the Council of State Historical Records Coordinators.

Alabama
Alabama Department of Archives and History
    624 Washington Ave., P.O. Box 300100, Montgomery, AL 36130-0100
    Phone: (334) 242-4435   www.archives.state.al.us/index.html

Alaska
Alaska Division of Libraries, Archives, and Museums
    141 Willoughby Ave., Juneau, AK 99801-1720
    Phone: (907) 465-2270   www.archives.state.ak.us/

Arizona
Arizona Department of Library, Archives, and Public Records
    1700 W. Washington, Suite 342, State Capitol, Phoenix, AZ 85007
    Phone: (602) 542-4159   www.lib.az.us/archives/

Arkansas
Arkansas History Commission and State Archives
    One Capitol Mall, Little Rock, AR 72201
    Phone: (501) 682-6900   www.ark-ives.com/

California
California State Archives
    1020 "O" St., Sacramento, CA 95814
    Phone: (916) 653-2246 (reference)
    www.ss.ca.gov/archives/archives.htm

Colorado

Colorado State Archives

    1313 Sherman St., Room 1B-20, Denver, CO 80203

    Phone: (303) 866-2358 (reference)

    www.archives.state.co.us/geneal.html

Connecticut

Connecticut State Library, History and Genealogy

    231 Capitol Ave., Hartford, CT 06106

    Phone: (860) 757-6580 (reference)   www.cslib.org/handg.htm

Delaware

Delaware Public Archives

    121 Duke of York St., Hall of Records, Dover, DE 19901

    Phone: (302) 739-5318   www.state.de.us/sos/dpa/

Florida

Florida State Archives

    Bureau of Archives and Records Management, Division of Library and
Information Services, 500 S. Bronough St., Tallahassee, FL 32399-0250

    Phone: (805) 245-6700   http://dlis.dos.state.fl.us/barm/fsa.html

Georgia

State Archives of Georgia

    330 Capitol Ave. SE, Atlanta, GA 30334

    Phone: (404) 656-2350 (reference)   www.sos.state.ga.us/archives/

Hawaii

Hawaii State Archives

    Department of Accounting and General Services, Kekauluohi Building, Iolani
Palace Grounds, Honolulu, HI 96813

    Phone: (808) 586-0329   http://kumu.icsd.hawaii.gov/dags/archives/

Idaho

Idaho Historical Society, Library and Archives

    1109 Main St., Suite 250, Boise, ID 83702

    Phone: (208) 334-3357   www2.state.id.us/ishs/index.html

Illinois

Illinois State Archives

    Margaret Cross Norton Building, Capitol Complex, Springfield, IL 62756

    Phone: (217) 782-4682

    www.cyberdriveillinois.com/departments/archives/archives.html

Indiana

Indiana State Archives

6440 E. 30th St., Indianapolis, IN 46219

Phone: (317) 591-5222

www.state.in.us/icpr/webfile/archives/homepage.html

Iowa

Iowa State Historical Society

600 E. Locust, Des Moines, IA 50319-0290

Phone: (515) 281-5111   www.iowahistory.org/archives/index.html

Kansas

Kansas State Historical Society

6425 SW Sixth Ave., Topeka, KS 66615

Phone: (785) 272-1099   www.kshs.org/

Kentucky

Kentucky Archives Research Room

Kentucky Department for Libraries and Archives,

300 Coffee Tree Rd., P.O. Box 537, Frankfort, KY 40602-0537

Phone: (502) 564-8300   www.kdla.state.ky.us

Louisiana

Louisiana Division of Archives and Records

3851 Essen Ln., Baton Rouge, LA 70809-2137

Phone: (504) 922-1208

www.sec.state.la.us/archives/archives/archives-index.htm

Maine

Maine State Archives

84 State House Station, Augusta, ME 04333-0084

Phone: (207) 287-5795   www.state.me.us/sos/arc/research/

homepage.htm

Maryland

Maryland State Archives

350 Rowe Blvd., Annapolis, MD 21401

Phone: (410) 260-6400   www.mdarchives.state.md.us

Massachusetts

Massachusetts Archives

220 Morrissey Blvd., Boston, MA 02125

Phone: (617) 727-2816   www.magnet.state.ma.us/sec/arc or

www.state.ma.us/sec/arc/arcidx.htm

Michigan

State Archives of Michigan

Michigan Historical Center, 717 W. Allegan St., Lansing, MI 48918-1800

Phone: (517) 373-1408

www.sos.state.mi.us/history/archive/archive.html

Minnesota

Minnesota Historical Society

345 Kellogg Blvd. West, St. Paul, MN 55102

Phone: (651) 296-2143 (reference)   www.mnhs.org

Mississippi

Mississippi Department of Archives and History

P.O. Box 571, Jackson, MS 39205-0571

Phone: (601) 359-6850   www.mdah.state.ms.us/

Missouri

Missouri State Archives

600 W. Main, P.O. Box 1747, Jefferson City, MO 65102

Phone: (573) 751-3280   www.sos.state.mo.us/archives/

Montana

Montana Historical Society

225 N. Roberts St., P.O. Box 201201, Helena, MT 59620-1201

Phone: (406) 444-2694   www.his.state.mt.us/

Nebraska

Nebraska State Historical Society

1500 "R" St., P.O. Box 82554, Lincoln, NE 68501-2554

Phone: (402) 471-4751   www.nebraskahistory.org/lib-arch/index.htm

Nevada

Nevada State Archives and Records Management

100 N. Stewart St., Carson City, NV 89710-4285

Phone: (775) 684-3360

http://dmla.clan.lib.nv.us/docs/NSLA/archives/nsa.htm

New Hampshire

New Hampshire Division of Records Management and Archives

71 S. Fruit St., Concord, NH 03301

Phone: (603) 271-2236   www.state.nh.us/state/index.html

New Jersey

New Jersey Division of Archives and Records Management

225 W. State St., Level 2, P.O. Box 307, Trenton, NJ 08625-0307

Phone: (609) 292-6260   www.state.nj.us/state/darm/

New Mexico

New Mexico State Records Center and Archives

 404 Montezuma St., Santa Fe, NM 87503

 Phone: (505) 827-7332 www.nmcpr.state.nm.us/

New York

New York State Archives

 Cultural Education Center, Room 11D40, Albany, NY 12230

 Phone: (518) 474-8955 www.archives.nysed.gov/holdings.htm

North Carolina

North Carolina State Archives

 109 E. Jones St., Raleigh, NC 27601-2807

 Phone: (919) 733-7305 www.ah.dcr.state.nc.us

North Dakota

North Dakota State Historical Society

 North Dakota Heritage Center

 612 E. Boulevard Ave., Bismarck, ND 58505-0830

 Phone: (701) 328-2091 (reference) www.state.nd.us/hist/sal.htm

Ohio

Ohio Historical Society

 Archives/Library Reference Questions

 1982 Velma Ave., Columbus, OH 43211-2497

 Phone: (614) 297-2300 www.ohiohistory.org

Oklahoma

Oklahoma State Archives

 200 NE 18th St., Oklahoma City, OK 73105-3298

 Phone: (405) 522-3579

 www.odl.state.ok.us/oar/archives/collections.htm

Oregon

Oregon State Archives

 800 Summer St., NE, Salem, OR 97310

 Phone: (503) 373-0701 http://arcweb.sos.state.or.us/

Pennsylvania

Pennsylvania State Archives

 350 North St., Harrisburg, PA 17120-0090

 Phone: (717) 783-3281

 www.phmc.state.pa.us/bah/DAM/overview.htm

Rhode Island
Rhode Island State Archives
  Department of Archives and History
  337 Westminster St., Providence, RI 02903-3302
  Phone: (401) 222-2353   www.state.ri.us/archives

South Carolina
South Carolina Department of Archives and History
  8301 Parkland Rd., Columbia, SC 29223
  Phone: (803) 896-6100   www.state.sc.us/scdah/newresearch.htm

South Dakota
South Dakota State Archives
  900 Governors Dr., Pierre, SD 57501-2217
  Phone: (605) 773-3804   www.sdhistory.org/archives.htm

Tennessee
Tennessee State Library and Archives
  403 Seventh Ave. N., Nashville, TN 37243-0312
  Phone: (615) 741-2764   www.state.tn.us/sos/statelib/pubsvs/

Texas
Texas State Library and Archives
  P.O. Box 12927, Austin, TX 78711-2927
  Phone: (512) 463-5460   www.tsl.state.tx.us/arc/index.html

Utah
Utah State Archives
  P.O. Box 141021, Salt Lake City, UT 84114-1021
  Phone: (801) 538-3031   www.archives.utah.gov/

Vermont
Vermont State Archives
  109 State St., Montpelier, VT 05609-1103
  Phone: (802) 828-2308   http://vermont-archives.org

Virginia
The Library of Virginia
  Archives and Research Services, 800 E. Broad St., Richmond, VA 23219
  Phone: (804) 692-3500   www.lva.lib.va.us/

Washington
Washington State Archives
  500 Union Ave., SE, P.O. Box 40220, Olympia, WA 98504-0220
  Phone: (360) 902-4151   www.secstate.wa.gov/archives

West Virginia
West Virginia State Archives
Archives and History Library, The Cultural Center
1900 Kanawha Blvd. East, Charleston, WV 25305-0300
Phone: (304) 558-0230   www.wvculture.org/history/wvsamenu.html

Wisconsin
State Historical Society of Wisconsin
Archives Division, Reference Services, 816 State St., Madison, WI 53706
Phone: (608) 264-6400   www.shsw.wisc.edu/archives/

Wyoming
Wyoming State Archives, Museums and Historical Department
Barrett Building, 2301 Central Ave., Cheyenne, WY 82002
Phone: (307) 777-7013   http://wyoarchives.state.wy.us/

Others

District of Columbia
District of Columbia, Office of Public Records
1300 Naylor Court NW, Washington, DC 20001-4225
Phone: (202) 671-1105   http://os.dc.gov/info/pubrec/pubrec.shtm

Puerto Rico
Puerto Rico General Archives
Ponce de Leon #500, Puerta de Tierra, San Juan, Puerto Rico 00902
Phone: (809) 722-0331

U.S. Virgin Islands
U.S. Virgin Islands Libraries, Archives, and Museums
23 Dronningens Gade, Charlotte Amalie, St. Thomas, USVI 00802
Phone: (809) 774-3407

National Archives and Regional Branches

National Archives and Records Administration
   700 Pennsylvania Ave. NW
   Washington, DC 20408
   Phone: (800) 234-8861 or (301) 713-6800
   E-mail: inquire@nara.gov
National Archives II
   8601 Adelphi Rd.
   College Park, MD 20740-6001
   Phone: (800) 234-8861
   E-mail: inquire@arch2.nara.gov
National Archives home page: www.archives.gov
National Archives—information on nationwide facilities, including regional
   branches and presidential libraries, holdings, research at each facility, hours,
   and directions to each location: www.archives.gov/facilities/index.html

Regional Branches of the National Archives
Alaska
National Archives, Pacific Alaska Region (Anchorage)
   654 W. Third Ave., Anchorage, AK 99501-2145
   Phone: (907) 271-2441
   Serving Alaska.

California
National Archives, Pacific Region
   24000 Avila Rd., Laguna Niguel, CA 92677-3497 or
   P.O. Box 6719, Laguna Niguel, CA 92607-6719
   Phone: (949) 360-2641
   Serving Arizona; southern California; Clark County, Nevada.
National Archives, Pacific Sierra Region
   1000 Commodore Dr., San Bruno, CA 94066-2350
   Phone: (650) 876-9001; genealogy and general inquiries: (650) 876-9009
   Serving northern California, Hawaii, Nevada except for Clark County,
   American Samoa, Pacific Trust Territories.

Colorado
National Archives, Rocky Mountain Region
   Bldg. 48, Denver Federal Center
   P.O. Box 25307, Denver, CO 80225-0307
   Phone: (303) 236-0806
   Serving Colorado, Montana, New Mexico, North Dakota, South Dakota,
   Utah, Wyoming.

District of Columbia
Washington National Records Center
4205 Suitland Rd., Suitland, MD 20746-8001
For information, visit the Web site:
www.archives.gov/facilities/md/suitland.html

Georgia
National Archives, Southeast Region
1557 St. Joseph Ave., East Point, GA 30344-2593
Phone: (404) 763-7474
Serving Alabama, Florida, Georgia, Kentucky, Mississippi, North Carolina, South Carolina, Tennessee.

Illinois
National Archives, Great Lakes Region (Chicago)
7358 S. Pulaski Rd., Chicago, IL 60629-5898
Phone: (773) 581-7816
Serving Illinois, Indiana, Michigan, Minnesota, Ohio, Wisconsin.

Massachusetts
National Archives, Northeast Region (Boston)
Murphy Federal Center, 380 Trapelo Rd., Waltham, MA 02452-6399
Phone: (781) 647-8104
Serving Connecticut, Maine, Massachusetts, New Hampshire, Rhode Island, Vermont.

National Archives, Northeast Region (Pittsfield)
10 Conte Dr., Pittsfield, MA 01201-8230
Phone: (413) 445-6885
A microfilm reading room, serving primarily the Northeast but with census, military, and other records with national coverage.

Missouri
National Archives, Central Plains Region (Kansas City)
2312 E. Bannister Rd., Kansas City, MO 64131-3011
Phone: (816) 926-6920
Serving Iowa, Kansas, Missouri, Nebraska.

National Archives, Central Plains Region (Lee's Summit)
200 Space Center Dr., Lee's Summit, MO 64064-1182
Phone: (816) 823-6272
Serving Department of Veterans Affairs; agencies and courts in New Jersey, New York, Puerto Rico, U.S. Virgin Islands.

New York
National Archives, Northeast Region (New York City)
201 Varick St., New York, NY 10014-4811
Phone: (212) 337-1300
Serving New Jersey, New York, Puerto Rico, U.S. Virgin Islands.

Ohio
National Archives, Great Lakes Region (Dayton)
3150 Springboro Rd., Dayton, OH 45439-1883
Phone: (937) 225-2852
Serving Indiana, Michigan, Ohio.

Pennsylvania
National Archives, Mid Atlantic Region (Center City Philadelphia)
900 Market St., Philadelphia, PA 19107-4292
Phone: (215) 597-3000
Serving Delaware, Maryland, Pennsylvania, Virginia, West Virginia.
Genealogical records are at this facility.
National Archives, Mid Atlantic Region (Northeast Philadelphia)
14700 Townsend Rd., Philadelphia, PA 19154-1096
Phone: (215) 671-9027
Serving Delaware, Maryland, Pennsylvania, Virginia, West Virginia.

Texas
National Archives, Southwest Region
501 W. Felix St., Bldg. 1, P.O. Box 6216, Fort Worth, TX 76115-0216
Phone: (817) 334-5515; genealogy/family history: (817) 334-5525
Serving Arkansas, Louisiana, Oklahoma, Texas.

Washington
National Archives, Pacific Alaska Region (Seattle)
6125 Sand Point Way NE, Seattle, WA 98115-7999
Phone: (206) 526-6501
Serving Idaho, Oregon, Washington.

APPENDIX E

Blank Forms

See pages 3, 5, and 6 for examples. These forms may be copied by the purchaser for personal use.

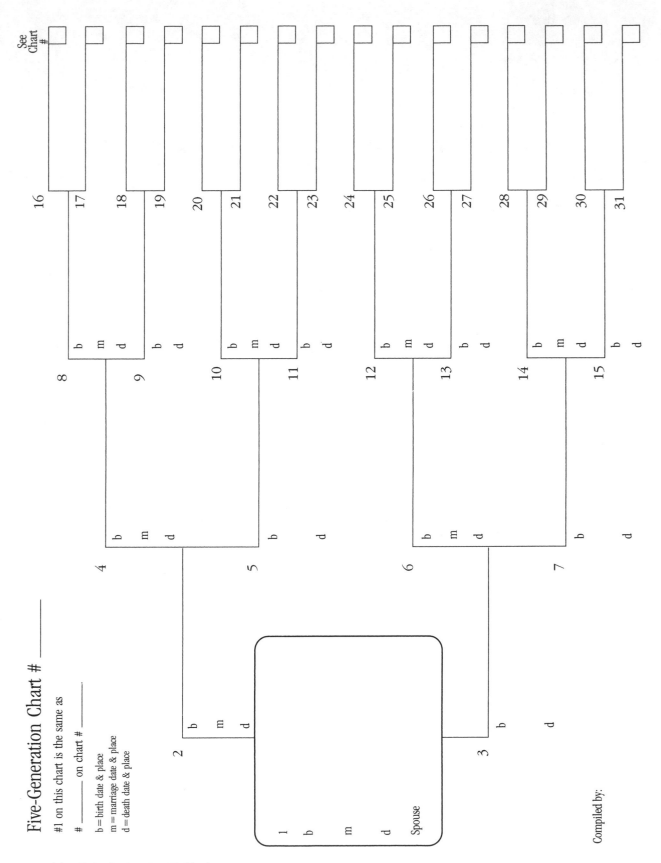

Five-Generation Chart # _____

#1 on this chart is the same as

_____ on chart # _____

b = birth date & place
m = marriage date & place
d = death date & place

See Chart #

16

17

18

19

20

21

22

23

24

25

26

27

28

29

30

31

8
b
m
d

9
b
d

10
b
m
d

11
b
d

12
b
m
d

13
b
d

14
b
m
d

15
b
d

4
b
m
d

5
b

d

6
b
m
d

7
b

d

2
b
m
d

3
b

d

1
b

m

d

Spouse

Compiled by:

Family Group Sheet of the _____ Family

Full name of husband	Birth date	
His father	Birth place	
	Death date	
	Death place	
His mother with maiden name	Burial place	

Full maiden name of wife	Birth date	
Her father	Birth place	
	Death date	
	Death place	
Her mother with maiden name	Burial place	

| Other Spouses | Marriage date, place, etc. |
| Source #s | Source #s |

Children of this marriage	Birth date & place	Death date, place, & burial place	Marriage date, place & spouse
Source #s			
Source #s			
Source #s			
Source #s			
Source #s			
Source #s			

Reprinted from Unpuzzling Your Past Workbook

Source #   Sources (Documentation)

Reprinted from Unpuzzling Your Past Workbook

Family Group Sheet of the _____ Family, continued

Father _____ Mother _____

Children of this marriage	Birth date & place	Death date, place, & burial place	Marriage date, place & spouse
Source #s			
Source #s			
Source #s			
Source #s			
Source #s			
Source #s			
Source #s			
Source #s			
Source #s			

Notes

Reprinted from Unpuzzling Your Past Workbook

Source #   Sources (Documentation)

Endnotes

About the Citations:

- The Family History Library is abbreviated FHL.
- The National Archives and Records Administration in Washington, D.C. is called simply National Archives.
- In citing census records from 1880 forward, *enumeration district* is abbreviated *e.d.*
- In keeping with standard form, the first citation of a source is the full and complete citation; subsequent citations of a source are shortened.

Chapter Two

1 U.S. Census of 1870, roll 737, Lincoln County, Mississippi, Township Six, p. 45.

2 U.S. Census of 1870, Agriculture Schedule, Lincoln County, Mississippi, p. 35, Mississippi Department of Archives and History, microfilm.

3 *Twenty Censuses: Population and Housing Questions 1790–1980* (Washington, D.C.: U.S. Department of Commerce, Bureau of the Census, 1979), 18, 22, 28, 33, 42, 52, 56–57 for the years 1870–1940.

4 U.S. Census of 1920, roll 69, Lee County, Arkansas, e.d. 120, sheet 2B, household of John Armstead.

5 U.S. Census of 1910, roll 55, Lee County, Arkansas, e.d. 72, sheet 3A, household of John Armstead.

6 U.S. Census of 1900, roll 65, Lee County, Arkansas, e.d. 49, sheet 10, household of Mary Blount.

7 U.S. Census of 1920, Lee County, Arkansas, Independence Township, e.d. 120, sheet 6, household of R.M. Dukes.

8 U.S. Census of 1910, Lee County, Arkansas, e.d. 72, sheet 4A, household of Monrow Dukes.

9 Marriage record of Fred Williams and Mary Blount, 1902, Lee County, Arkansas, Marriage Book F:245, FHL microfilm 1017654.

10 U.S. Census of 1880, roll 1261, Haywood County, Tennessee, e.d. 73, sheet 25, family 128, household of Elias Weems (Jr.), and family 126, household of Elias Weems (Sr.).

11 Ibid., sheet 28, family 152, household of Sam Blount.

12 Marriage record of Fayette Blount and Mary Weems, 1881, Haywood County, Tennessee, Marriage Book 10:80, FHL microfilm 1006853.

13 Marjorie Hood Fischer, comp., *Haywood County, Tennessee, Marriage Records, Books 1–8, 1859–1878* (Vista, Calif.: the compiler, 1987), 6, from county Marriage Book 8:281, dated 29 July 1877.

14 U.S. Census of 1870, roll 1536, Haywood County, Tennessee, p. 396, household of Elias Weems.

15 U.S. Census of 1880, roll 6, Cherokee County, Alabama, p. 238, household of S. Blount.

Chapter Three

1 U.S. Census of 1870, Lincoln County, Mississippi, Brookhaven post office, Township Eight, p. 83, family 165, household of Joe Paxton; U.S. Census of 1880, roll 655, Lincoln County, Mississippi, Brookhaven post office, Macedonia precinct, e.d. 36, sheet 4, no family numbers given, household of Joseph Paxton; U.S. Census of 1900, roll 817, Lincoln County, Mississippi, Red Star post office, Beat 5, e.d. 102, sheet 5, family 91, household of Joe Paxton; U.S. Census of 1910, roll 749, Lincoln County, Mississippi, Red Star village, on Brookhaven and Medville Road, Beat 5, e.d. 92, sheet 10B, family 169, household of Joe Paxton; Paxton apparently died before 1920.

2 U.S. Census of 1890, special schedule of Union veterans and widows, National Archives microfilm M123, roll 4, Louisiana, New Orleans, e.d. 43, p. 1, entries of Joseph Harris and William James.

3 Ibid., roll 4, Louisiana, New Orleans, e.d. 77, 5th ward, p. 1, line 2, entry of Octave Lavaux.

4 Ibid., roll 26, Lincoln County, Mississippi, Caseyville District, e.d. 89, p. 1, line 1, entry of George Thomas.

5 David M. Ludlum, *Early American Winters II, 1821–1870* (Boston: American Meteorological Society, 1968), 133–137.

6 U.S. Census of 1880, roll 23, Marengo County, Alabama, Jefferson, e.d. 99, sheet 39, family 444, household of Louisa Finch.

7 Marriage of Robert Benson and Louisa Massey, Marriage Register, p. 28, frame 20, Vicksburg, Mississippi, Field Office, in Indentures and Marriages, *Records of the Assistant Commissioner for the State of Mississippi, Bureau of Refugees, Freedmen, and Abandoned Lands, 1865–1869*, National Archives microfilm M826, roll 42.

8 Indenture of apprenticeship of orphan Jane, dated 14 September 1865, in Indentures, September 1865–August 1867, *Records of the Assistant Commissioner for the State of North Carolina, Bureau of Refugees, Freedmen, and Abandoned Lands, 1865–1870*, National Archives microfilm M843, roll 35.

9 Depositor record of Mrs. Ellen Baptiste Lubin, 2 July 1866, in register of New Orleans, Louisiana, 20 June 1866–29 June 1874, *Registers of Signatures of Depositions in Branches of the Freedman's Savings and Trust Company, 1865–1874*, National Archives microfilm M816, roll 12.

10 Depositor record of Ancel Bunton, #83, ibid.

11 Depositor record of Violet Ann Shields, #1467, in register of New York City, 20 February 1871–6 July 1874, ibid., roll 17.

12 Depositor record of Robert Hammonds, #50, in register of Atlanta, Georgia, 15 January 1870–2 July 1874, ibid., roll 6.

13 Depositor record of William Guilford, #86, ibid.

14 Depositor record of Peter Williams, #142, ibid.

15 U.S. Census of 1870, roll 151, Fulton County, Georgia, Atlanta, 4th Ward, p. 252, family 48, household of Elbert Green.

Chapter Four

1 J.A. McDaniel, transcriber, *Panola County Voter Registration of 1867/1870* (Carthage, Tex.: the transcriber, 1993), 1; taken from the microfilm of the originals in the Texas State Archives.

2 Nebraska State Census, 1885, Custer County, Westerville Township, e.d. 171, Schedule 1, p. 1A, family 4, household of Jerry Shores; Schedule 2, Agriculture, p. 1, line 4, Jerry Shores, National Archives microfilm M352, roll 11.

3 Testimony of claimant Jerry Shores for homestead proof, dated 2 April 1889, in land entry file for homestead Final Certificate 8483, previously cited.

4 Birth record of Mary Elizabeth Wilson, 26 September 1855, Botetourt County, Virginia, Register of Births, 1853–1870 (pages not numbered, but entries fairly chronological), Library of Virginia, microfilm.

5 Death record of Billy Goff, February 1867, Cumberland County, Virginia, Death Records, p. 83, in Virginia Vital Statistics: Death Records, Library of Virginia, Richmond.

6 Deed of J. Edward Sullivan and wife to Nelson White, 1911, Marion County, Kentucky, Deed Book 34:240, County Clerk's Office, Courthouse, Lebanon.

7 Affidavit of descent filed by Lucian Vaughn, 16 June 1942, Green County, Kentucky, Deed Book 70:590, County Clerk's Office, Courthouse, Greensburg.

8 A. Leonard, comp., *Houston City Directory for 1866* (Houston: Gray, Strickland & Co., 1866; reprint, Dallas: R.L. Polk & Co., undated), 112.

9 Frederick Douglass, *Autobiographies* (New York: Literary Classics of the United States, Inc., 1994), *Life and Times of Frederick Douglass*, reprint of 1893 edition, 475–476.

10 Eugene D. Genovese, *Roll, Jordan, Roll: The World the Slaves Made* (New York: Vintage Books, 1972), 293.

11 Letter to Emily Croom from Yvonne Corey, Brooklyn, New York, 30 May 2001.

12 Marriage license of William Collins to Hattie White, Craven County, North Carolina, license #1113, dated 11 December 1912, Craven County Marriage Licenses, 1908–1914, FHL microfilm 0288285, pages not numbered but licenses filed chronologically; letter from Yvonne Corey, 8 February 2001, naming William's first wife as *Carrie* White, who had one son before she died; no other marriage records have been found for a William Collins in that time period and several-county area to a bride named White.

13 Marriage license of William Collins to Louna Croom, Craven County, North Carolina, license #1787, dated 20 January 1915, Craven County Marriage Licenses, 1915–1919, FHL microfilm 0288286, pages not numbered but licenses filed chronologically.

14 U.S. Census of 1920, roll 1293, Craven County, North Carolina, e.d. 17, sheet 4B, family 89, household of William Collins; census day was January 1 and ages reported were supposed to be the age each person was on January 1, having turned that age on the most recent birthday; 1920 minus 60 means that William was already born by 1 January 1860. (See chapter two.)

15 Death certificate of William Collins, Craven County, North Carolina, Death Register, vol. 1924:549, Office of the Register of Deeds, Courthouse, New Bern.

16 U.S. Census of 1880, roll 978, Pitt County, North Carolina, Pactolus post office, e.d. 129, sheet 55, family 508, household of Burton Clark, age 50, and his wife, Jane Clark, age 45.

17 Ibid., sheet 54, family 502.

18 Ibid., sheet 54, family 496, household of Clarncey Shepard, whose niece Mary Clark was listed as age 20; marriage record of Burton Clark Jr. and Mary Clark, license dated 12 January 1881, wedding dated 13 January 1881, Pitt County, North Carolina, Marriages (Colored), Vol. 1 (1866–1924), recorded chronologically under initial C.

19 U.S. Census of 1870, roll 1155, Pitt County, North Carolina, Pactolus Township, p. 173, family 158, household of Bert Clark.

20 *1880 United States Census and National Index*, FamilySearch Family History Resource File (Salt Lake City: The Church of Jesus Christ of Latter-day Saints, 2001), CD 4—National Index to the 1880 U.S. Census for names beginning C-Cn, and CD 14—Cumberland region, North and South Carolina for names beginning A–R; those William Collinses shown as sons in households with parents by names other than John and Jane or Burton and Jane have been eliminated for the time being; the remaining candidates were single men living in households with surnames other than Collins and one married William Collins with a young son named Jimmie (James).

21 U.S. Census of 1880, roll 952, Beaufort County, North Carolina, Bath Township, e.d. 1, sheet 31, family 326, household of Robert Clark.

22 FamilySearch, *1880 United States Census*, North Carolina, CD 14.

Chapter Five

1 *A Century of Population Growth: From the First Census of the United States to the Twelfth, 1790–1900* (Washington, D.C.: Government Printing Office, 1909; reprint, Orting, Wash.: Heritage Quest Press, 1989), figured from chart on p. 80.

2 Ira Berlin, *Slaves Without Masters: The Free Negro in the Antebellum South* (New York: The New Press, 1974), calculated from census figures in chart on p. 136.

3 Emancipation of Rhoda Hamilton, Petersburg, Virginia, Deed Book 10:482, Library of Virginia.

4 Gibson Jefferson McConnaughey, comp., *Miscellaneous Records, Amelia County, Virginia, 1735–1865* (Amelia, Va.: Mid South Publishing Co., 1995), 80.

5 Petition of Cynthia Ewing on behalf of Delilah, 1847, Memorials and Petitions, Records of the Texas Legislature, Record Group 100, Texas State Archives, Austin.

6 U.S. Census of 1830, roll 18, Jones County, Georgia, upper regiment, pp. 436–437, household of Nat Matthews; lower regiment, p. 442–443, households of Free Anthony and Free Milla; other free persons of color listed on pp. 433, 435, 440, 442, 457, 466, 467, 472.

7 Entries of Nathaniel Mathews and family, Jones County, Georgia, Inferior Court Records, Book of Writs, 1818–1846, register of free persons of color, pages unnumbered but arranged chronologically, 8 April 1818, 29 February 1820, 6 Mar 1821, 9 July 1822, 8 July 1823, 3 April 1826, FHL microfilm 0454256.

8 U.S. Census of 1830, Jones County, Georgia, upper regiment, sheet 14, labeled as pp. 441–442, household of Daniel Nivin.

9 Instructions for 1910, *Twenty Censuses*, 42.

10 Berlin, *Slaves Without Masters*, note, 174–175.

11 Guardianship of Cozens, Jones County, Georgia, Inferior Court, Book of Writs 1818–1846, p. 64, FHL microfilm 0454256.

12 Registration of six Cozens/Cousins free persons, Jones County, Georgia, Inferior Court, Book of Writs, 1818–1846, register of free persons of color, 29 February 1820, FHL microfilm 0454256; Registration of Thomas and James Cousins, 6 March 1821, ibid.

13 Registration of Sally Cousins, 11 June 1823, ibid.

14 Court appointment of guardian for Sally Cousins, Jones County, Georgia, Minutes of the Inferior Court, volume not numbered, pages not numbered, page facing this page dated January term 1830, FHL microfilm 0454255.

15 U.S. Census of 1860, Free Schedule, roll 895, Currituck County, North Carolina, Tulls Creek Bridge, Tulls Creek District, p. 548, household of William Etheridge.

16 U.S. Census of 1820, roll 9, Captain William Evans district, Putnam County, Georgia, p. 84B, household of William Turner.

17 H.P.N. Gammel, *The Laws of Texas, 1822–1897* (Austin: The Gammel Book Company, 1898), II:549, again on 648 (act on behalf of Ainsworth/Ashworth and Thomas families, 12 December 1840), 879.

18 John Hope Franklin, *The Free Negro in North Carolina, 1790–1860* (Chapel Hill: The University of North Carolina Press, 1943, reprint 1995), 232–233, 234–237.

19 Villamae Williams, ed., *Stephen F. Austin's Register of Families: From the Originals in the General Land Office, Austin, Texas* ([St. Louis, Mo.: distributed by Ingmire Publications], c. 1984), Book 1, 81–82 (Wilson, entry #488), 91–92 (Jones, entry #605).

20 Genovese, *Roll, Jordan, Roll*, 400.

21 Berlin, *Slaves Without Masters*, 252.

22 Leon F. Litwack, *North of Slavery: The Negro in the Free States, 1790–1860* (Chicago: The University of Chicago Press, 1961), 155.

23 James W. Hagy, *Directories for the City of Charleston, South Carolina for the Years 1830–1831, 1835–1836, 1836, 1837–1838, and 1840–1841* (Baltimore: Clearfield Co., 1997), 2, 14, 15, 32, 45, 46, 82, 83, 110, 112; used with permission.

24 Ibid., 14, 15, 114.

Chapter Six

1 U.S. Census of 1920, roll 1315, Pitt County, North Carolina, Winterville township, enumerated 24 January 1920, e.d. 58, sheet 8–9, no family num-

ber given, household of Tea Dixon; letters to Emily Croom, 30 May and October 2001, from Yvonne Corey, Brooklyn, New York; marriage records of Teat Dixon's children all from Pitt County Marriage Records (Colored), 1851–1948, Vol. 1 (1866–1924) and Vol. 2 (1924–1948), FHL microfilm 033704, records alphabetical by initial letter of groom's surname and chronological by license date; copies of original marriage licenses obtained from Register of Deeds, Pitt County Courthouse, Greenville, some of which clarified what had been copied in the marriage register on microfilm.

2   U.S. Census of 1900, roll 1212, Pitt County, North Carolina, Swift Creek Township, e.d. 97, sheet 4B, family 74, household of Teat Dixon; U.S. Census of 1880, Pitt County, North Carolina, Belvoir-west division of township, e.d. 122, sheet 11, family 1, household of Emley Dixon; marriage record cited with others above; birth certificate of Gentry Dixon, certificate 63, dated 30 July 1918, and death certificate of Feate Dixon, certificate 3, dated 14 January 1937, both from Register of Deeds, Pitt County Courthouse, Greenville.

3   Harland C. Skinner, "Slavery and Abolition in New Hampshire" (master's thesis, University of New Hampshire, 1948), 9.

4   Genovese, *Roll, Jordan, Roll*, 446.

5   William D. Pierson, *Black Yankees: The Development of an Afro-American Subculture in Eighteenth-Century New England* (Amherst: The University of Massachusetts Press, 1988), 35.

6   Genovese, *Roll, Jordan, Roll*, 446.

7   Pierson, *Black Yankees*, 35, using the father's given name.

8   Genovese, *Roll, Jordan, Roll*, 446, using the father's surname.

9   Herbert G. Gutman, *The Black Family in Slavery and Freedom, 1750–1925* (New York: Pantheon Books, 1976), 232.

10   Ibid., 256, quoting from *War-Time Journal of a Georgia Girl, 1864–1865* (published 1908).

11   Joel Williamson, *After Slavery: The Negro in South Carolina During Reconstruction, 1861–1877* (Hanover, N.H.: University Press of New England, 1990, reprint of 1965 edition by University of North Carolina Press), 311.

12   George P. Rawick, ed., *The American Slave: A Composite Autobiography* (Westport, Conn.: Greenwood Publishing, 1972), Series 2, vol. 16, Kentucky section, 18–19.

13   Inventory and appraisal of Lodwick L. Weathersby, 1844, Amite County, Mississippi, Probate Records, Vol. 9:614, Chancery Clerk's Office, Courthouse, Liberty.

14   Will of Lewis Weathersby, 1843, Amite County Wills, Vol. 1:248–252, Chancery Clerk's Office.

15   Petition of Walter B. Weathersby et al, 1846, Amite County Estate Papers, File 204, Chancery Clerk's Office.

16   Division of Lodwick Weathersby's estate, 1853, Amite County Probate Records, Vol. 16:604, Chancery Clerk's Office.

17   Dale Edwyna Smith, *The Slaves of Liberty: Freedom in Amite County, Mississippi, 1820–1868* (New York: Garland Publishing, 1999), Garland Reference Library of the Humanities, vol. 2081; Crosscurrents in African-American History, vol. 2:37–48.

18 U.S. Census of 1870, Lincoln County, Mississippi, District 5, p. 3.

19 Ibid., p. 1.

20 Division of Lodwick Weathersby's estate, 1853, Amite County Probate Records, Vol. 16:604.

21 Registry of Freedmen, August to October 1865, File 2278, Natchez Office, Southern District of Mississippi, Records of the Field Offices of the Bureau of Refugees, Freedmen, and Abandoned Lands, Record Group 105, National Archives.

Chapter Seven

1 Manifest for the Brig John A. Lancaster of Richmond, Benjamin Sooy, Master, dated 27 December 1849, *Inward Bound Slave Manifests, 1807–1860, Port of New Orleans*, Records of the U.S. Customs Service, Record Group 36, National Archives, Washington, Scholarly Resources microfilm S3348, roll 10 (1850–1851).

2 U.S. Census of 1880, roll 1253, Fayette County, Tennessee, District 2, e.d. 18, sheet 5, family 164, household of Thornton Alexander.

3 U.S. Census of 1870, roll 1526, Fayette County, Tennessee, Somerville, p. 212, family 8, household of Thornton Alexander.

4 Quinnie Armour, abstractor, *Hardeman County Freedmen's Marriage Records, 29 November 1865–31 December 1870, Marriage Book IV-A* (Bolivar, Tenn.: the abstractor, 1966; mimeographed, 1972), 26, marriage bond and record for Alexander Thornton and Lizzie Blaylock.

5 U.S. Census of 1870, roll 1533, Hardeman County, Tennessee, District 3, Bolivar, p. 139, family 52, household of J. Blaylock.

6 U.S. Census of 1860, Slave Schedule, roll 1282, Hardeman County, Tennessee, District 3, p. 33, entry of Jesse Blaylock.

7 U.S. Census of 1850, Slave Schedule, roll 903, Hardeman County, Tennessee, p. 1023, entry of Jesse Blaylock.

8 U.S. Census of 1840, roll 522, Hardeman County, Tennessee, p. 25, line 9, household of Jesse Blaylock.

9 Lisa Clayton Robinson, "Slave Narratives," in *Africana: The Encyclopedia of the African and African American Experience*, Kwame Anthony Appiah and Henry Louis Gates Jr., editors (New York: Basic *Civitas* Books, 1999), 1718.

10 George P. Rawick, ed., *The American Slave: A Composite Autobiography* (reprint; Westport, Conn.: Greenwood Publishing Co., 1972), Series 2, Vol. 16: Ohio section, 1–5, interview with Charles H. Anderson, undated but details in interview point to 1937, in Cincinnati, Ohio.

11 Ibid., 26–32, interview with Mrs. Hannah Davidson, 1937, Toledo, Ohio.

12 U.S. Census of 1870, Claiborne County, Mississippi, p. 556, family 340, household of Thomas Bowen; family 342, household of Ned Bowen.

13 Ibid., p. 555, family 337, household of C.H. Barland; family 331, household of E.S. Jefferies Jr.; p. 553, family 313, household of E.S. Jefferies Sr.

14 U.S. Census of 1860, Slave Schedule, roll 596, Claiborne County, Mississippi, p. 126.

15 U.S. Census of 1850, Slave Schedule, roll 384, Claiborne County, Mississippi, p. 112.

16 U.S. Census of 1860, Free Schedule, roll 580, Claiborne County, Mississippi, district 5, p. 576, family 64 (C.H. Barland) and p. 577, family 68 (E.S. Jefferies).

17 U.S. Census of 1850, Free Schedule, roll 370, Claiborne County, Mississippi, p. 138, family 551, household of Evan S. Jefferies.

18 Mississippi State Census of 1866, Claiborne County, p. 3, Barland and Jefferies entries, Mississippi Department of Archives and History, microfilm.

19 Land tax roll, 1866, Claiborne County, Mississippi, Chancery Clerk's Office, Courthouse, Port Gibson.

Chapter Eight

1 U.S. Census of 1900, Lincoln County, Mississippi, e.d. 37, sheet 14, household of James W. Hilson.

2 U.S. Census of 1870, Lincoln County, Mississippi, p. 72, household of Perry Cotton.

3 U.S. Census of 1880, Lincoln County, Mississippi, Macedonia precinct, e.d. 36, sheet 29, household of Perry Cotton, no family numbers given for this county.

4 Ibid., sheet 27, household of Robert Short.

5 Ibid., sheet 26, household of Richard Nelson.

6 List of discharges of colored soldiers from the U.S. service at the Brookhaven office for collection of additional bounty, Register of Complaints, Records for the Brookhaven Sub-district Office, Mississippi, Bureau of Refugees, Freedmen and Abandoned Lands, Record Group 105, National Archives, Washington.

7 Civil War military service information for Perry Cotton (private, Co. B, 6th U.S. Colored Heavy Artillery), in pension application for widow Tamer Cotton, file no. 390714, Civil War Pension Application Files, Records of the Veterans Administration, Record Group 15, National Archives.

8 Civil War pension application for widow Tamer Cotton, no. 390714, ibid.

9 1867 personal tax rolls, Franklin County, Mississippi, Record Group 29, Auditor of Public Accounts, Mississippi Department of Archives and History, microfilm.

10 U.S. Census of 1870, Lincoln County, Mississippi, p. 72, family 353, household of P.M. Smith.

11 U.S. Census of 1880, Lincoln County, Mississippi, e.d. 36, p. 30, household of P.M. Smith.

12 U.S. Census of 1870, Lincoln County, Mississippi, p. 72, family 369, household of W. [sic] Calcote.

13 U.S. Census of 1860, Free Schedule, roll 581, Franklin County, Mississippi, p. 74, family 510, household of Thomas R. Short; U.S. Census of 1860, Slave Schedule, roll 597, Franklin County, Mississippi, p. 52.

14 U.S. Census of 1850, Free Schedule, roll 368, Amite County, Mississippi, p. 53, family 5, household of D.C. Short.

15 Marriage record of Thomas R. Short and Mahala Calcote, East Feliciana Parish, Louisiana, Marriage Book A:360, from Albert Eugene Causey,

Amite County, Mississippi, 1699–1890 (Birmingham, Ala.: Amite County Historical Fund, 1957), III:81.

16 U.S. Census of 1850, Free Schedule, roll 372, Franklin County, Mississippi, p. 26, family 274, household of Willis M. Calcote.

17 Estate of Willis Calcote, June term 1863, Franklin County, Mississippi, Probate Court Minutes, Book G (1863–1868):24, FHL microfilm 890435.

18 Amite County, Mississippi, probate files, file 178, Chancery Clerk's Office, in Causey, *Amite County, Mississippi, 1690–1890*, III:364.

19 Application for widow's dower, file 178, ibid.

20 U.S. Census of 1850, Slave Schedule, roll 383, Amite County, Mississippi, entry of D.C. Short.

21 Marriage record of Mahala Short and William L. Howard, Franklin County, Mississippi, Marriage Book 4:377, Circuit Clerk's Office, Courthouse, Meadville.

22 U.S. Census of 1870, Lincoln County, Mississippi, p. 72, household of W. [*sic*] Calcote.

23 Ibid., p.69, family 326, household of Lee Calcote.

24 U.S. Census of 1880, Lincoln County, Mississippi, e.d. 36, sheet 26, household of L.E. Calcote; ibid., sheet 26, household of Robert Short; ibid., sheet 26, household of Mann Middleton.

25 1878 List of educable children, Lincoln County, Mississippi, Record Group 28, R003-B07-S5-02651, Mississippi Department of Archives and History.

26 Francis Calcote Brite, *Calcote Family Journey* (Baltimore, Md.: Gateway Press, 1997), 51–59.

27 Ibid., 51.

28 WPA Project, Lincoln County, Mississippi, Mississippi Department of Archives and History, microfilm.

29 Brite, *Calcote Family Journey*, 51–59.

30 1810 Mississippi Territorial Census, Franklin County, *Journal of Mississippi History* 13:251; 1813 and 1817 combination tax rolls, Amite County, Record Group 29, Mississippi Department of Archives and History, microfilm; 1816 Mississippi Territorial Census, Amite County, Mississippi Department of Archives and History, microfilm; U.S. Census of 1820, roll 57, Franklin County, Mississippi, p. 37; U.S. Census of 1830, roll 70, Franklin County, Mississippi, p. 159.

Chapter Nine

1 Receipt of A.S. Coleman, dated 26 October 1860, Hardeman County, Tennessee, Deed Book Q:635, Office of the Register of Deeds, Courthouse, Bolivar.

2 Deed of trust from Thomas Patton to H.B. Buckley and James W. McCalley [*sic*], 17 May 1842, Fayette County, Tennessee, Deed Book J:492, Office of the Register of Deeds, Courthouse, Somerville; bill of sale from Jesse Day to Thomas Patton, 17 May 1842, ibid., J:509.

3 Deed of trust from Thomas Patton to James W. McCaully [*sic*], 5 July 1843, ibid., K:475.

4 Deed of gift from Thomas Patton to Sarah Jane Day, 18 January 1845,

ibid., L:434.

5 Will of John Wright, 9 December 1852, Original Wills P–W, Yadkin County, North Carolina, FHL microfilm 1605076, item 1, frames 657–659.

6 Will of A.P. Woodruff, 15 March 1851, ibid., frames 644–646.

7 U.S. Census of 1880, roll 988, Yadkin County, North Carolina, East Bend Township, e.d. 229, sheet 25, family 256, household of Lewis (67) and Mary (40) Poindexter, showing five children, of which Harriet (23) could have been alive in 1860; U.S. Census of 1870, roll 1166, Yadkin County, North Carolina, East Bend Township, p. 666, family 61, household of Lewis (50) and Mary (34) Poindexter, showing four children, of which James (14) and Harriet (10) could have been alive in 1860.

8 U.S. Census of 1860, Free Schedule, roll 919, Yadkin County, North Carolina, family 578, household of John G. Poindexter (81), $3,325 personal property; U.S. Census of 1860, Slave Schedule, roll 927, Yadkin County, North Carolina, p. 484, John G. Poindexter entry, showing two females, ages 49 and 19, and a male, 40.

9 Yadkin County, North Carolina, Inventories 1851–1888, volume beginning 1859, p. 287–291, estate of John G. Poindexter, sale of Lewis on p. 289, FHL microfilm 0802522; Yadkin County Original Wills, P–W, FHL microfilm 1605076, item 1, did not reveal a will for John G. Poindexter.

10 Estate division of William Daniel, Cumberland County, Virginia, Will Book 4:186–192, microfilm.

11 Will of William Doss, Surry County, North Carolina, Will Book 4 (1827–1853):230, microfilm; Executor's return on Doss estate, Yadkin County, North Carolina, Inventories of Estates, volume 1851–1858, p. 42, FHL microfilm 0802522.

12 Superior Court Minutes, 1829–1839, September 1833 term, Putnam County, Georgia, pages in volume not numbered but in chronological order, FHL microfilm 0400927.

13 Letter from E.G. Coleman, Bolivar, Tennessee, to Ferdinand G. Coleman, Cumberland County, Virginia, 7 September 1855, transcribed from the original by Emily Croom, 1972, at the home of Thyrza McCollum, Greenville, Mississippi, who later supplied a photocopy of the original.

14 Presbyterian Church Register, Book I, p. 22–23 (membership), p. 77 (baptisms), copied by Emily Croom, June 1972, in Bolivar, Tennessee, from a copy made by Louise J. McAnulty of Bolivar in 1969.

15 U.S. Census of 1870, roll 1533, Hardeman County, Tennessee, Bolivar, p. 199, household of Pleasant Coleman; U.S. Census of 1860, Slave Schedule, roll 1282, Hardeman County, Tennessee, p. 62, slaveholders E.G. Coleman and C.E. Patton.

16 Barbara Smith, transcriber, *Ballard County, Kentucky, Births and Deaths, 1852–1910* (Melber, Ky.: Simmons Historical Publications, 1998), p. 19, #256, transcribed from microfilm at Kentucky State Archives.

17 Register of Births, 1853–1870, Botetourt County, Virginia, p. 1, line 23, microfilm.

18 Register of Births and Deaths, 1853–1870, Lee County, Virginia, first page for 1855 (pages not numbered), line 11.

Chapter Ten

1 Death certificate for Henry Dodson [*sic*], 1918, Claiborne County, Mississippi, certificate no. 17977, State of Mississippi Department of Health and Vital Records.

2 U.S. Census of 1910, roll 735, Claiborne County, Mississippi, Beat 3, e.d. 37, sheet 1, family 8, household of Henry Dotson.

3 Marriage of Henry Dotson and Angeline Walters, Claiborne County, Marriage Book 8:299, Circuit Clerk's Office, Courthouse, Port Gibson.

4 U.S. Census of 1900, roll 804, Claiborne County, Mississippi, Beat 3, e.d. 160, sheet 1, family 10, household of Henry Dotson.

5 U.S. Census of 1880, roll 644, Claiborne County, Mississippi, Beat 3, e.d. 67, sheet 38, family 258, household of Henry Dotson.

6 Ibid., family 259.

7 U.S. Census of 1870, roll 726, Claiborne County, Mississippi, Rocky Springs District, p. 657, family 318, household of Henry Dodson, family 317, household of Winnie Jones.

8 Deed of Henry Dotson and Winnie Jones, Claiborne County, Mississippi, Deed Book HH:434, Chancery Clerk's Office, Courthouse, Port Gibson.

9 Deed of Henry Dotson, ibid., Book 3B:527.

10 Deed of Henry Dotson, ibid., Book 3K:532.

11 William Dotson Family Bible, in possession of Wilamena (Jones) Grisby of Jones Village, Claiborne County, Mississippi, in 1996.

12 Will of William Dotson, 1858, Claiborne County, Mississippi, Will Book B:272, Chancery Clerk's Office.

13 Inventory and appraisal of the estate of William Dotson, Claiborne County, Mississippi, Probate Record Book for 1858–1860:39, Chancery Clerk's Office.

14 File of William Dotson, D-4, Papers of Decedents, Claiborne County, Mississippi, Chancery Clerk's Office.

15 Conversation with Charlie B. (Campbell) Weddington, by Franklin Smith, at Port Gibson, Mississippi, 1999.

16 File of William Dotson, D-4, Papers of Decedents, Claiborne County, Mississippi.

17 File of George Tannyhill, T-5, Papers of Decedents, ibid.

18 Ibid.

19 Tannyhill Wards, T-1, Orphan Files, Claiborne County, Mississippi, Chancery Clerk's Office.

20 William Dotson entries, 1824–1841 Combination Tax Rolls, Claiborne and Adams Counties, Mississippi, and 1842–1849 Personal Tax Roll, Claiborne County, Record Group 29, Auditor of Public Accounts, Mississippi Department of Archives and History, microfilm.

21 U.S. Census of 1830, roll 70, Adams County, Mississippi, p. 30.

22 Marriage of William Dodson and Mary Jane Brice, Claiborne County, Mississippi, Marriage Book B:61, Circuit Clerk's Office.

23 File for William Harman, H-6, Papers of Decedents, Claiborne County, Mississippi.

24 U.S. Census of 1840, roll 213, Claiborne County, Mississippi, p. 69.

25 U.S. Census of 1850, Slave Schedule, roll 384, Claiborne County, Mississippi, p. 68.

26 Mississippi Territorial Census of 1810, Claiborne County, *Journal of Mississippi History* 13:50–63.

27 In Claiborne County deed records between 1823 and 1830, three women, as joint heirs, released interest in estate property to each other, stating they were sisters and the wives of William Dotson, George Tannyhill, and James Hutcherson.

28 U.S. Census of 1850, Free Schedule, roll 370, Claiborne County, Mississippi, District 3, p. 125B, family 353, household of William Dotson.

29 Tombstone of William Dotson, Clarke Cemetery, Claiborne County, Mississippi, in Katy McCaleb Headley, comp., *Claiborne County, Mississippi: The Promised Land* (Port Gibson: Claiborne County Historical Society, c. 1976), 294.

30 Mrs. Sherman Williams, comp./ed., *The Dodson (Dotson) Family of North Farnham Parish, Richmond County, Virginia: A History and Genealogy of Their Descendants* (Easley, S.C.: Southern Historical Press, 1988), 54.

31 U.S. Census of 1810, roll 62, Fairfield County, South Carolina, p. 867, household of Esau Godson; U.S. Census of 1820, roll 118, Fairfield County, South Carolina, p. 226, household of Esau Dotson.

32 Deed of Isaac Dansby to William Dodson, Fairfield County, South Carolina, Deed Records, Book Y:412, FHL microfilm 1294133.

33 Will of William Harmon, 1838, Claiborne County, Mississippi, Will Book B:157, Chancery Clerk's Office.

34 Deed of L.N. Baldwin to J.I.B. Rundell, 1870, Claiborne County, Mississippi, Deed Book HH:434, Chancery Clerk's Office.

35 Deed of J.I.B. Rundell to Henry Dotson and Winnie Jones, 1870, ibid., p. 436.

36 Deed of J.I.B. Rundell to William Campbell, 1874, ibid., Deed Book NN:343.

37 Deed of L.N. Baldwin to J.I.B. Rundell, 1878, ibid., Deed Book UU:264.

Chapter Eleven

1 Information learned by Franklin Smith from family members from the late 1970s until the early 1990s.

2 U.S. Census of 1920, roll 872, Claiborne County, Mississippi, e.d. 36, sheet 4, family 103, household of Willis Smith.

3 U.S. Census of 1910, Claiborne County, Mississippi, e.d. 40, sheet 12, family 265, household of Willis Smith.

4 Marriage of Willis Smith and Sarenthia Hilson, Lincoln County, Mississippi, Marriage Book 4:35, Circuit Clerk's Office, Courthouse, Brookhaven.

5 U.S. Census of 1900, Lincoln County, Mississippi, e.d. 103, sheet 14, family 244, household of James W. Hilson.

6 U.S. Census of 1880, Lincoln County, Mississippi, e.d. 36, sheet 35, no family numbers given, household of George W. Smith.

7 U.S. Census of 1870, Lincoln County, Mississippi, p. 36, family 219, household of Eli Hilson.

8 Undated program from a family reunion, in possession of Beverly Bingham, Red Lick, Jefferson County, Mississippi, when Franklin Smith visited her at her home about 1997.

9 Census of educable children, 1878, Lincoln County, Mississippi, Record Group 28, Agency R003-B07-S5-02651, Mississippi Department of Archives and History, Jackson.

10 Social Security application (SS-5) for Other Hilson, SS no. 271-26-5261, 6 June 1945, microprint copy from Social Security Administration, Baltimore, Maryland.

11 U.S. Census of 1870, Lincoln County, Mississippi, p. 36, family 219.

12 U.S. Census of 1880, Lincoln County, Mississippi, e.d. 34, sheet 18, family 137, household of Eli Hilson.

13 U.S. Census of 1900, Lincoln County, Mississippi, e.d. 103, sheet 16, family 264, household of Abram Brown.

14 U.S. Census of 1880, Lincoln County, Mississippi, e.d. 36, sheet 29, no family numbers given, household of Abram Brown; he was living next door to Perry Cotton, one subject of the case study in chapter eight.

15 U.S. Census of 1870, Lincoln County, Mississippi, p. 35, family 205, household of Anson Runnels.

16 U.S. Census of 1880, Lincoln County, Mississippi, e.d. 34, sheet 12, family 100, household of Jack Hilson.

17 Death certificate of Jack Hilson, dated March 12, 1928, Lincoln County, Mississippi, certificate 5935, Mississippi State Department of Health and Vital Records, Jackson.

18 Personal tax rolls for 1868, Franklin County, Mississippi, Record Group 29, Auditor of Public Accounts, Mississippi Department of Archives and History, microfilm.

19 U.S. Census of 1870, Lincoln County, Mississippi, p. 36, family 221, household of John Martin.

20 Ibid.

21 U.S. Census of 1880, Lincoln County, Mississippi, e.d. 34, sheet 1, family 1, household of John O. Martin.

22 U.S. Census of 1860, Free Schedule, roll 577, Amite County, Mississippi, p. 28, family 194, household of John Martin.

23 U.S. Census of 1860, Slave Schedule, roll 595, Amite County, Mississippi, p. 16–17.

24 U.S. Census of 1850, Free Schedule, Amite County, Mississippi, p. 64, family 182, household of John Martin.

25 Marriage of Lodwick L. Weathersby and Elphany Obier, Amite County, Mississippi, Marriage Book 2:410, Circuit Clerk's Office, in Causey, *Amite County Mississippi, 1699–1865*, I:33.

26 U.S. Census of 1860, Free Schedule, Amite County, Mississippi, p. 28, family 199, household of Lewis (L.L.) Weathersby.

27 Letters of administration for Elphany Weathersby and William A. Obier, in Causey, *Amite County Mississippi, 1699–1865*, I:232, Amite County,

Mississippi, Letters of Administration, 1838–1866.

28 Inventory and appraisal of Lodwick L. Weathersby, 1844, Amite County, Mississippi, Probate Records, Book 9:614, Chancery Clerk's Office, FHL microfilm 864473.

29 Estate division of Lodwick L. Weathersby, 1853, ibid., Book 16:604, FHL microfilm 864476.

30 Bertha Ann Hubbard Allen, *Weathersby Family, 1711–1955* (Chattanooga, Tenn.: the author, 1955), 11.

31 Stewart E. Tolnay and E.M. Beck, *A Festival of Violence: An Analysis of Southern Lynchings, 1882–1930* (Urbana: University of Illinois Press, 1995), 24–25; U.S. Census of 1900, Lincoln County, Mississippi, e.d. 36, sheet 15, family 260, household of Eli Hilson Jr.

Chapter Twelve

1 Death certificate of Archie Davis Sr., 1923, certificate no. 15351, Claiborne County, Mississippi State Department of Health, Vital Records, Jackson.

2 U.S. Census of 1920, Claiborne County, Mississippi, e.d. 39, sheet 9, household of Arch Davis Sr.

3 U.S. Census of 1910, Claiborne County, Mississippi, e.d. 37, sheet 1, family 6 (Arch Davis Sr.) and family 7 (Archie Davis Jr.).

4 U.S. Census of 1900, Claiborne County, Mississippi, Beat 3, e.d. 160, sheet 1, family 7, household of Archie Davis Sr.

5 Marriage of Archie Davis and Harriett Brown, 1887, Claiborne County, Mississippi, Marriage Book 10:385, Circuit Clerk's Office, Courthouse, Port Gibson.

6 U.S. Census of 1880, Soundex for Mississippi, roll 15, Code D120, family card for Archie Davis, Claiborne County; U.S. Census of 1880, Claiborne County, Mississippi, Beat 2, e.d. 66, sheet 26, family 417, household of Archie Davis, beginning line 35.

7 U.S. Census of 1870, Claiborne County, Mississippi, Grand Gulf district, p. 572, family 231, household of Nella Davis.

8 Ibid., p. 571, family 228, household of Archie Davis.

9 Marriage of Richard Wallace and Harriett Woods, 1876, Claiborne County, Mississippi, Marriage Book 8:93, Circuit Clerk's Office.

10 U.S. Census of 1880, Claiborne County, Mississippi, Beat 2, e.d. 66, sheet 26, family 418.

11 U.S. Census of 1870, Claiborne County, Mississippi, Grand Gulf district, p. 571, family 227, household of Jesse Humphreys; p. 572, family 230, household of James Humphreys.

12 Visit with Sylvia Lee (Boines) Smith and Georgia Helen (Boines) Rucker, by Franklin Smith, at the Rucker home, Grand Gulf, Claiborne County, Mississippi, March 1996.

13 Visit with Johnnie Johnson, by Franklin Smith, at the Johnson home, Port Gibson, Claiborne County, Mississippi, July 1997; Mrs. Johnson was a great-granddaughter of Martha and Archie Davis Sr. and a granddaughter of Harriett Davis.

14 Marriage of Jordan Haywood and Lucinda Humphreys, 1870, Claiborne

County, Mississippi, in Automated Archives, *Marriage Records: Arkansas, Mississippi, Missouri, Texas*, CD-ROM, #CD5 (General Research System, now Novato, Calif.: Brøderbund, 1993), grooms listed alphabetically.

15 U.S. Census of 1870, Claiborne County, Mississippi, Grand Gulf district, p. 583, family 437, household of Willoughby Humphreys.

16 U.S. Census of 1870, Claiborne County, Mississippi, Grand Gulf district, p. 572, family 233, household of John P. McIntyre; U.S. Census of 1880, Claiborne County, Mississippi, Beat 2, e.d. 66, sheet 26, family 415, household of J.P. McIntyre.

17 U.S. Census of 1880, Claiborne County, Mississippi, Beat 2, e.d. 66, sheet 28, line 11, household of James Humphreys, and line 15, household of Willoughby Humphreys (no family numbers given).

18 U.S. Census of 1860, Free Schedule, Claiborne County, Mississippi, Police District 3, p. 55, family 14, household of Dr. E. Pollard; U.S. Census of 1860, Slave Schedule, Claiborne County, p. 440, slaves of Jno. McIntyre.

19 U.S. Census of 1850, Free Schedule, Claiborne County, Mississippi, p. 123, family 316, household of A.C. McIntyre; U.S. Census of 1850, Slave Schedule, Claiborne County, pages not numbered, 6 September 1850, A.C. McIntyre entry.

20 U.S. Census of 1840, Claiborne County, Mississippi, p. 72, line 17, household of D.H. McIntyre (age 30–40), with 48 slaves; U.S. Census of 1830, roll 70, Franklin County, Mississippi, p. 166, line 1, household of D.H. McIntyre (age 30–40), with 13 slaves; Claiborne County, Mississippi, Record of Probate, Book 1849–1851:2, widow A.C. McIntyre received her dower as part of the estate of D.H. McIntyre, 1849, Chancery Clerk's Office.

21 Inventory and appraisal of D.H. McIntyre estate, 1842, Claiborne County, Mississippi, Record of Probate, Book K:40ff; Sale of slaves from D.H. McIntyre estate, 1848, probate file M-9, Claiborne County, Mississippi, Chancery Clerk's Office.

22 U.S. Census of 1900, Claiborne County, Mississippi, e.d. 157, sheet 9, family 120, household of Wilson Humphreys.

23 U.S. Census of 1840, Claiborne County, Mississippi, p. 72, line 31, household of Peter McIntyre (age 60–70), with 72 slaves; U.S. Census of 1830, Franklin County, Mississippi, p. 153, line 11, household of Peter McIntyre (age 50–60), with 24 slaves.

24 Deed from Peter McIntyre to D.H. McIntyre, 1841, Claiborne County, Mississippi, Deed Book V:64, Chancery Clerk's Office.

25 Dorris D. Hendrickson and Paul L. Hisaw, *From a Sow or a Sparrow: A History of the Sugg Family* ([Fayetteville, Ark: D.D. Hendrickson], 1988), 352, J.B. Sugg-McIntyre marriage.

26 Deed from Josiah B. Sugg to Duncan H. McIntyre, 1838, Claiborne County, Deed Book R:347, and deed from Josiah B. Sugg to Peter McIntyre, 1838, Deed Book R:453, Chancery Clerk's Office.

27 Hendrickson and Hisaw, *Sugg Family*, 351, citing Claiborne County Marriage Book 5:151, W.R. Sugg-McIntyre marriage.

28 Land tax rolls, 1848, Claiborne County, Mississippi, p. 17, Record Group

29, Records of the Auditor of Public Accounts, Mississippi Department of Archives and History, microfilm.

29 Inventory and appraisal of William Sugg's estate, 1824, Claiborne County, Mississippi, Orphans Court Records, Book C (1822–1826):238–239; Annual report of William Sugg's estate, 1829, Orphans Court Records, Book of July 1829–June 1832:38, both in Chancery Clerk's Office.

30 U.S. Census of 1830, roll 70, Claiborne County, Mississippi, p. 81, household of Margaret Sugg.

31 Ibid., p. 73, household of Josiah B. Sugg.

32 Inventory and appraisal of Margaret Sugg's estate, 1831, Claiborne County, Mississippi, Orphans Court Records, Book of July 1829–June 1832:310–312; inventory of William R. Sugg's estate by his guardian, 1832, ibid., 352, both in Chancery Clerk's Office.

33 U.S. Census of 1840, Claiborne County, Mississippi, p. 54, household of W.R. Sugg.

34 Hendrickson and Hisaw, *Sugg Family*, 353, indicating that the children of Josiah Bryan Sugg and Elizabeth McIntyre were born in Bossier Parish, Louisiana; Inventory of Sugg estate by guardian Peter McIntyre, January 1842, Claiborne County, Mississippi, Record of Probate, Book K:17, Chancery Clerk's Office.

35 Deed from William R. Sugg to John P. McIntyre, 1860, Claiborne County, Mississippi, Deed Book EE:192, Chancery Clerk's Office.

36 Deed from Bryan and Sugg to the Sugg brothers, January 1804, Claiborne County, Mississippi, Deed Book A:55–56, Chancery Clerk's Office; Hendrickson and Hisaw, *Sugg Family*, 350.

37 Inventory and appraisal of Britton Bryan's estate, 1804, file B-11, Claiborne County, Mississippi, Papers of Decedents Estates, Chancery Clerk's Office.

38 *Heads of Families at the First Census of the United States Taken in the Year 1790: North Carolina* (Washington, D.C.: Government Printing Office, 1908; reprint, Baltimore: Genealogical Publishing Co., 1966), 54.

39 Marriage record of William Sugg and Margaret Daniel, 1822, Claiborne County, Mississippi, Marriage Book 2:28, Circuit Clerk's Office.

40 Mississippi Territorial Census of 1810, Claiborne County, in *Journal of Mississippi History* 13:50–63.

41 Will of Ann Daniel, 6 July 1830, Claiborne County, Mississippi, Will Book A:218, Chancery Clerk's Office.

42 Inventory and appraisal of William Daniel's estate, 1815, Claiborne County, Mississippi, Estate Inventory 1804–1815:414, Chancery Clerk's Office.

43 Division of William Daniel's estate, 1821, Claiborne County, Mississippi, Probate Records, Book for July 1821–August 1822:208, Chancery Clerk's Office.

Bibliography

Reference Lists in the Text:

Free people of color, pages 103–105
Military records and research, page 36
Native Americans, pages 101–102
Newspaper research, page 78
Published diaries, pages 158–159
Slave narrative indexes, page 124
State research guides, page 85
Vital records, page 65

Selected Works for Further Reference

Bentley, Elizabeth Petty. *County Courthouse Book*. Latest edition. Baltimore: Genealogical Publishing Co.

Burroughs, Tony. *Black Roots: A Beginner's Guide to Tracing the African American Family Tree*. New York: Fireside, 2001. Focuses on genealogy from the present back to 1870.

Byers, Paula K., ed. *African-American Genealogical Sourcebook*. Detroit: Gale Research, 1995.

Carmack, Sharon DeBartolo. *A Genealogist's Guide to Discovering Your Female Ancestors*. Cincinnati: Betterway Books, 1998.

———. *A Genealogist's Guide to Discovering Your Immigrant & Ethnic Ancestors*. Cincinnati: Betterway Books, 2000.

———. *Your Guide to Cemetery Research*. Cincinnati: Betterway Books, 2002.

Crawford-Oppenheimer, Christine. *Long-Distance Genealogy: Researching Family History from Home*. Cincinnati: Betterway Books, 2000.

Croom, Emily Anne. *The Genealogist's Companion & Sourcebook*. Latest edition. Cincinnati: Betterway Books. Focuses on U.S. sources for genealogical research.

———. *The Sleuth Book for Genealogists*. Cincinnati: Betterway Books, 2000. Focuses on techniques for problem solving in genealogical research.

———. *Unpuzzling Your Past*. 4th ed. Cincinnati: Betterway Books, 2001. A beginner's guide to genealogy.

———. *The Unpuzzling Your Past Workbook*. Cincinnati: Betterway Books, 1996.

Drake, Paul. *What Did They Mean By That?: A Dictionary of Historical Terms for Genealogists*. 2 vols. Bowie, Md.: Heritage Books, 1994, 1998.

Eichholz, Alice, ed. *Ancestry's Red Book: American State, County & Town Sources*. Rev. ed. Salt Lake City: Ancestry, 1992.

Evans, Barbara Jean. *A to Zax: A Comprehensive Genealogical Dictionary for Genealogists and Historians*. 3d ed. Alexandria, Va.: Hearthside Press, 1995.

Everton, George B., Sr., ed. *The Handy Book for Genealogists*. Latest edition. Logan, Utah: The Everton Publishers.

Fears, Mary L. Jackson. *Slave Ancestral Research: It's Something Else*. Bowie, Md.: Heritage Books, Inc., 1995.

Harris, Maurine, and Glen Harris. *Ancestry's Concise Genealogical Dictionary*. Salt Lake City: Ancestry, 1989.

Hatcher, Patricia Law. *Locating Your Roots: Discover Your Ancestors Using Land Records*. Cincinnati: Betterway Books, 2003.

Hinckley, Kathleen W. *Locating Lost Family Members & Friends*. Cincinnati: Betterway Books, 1999.

———. *Your Guide to the Federal Census*. Cincinnati: Betterway Books, 2001.

Hone, E. Wade. *Land and Property Research in the United States*. Salt Lake City: Ancestry, 1997.

Kemp, Thomas Jay. *International Vital Records Handbook*. Latest edition. Baltimore: Genealogical Publishing Co.

Lainhart, Ann S. *State Census Records*. Baltimore: Genealogical Publishing Co., 1992.

McClure, Rhonda. *The Genealogist's Computer Companion*. Cincinnati: Betterway Books, 2001.

Melnyk, Marcia Yannizze. *The Weekend Genealogist: Time-Saving Techniques for Effective Research*. Cincinnati: Betterway Books, 2000.

Neagles, James C. *The Library of Congress: A Guide to Genealogical and Historical Research*. Salt Lake City: Ancestry, 1990.

———. *U.S. Military Records: A Guide to Federal & State Sources, Colonial America to the Present*. Salt Lake City: Ancestry, 1994.

Schaefer, Christina Kassabian. *The Center: A Guide to Genealogical Research in the National Capital Area*. Baltimore: Genealogical Publishing Co., 1997.

———. *The Hidden Half of the Family*. Baltimore: Genealogical Publishing Co., 1999. Focuses on references for researching female ancestors.

Streets, David H. *Slave Genealogy: A Research Guide with Case Studies*. Bowie, Md.: Heritage Books, 1986. Guide to research using records of Wayne County, Kentucky.

Sturdevant, Katherine Scott. *Bringing Your Family History to Life Through Social History*. Cincinnati: Betterway Books, 2000.

Taylor, Maureen A. *Uncovering Your Ancestry Through Family Photographs*. Cincinnati: Betterway Books, 2000.

Thorndale, William, and William Dollarhide. *Map Guide to U.S. Federal Censuses, 1790–1920*. Baltimore: Genealogical Publishing Co., 1987. Important reference, with maps.

Warren, Paula Stuart, and James Warren. *Your Guide to the Family History Library: How to Access the World's Largest Genealogy Resource*. Cincinnati: Betterway Books, 2001.

Witcher, Curt Bryan. *African American Genealogy: A Bibliography and Guide to Sources*. Fort Wayne, Ind.: Round Tower Books, 2000. Important reference.

Woodtor, Dee Parmer. *Finding a Place Called Home: A Guide to African-American Genealogy and Historical Identity*. New York: Random House, 1999.

Index